African Novels
in the Classroom

African Novels
in the Classroom

edited by
Margaret Jean Hay

LYNNE
RIENNER
PUBLISHERS

BOULDER
LONDON

Published in the United States of America in 2000 by
Lynne Rienner Publishers, Inc.
1800 30th Street, Boulder, Colorado 80301
www.rienner.com

and in the United Kingdom by
Lynne Rienner Publishers, Inc.
3 Henrietta Street, Covent Garden, London WC2E 8LU

Library of Congress Cataloging-in-Publication Data
African novels in the classroom   /   edited by Margaret Jean Hay.
     p.   cm.
     Contents: Peter Abrahams's A wreath for Udomo—Chinua Achebe's Things fall apart—
Ayi Kwei Armah's The beautyful ones are not yet born—Mariama Bâ's So long a letter—
Driss Chraïbi's Mother comes of age—Lindsey Collen's The rape of Sita—Maryse
Condé's Segu—Tsitsi Dangarembga's Nervous conditions—Modikwe Dikobe's The
Marabi dance—Buchi Emecheta's The joys of motherhood—Buchi Emecheta's The slave
girl—Nuruddin Farah's Gifts—Elsa Joubert's Poppie Nongena—J. Nozipo Maraire's
Zenzele : letters to my daughter—Meja Mwangi's Going down River Road—Ngugi wa
Thiong'o's A grain of wheat—Djibril Tamsir Niane's Sundiata—Flora Nwapa's Efuru—
Ferdinand Oyono's Houseboy—Tayeb Salih's Season of migration to the north—Ousmane
Sembene's God's bits of wood—Wole Soyinka's Ake : the years of childhood—Moyez
G. Vassanji's The gunny sack—Paul Tiyambe Zeleza's Smouldering charcoal.
     ISBN 1-55587-853-9 (hc   :   alk. paper)
     ISBN 1-55587-878-4 (pbk.   :   alk. paper)
     1. African fiction—Study and teaching.   2. African fiction (English)—Study and
teaching.   3. Africa—Civilization—Study and teaching.   I. Hay, Margaret Jean.
     PL8010.6.A34   2000
     809.3'0096—dc21   00-022780

British Cataloguing in Publication Data
A Cataloguing in Publication record for this book
is available from the British Library.

Printed and bound in the United States of America

The paper used in this publication meets the requirements
of the American National Standard for Permanence of
Paper for Printed Library Materials Z39.48-1984.

5 4 3 2 1

Contents

Introduction

Margaret Jean Hay

I HAVE FOUND THAT MOST AFRICANIST SCHOLARS ARE passionate about their teaching. Conversations over dinner at a professional conference or informal messages over email often involve discussion of how a particular class is going, exchange of relevant syllabuses, and comments on a new textbook, approach, novel, or film that has been tried and found helpful—or just the opposite. Publishing a persuasive article or an award-winning book represents critical recognition from our peers, but the interest and effectiveness of our teaching often makes more of a difference in our everyday lives. I feel strongly that the publishing world has overlooked this aspect of our experience. Literally hundreds of books aimed at elementary and secondary schoolteachers present new methods and advice on teaching particular subjects, stimulating students' creativity, encouraging them to write, and so on—the list is vast. In contrast, once college teachers have demonstrated mastery in their field of academic expertise (in most cases through the successful completion of a Ph.D. dissertation), they are expected to become effective teachers without any specific training or guidance in that dimension.

Along with its predecessor, *Great Ideas for Teaching About Africa*, edited by Misty Bastian and Jane Parpart, the present collection is intended to address that need. Here, twenty-four college teachers from different disciplines discuss how they use specific African novels in the classroom—why they choose a certain novel, what corollary readings they assign, what background information they present in lecture, what major themes emerge in discussion, and what written assignments then explore the students' engagement with that particular novel.

1

If you teach a unit or a course on some aspect of African studies and would like to diversify your reading assignments or to enliven class discussions, this book is for you. It has been written primarily with college teachers in mind, but will be useful for secondary teachers as well. Let me say right up front what it is not: this is not a work of literary criticism, nor is it about African novels or African literature as such. It is something quite different: hands-on personal accounts from teachers who have used one of twenty-four African novels in the classroom, with plot summaries, background information on historical context and on the novelist's life and work, related reading and writing assignments, and the major themes that come up in discussion, as well as advice on specific problems students might encounter. It is intended to be informal, helpful, and relevant to day-to-day teaching.

The works discussed in these pages are drawn from across the African continent, although more come from West Africa than from any other region, reflecting the historical dominance of literature from that area in both anglophone and francophone literary traditions. The great majority of novels presented here are set in the twentieth century; Maryse Condé's *Segu*, D. T. Niane's *Sundiata*, and Buchi Emecheta's *Slave Girl* are the striking exceptions. Indexes at the end of the collection list the novels by region and by principal theme.

Two of the essays included here involve books that are not technically novels at all: Niane's *Sundiata* is a short, accessible version of a historical epic about the founding of the kingdom of Mali, and Wole Soyinka's *Ake* is an autobiographical account of growing up in a Nigerian village. The essays on these books fit comfortably with the other chapters here and suggest that African epics and life histories offer additional possibilities for teaching. I did not preselect the list of books to be included and then search for authors to write about them. In most cases the scenario was reversed; I approached individuals I knew to be good teachers, asked whether they used novels in their teaching, and if so, what novel they might like to write about. The process confirmed my impression that a great many teachers assign novels as part of the required reading for African studies classes in anthropology, history, political science, religion, and women's studies, as well as literature. I believe there are three broad reasons why this is the case.

First, Western students with little or no first-hand experience of African societies will pick up a vast array of information from reading a novel, including such details as what houses and cities and villages look like; what a meal might consist of; what kinds of work people do; how leisure time might be used; how a prosperous government minister, a hard-working peasant, or a call girl might dress or behave; but perhaps most important of all, they will absorb many clues about relationships—the extended family in its urban and rural permutations, the bonds or conflicts between workers, or the varying relationships between the sexes, between officials and peasants, black and white, young and old.

Second, it quickly becomes apparent that students really enjoy the change of pace involved in reading African novels in the midst of other more scholarly writings. Instructors also find pleasure in class discussions that are usually a break from normal routines. (One of my colleagues at a large midwestern university, perhaps too close to the fictional Lake Wobegon, warned me that not only did she not use novels in her teaching, she felt it was counterproductive and perhaps dangerous to have assignments that students actually enjoyed.)

Perhaps most important, however, is the students' ability to relate to fictional characters as human beings, to conceive of African societies as populated by distinct individuals whose behavior, personal concerns, and perceived self-interest can differ widely from one to another. This is quite different from the perception some students might have developed of Africans as faceless victims oppressed by Western colonialism—a sympathetic stance from the students' point of view, no doubt, but one that tends to distance and dehumanize.

Each of the twenty-four teachers whose essays are included here have personal reasons for assigning one African novel instead of another in a particular class, but a number of common themes arise from their discussions. Richard Rathbone, for example, feels that students are often alienated by the fact that much of modern African history tends to be rather impersonal. He enjoys using Peter Abrahams's *A Wreath for Udomo* (Chapter 1) when he's teaching about modern Ghana because the novel's portrayal of fictional African radicals makes the epic figures who dominate the nationalist epic of the mid twentieth century—especially Kwame Nkrumah himself—come to life. Abrahams also provides a wealth of detail about the actual founding and day-to-day operation of political movements and parties. The same might be said about D. T. Niane's *Sundiata* (Chapter 17), a short and engaging epic account of the thirteenth-century foundation of the Mali empire. The legendary hero is first introduced as a toddler who is unable to walk properly but who accumulates both strength and wisdom sufficient to guarantee his place in history. Curtis Keim uses Niane's version of the Sundiata epic to help his students appreciate that historical fiction is a story about the past as well as evidence for the time it was written. *Sundiata* is one of only a handful of works suitable for classroom use that focus on precolonial African history.

Many teachers find novels helpful for the way they make broad historical processes more understandable through the constraints and opportunities faced by individual characters and the choices and decisions they make. Joye Bowman assigns Maryse Condé's historical novel *Segu* (Chapter 7) because she likes the way it presents the sweeping historical themes of the nineteenth century in West Africa—the spread of Islam, the abolition of the slave trade, and the development of "legitimate commerce" through the experiences of a single family. In a similar vein, Vassanji's *The Gunny Sack* (Chapter 23) is a wide-ranging historical novel, covering approximately 150 years of East African history through the experiences of one extended Asian family in Tanzania. Jamie Monson assigns the novel because it integrates several themes she feels are central to understanding East African history: oral narrative, collective memory, cultural identity, race, gender, and nationalism.

God's Bits of Wood (Chapter 21) is one of a few African novels that recreate a specific historical event—in this case, a railway workers' strike in late 1940s French West Africa. Dennis Cordell finds Sembene's novel a wonderful novel for teaching about the complexity of social movements and social change, ranging from labor organizing and gender relations to race relations and nationalism. The book is also very useful for class discussions about the nature of history, the "truth" of the historian, and the "truth" of the novelist. Ngugi wa Thiong'o's novel *A Grain of Wheat* (Chapter 16) is a moving depiction of the involvement of ordinary people in Mau Mau resistance and their ultimate disillusionment with the political independence for which they had sacrificed so much. In my own teaching I especially value *A Grain of Wheat* for the ways it muddies the waters of resistance and collaboration by showing individual calculations and compromises; it is thus a useful antidote to students' tendency to simplify (and perhaps to glorify) notions of African resistance without understanding the ultimate costs involved.

Because *The Marabi Dance* (Chapter 9) covers so many aspects of both urban and rural life in South Africa—from squalid housing, gangs, and the vibrant appeal of marabi music to transitions in religious and marriage ceremonies—it offers students a window into a broad range of cultural and social issues during a time of rapid social transformation. But Iris Berger appreciates the way author Modikwe Dikobe avoids simple dichotomies in representing the choices open to individuals and neither idealizes rural culture nor condemns it. James Pritchett finds that Mariama Bâ's *So Long a Letter* (Chapter 4) forces students to focus on the individual strategies of both men and women in late colonial Senegal. Bâ's novel shows how individuals rethink fundamental issues about work, polygyny, family, and Islamic faith and customs, and how their different positions within society present them with different options and constraints. African responses to colonialism are infinitely varied and complex, and *So Long a Letter* helps the class deconstruct previous assumptions about the opposition between "tradition" and "modernity." Many other essays mention the value of encouraging students to rethink these dichotomies. Martin Klein feels that Chinua Achebe's classic *Things Fall Apart* (Chapter 2) gives students an African perspective on indigenous social patterns and the British colonial impact from the standpoint of a decentralized Nigerian society; it also challenges their assumption that "civilization" is identified with the existence of large-scale political systems. After students read *Things Fall Apart*, they no longer associate Igbo village life with "primitive society."

Tsitsi Dangarembga's *Nervous Conditions* (Chapter 8) usually provokes an enthusiastic response from undergraduates because the main character is a teenage girl whose conflicts with her father echo familiar themes from their own lives. Bill Bravman and Mary Montgomery also value Dangarembga's novel because of the way it challenges students to rethink staple dichotomies like African/Western, rural/urban, and traditional/modern. They find that the ambivalences and contradictions of all the major characters help students grasp the complexities of gender, generation, and Westernization in mid-twentieth-century Zimbabwe.

In many of the essays included here, teachers assign specific African novels for the purpose of sparking discussions about the changing roles of women in particular regions and time periods. Janice Spleth finds that Driss Chraïbi's *Mother Comes of Age* (Chapter 5) is most valuable for incorporating the theme of women's status under Islam—the novel's sympathetic male characters make it easier for her students to question issues of seclusion, education, and the veil. In this warm-hearted account, two young men in a fairly cosmopolitan Moroccan household consciously decide to liberate their very traditional mother. For Sandra Greene, Flora Nwapa's presentation of Igbo women in *Efuru* (Chapter 18) provides a useful forum to discuss controversies surrounding the issues of female circumcision, bridewealth, and polygyny in early colonial Nigeria. *Efuru* was written partly in response to Chinua Achebe's *Things Fall Apart* and is also a text to which other authors in turn have responded. This situation gives students a chance to explore the intertextual conversations that have taken place between African men and women, and among African women writers themselves, over how the historical lives of African women should be presented to a broader public.

Lindsey Collen's *The Rape of Sita* (Chapter 6), which presents rape in actual and metaphorical contexts in Mauritius, provides Beverly Mack's students with a new perspective on women's responses to patriarchal control. Mack particularly appreciates the multifaceted style and subject matter; Collen's integration of epic and oral narrative styles, Western literature, and a broad Islamic context forces students to acknowledge the complexity of contemporary African societies, while her conscious manipulation of an old Beatles' tune ("Jojo was a man who thought he was a woman") startles everyone and stimulates discussion.

Misty Bastian has found that *Joys of Motherhood* (Chapter 10) works well as a detailed description of Western Igbo experience in the high colonial period of Nigeria and particularly the ways in which women were integrated into urban economies during the 1930s and 1940s. Along the way, readers learn that motherhood may be universal, but its social expression can vary widely from place to place and from one historical period to another. Bastian is especially careful to point out the ambivalent reception of Emecheta's work in Nigeria to her students. Kathleen Sheldon has taught Buchi Emecheta's novel *The Slave Girl* (Chapter 11) in order to provide an example of African women's voices, to present the historical theme of internal African slavery through accessible fiction, and to raise a series of questions about women's position in African societies. She particularly values Emecheta's ambivalence toward aspects of both Nigerian and Western culture and the ultimate ambiguities of the story's outcome as enabling wide-ranging discussions in the classroom.

Jeanne Penvenne believes that assigning novels and biographies focusing on ordinary women's experiences can help compensate for the elitism and androcentricity that still characterize much of the historical literature. In addition to valuable suggestions about the day-to-day lives of working people in apartheid South Africa, Elsa Joubert's *Poppie Nongena* (Chapter 13) raises valuable questions about authorship and form, history and memory. Karen Keim chooses J. Nozipo Maraire's novel *Zenzele* (Chapter 14) because it offers her students a highly accessible introduction to upper-middle-class life in Zimbabwe. In the form of a letter from an African mother in Harare to her undergraduate daughter at Harvard University, *Zenzele* portrays a clear statement of one African woman's core values: dignity based on an appreciation of one's heritage, respect for the family, the wise use of education, the importance of building long-lasting relationships, and the promotion of racial understanding.

The blunt racism inherent in colonial rule is another theme that emerges in many of these chapters. In *Houseboy* (Chapter 19), Cameroonian writer Ferdinand Oyono has an acute eye for the nuances of social interactions between African and European, for the subtle violence of daily life in late colonial Cameroon, and for the tragicomic dimensions of the spectacle of French power. Barbara Cooper particularly enjoys the tremendous sympathy and humor of Oyono's writing and the fact that *Houseboy* confronts students with a clear case in which the construction of gender affects men as well as women. Farouk Topan uses *Season of Migration to the North* by Sudanese author Tayeb Salih (Chapter 20) to teach about expressions of Islam in Sudanese society. While studying in Britain, the novel's African protagonist makes a career of sexually exploiting English women, clearly a response to the British exploitation of the Sudan. Topan appreciates the tensions involved in the novelist's depictions of the cross-cultural negotiations of the self and the other, both in Britain and subsequently in Africa. Wole Soyinka's memoir, *Ake: The Years of Childhood* (Chapter 22), allows readers to interpret one African's perspective on what it was like to grow up in an elite, educated Christian family in colonial Nigeria. Tamara Giles-Vernick appreciates the particular glimpse that *Ake* provides into the direct and indirect ways that British colonialism could shape education and families, and the different ways African women and men could negotiate and reshape these influences.

Several teachers choose novels set in the 1960s, 1970s, and later as representing individual African intellectuals' perspectives on the troubling transformations within postcolonial society. Ayi Kwei Armah's *The Beautyful Ones Are Not Yet Born* (Chapter 3) illuminates the political and moral decay of Ghana in the mid-1960s and, by extension, casts light on today's situation as well. Emmanuel Akyeampong appreciates Armah's intimate descriptions of working-class life, which show how ordinary people are affected by larger issues of political economy. Meja Mwangi's novel of urban Nairobi in the 1970s, *Going Down River Road* (Chapter 15) can be read both as a gritty depiction of urban life during the first decade of independence and as a pessimistic document of its time. By 1976 a sense of decay and decline had begun to undermine the optimism and confidence of the immediate postindependence years in Kenya. Charles Ambler uses *Going Down River Road* in class to complement broad arguments regarding neocolonialism and underdevelopment, showing how the broad forces of change impact ordinary lives and how individuals resist those forces or attempt to profit from them.

Historian Melvin Page assigns novels in his teaching to lend a feeling of authenticity to his courses and to highlight indigenous perspectives on the troubles that have plagued many African countries after independence. P. T. Zeleza's novel, *Smouldering Charcoal* (Chapter 24), provides an artistically satisfying and politically astute analysis of postcolonial problems in Malawi through the fictional experiences of several friends who dare to challenge the establishment. Lidwien Kapteijns uses Nuruddin Farah's beautiful novel *Gifts* (Chapter 12) to introduce her students to an African intellectual's perspective on the disintegration of the Somali state in the late 1980s. Farah's novel also allows her students to experience a particular African context through particular fictional individuals, in this case a young, middle-class Somali nurse in Mogadishu. Kapteijns believes that true social history begins when students try to understand that in Africa as elsewhere, the social institutions of the present are the crystallization of social struggles of the past, and that these institutions are maintained or changed by people both like and unlike themselves who face circumstances not of their own making.

After paging through this collection, it should be clear to readers that none of these essays attempts to present a novel as representing historical truth. Nevertheless, as Keith Booker reminds us, historical novels constitute a major component in the processes of historical recovery and the reconstruction of cultural identities that are underway across Africa (see Booker 1998: 27–28). Many of those who write historical novels, of course, have done a great deal of background research on their subjects. See, for example, the fascinating essay by novelist Margaret Atwood and responses by three historians comparing history and historical fiction in the 1998 *American Historical Review*.[1] The African novelists described here often write about events or periods with which they are personally familiar—Ngugi wa Thiong'o's various portrayals of Mau Mau, Buchi Emecheta's account of Lagos in the 1940s, Ousmane Sembene's presentation of the 1947 railway strike, or P. T. Zeleza's critique of the repression of political opposition in postcolonial Malawi. What is important is that a particular writer has chosen to interpret history or society in a particular way.

A number of African literature scholars have expressed their concerns about the potential misuse of African novels in the classroom by those in other disciplines, where they feel students can too easily fall into the trap of assuming that any particular novel represents literal and historical truth. For a considered expression of these concerns, see the collection edited by Eileen Julien, Biodun Jeyifo, and Mamadou Diouf entitled *African Literature Between Humanism, Theory, and Ethnic/Area Studies.* This forthcoming collection of papers grew out of two African Studies Association roundtables and a workshop on the ways members of different disciplines use and refer to African novels. Julien and her coeditors are concerned that we remind students that novels are literary works in which the time and setting portrayed are mediated through the time and setting of the writer's location and the time and setting of the reader's location—where location is defined in terms of history, class, gender, and identity. It is useful to remind our students periodically that these are works of literature and not case studies of anthropology, politics, or history, although they will learn much about a particular African region during a certain period of time from reading any of these novels. In the present collection, there are particularly useful accounts of engaging students on the issues of fiction, representation, and historical truth in Chapters 10, 21, and 24.

I have found much of interest in the following chapters, even when they deal with novels I am already quite familiar with, and hope to apply some of the innovative teaching methods next semester. It is my hope you will find them useful as well.

NOTE

1. Unfortunately for our purposes here, the three historians are discussing the links and similarities between history and historical fiction, rather than using the latter to teach the former.

SUGGESTIONS FOR
FURTHER READING AND RESOURCES

Atwood, Margaret. 1998. "In Search of *Alias Grace*: On Writing Canadian Historical Fiction," *American Historical Review* 103, 5: 1503–1516. Along with responses from historians Lynn Hunt, Jonathan Spence, and

John Demos, Atwood's piece comprises a special "AHR Forum: Histories and Historical Fictions."

Bastian, Misty L., and Jane L. Parpart, eds. 1999. *Great Ideas for Teaching About Africa*. Boulder, Colo.: Lynne Rienner.

Booker, M. Keith. 1998. *The African Novel in English: An Introduction*. Portsmouth, N.H.: Heinemann. A useful guide to teaching African literature, with discussions of the major issues students will need to confront, a historical survey of the development of the African novel, and specific chapters on eight representative novels.

Cazenave, Odile. 1999. *Rebellious Women: The New Generation of Female African Novelists*. Boulder, Colo.: Lynne Rienner.

D'Almeida, Irene Assiba. 1994. *Francophone African Women Writers: Destroying the Emptiness of Silence*. Gainesville: University Press of Florida.

Davies, Carole Boyce, ed. 1986. *Ngambika: Studies of Women in African Literature*. Trenton, N.J.: Africa World Press.

Gunner, Elizabeth. 1987. *A Handbook for Teaching African Literature*, 2nd ed. Portsmouth, N.H.: Heinemann. A marvelous introduction to using African literature in all forms in the classroom: novels, plays, short stories, poetry. Gunner includes teaching suggestions, discussion questions, audiovisual resources. While aimed at nonspecialist precollegiate teachers, contains useful tips for college teachers as well.

Harrow, Kenneth W., ed. 1991. *Faces of Islam in African Literature*. Portsmouth, N.H.: Heinemann.

Irele, Abiola. 1990. *The African Experience in Literature and Ideology*. Bloomington: Indiana University Press.

JanMohamed, Abdul R. 1983. *Manichean Aesthetics: The Politics of Literature in Colonial Africa*. Amherst: University of Massachusetts Press. Discusses the writings of six authors in interesting pairings. I learned much from his discussion of Ngugi's novels.

Julien, Eileen. 1992. *African Novels and the Question of Orality*. Bloomington: Indiana University Press.

Julien, Eileen, Biodun Jeyifo, and Mamadou Diouf, eds. Forthcoming. *African Literature Between Humanism, Theory, and Ethnic/Area Studies*.

Mortimer, Mildred P. 1990. *Journeys Through the French African Novel*. Portsmouth, N.H.: Heinemann.

Owomoyela, Oyekan, ed. 1993. *A History of Twentieth-Century African Literatures*. Lincoln: University of Nebraska Press.

Research in African Literatures. The preeminent scholarly journal of African literary criticism, beginning in 1970. Readers browsing through back issues will find articles of interest on all of the authors whose works are mentioned here.

Zell, Hans, Carol Bundy, and Virginia Coulon. 1983. *A New Reader's Guide to African Literature*. New York: Africana. This exceptionally useful annotated reference work unfortunately ends in 1983 and is sadly in need of updating. Includes author biographies and country-by-country listing of published works.

1

Peter Abrahams's
A Wreath for Udomo

Richard Rathbone

A SESSION WITH A LIE DETECTOR WOULD PROBABLY elicit the real reason for my classroom use of Peter Abrahams's novel. The truth is that I always enjoy rereading it, and that my claim about its pedagogic value is, in some measure, an excuse for doing so. It does require some serious excusing. By no stretch of the most indulgent imagination is it great literature. It is unremittingly didactic, the dialogue is often desperately unreal, and the plot is extremely contrived. The characters are for the most part two-dimensional; the handful of women in the story enjoy or endure walk-on—or rather lie-down—parts. But it is a curiously powerful novel for reasons I try to outline in the course of this chapter.

But first, how do I use this book, and with whom? It finds its place in two history courses I teach. The first is a tightly focused, final-year undergraduate course on the late colonial period of Ghanaian history. Before commencing the course, the students must have read, over the summer vacation, Dennis Austin's *Politics in Ghana* and Kwame Nkrumah's autobiography *Ghana*, and they are asked for book reviews of one or another of these before admission to the course. For those claiming total ignorance, I recommend the later chapters of F. M. Bourret's short book *Ghana: The Road to Independence*, which still remains the most concise introduction to the place and the period.

The class is usually about fifteen strong, and they are all history majors. Although we are looking in detail only at the years between

Peter Abrahams, *A Wreath for Udomo* (London: Faber and Faber, 1956).

1940 and Ghana's independence in March 1957, the bibliography is long and intimidating. Students write four assignments—we call them essays—in the course of the year. Each of these is prompted by a historiographical question that is chosen from a list of twenty-four "sample" titles; to each of these is appended a starter bibliography, although smart students expand their reading by picking up on footnotes and using the course bibliography. Each answer of about four thousand words will have demanded the kind of extensive reading of books and articles that gives them a real grasp of significant analytical problems connected with either a running theme—nationalism, trade unionism, the political role of women, or ethnicity, for example—or a period-specific problem, such as why rioting broke out in 1948, why the radical rather than the moderate nationalists triumphed in 1951, or why violence erupted in late 1955. In addition they are required to complete a ten-thousand-word dissertation usually based on primary material dug out of archives of one sort or another.

The objective of the course is relatively simple. Having studied African history for two years, students are confronted in their final year with all the problems of researching and writing, and not just reading history. In the course of the year they are expected to have mastered the secondary literature and once they get around to assignment writing, the assumption is that they are familiar with it in considerable detail. By the middle of the year they must confront the selection and design of the dissertation. Being based in London, they have about them many of the raw materials of the historian; they are expected to use archives, newspaper collections, and ephemera. By February they are to be seen about the college, teetering under the weight of photocopies of party manifestos, assembly debates, reports of commissions of enquiry, and boxes of note cards. By the end of the year the best of them know much more about particular historical problems and events in recent Ghanaian history than does their teacher. As a political historian teaching a course dominated by a dramatic political narrative, I recognize that many students need to be made aware of the wider context of that political history. Few have been to Ghana, and thus we use slides, maps, films, and recordings to gain a sense of place, and especially place in time, throughout the year. I am always in search of fiction that underlines the rich and engaging particularity of time or place. *A Wreath for Udomo*, Cameron Duodo's sadly undervalued novel *The Gab Boys*, and Ayei Kwei Armah's much more famous *The Beautyful Ones Are Not Yet Born* are those most enjoyed by the class (see Chapter 3 in this collection on Armah's novel). Most students read these for fun, for a sense of contemporary texture, rather than with a paragraph in an assignment in mind.

Additionally, this novel finds its place in a master's-level course on West African coastal societies in the nineteenth and twentieth centuries. This is a graduate seminar with an even more intimidating bibliography. But here students have their own particular interests that they are encouraged to develop in the course of writing three seminar presentations throughout the year. The majors will also spend the period from mid-May to September (and of course it's a long, long way from May to September) researching and writing their dissertations. The best of these are usually publishable. Student interests vary from year to year. But a running theme is, necessarily, the role of the African diaspora in the construction of the cultures of West African coastal societies. The variety of those dialogues—and trialogues—is enormous; the recent histories of Dakar and Ibadan are, for example, very unlike one another and quite instructively so. But the problem of understanding the importance of the political activities of Africans in the metropoles especially in the 1930s and 1940s is also a significant theme. And here *A Wreath for Udomo* comes into play for reasons that will perhaps become more obvious in the course of this chapter.

A WREATH FOR UDOMO

So what is the book about? The plot line is simple enough. A bunch of highly politicized African students are, for a variety of reasons, in London in the mid-1940s. All of them are technically studying for degrees. But more important, they are all deeply committed to the overthrow of colonial rule in their respective home states. They are busy organizing and attending meetings; they debate endlessly among themselves; and they live very frugally and have tender love affairs. Each of them has a different personal history. One, Mhendi, has led a doomed revolt in the settler-dominated colony, Pluralia, from which he has fled. In the process, many of his supporters have been massacred, and those victims include his wife and child. Others, Adebhoy and Mabi, are less obviously scarred but no less militant. The epicenter of their intellectual and personal universe is the compelling figure of Thomas Lanwood, a voluntary exile from another colony, the settler-free colony of Panafrica. An ex-member of the

Communist Party and a much-published veteran anticolonial activist, Lanwood is an intimidating icon to these younger men. Early in the novel, the central figure of Michael Udomo, another temporary exile from Panafrica, appears on the scene. Idealistic, shy, but immensely intelligent and attractive, his political affectivity is sharpened by his comrades, and especially by the experience and guidance of Lanwood. His personal life, and that of the others, is softened by the ministrations of a clutch of tender but radical white women who can cook.

Udomo returns home, where his creative political skills and the growing love of the people outflank both the colonial administration and the local forces of reaction, a grim constellation of merchants and "chiefs and elders." After a short period of martyrdom in prison, he becomes the prime minister of his self-governing state in a process of bloodless revolution and negotiation. Local self-government achieved, his old friend Mhendi joins Udomo in Panafrica. Mhendi's home state of Pluralia is, however, still under settler domination. Conveniently for the narrative, Pluralia physically abuts the now independent Panafrica. And now Mhendi commences the revolution from the base in Panafrica afforded him by Prime Minister Udomo and with Udomo's encouraging advice. Udomo, however, eventually sacrifices Mhendi to the brutal security forces of Pluralia; this is part of a deal with a cluster of imperialist interests that Udomo believes will ultimately benefit the welfare and development of his own country. Mhendi is killed. Once these cruel workings of *realpolitik* are discovered, Udomo's cynical betrayal alienates his old London comrades, who have become ministers in his government; it also loses him the support and affection of the old market trader, Selina, who bankrolled Udomo's party in its early years and had organized the market women to support him. Even before the tragedy of Mhendi unfolds, Lanwood (who had joined Udomo in the newly free Panafrica) quietly leaves the country, appalled at what he sees as Udomo's cynical pragmatism and loss of principles in dealing with the old enemy. Udomo is finally hacked to death as his traditionalist opposition overwhelms his living quarters.

Set out baldly like that, the story is in some respects operatic and almost ridiculous. Most modern historians would suggest that it hopelessly overinflates the role of individuals in historical processes; this is, however, a debatable matter to which we will return. In terms of character development, Abrahams's great technical weakness is manifest; because each of the protagonists is forced to represent this or that political viewpoint, they all lack credible personalities. They are congeries of ideas, not breathing flesh and blood. They are forced to deliver long, set-piece monologues of the sort that do not typify interpersonal exchange between friends, at least in my experience. The colonial officials come close to the "nice policeman/nasty policeman" stereotypes. And the women are usually saintly moral onlookers, providers of refreshment of all sorts; they also serve as occasional Greek choruses who nonetheless do the bidding of their menfolk. Only a woman could judge whether Abrahams's women in this novel think, let alone talk, like women. My guess is that they do not.

So why bother with this book at all? There are several answers to that question. The first emerges as a general response to the impersonality of much modern African history. Scholars for the most part have done no better than Peter Abrahams in making the epic figures who dominate the factual nationalist epics of the mid twentieth century come to life. They are cardboard cutouts, heroes or villains, and as such very unlike the far more accessible personalities of those who have played major roles in, and even commanded, the political fates of the West in the same period. African historical studies have denied humanity to the actors less out of spite than because of ignorance; it is a field starved of autobiographies and biographies. Although Abrahams is really not much concerned with personality in the way of many modern novelists, his story does at least insist that these larger-than-life figures played vital roles in great events. He also suggests that great men and women have their moral weaknesses while the less obviously successful, the ostensibly fragile, can retain their moral organizing principles.

From long experience I would suggest that the impersonality of modern African history acts as a serious deterrent to young scholars. Most of us wish to get inside narrative, to understand why people do as they do, to answer those teasing "What would I have done?" questions. The answers proposed by scholarship are inevitably materialist; we tend to suggest that people act as they do because of the proddings of the processes of class, race, or gender. We have given scant attention to personality or intellectual proclivity. Students habitually enjoy the scatter of gossip in what they read, and they are utterly right to do so. The scuttlebutt—the material left out of the somber official documents and the material suppressed by those on all sides with a serious interest in deceiving us—is often important.

Abrahams's strength in this respect is very considerable, and that is why I use his book. This strength does not so much lie in the novel as an artistic achievement (for here it surely fails) as in the many things that this novel is about. For the novel is quite obviously the result of his own personal experiences of London in the 1940s, of the hectic anticolonial politics of that period. Abrahams was born in 1918 and, as a black, radical South African intellectual, decided to escape the dangers and constraints of state racism. He chose to make his home in London before making his final home in Jamaica; there he played a very significant role in the development of that country's broadcasting services. He wrote twelve books and innumerable articles. Some of his novels, especially *Mine Boy* (1946) and *Wild Conquest* (1950), are important elements in the development of the South African novel.

A Wreath for Udomo is beyond any shadow of a doubt a teasing puzzle, a roman à clef. It is possible that one of the reasons for the flatness of Abrahams's treatment of personality is very precisely because, almost without exception, his protagonists are based on real people whom he knew and who were very much alive when he published this deeply despairing book in 1956. Some of the models were towering, larger-than-life, iconic figures by the time he delivered his typescript to his publishers; and what he was saying about these demigods was subversive, for he was far from flattering. He was asserting, and asserting very strongly, that some of the people he had worked with in London had sold their ideological birthrights, had abandoned their principles, and were capable of the most cynical, murderous acts of betrayal.

Although there is no way of knowing whether my reading, my own attempt to turn the key in this roman à clef, is entirely accurate, there can be little doubt that Michael Udomo is none other than Kwame Nkrumah. Turning the key further, it is clear to me at least that the description of Thomas Lanwood does more than merely suggest that he is the great West Indian radical intellectual George Padmore. The doomed, unhappy figure of Mhendi matches in some respect the ultimately much less doomed and unhappy Jomo Kenyatta. The very thoroughly dislikable leader of the Panafrican opposition, Dr. Endura, is, I have no doubt, a fictional Dr. Joseph Boakye Danquah, while the pragmatically liberal and manipulative governor, Rosslee, is a composite of Sir Charles Arden Clarke, Arthur Creech Jones, and Lord Listowel. Such identifications creep off the page (when they do not leap off) as Abrahams, surely intentionally, drops clue after clue. But just as he laces the text with a scatter of evidence, he also tries to erase the fingerprints, to remove the smoking guns and generally disturb the scene of the crime. Although the fictional protagonists have their alternates in the real historical world, the central event, Mhendi's betrayal, has no such factual basis. For those who were part of this world, now sadly a much-reduced cohort, and for those of us who study it a half century later, there is almost something playful about all of this, even if the novel's intention is in every sense deadly serious. This book is a stark and savage denunciation, a personal attack mounted, in the manner of the satirists of the eighteenth century, in carefully encoded language.

Now Abrahams, a radical "colored" South African communist in exile, knew and worked with many of these figures in the period. As well as being a political activist, Abrahams was an experienced and much-published writer of fiction. He knew all about character and character development. The flatness of personality in this novel is, I believe, the upshot of being cautious about being overly specific and not merely because of the restrictive libel laws of the United Kingdom. Suggesting, as Abrahams does, that Nkrumah had "sold out" for pragmatic reasons was not exactly a popular view in this period, one in which Nkrumah was gracing the cover of *Time* magazine and being hailed as the leader of not only Ghana but also Africa and all people of African descent. It was certainly not the view of most radicals at the time and especially not of those with whom Abrahams was intimate, such as C. L. R. James.

My suspicion about his wish to expose but also to be seen to be unspecific, to be writing about a fictional rather than a real world, is reinforced by the almost absurd names he chooses for African states. "Pluralia" is surely a pun on the sordid and dishonest pretensions of the placatory ideology of "multiracialism" in Kenya at the time, although the literary critic Ensor believes, wrongly I think, that Pluralia represents South Africa itself (Ensor 1992). Panafrica is also a pun, for it is a name that captures Nkrumah's early political ambitions. Neither of them sound even remotely convincing as place names, and I do not believe that they were intended to be so. Their very verbal awkwardness creates space between the possibility of these being real places and Abrahams's perceived need to fictionalize reality. We might regard them as, perhaps, Peter Abrahams's Laputas, his Brobdignags, his Lilliputs.

This is, I believe, a biting satire written without much evidence of humor but full of withering irony. It is a book about the ways in which access to real power, rather than youthful idealism about achieving it, might come to destroy those very ideals; indeed, the first section of the book is actually called "The Dream." The nightmare that gradually unfolds is very much about Abrahams's reading not just of things that had happened, but of what he feared might happen. It is a prophecy because the excesses of Nkrumah's period in office (1951–1966), which came to include imprisonment without trial, internal exile, and large-scale deportations, lay in the future. But it is also a meditation on the price Abrahams believed Nkrumah had already paid for abandoning the revolution they had all planned in London in favor of negotiation with the colonial authorities so that the eventual achievement of self-rule could be achieved without bloodshed.

This strategy of negotiation rather than revolutionary confrontation is clearly regarded by Peter Abrahams as the betrayal of radical intentions by people with whom he had shared a common belief; that belief was in the need not only to liberate Africa but also to destroy every last corrosive vestige of the colonial connection, including capitalism itself. Toward the end of the novel Udomo/Nkrumah is allowed long passages of self-justification; here he very lucidly argues that dealing with the West is, in the real world rather than in theory, the only way to alleviate the primordial enemies of development and human elevation—degrading poverty, illness, and illiteracy. These justificatory passages are convincing enough. But it is a path, Abrahams suggests, that involves compromise; all compromises corrupt, he suggests, and the most dramatic symptom of such corruption ultimately involves the literal betrayal of Udomo's best friend.

So here is a novel that has its uses in the classroom as a very early, very articulate criticism of the nonrevolutionary path to independence. It predates Fanon's better-known critiques of politically acquired rather than violently seized independence by many years. It is a representative if somewhat silenced voice of the Far Left who, by the mid-1950s, were being trumped by what was actually happening in Africa, the triumph of bourgeois nationalism. By the mid-1950s gradualism, accommodation, and dialogue had extracted considerable concessions from some colonial regimes in some states far more effectively than revolutionary struggle. Abrahams, a South African, remember, deeply distrusted this drift.

The novel's uses go beyond being an accessible, excitingly discordant point of view. It is also a very remarkable piece of social history. As mentioned earlier, it is my belief that most people, and not only young people, who are interested in the study of history yearn for the sense of what it was like to be there, then. I share this need. Sometimes the historical novel, and especially the well-researched historical novel, can impart that sense better than the scrupulously footnoted monograph. For example, while there is a massive amount of historical scholarship on the French Revolution, it is initially easier to imagine what the revolution felt like for those involved from a marvelous novel like Hilary Mantel's *A Place of Greater Safety* or a stunning movie like *Danton*. In some ways *A Wreath for Udomo* can be read as one might read Georg Buchner's similarly flawed, overdidactic mid-nineteenth-century play *Danton's Death,* upon which the movie was loosely based.

Although there is some memoir material and scholarly literature on African politics in London in the 1940s, few evoke what it all felt like quite so well as Abrahams's novel. Hakim Adi and Marika Sherwood's *The 1945 Manchester Pan-African Congress Revisited* (1995), and Hakim Adi's detailed account of the history of the West African Students' Union (*West Africans in Britain*, 1998), along with Nkrumah's own autobiography and Joe Appiah's *Joe Appiah: The Autobiography of an African Patriot* certainly provide us with a great deal of information about what happened and who made it happen. But Abrahams is a better scene painter in his attention to the seemingly unimportant detail.

Asking students to imagine what it was like to be an African student politician in 1940s London is a tough demand. The London that Nkrumah, Solanke, Kenyatta, and Padmore lived in or endured is long gone. Their London was a postwar wreck of a city that had been ravaged by years of aerial bombing. Great tracts of the town were still massive bomb craters, holes in the ground being slowly overwhelmed by rose-bay willow herb, the pioneering weed that colonizes recently burned sites. There were wrecked buildings everywhere, informal memorials to those who had been killed or maimed in the nightly air raids. Clothing, gasoline, and food were strictly rationed; meat, fruit, butter, and eggs were rarities, luxuries for which people stood in line for hours. And it was terribly cold and damp in this era before central heating. The power supply was uncertain, coal was rationed, and power outages were frequent.

This bleak place, almost unimaginable to students living in the comparative comfort of late twentieth-century London, was where these remarkable people planned the 1945 Manchester Pan-African Congress in smoke-filled rooms, where the West African National Secretariat was initiated, and where the personal relationships that facilitated postindependence diplomacy were forged. It was a world of drafty meeting halls filled with ill-nourished people swaddled against the cold in poor-quality coats. Because bombing had drastically reduced the housing stock, accommodation was hard to find, and even harder if you were black, for this was also a world in which racial discrimination had yet to be made illegal. How did it feel to be black and to be poor in such a cold city? That is what needs to be understood.

Abrahams summons all of this quite excellently. He explains why such a harsh environment made for group intimacy. Beyond race and political sympathy, you needed a network if you were to get a room, to get clothing, to get a meal. He is so good at explaining how the personal and the political become entwined. How exciting it was to encounter like-minded people of any race; but how much better it was if they were to give you a mug of cocoa or to make you a meal. Abrahams steers us around from cold, dingy, ill-lit apartments to gloomy meeting halls. You can hear—and smell—the hiss of gas from the single-ring cookers. You can smell the wet-dog reek of damp clothing worn by people for whom a hot bath was at best a weekly luxury.

He is no less illuminating about the sheer effort of "doing" politics. We seldom think about what it meant to generate journals, minutes of meetings, posters, or handbills with the primitive technology of those days. If you were lucky, you had a manual typewriter all of whose keys worked; if you were lucky, you could find a fresh typewriter ribbon. You then ran off multiple copies by cutting stencils for a hand-cranked copying machine. Any misprint on those stencils required correction by hand. And when you wanted to organize meetings, you were not afforded the luxury of contacting people by telephone or electronic mail; very few people owned telephones, and those who wished to have a "phone" had to wait years for connection. There are very few cars in Abrahams's London; covering distance in what was even than a vast city was dependent upon uncomfortable public transport, much of which shut down by eleven o'clock at night. This was the very unlovely, bleak world of the envied "Been tos," the cold, utterly unromantic universe of exile.

If much of Abrahams's opening chapters provide us with this textured understanding of the experience of the lives of these heroes to be, it is reasonable to ask whether any of this matters. I have suggested that it does matter to the student who is ever alert to the inspiration of empathy. I also believe that it matters greatly to the professional historian too. Here is a powerful and very believable account of the forge of policies, attitudes, and strategies. London was where young Africans experienced the metropole and mingled with its inhabitants. Encountering colonialism and its agencies in Africa was not an encounter with, in this case, Britain. In the "real" Britain, rather than in its strange representation as colonial authority, and in the diverse, cosmopolitan world of a great capital, things seemed much more complicated. Abrahams is exquisitely sensitive to the ironies of the kaleidoscope of "race" and their lasting political significance.

Although it is white British people who hold down Udomo's countrymen and -women, any simple binary opposition based upon the happenchance of pigmentation comes apart in London. Lanwood, Udomo's hero, his role model, lives with his indispensable and always critical companion, the white communist Mary. Udomo's loneliness in London is softened by Lois, who is also white. Although Lois and her love are sacrificed for the great task of liberation, it is the chances of happiness she has shown him that flood back as memory in the tormented moments before he, now bereft of friends or a future, meets his harrowing death. There are brutal, racist whites in this novel, but Abrahams is keen to avoid essentialism. Even the colonial establishment figures are an assorted bunch. There are genuine idealists as well as dismissive, paternalist louts. Turning over the same coin, we find a further reprise of Abrahams's inherent universalist ideas. Of all the villains of the piece, it is the Endura/ Danquah character who wins the gold medal for Olympic-class nastiness. Black and white, Abrahams suggests, are equally capable of perfidy or generosity because they really are equal.

That much is straightforward enough and is pretty uncontroversial. What is of considerable value in the classroom is Abrahams's quite remarkably good depiction of how the relationships between black ministers and white civil servants worked. In all of the British-ruled territories, final independence was approached by a period of joint rule, of diarchy. Bewilderingly, African politicians who had made their careers demanding immediate independence now sat down and ruled with the active assistance of the very colonial officials whose instant removal they had once called for.

Although the documentary record for these periods of diarchy is very solid, there are few glimpses of the day-to-day realities of this abrupt role reversal when master became man and man, master. It is a credit to Abrahams's ability to understand the everyday politics of human relationships in government that he helps us see why what was so implausible in the 1940s becomes the norm by the 1950s. It is all the more remarkable because it is just this sort of cooperation that Abrahams sees as the fatal compromise, the failure to make the clean break, to cast off from the sow that murders its farrow, the old vampire, Empire. Any student reading these brief sections of the novel alongside the detailed documentary record to be found in Rathbone, *Ghana: British Documents on the End of Empire,* learns more than she or he could possibly get from the documents alone.

There is much more in this book that my students and I have found useful, but we are getting close to the point where the editor will call a halt. Allow me two more justifications for the classroom use of this novel. First, with guidance, students find Abrahams's brief account of Udomo's return to Panafrica very stimulating. In the "real world" Nkrumah is asked back to serve as general secretary of a political party formed only months before his return to Ghana in November 1947. This party, the United Gold Coast Convention, was led by a group of Africans Nkrumah was later to denounce as "reactionaries, middle class lawyers, and businessmen." Udomo is also to serve, before breaking with them, just such a group. They censor his newspaper and tone down his editorials because they own it and, of course, aspire to own him. We do not need Abrahams to help us understand that, as we have good accounts from the actors about these events. But with those contemporary accounts on board, we can start dipping into Abrahams. Here we can think about the previously unproblematized. Who owned African newspapers, and how much control did they seek to impose on their editors? What was producing a newspaper like, in technical terms? How did one distribute papers? Abrahams provides us with a hole-in-the-wall at the newspaper office, where the relationships between editor, printer, and proprietor are intriguingly acted out. That then throws the scholar back to basics. Newspapers were, we know, vital elements in the post-1945 radicalization of Africa. How did the presses run? Once again Abrahams provides us with some textured understanding of what these broad scholarly statements actually meant as lived experiences.

Finally, Nkrumah is always credited with having charisma. Udomo has this in full measure. He is an affective as well as an effective man who is instantly noticed, unignorable. Abrahams shows how charisma works. He is absolutely at his best in suggesting how it works in Africa. Nkrumah returns to Africa after more than a decade away from Africa. Udomo also returns after a long absence. Nkrumah managed in a remarkably short time to inspire amazing degrees of loyalty among a huge variety of people. How did he do that?

Well, we can let Udomo suggest some of the ways his factual alter ego managed it. In a series of vignettes Abrahams shows Udomo's unerring sense of who mattered and who did not. Udomo's cultivation of Selina, the illiterate but wealthy market woman, provides him with much-needed capital when his middle-class employers pull the plug on him. But Selina also stands at the head of a network, that of the market women. He impresses her and by so doing is able to look to her as an effective recruiting sergeant. The trick is his apparent humility. He is a member of the African middle class; like Nkrumah, his educational attainments connote a superior class position. But unlike others members of the educated elite—Endura in the fiction, Danquah in real life, for instance—Udomo and Nkrumah refuse to adopt the disdain for ordinary men and women that such status usually promoted. Udomo/Nkrumah are ardent pressers of flesh, refuse to be called "sir" or "massa," are happy to sit down in the dust to talk with the poor and weak. The novel conveys the ways in which this atypical warmth becomes a widely diffused personal myth. But it also carries with it a surgeon general's warning. Being "nicer" than other people and being a successful cultivator of the image of warmth and openness is nothing if personal principles are not maintained alongside them. Udomo dies partly because he has come to assume that his personal reputation is more important than his deeds. This is not a bad analysis of Nkrumah's removal from power in 1966, a moment that was not much mourned, at the time, by many of those who had adored him a decade before.

When I next read *A Wreath for Udomo,* I will, almost certainly, find more to enthuse about. My slow decoding of the novel has taken years, and, such as they are, my deciphering skills have developed as my knowledge of the more formal primary material has grown. In this, as in so much more, I am aided annually by a team of young sleuths, for there is always someone who notices something that I have missed. It is over thirty years since I first read Nkrumah's autobiography, for example, a book I have read closely and many times. In 1997 one of my students pointed out in an acute essay that Nkrumah quite intentionally and instrumentally misquotes a poem of Walt Whitman's on the first page. She had been smart enough to go back to Whitman; I had trusted Nkrumah.

A Wreath for Udomo is most assuredly not a biography of Nkrumah in disguise. If it was presented as such, then it is chock-full of inaccuracy and distortion. But it is an unusually stimulating way of coming at the well-documented "facts." It constantly demands that we think about things that are not covered by the documentary record. Some of the questions posed by Abrahams are incapable of being answered by that record. But some of them are very important indeed. Their importance is in part a function of the fact that Peter

Abrahams "was there," and these things, personal relationships, mood, sense of place, seemed important enough for him to include in his narrative. Our annual judgment is that he is at the very least a wonderful witness.

SUGGESTIONS FOR FURTHER READING

Abrahams, Peter. 1946. *Mine Boy*. London: Crisp.

———. 1950. *Wild Conquest*. London: Faber and Faber.

Adi, Hakim. 1998. *West Africans in Britain: Nationalism, Pan Africanism, and Communism*. London: Lawrence and Wishart. Much the best evocation of the political world Abrahams lived in and the comrades with whom he worked. See especially the chapter "Africanisation and Radicalization: Cold War Responses 1945–49."

Adi, Hakim, and Marika Sherwood. 1995. *The 1945 Manchester Pan-African Congress Revisited*. London: New Beacon Books.

Appiah, Joe. 1990. *Joe Appiah: The Autobiography of an African Patriot*. Westport, Conn.: Praeger.

Armah, Ayei Kwei. 1975. *The Beautyful Ones Are Not Yet Born*. Portsmouth, N.H.: Heinemann. First published in 1968. (See Chapter 3 of this volume).

Austin, Dennis. 1964. *Politics in Ghana*. London: Oxford University Press.

Bourret, F. M. 1960. *Ghana: The Road to Independence*. London: Oxford University Press. Bourret's short classic still remains the most concise introduction to the place and the period.

Buchner, Georg. 1961. *Danton's Death*, trans. James Maxwell. San Francisco: Chandler. A mid-nineteenth-century play.

Duodo, Cameron. 1967. *The Gab Boys*. London: Deutsch. The "gab boys" (named for their gabardine trousers) are the sharply dressed youngsters who hang around Ghanaian villages. A sadly undervalued novel of 1960s Ghana.

Ensor, R. 1992. *The Novels of Peter Abrahams and the Rise of Nationalism in Africa*. Essen: Verlag die Blaue Eule. Those who like chapters called "Interdiscourse and Intersemiosis: Towards an Iconology of Abrahams's Novels" could try this work, which I personally find very heavy going.

Mantel, Hilary. 1993. *A Place of Greater Safety*. Harmondsworth: Penguin. First published by Viking in 1992.

Nkrumah, Kwame. 1957. *Ghana*. Edinburgh: Thomas Nelson. Nkrumah's autobiography.

Ogungbesan, K. 1979. *The Writing of Peter Abrahams*. London: Hodder and Stoughton. Among the most accessible writing on Abrahams's literary career.

Rathbone, Richard, ed. 1992. *Ghana: British Documents on the End of Empire*. 2 vols. London: Her Majesty's Stationery Office.

Wade, M. 1972. *Peter Abrahams*. London: Evans. Another very accessible account of Abrahams's literary career.

2

Chinua Achebe's
Things Fall Apart

Martin A. Klein

ONE OF THE MAJOR PROBLEMS IN TEACHING AFRICAN history is that few of our students have a real sense of what Africa is like. Most have highly stereotypic images of Africa and African life, often based on television—reruns of "Tarzan," starving children in Ethiopia, or Humphrey Bogart pushing the *African Queen* up a muddy but unpopulated stream. The Africa in their minds is almost always an Africa of the jungle and rarely an Africa of cleared fields or open savanna. It is sometimes an Africa of kings and warriors, rarely an Africa of simple and practical peasants, and usually an Africa of victims. Both films and novels are useful in giving students a sense of what Africa looks and feels like and how Africans think and relate to each other. Chinua Achebe's *Things Fall Apart* goes beyond this and introduces a series of themes that I deal with in my courses. I have used a number of novels over the years, but *Things Fall Apart* is by far the most effective.

I have used *Things Fall Apart* in a first-year history course on the world outside the West, where it is designed to give students an African view of traditional society and colonization. I have also used it in a third-year course on twentieth-century Africa, where it introduces a series of major themes. A number of things make it useful. First, the text is only 148 pages long, readable, and very engrossing, an assignment most students can handle in a week. It also covers with incredible terseness a wide range of topics. It is the perfect novel for a discussion section or an undergraduate seminar. Second,

---

Chinua Achebe, *Things Fall Apart* (Portsmouth, N.H.: Heinemann, 1997).

the novel deals with a decentralized society. If the instructor wants to call into question the association of large states with progress and "civilization," this novel helps do so effectively.

Third, it vividly recreates Igbo society in the early twentieth century. Achebe uses proverbs and tries to recreate the speech and patterns of thought of his Igbo ancestors. His characters deal with problems of day-to-day life. They negotiate marriages, fall in love, and raise children. They play and they work. They also struggle with deeper problems of life and death. Achebe makes no effort to hide those aspects of traditional values he and most of his readers find unattractive. Rather, he makes those values comprehensible and sets them in context. It is the tensions within Igbo society itself that produce the climax.

A NOTE ON ACHEBE'S LIFE AND WORK

Chinua Achebe was born in 1930 into a pioneer Christian family in Ogidi, eastern Nigeria, and attended a missionary-run primary school there. An early graduate of the University of Ibadan (where he studied literature), Achebe worked for the Nigerian Broadcasting Company and was director of external broadcasting from 1961 to 1966. During the political upheavals that followed the military coup of July 1966, he was forced to flee to Biafra, where he became a spokesman for the breakaway state during the Nigerian Civil War. After the defeat of Biafra, he taught for a number of years in the United States before returning in 1976 to teach at the University of Nigeria. He was made emeritus professor in 1985. In recent years Achebe has made his home in New York, teaching at Bard College.

Things Fall Apart was first published in 1958 at a time when there was hardly any market for contemporary African fiction, either inside Africa or in the West. Publisher William Heinemann decided to take a chance on this unknown author with a print run of only two thousand copies. The rest is history: at this point the novel has been translated into roughly forty-five languages and has sold over eight million copies. In 1962 *Things Fall Apart* was republished as the first book in the African Writers Series, and Achebe served as editor of that series for many years.

In *Things Fall Apart* Achebe introduces us to Igbo society in the late nineteenth century and gives us an Igbo view of the beginnings of colonial rule. This portrayal is so simple and so effective that the book has been reprinted more than thirty times. It was the first African novel to be successful outside the continent and is probably the most successful African novel ever. *Things Fall Apart* was the first of a trilogy of novels that highlight the ambiguities of colonization. The others are *No Longer at Ease* (1960), which dealt with decolonization, and *Arrow of God* (1964), based on a real incident in which a traditional priest refused a chiefly appointment. Achebe's later involvement in the events of his time increasingly pulled him away from the exploration of the past. *Man of the People* (1966) was a more disillusioned book, an attack on the corruption of Nigeria's new elites and an analysis of the political crisis that led to the civil war. *Anthills of the Savanna* (1987) later picked up on these political themes.

SUMMARY OF THE PLOT

The novel begins with a wrestling match in which the young Okonkwo defeats the reigning champion of his region. Achebe thus introduces him as a man who is large, strong, and fast, a physically powerful man, but also one who demands much of himself. Okonkwo's determination has been shaped by the shame of a ne'er-do-well father—a convivial man who enjoyed playing the flute and socializing, a good drinking companion but a poor farmer who never took a title and was mired in debt. Okonkwo is determined to be everything his father was not. Because of that compulsion, he is the embodiment of Igbo values in all regards but one: he does nothing in moderation. Sometimes this is good. Okonkwo does not inherit a barn full of yams, but he is able to borrow yams because he sees a good investment. He becomes a successful farmer, takes three wives, and has over a dozen children. He is also feared as a warrior and has taken five human heads in combat. He is respected and has loyal friends. He is also harsh, demanding of his wives and children, uncompromising in his convictions, and afraid of ever expressing his emotions. Just as Okonkwo reacted to his father's softness, so his oldest son, Nwoye, responds to Okonkwo's harshness. Nwoye is a gentler and softer person, which Okonkwo sees as weakness.

The action of the novel centers on two crises. The first begins when a woman from Umuofia is killed at a nearby market. The nine villages of Umuofia are called to a meeting, where they decide to go to war if compensation is not given. Such is Umuofia's military reputation that the neighboring community submits and gives Umuofia a boy and a girl. Okonkwo carries out the ultimatum and brings the children back with him. The girl goes to the man who had lost a wife. The boy, Ikemefuna, a fifteen-year-old, belongs to the whole clan but is entrusted to Okonkwo's keeping. Though at first depressed, Ikemefuna speedily becomes part of the family. He is lively and knows many stories; he can make flutes, trap rodents, and identify birds. Most important, he and Nwoye become good friends and work together with Okonkwo. Okonkwo is pleased with Ikemefuna, and increasingly with Nwoye, though he cannot bring himself to show his pleasure. Okonkwo increasingly treats Ikemefuna like a son. Then, after three years, the Oracle of the Hills and the Caves decides that he must be killed. One of Okonkwo's friends tells him: "The boy calls you father. Do not bear a hand in his death." Okonkwo cannot allow himself to be soft. He goes with the men who take Ikemefuna away, and when the first blow with a machete does not kill the boy, Okonkwo himself deals the fatal blow. The price he pays is the disaffection of his oldest son.

Not long afterward, at the funeral of a friend, Okonkwo's gun explodes, accidentally killing another mourner. Taking the life of a clansman, even accidentally, is a crime against the Earth Goddess and pollutes the earth. After Okonkwo gives all of the yams in his barn to a friend, his compound is destroyed and he goes into exile with his family for seven years. They go to the village of his mother's clan, where they are well received and he is able to reestablish his fortune speedily. While Okonkwo is in exile, British missionaries and colonial officials arrive. When a white man on a bicycle arrives in a village not far from them, he is killed and the British respond by massacring the village. No village is likely to challenge British power after this, although some men, like Okonkwo, are determined to fight the invaders. The last part of the novel describes the development of Christianity, the establishment of the colonial state, and the penetration of the colonial economy. It also describes the inability of Okonkwo, now back in Umuofia, to cope with these changes.

Most early converts were people of low status, for example, men who never took a title or people alienated by their own society, such as the mothers of twins. The first member of a good family to join the Christians is Nwoye, who rapidly becomes a good student and is sent to school by the mission. Okonkwo cannot accept this rejection of his ancestors' beliefs and treats Nwoye as if he were dead. Christianity thus polarizes the community. When Enoch, one of the more passionate Christian converts, unmasks one of the masked *egwugu*, the masked spirits descend on the Christian community and destroy Enoch's compound and the church. Six of the leaders of Umuofia are then called to a meeting with the District Commissioner, at which they are arrested. Umuofia is then forced to pay a fine for their release. Through all of this, Okonkwo is determined to make war. When a meeting is called to discuss whether to revolt, a band of messengers from the District Commissioner arrives to tell them to disperse. Okonkwo takes out his machete and kills the head messenger with one blow, but no one follows his example, and the other messengers withdraw. Knowing he has lost the debate and will be called before the white man's justice, Okonkwo goes into the bush and hangs himself. Ironically, this man who was determined to be the perfect Igbo pollutes the earth in his death by taking his own life. His best friend, who stood by him through all of his difficulties, tells the District Commissioner: "That man was one of the greatest men in Umuofia. You drove him to kill himself; and now he will be buried like a dog" (p. 147).

CLASSROOM DISCUSSION AND MAJOR THEMES

A series of themes woven through the novel initiate useful discussions of issues that will come up in these history courses. The first of these is a very vivid depiction of precolonial Igbo culture. Achebe depicts the intense Igbo attachment to the earth and its cultivation. He describes family life, gender roles, and the raising of children. There is a contrast between Okonkwo's relationship with Nwoye and with his favorite daughter, Ezinma. Reluctant as Okonkwo is to show emotion, he feels freer to do so with a daughter, and she remains more loyal to him. The student confronts the importance of kinship and community, the ties that bind a man to his wives and children, and those that link all of the people of Umuofia. Okonkwo's exile introduces the importance of matrilineal linkages in a patrilineal society. The novel depicts the broader values of the society, perhaps most strongly in the contrast between Okonkwo's excessive fear of showing emotion or yielding to weakness and the more humane values of the others. When Ikemefuna is led away, there is sorrow in Okonkwo's compound and even those who take him away find the obligation painful.

The second theme is government. This produces some of the

most interesting discussions among students because the study of
Igbo government calls into question many assumptions about politics. We tend to objectify political authority and see it as the emana-
tion of presidents, governors, and kings. We also assume that
progress is associated with bigness, with empires and kingdoms, with
great conquerors and powerful states. Achebe confronts us with a
society that had neither hereditary roles nor any person with the
capacity to decide for others. All authority is achieved and transient.
Okonkwo becomes a powerful man though he inherits no wealth and
his father has no titles. Men achieve authority by purchasing titles
with the wealth they acquire by being good farmers and producing
surplus.

The only woman who possesses any authority is the priestess of
the Oracle of the Hills and the Caves, who is by day an ordinary
woman who sells in the market. At night, at the shrine, she has the
power to settle conflicts and to stop wars, and in the case of
Ikemefuna, she has the power of life and death. *Things Fall Apart*
has been criticized for its depiction of female passivity, but even
there, the novel opens up for discussion a question of female roles. I
often suggest that students unhappy with Achebe's portrayal of
women in the novel write a paper on Igbo women. Interested students might also be encouraged to read Flora Nwapa's *Efuru*, a novel
written at least in part to present a different vision of Igbo women's
roles (see Chapter 18 in this volume).

There are two crucial aspects of government. One is the resolution of conflict. When negotiation between clans fails to resolve conflicts, Igbo can appeal to either the god Agbala at the Oracle of the
Hills and the Caves or to the masked *egwugu* spirits. The *egwugu* are
village elders; once masked, however, they become ancestors and
can either act to intimidate wrongdoers or hear cases. Both the shrine
and the *egwugu* hear cases.

Igbo society is not so simple that interclan discussions and an
occasional appeal to the spirits can resolve all problems. Eastern
Nigeria is densely populated, and communities frequently come into
conflict with each other. A typical Igbo polity, Umuofia consists of
nine villages that come together in periods of stress. The most important decisions center on matters of war and peace. When there is an
issue to be decided, the village criers announce a meeting and the
nine villages assemble. These are not democratic town meetings.
There are about ten thousand men at a Umuofia meeting, and the
only speakers are elders, men who hold titles. Those who carry the
day are generally men with powerful voices and persuasive argu-

ments. There is no vote, but rather a search for consensus, usually a consensus dominated by the major title holders. When Okonkwo kills the messenger and no one kills the other messengers, he knows he has lost the argument before he has even spoken.

The third theme is traditional religion. The behavior of the novel's major characters is bounded by Igbo cosmology. Life is regulated by rituals, each of which expresses fundamental religious values. There is a concern with pollution, which is rooted in a respect for the sanctity of life. Every person has a *chi*, a personal god who provides protection—in a sense, a guardian angel. Perhaps most important, Achebe forces the reader to recognize the spirituality of Igbo life. There is a sense of awe rooted in fear of death and uncertainty about the future. This fear of death lies behind many Igbo religious practices. The Igbo are concerned about signs of divine displeasure. Thus, twins are left out to die. There is also a belief that when a woman's children repeatedly die, she is cursed by an *ogbanje*, a child who repeatedly dies and returns to its mother to be reborn. To dissuade the *ogbanje* from returning, the child's body is mutilated and cast into the Evil Forest.

Ethnicity is not a theme that is highly developed in the novel, and yet certain passages open up interesting discussions of identity. The main actors in the novel do not think of themselves as Igbo because everyone around them is Igbo. They identify, rather, with Umuofia. When the British move into the area, both the missions and the colonial state have recruited Igbo, but mostly from coastal or riverine areas that were colonized earlier. They address the local people in Igbo, but their dialect is very different. The word "myself" sounds to Umuofia people like "my buttocks," which produces much jesting. They are eventually referred to as the "ashy buttocks" because of the gray pants they wear. The court messengers are hated "because they were foreigners and also arrogant and high-handed" (p. 123). They do not bond with local people, are often abusive, and use their intermediary role to exploit. They are strangers, see themselves as strangers, and are seen as strangers.

Igbo society is based on individual achievement, with no commitment to equality. It is interesting that Achebe does not deal with slaves or the slave trade, which were still important at the end of the nineteenth century. Outcasts play a marginal role in the novel, but Okonkwo has only contempt for weak men and those who are not good producers. Achebe portrays an Igbo society clearly based on hierarchy. Of course inheritance is important—life is easier for a man who inherits a full barn or whose father buys his first title, as

Okonkwo intends to do for his oldest sons. None of this can guarantee, however, that these sons will accumulate more titles or will have their voices heard in Igbo assemblies. Nor does it bar the son of a failure from becoming one of the most powerful men in the village.

European penetration is profoundly disruptive in the long run, yet the impact of the colonial state is at first limited. "They had built a court," Achebe tells us, "where the District Commissioner judged cases in ignorance" (p. 123). The District Commissioner understands neither Igbo values nor Igbo law. People have more positive feelings toward the shops where they can sell palm oil and buy consumer goods, but these shops extend only market relations that are already highly developed among the Igbo. Achebe's Europeans tend to be flat, a series of stereotypes, as they probably were to the early Igbo. In the period covered by this novel, it is the missions that have the deepest impact, both because religion lies at the heart of so much Igbo behavior and because the missionaries are present in the villages. This is a theme Achebe picks up again in *Arrow of God*, where the inability of the priest to preside over the annual yam festival leads to a religious crisis and opens a door to the missions. The elders are hostile to the first missionaries, who threaten the unity of their communities and claim that Igbo gods are false gods. When the missionaries at Mbanta, the village of Okonkwo's exile, ask for land, they are given a plot in the Evil Forest, a sinister area of darkness where those who die of horrible diseases like smallpox and leprosy are buried. Everyone expects the Christians to die within days. When they build their church and do not die, everyone realizes that they have a fetish with "unbelievable power" (p. 106). In Mbanta, conflict takes place when a zealous convert kills a python, the totem of the clan, and the village assembly decides to ostracize the Christians. Christian women are even denied the right to take water at the stream. The conflict is resolved when the zealot suddenly dies. For a moment, the gods seem to be taking care of their own problems.

Achebe describes two missionaries, Mr. Brown and James Smith. Mr. Brown is open-minded, curious, and tolerant. He discourages excesses of zeal that might produce conflict and becomes friends with many leading men in the village. A conversation with one of those men underlines the differences between Igbo and Christian religious belief. "Your Queen sends her messenger, the District Commissioner," the elder explains: "He finds that he cannot do the work alone and he appoints *kotma* [messengers] to help him. It is the same with God or Chukwu. He appoints the smaller gods to help Him because his work is too great for one person" (p. 127).

Mr. Brown thus learns the Igbo conception of God and learns to respect Igbo ways. He first gathers outsiders, people of low status, and then those who are alienated—women who have borne twins and *ogbanje*, and young men like Nwoye. When illness forces Brown to return to Britain, his successor, James Smith, is intolerant and unhappy at the laxness of many of these early converts. Smith's intolerance and Enoch's zeal produce the final crisis.

Both state and mission are dependent on African intermediaries, but the missionaries are in the village, and their catechists are more committed than the messengers and interpreters of the colonial state. Kiaga, the African minister in Mbanta, is an attractive figure. Inevitably, the missions need protection and the state is able to use its intervention to extend its control. The elders arrested after the destruction of the mission are abused in detention by their guards. When the District Commissioner imposes a fine of 200 bags of cowries, the guards translate the amount into Igbo as 250 bags, keeping the extra 50 bags for themselves.

An element of nostalgia characterizes the early part of the novel. Igbo society functions well and deals with most of its own problems. The reader feels regret for a world that no longer exists, but much of the action flows from tensions within that world. Okonkwo's efforts to prove himself in a very achievement-oriented society lead to his own destruction. The early success of Christianity is rooted in the existence of people of low status and people alienated by the harsher Igbo customs. Those who bear twins are attracted to a religion that rejects the killing of twins. Nwoye is attracted to the poetry of Christianity, largely because he is alienated by both his father's harshness and the killing of Ikemefuna. When Nwoye comes to tell his father that he has become a Christian, Okonkwo is prevented from killing him only by the timely intervention of a friend. Nwoye leaves for school without his father's blessing.

Nwoye never sees his father again, but Achebe tells us that after Okonkwo's death, Nwoye returns and converts other members of his family. In Achebe's subsequent novel *No Longer at Ease*, we return to the character of Nwoye. By this time, Nwoye is an elder in the Church, a defender of traditional values being challenged by his son, Obi Okonkwo, who wants to marry an outcast. *No Longer at Ease* is a less widely read novel. It deals with a different period of change, this time to independence, but it complements *Things Fall Apart* and underlines the continuities that exist, even during a period of disruptive change.

The chief virtue of *Things Fall Apart*, for a history teacher, is thus that it not only gives the student a feel for one particular society, but that it opens a series of questions that most instructors will or should deal with at some point in a course on African history. Achebe's terseness means that the student covers a range of questions in a short but pleasant read. The book ends on an ironic note with the musings of the District Commissioner, whose soldiers have to remove Okonkwo's dangling body from the tree on which he has hanged himself. He is told that Okonkwo's clansmen cannot take the body down because Okonkwo committed an abomination by killing himself. After burying the body, the clansmen will have to perform sacrifices to cleanse the desecrated land. All this seems quite exotic to the Distrct Commissioner, who intends to devote a paragraph on the case in his book on *The Pacification of the Primitive Tribes of the Lower Niger*. Achebe has so successfully immersed us in the Igbo worldview that most readers will stop to wonder who and what was primitive.

SUGGESTIONS FOR
FURTHER READING AND RESOURCES

Achebe, Chinua. 1960. *No Longer at Ease*. London: Heinemann.
———. 1964. *Arrow of God*. London: Heinemann.
———. 1988. *Anthills of the Savanna*. Garden City, N.Y.: Anchor/ Doubleday.
———. 1996. *Things Fall Apart*. Portsmouth, N.H.: Heinemann. This "Classics in Context" edition contains notes, maps, a glossary, and background material that may be particularly helpful to nonspecialists.
Ekechi, Felix N. 1971. *Missionary Enterprise and Rivalry in Igboland 1857–1914*. London: Frank Cass.
Gikandi, Simon. 1991. *Reading Chinua Achebe: Language and Ideology in Fiction*. London: Heinemann.
Innes, C. L. 1990. *Chinua Achebe*. Cambridge: Cambridge University Press.
Isichei, Elizabeth. 1976. *A History of the Igbo People*. London: Macmillan.
Nwapa, Flora. 1966. *Efuru*. Portsmouth, N.H.: Heinemann. A portrayal of Igbo society from the perspective of a strong and independent woman. See Chapter 18 in this volume.
Ogbaa, Kalu, ed. 1999. *Understanding* Things Fall Apart*: A Student Casebook to Issues, Sources, and Historical Documents*. Westport, Conn.: Greenwood. A casebook of excerpts from a wide range of previously published materials, with more attention to Igbo history and culture than to literary assessments of Achebe's work.
Ohadike, Don C. 1994. *Anioma: A Social History of the Western Igbo People*. Athens: Ohio University Press. A broad overview of the Igbo

people living west of the Niger River from earliest settlements to modern times.

Ohaeto, Ezenwa. 1997. *Chinua Achebe: A Biography.* Bloomington: Indiana University Press, and Oxford: James Currey.

Uchendu, Victor. 1965. *The Igbo of Southeastern Nigeria.* New York: Holt, Rinehart and Winston. A somewhat dated but very accessible introduction.

Wren, Robert M. 1980. *Achebe's World: The Historical and Cultural Context of the Novels.* Washington, D.C.: Three Continents.

3

Ayi Kwei Armah's *The Beautyful Ones Are Not Yet Born*

Emmanuel Akyeampong

ARMAH'S *BEAUTYFUL ONES* IS THE MOST POWERFUL novel written on political and moral decay in independent Ghana. Based on the twilight years of Nkrumah's government (1951–1966), the novel's major attraction lies not only in its dramatic depiction of life in Nkrumah's Ghana, but also in how the events and developments it describes fictionally for the mid-1960s equally hold true under subsequent regimes in Ghana. For Western societies, where bribery and corruption are seen as anomalies, the novel sets up a different context in which honesty and integrity are anomalies, and explores the social and cultural factors underpinning corruption. The novel is set in the railway and harbor town of Sekondi-Takoradi, and its intimate description of working-class life is the social historian's dream. Armah explores how ordinary people are affected by the larger issues of political economy, and their coping mechanisms for survival in a declining national economy.

For many readers, including my students, what is most striking about the novel—in their initial impression—is its strong language. Rot (especially of wood), filth, and human excrement are major images in the novel. Together, they conjure the inexorable, natural trend toward decay in all living organisms, and provide an interesting argument against striving for moral rectitude in this context. Most of the characters in the book are obsessed about material acquisitions and urge relations or loved ones forward in the mad scramble to

Ayi Kwei Armah, *The Beautyful Ones Are Not Yet Born* (Portsmouth, N.H.: Heinemann, 1975).

acquire wealth. In the past two decades or so, when bribery and corruption in African countries have provoked international attention
and censure, Armah's novel leads us into the world of accumulation
and conspicuous consumption in Ghana. Read alongside Thomas
McCaskie's two essays titled "Accumulation, Wealth and Belief in
Asante History," the reader gains an important understanding about
the culture of wealth and power in southern Ghana. For former students who have written to me after their time at Harvard, it is
Armah's novel that left the strongest imprint on their understanding
of contemporary West Africa.

I use Armah's novel in my History 1907 course, West Africa
from 1800 to the Present. The course is a sequel to History 1906,
West Africa from the Earliest Times to 1800. Africa is gradually
emerging as a major field of inquiry at Harvard University, and several faculty members teaching on Africa coordinate their efforts
through a Committee on African Studies. This committee offers a
Certificate in African Studies at the undergraduate level. The history
department at Harvard is noted for American and European history,
and several students seldom take more than one or two courses in
African history. Graduate recruitment in Africa programs is growing
in the social sciences, and history, art history, government, anthropology, and economics are major beneficiaries. Graduate and undergraduate students interested in West African history enroll in History
1906 and History 1907. The modern West Africa survey is the more
popular course, and it is often the first Africa course for some of the
enrolled students. Maps, African novels, and film are crucial to the
course as visual aids for those who have never been to Africa, and to
heighten the human drama and sense of immediacy. These include
Basil Davidson's documentary series *Africa: A Voyage of Discovery*,
Chinua Achebe's *Things Fall Apart* (see Chapter 2), Ferdinand
Oyono's *Houseboy* (see Chapter 19), and Mongo Beti's *Remember
Ruben*. Student enrollment ranges from ten to thirty.

Armah's *Beautyful Ones* is set in Sekondi-Takoradi, and much of
the events described in the book take place in a ten-day phase. In all,
the novel stretches probably over not more than a year, and ends with
the overthrow of Kwame Nkrumah's Convention People's Party
(CPP) in a military coup in February 1966. The main character,
called only "the man," has some secondary school education and
works at the Railway and Harbor Administration in Takoradi. The
novel opens on a Wednesday with the man working the 5 A.M. to 7 P.M.
shift as a traffic controller, monitoring the movement of trains. He is
married to Oyo and has three children. An interesting early tension is

set up in the novel between "passion week" and "payday." In this working-class town with its meager wages, wages ensure a modicum of comfort only in the first week; then follows a period of belt tightening. The last week before "payday" (on a monthly cycle) is "passion week," when deprivation peaks. Workers barely have enough money for public transport to and from work, and many are compelled to skip lunch. Though the government has declared the country a socialist country, the opulence of public officials stands in stark contrast to the working poor. A dog-eat-dog mentality is created: the rich prey on the poor, and the poor on the poor. Survival, or getting ahead, is the name of the game.

Against this context, a timber merchant, Amankwa, comes to the man's office and offers him twenty Ghanaian cedis to facilitate the transport of his felled logs from his inland concession to the harbor. The man declines and instructs Amankwa to come in during regular hours the following day and apply to the booking clerk. After his protracted cajoling fails, the timber contractor actually gets offended: "But why?" he shouts. "Why do you treat me so? What have I done against you? Tell me, what have I done?" "Scratch my back and I'll scratch your back" has become so ingrained in Ghanaian social relations that the timber merchant is confounded in his confrontation with a man of integrity. The man is perverse, not the timber merchant. The irony here is that this is such a routine procedure that the man does not understand why the timber contractor is offering him a bribe. But economic difficulties have created an environment where nothing is for free. The exchange of money and gifts lubricate even the most trivial requests. At the bus station after work, a powerful new car pulls up, and the driver alights to buy oranges. The suited owner of the car follows to buy bread. This is Joseph Koomson, a CPP stalwart and a minister in the Nkrumah government. He is an old schoolmate of the man's, and their families remain friends. He spies the man waiting for a bus, and he leads him to the car to greet Estella, his perfumed, expensively dressed wife. Koomson apologizes for not being able to drop the man off at home: they are late for a rendezvous with friends at the Atlantic-Caprice Hotel. They promise to visit the man and his wife on Sunday. The author juxtaposes the world of the Railway and Harbor office and that of the Atlantic-Caprice, a stone's throw away, in his examination of the lifestyles of the poor and the rich.

The man arrives home to his chamber-and-hall (two-room residence), and the flat look in his wife's eyes—"eyes totally accepting and unquestioning in the way only a thing from which nothing is ever expected can be accepted and not questioned"—immediately alerts the reader to a tense domestic situation. In fact, it seems to the man that his three little children are learning the same flat look from their mother—a defense against hope. The man tells his wife of his encounter with the Koomsons. "She has married well," replies Oyo in reference to Estella, a not-so-subtle indictment of the man. But Oyo's barbs are nothing in comparison to her mother's, who seems to specialize in throwing the man's poverty in his face. The man informs Oyo that the Koomsons will be visiting on Sunday. Koomson is planning on buying a motorized fishing boat. Because the ministers of a "socialist" regime ought to be circumspect in their dealings, he has proposed buying the boat in the name of Oyo and Oyo's mother. The man is uneasy about this arrangement and its possible repercussions. He mentions his reservations to Oyo and draws his wife's ire. Indeed, Oyo calls him *chichidodo*, a reference to a bird that detests human excrement but relishes maggots, which feed on excrement. How can a man who brings so little money home dare to criticize the efforts of others to uplift the finances of the same home! This is obviously not the time to mention that a timber contractor has offered him a bribe for a very simple request. But the man does, and his wife knows offhand that the husband would refuse. Her retort is illuminating: "When you shook Estella Koomson's hand, was not the perfume that stayed on your hands a pleasing thing? Maybe you like this crawling that we do, but I am tired of it." Like Estella, Oyo would like to ride in their car. At least there would be sufficient food at home and shoes on her children's feet.

The man often seeks refuge with his friend, "the teacher," when he feels besieged at home. It appears that the two people with integrity in the novel lack names: they are an endangered species in independent Ghana. The teacher has cut himself away from his relations and has chosen to remain single in his endeavor to remain pure. The implication here is that families and relatives push individuals into aggrandizement and moral corruption. Chapter 6, where these two characters reflect over their lives and the nation's destiny, is perhaps the most important and informative chapter in the novel. Preparing for the Koomsons' visit is a major enterprise. The visit coincides with payday, and the man visits High Street to buy the expensive food items and liquor required by Oyo for the occasion. In spite of himself, the man cannot ignore the thrill of wealth and power he experiences through buying these items, and especially the admiring glances of fellow shoppers. Eventually, Oyo signs the papers for the boat business. As the man suspected, Oyo and her mother receive no financial gain from the venture aside from the occasional packages of fish, which cease after a time. Oyo resigns herself to her fate, perhaps wondering inwardly if her husband has not been right all along.

The climax of the book is the coup of February 1966. Government ministers and high party officials are being arrested, and a cowering Koomson seeks refuge in the man's bedroom. The man returns home from work to find a new look in his wife's eyes: the look of respect and trust. At a time when those associated with the toppled regime walk in fear, the man walks tall and fearless. Koomson is so immobilized by fear that he exudes, literally, an overpowering stench. Oyo now confesses to her husband: "I am glad you never became like him." Eventually, the military forces track Koomson to the man's house, and Koomson and the man are forced to make their escape through the hole in the pit latrine in the man's house. This latrine is so decrepit and stinking that the man himself prefers to use the latrine at work, another oversubscribed latrine. It seems a fitting end to Koomson and the likes of him, considering the use of excrement as a leitmotif in this novel: from shit to shit.

HISTORICAL CONTEXT

Sekondi grew from a fishing village into an important railway town when it became the terminus of the railway network in 1898. The colonial government constructed railway lines to link the interior mines with the natural harbor at Sekondi. Shortage of labor led to the immigration of numerous ethnic groups to Sekondi, and stevedores and railway workers became a significant constituency. The government built a deep-water harbor at adjacent Takoradi in 1927, and the two towns merged into the twin city of Sekondi-Takoradi. Housing conditions in Sekondi-Takoradi were far from congenial even at the time of K. A. Busia's *Social Survey* (1950). Social life was lived mostly outdoors.

The rigors of railway labor forged the workers into a strong union, and the politicized railway workers were a potent force in Nkrumah's CPP. Indeed, Sekondi-Takoradi was one of the few places that gave some attention in the 1930s to the communist agitation of the labor activist, I. T. A. Wallace Johnson. The railway workers were instrumental in the effectiveness of Nkrumah's "Positive Action" campaign in January 1950, which revised the colonial government's estimation of the popularity of the new CPP. Nkrumah

abandoned the railway workers shortly after independence, and a far-
cical regime acquired wealth while preaching socialism as official
policy from 1960. The brutal suppression of the railway workers'
strike in 1961 underscored the great divide that had emerged between
Nkrumah and his former allies. The years between 1960 and 1966
were painful ones for Sekondi-Takoradi inhabitants. For political
skeptics such as the railway workers, they had identified with the
simple lifestyle and the revolutionary vision of Nkrumah. They wondered about what had changed Nkrumah, and if Nkrumah had
changed, whether virtue could be found in any politician.

Students in my History 1907 course are always curious about the
author after reading *Beautyful Ones*, and what sparked such disgust
in him against his own society. Ayi Kwei Armah (also known as
George Armah) is a product of the renowned Achimota College, one
of the leading secondary schools in Ghana, and the alma mater of
Nkrumah and Flight Lieutenant John Jerry Rawlings, the present
head of state. His literary talents were abundantly manifest even in
his formative years, and the relevant chapters in Bernth Lindfors's
African Textualities provide the necessary biographical background.
At Achimota, Armah excelled academically and in extracurricular
affairs, ending up as chief editor of the campus magazine, *The
Achimotan*. He graduated from Achimota in 1958, a year after
Ghana's independence, and worked for eight months as a Radio
Ghana scriptwriter, reporter, and announcer. In the fall of 1959, he
gained admission to Groton School in Groton, Massachusetts,
through the American Field Service (AFS) program and spent a year
there before his entry to Harvard University in 1960. He graduated
from Harvard in 1964.

It is obvious even from his Groton writings in *The Grotonian*
that Armah had an agile, mature mind and read far beyond course
requirements. He had begun to tackle the issues of colonialism, the
East-West divide in the era of cold war, and the place of nonalign-
ment in global politics. These are heavy subjects, and his immersion
in social studies at Harvard provided the theoretical grounding for
his literary forays into issues of race, power, class, gender, and age.
The fate of the fledgling Harvard African and Afro-American
Students' Association, denied recognition in 1963, the Congo crisis
and the assassination of Patrice Lumumba, and the violence of the
civil rights crusade generated disillusion and despair for a sensitive
intellectual like Armah. Armah's identity had undergone important
changes in his years in the United States, and as he became
"African" in intellect and disposition, he dropped the "George" and

reverted to "Ayi Kwei." His writings reflect these mental processes, and one of his essays at Harvard won the Harvard prize for best short fiction in 1963. He quit Harvard in 1963 and went to Algeria to work as an English translator for *Révolution Africaine*. His health broke down in less than a year, and he returned to hospitalization in Boston. He completed his degree at Harvard at this time and returned to Ghana with a bachelor's degree in 1964. Armah's first novel was *Beautyful Ones* (1968). In this novel and a subsequent one, *Fragments*, Armah's heroes—against the general trend—turn their backs on the materialist world of the West. His work introduced the themes of isolation, loneliness, and anomie into Ghanaian literature. His lead characters are "thinkers," and they reflect Armah's personal search to define his role as an African intellectual in Africa during a phase of reconstruction. In fact, Lindfors describes Armah as a "romantic revolutionary."

In addition to teaching for brief periods at the universities of Massachusetts and Wisconsin, Armah spent some five years traveling in East and southern Africa, writing and teaching in various colleges and universities. He has consistently refused to be interviewed or to discuss his work. At the present, Armah lives in Dakar, where he has established a publishing house and is affiliated with CODESRIA (Council for the Development of Social Science Research in Africa). In 1997 he gave a series of lectures on "Pan-Africanism and the African Heritage" at Harvard's W. E. B. DuBois Center, which was televised on national television.

History 1907 is a survey course that takes place over fourteen weeks. The course explores broadly the internal dynamics of West African states from 1800, and West Africa's relations with the wider world. The course requirements are a midterm exam, a final exam, and a ten-to-twelve-page research paper, chosen by the student in conjunction with the professor. Exploring African novels has been a popular research topic. Between 150 and 200 pages of reading are assigned each week. Some of the key texts include A. A. Boahen's *African Perspectives on Colonialism*, Boahen and Webster's *The Revolutionary Years*, and Patrick Manning's *Francophone Sub-Saharan Africa*. Weeks eleven and twelve feature lectures on African nationalism and the transfer of political power. In addition, we screen Basil Davidson's "The Rise of Nationalism" and "The [Colonial] Legacy." Armah's novel is assigned for week thirteen, with the focus on independence and after. The readings for the thirteenth and four-teenth weeks also include Basil Davidson's *Black Man's Burden* and David Sandbrook's *The Politics of Africa's Economic Stagnation*.

The context for Armah's novel is provided by an earlier reading of Jean Allman's *Quills of a Porcupine* and the relevant sections of my *Drink, Power, and Cultural Change.*

None of the students miss the key themes of bribery and corruption portrayed in the novel, with their implied moral lessons. The issue of systemic corruption comes up, along with the question of whether Ghanaian society is indeed rotten to the core. A. N. Mensah (1972) raises this question of exaggeration in a sensitive reading of Armah's early novels. Armah's novel is remarkable in its foresight, and it describes even more accurately Ghana today. Maybe this was Armah's clarion call for Ghanaians to get their act together before they sank to the level described in *Beautyful Ones.*

What has needed to be teased out in class discussion is pertinent commentary on World War II and the lives of ex-servicemen, the nature of party politics and the United Gold Coast Convention (UGCC) confrontation with the Convention People's Party (CPP), and the significance of the railway workers to the nationalist movement. African soldiers returned from World War II with psychological problems. The amusing but sad example of Home Boy, a mad ex-serviceman who marched endlessly to military commands learned in foreign countries, drives the point home. The violence ex-servicemen introduced into their communities led to the 1940s and 1950s being called the age of the "jackknife and the chuke."[1] Their impact on the violent confrontation between the Convention People's Party and the Asante-based National Liberation Movement is evident. These intimate portraits of soldiers' lives are not contained in the standard history works.

The social distance between the elitist UGCC and the workers of Sekondi-Takoradi is cataloged in the novel; Armah shows why the city became a stronghold of the commoners' party, the CPP. The lawyers and the merchants of the UGCC, with their big suits and their British accents, were caricatured by the workers, who had great fun imitating these politicians after rallies. The antics of these elitist politicians had ceased to amuse the railway workers, and they had to be cajoled into attending the first rally Kwame Nkrumah gave in Sekondi-Takoradi. They were mesmerized by Nkrumah's powerful rhetoric about seizing control of their own destiny, his simple appearance, and his slight build. They became converts to Nkrumah's cause. Even when evidence of corruption among the CPP was rife, the railway workers of Sekondi-Takoradi refused to defect to any rival political party. They were workers, and the CPP remained for them the bona fide workers' party.

Was this an expression of class solidarity? The concepts of class, socialism, and populism are highlighted in this novel. The workers of Sekondi-Takoradi have a sharpened sensitivity to public corruption, especially as these accumulators are often ordinary workers elevated to prominence through political patronage. Railway men discuss the latest material acquisitions of CPP politicians, often ending with the refrain: "Ah, but he was my classmate." A lunchtime conversation of railway workers as they eat the poor workers' staple, gari, and beans with palm oil, provides a vivid illustration: "'He is only a small boy....' 'Yes, it's the CPP that has been so profitable for him....' 'Two cars now....' 'No, you're behind. Three. The latest is a white Mercedes. 220 Super.' 'You will think I am lying but he was my classmate, and now look at me.' 'Ah, life is like that,' 'Ei, and girls!' 'Running to fill his cars. Trips to the Star for weekends in Accra. Booze'" (p. 110).

The conversation ends with an interesting comment: "Contrey, you would do the same" (p. 110). Social and family ties between rich and poor people, such as the man and Koomson, vitiated the forging of a strong working-class consciousness. Indeed, conspicuous consumption and the need to be admired dictated that you impress your have-not friends with your new wealth. Hence, the cover of the Heinemann edition of Armah's novel shows people worshiping television sets, cars, imported liquor, washing machines, and other material objects. Railway workers did not scorn wealth; they aspired to be wealthy. They criticized ill-gotten wealth, but some wondered if they would behave any differently if they were elevated to political power. The connections between political power and accumulation are made explicit in this book. This was certainly not a fertile ground for socialism and communism.

And the novel's vivid description of social life in this port and railway town, the importance of drink to perceptions of power, and tidbits about prostitution and the introduction of marijuana in post–World War II Ghana provide fascinating material for the social historian. I cannot count the number of times I have read Armah's novel, and each reading yields new findings. It is important that the reader transcend the strong language of the novel to plumb its rich findings. Perhaps the strongest message in the book is the betrayal of Africa by its leaders. The author laments, "How long will Africa be cursed with its leaders?" (p. 80). African leaders hunger after things Western and yearn to be more European than the Europeans. They form alliances with the old colonial masters, which perpetrate neo-colonial relations. They loot national coffers and have no perception of the national good. The crisis in leadership is underscored in the man's lack of faith in the new military leaders of 1966. He opines that: "New men would take into their hands the power to steal the nation's riches and to use it for their own satisfaction." He concludes pessimistically that this is the "Ghanaian way of life" (p. 162).

NOTE

1. I suspect the "chuke" is a kind of wrestling grip in which one grabs his opponent by the throat—something akin to a "full Nelson."

SUGGESTIONS FOR
FURTHER READING AND RESOURCES

Fiction by Ayi Kwei Armah

Armah, Ayi Kwei. 1968. *The Beautyful Ones Are Not Yet Born.* Boston: Houghton Mifflin.
———. 1970. *Fragments*: Boston: Houghton-Mifflin. The shattered spiritual experience of a young African returning home after five years in the United States.
———. 1972. *Why Are We So Blest?* New York: Doubleday. The cause of revolution brings together two men and one woman.
———. 1973. *Two Thousand Seasons.* Portsmouth, N.H.: Heinemann. An epic novel of the ability of Ghanaian people to survive the projected "two thousand seasons" of Western colonialism and neocolonialism.
———. 1975. *The Beautyful Ones Are Not Yet Born.* Portsmouth, N.H.: Heinemann. First published in 1968.
———. 1978. *The Healers.* Nairobi: East Africa Publishing House. A historical novel set in the context of the nineteenth-century Asante kingdom; a young man refuses a kinship and wants to join the Healers, a group of people who work to heal social fragmentation as well as ordinary illnesses.

Other Reading

Akyeampong, Emmanuel. 1996. *Drink, Power, and Cultural Change: A Social History of Alcohol in Ghana, c. 1800 to Recent Times.* Portsmouth, N.H.: Heinemann.
Allman, Jean. 1993. *The Quills of the Porcupine: Asante Nationalism in an Emergent Ghana.* Madison: University of Wisconsin Press.

Austin, Dennis. 1964. *Politics in Ghana 1940–1960*. London: Oxford University Press.

Boahen, A. A. 1987. *African Perspectives on Colonialism*. Baltimore: Johns Hopkins University Press.

Boahen, A. A., and J. B. Webster. 1980. *The Revolutionary Years: West Africa Since 1800*. London: Longmans.

Busia, K.A. 1950. *Report on the Social Survey of Sekondi-Takoradi*. London: Crown Agents.

Davidson, Basil. 1984. "The Rise of Nationalism" and "The [Colonial] Legacy." Segments of his video series, *Africa: A Voyage of Discovery*. Chicago Home Vision.

———. 1992. *The Black Man's Burden: Africa and the Curse of the Nation-State*. New York: Times Books.

Fraser, Robert. 1980. *The Novels of Ayi Kwei Armah: A Study in Polemical Fiction*. London: Heinemann.

Jeffries, Richard. 1978. *Class, Power and Ideology in Ghana: The Railwaymen of Sekondi*. Cambridge: Cambridge University Press.

Lazarus, Neil. 1990. *Resistance in Postcolonial Fiction*. New Haven: Yale University Press. Includes much on Armah.

Lindors, Bernth. 1997. *African Textualities: Texts, Pre-Texts and Contexts of African Literature*. Trenton: Africa World Press.

Manning, Patrick. 1988. *Francophone Sub-Saharan Africa*. Cambridge: Cambridge University Press.

McCaskie, Thomas. 1983. "Accumulation, Wealth and Belief in Asante History I," *Africa* 53, 1: 23–43.

———. 1986. "Accumulation, Wealth and Belief in Asante History II," *Africa* 56, 1: 3–23.

Mensah, A. N. 1972. "The Crisis of a Sensitive Ghanaian: A View of the First Two Novels of Ayi Kwei Armah," *Universitas* 2, 2: 3–17.

Sandbrook, David. 1985. *The Politics of Africa's Economic Stagnation*. Cambridge: Cambridge University Press.

Wright, Derek, ed. 1992. *Critical Perspectives on Ayi Kwei Armah*. Washington, D.C.: Three Continents Press.

4

Mariama Bâ's
So Long a Letter

James A. Pritchett

SO LONG A LETTER PRESENTS A UNIQUE AND INTIMATE
portrait of rapid social transformation as experienced by a range of
individuals in French West Africa during the colonial and postcolonial periods. I frequently assign this novel to highlight and transcend
what I see as the three most common shortcomings of traditional historical and anthropological texts on colonialism and social change in
Africa. First, the colonial enterprise is variously portrayed as an
exercise in European machismo or empire building, a by-product of
the breakdown of the Concert of Europe, the outgrowth of machina-
tion by a small capitalist class, or an inevitable stage in the development of the Industrial Revolution. These top-down, grand synthetic
models may be acceptable heuristic devices for quickly encapsulat-
ing the confusing and often contradictory array of European political
and economic acts associated with colonialism, but they provide a
weak platform from which to explore African reactions. *So Long a
Letter* reminds students that society, from the bottom-up perspective
of the individual, is first and foremost a system of opportunities and
constraints. Individual strategies for life are most often centered on
gaining the benefits that accrue to those who master the nuances of
their social circumstances and who make the kinds of decisions that
propel them over, around, or through the embedded obstacles.
Colonialism thus primarily represented a comprehensive shift in
African social equations. It brought vastly different challenges and
raised never-before-seen hurdles. Yet it also offered new forms of

---

Mariama Bâ, *So Long a Letter* (Portsmouth, N.H.: Heinemann, 1981).

rewards to those strategically positioned to seize them. In *So Long a Letter* we witness individuals rethinking fundamental issues, exploring the contours of the new social terrain, and seeking their own best options within the new dispensation. Most important, the novel demonstrates how differentially positioned subjects in the old order are invariably presented with fundamentally different options in the new order, thus resulting in African responses to colonialism more varied and complex than is observable or explainable from a top-down view.

Second, I find *So Long a Letter* an excellent tool for deconstructing the perceived categorical opposition between "tradition" and "modernity" that students tend to bring with them into introductory courses in African studies. Precolonial Africans, most seem to think, were comfortably ensconced in a world of long-standing traditions. Europeans with superior technology arrived, conquered, and began the process of transplanting "Western" values on African soil. Africans had two choices: to fight against the odds to maintain their own traditions, or to acquiesce and accept Western ways. I find several problems inherent in this set of suppositions. It assumes that technology and values come in discrete, inseparable packages. It labels values as modern or traditional, Western or African in accordance with their technological association. It underestimates the willingness and creative capacity of Africans to borrow, reconfigure, and reconstruct their technological and normative worlds. It overestimates European resistance to all things African, be they values or technology. But perhaps most important, this dichotomized view of Africa constrains the imagination, the ability of students to conceptualize the complex bricolage that characterizes contemporary Africa. *So Long a Letter* is an excellent corrective. It pulls students into a world that defies easy categorization. It decenters and disorients students, leaving them ripe for the search for new explanatory frameworks.

Finally, *So Long a Letter* adds one more female voice to the all too male-centered corpus of historical and anthropological texts on Africa. It is refreshing to hear women talking to women about things that matter most to them. Thoughts on constitutional politics, economic development, and international relations combine easily with thoughts on life, love, marriage, childrearing, duty to others and self. There is an extended focus on polygyny, Islam, and urban lifestyles in contemporary Senegal. All are treated with such brutal honesty and intimacy of detail that it leaves the reader feeling a bit like a voyeur. However, at less than one hundred pages, *So Long a Letter* is a remarkably painless point of entry into a world dense with motives, meanings, and social maneuvering.

BASICS OF NOVEL AND AUTHOR

The novel takes the form of a long letter from Ramatoulaye, a Senegalese schoolteacher, to her best friend, Aissatou. The occasion is the sudden death of Ramatoulaye's husband. Yet the novel is not about death, but rather about figuring out life. Under the guise of working through her grief, Ramatoulaye uses the letter as a vehicle for reminiscing about her emotional journey through a period of history unimagined by past generations and toward a future unforeseeable by the present one. It is a journey that was embarked on with great passion—a passion that still lingers even as the cautiousness and apprehensions of old age replace the fearlessness and reckless abandon of freshly unbridled youth. Aissatou is the perfect target for Ramatoulaye's musings. Their grandmothers had been friends back in the village. Their mothers' compounds had shared a fence over which they had gossiped and teased one another daily. Ramatoulaye and Aissatou had learned to tie their wrappers together, had walked up the stony road to school each morning and returned to Koranic lessons each evening. They had both been selected to attend the Teachers' College in Ponty-Ville, the elite boarding school that attracted and trained a new generation of progressive-thinking African women from throughout French West Africa. Ramatoulaye and Aissatou each went on to marry radical young activists for the cause of Senegalese independence. Each did so against the wishes of her family. Both husbands would subsequently rise rapidly to the top of their respective professions, moving into the spaces left vacant by the receding colonial regime. And each would ultimately take on a second wife.

Although both tradition and Islamic law acknowledge the right of men to have more than one wife, Aissatou felt her husband's remarriage was an act of betrayal, a blasphemy against their own marriage vows. Polygyny was an affront to their long-shared dreams of a liberated nation and to their shared struggled against both family and the forces of colonialism to live life on their own terms. Aissatou immediately walked out on her husband, went back to school, forged a lucrative career, and created a new life for herself and her two sons.

Years later Ramatoulaye's husband would announce his own

intention to remarry. By this time Ramatoulaye was no longer the young radical. She was a well-settled schoolteacher, mother of twelve, looking forward to growing old, and more intensely in love with the man at the center of all her identities: wife, mother, teacher, and person. Ramatoulaye's heart now experienced the hurt that her friend Aissatou had had to endure years earlier. But Ramatoulaye's head led her in a different direction. She would not divorce. She would not relinquish her status or her claim on her husband's resources. Yet ever-declining attention from her husband ultimately reduced her to the status of wife in name only. Ramatoulaye's anguish is all the more complete when her husband's new wife is revealed to be a friend of their daughter, a mere child who had spent much time in Ramatoulaye's company. This young girl had on more than a few occasions spoken of her "sugar daddy" and complained about the pressure from her own mother to marry the "fat old bastard." This seemingly naive little child had actually asked Ramatoulaye for advice on the matter without ever revealing that her elderly suitor was none other than Ramatoulaye's own husband. This was the ultimate humiliation. The sudden death of Ramatoulaye's husband by a heart attack, five years after his new marriage, provides the impetus for her to rethink, via "so long a letter," the path she had chosen to navigate through the constraints and opportunities of her rapidly changing world.

The text of the novel contains no actual dates. Ramatoulaye's ruminations, however, cover five generations, pushing us well back into the precolonial era, and bringing us forward into the second decade of Senegalese independence.

Mariama Bâ was born in Dakar, Senegal, in 1929 and was raised in a Muslim household by her maternal grandparents. She attended the French School in Dakar and the Ecole Normale for girls in Rufisque. She would go on to become a primary-school teacher, marry a government minister, and have nine children. Bâ was an active participant in several international women's organizations and is credited with being one of the leaders of the feminist movement in Senegal. *So Long a Letter*, originally written in French as *Une Si Longue Lettre* (1979), was Bâ's first novel. The parallels between her own life and that of her lead character, Ramatoulaye, are apparent throughout, making this novel a deeply personal account, if not outright autobiographical. The novel was honored as the first recipient of the Noma Award for publishing in Africa in 1980. Mariama Bâ died the following year, leaving behind one unpublished manuscript, *Un Chant Escarlate*. In that work Bâ would again focus her critical gaze on gender relations and the construction of identity in Senegal. This time, however, the themes are filtered through the lens of race as Bâ examines the cultural conflict of a white European woman married to a black Senegalese man who is himself conflicted over his sexual identity.

COURSE CONTEXT

I use this novel in a course entitled Peoples and Cultures of Africa. It was designed as an upper-level undergraduate anthropology course, but is in fact open to all. Few students at any rank tend to have much experience with Africa. Enrollment usually includes fifty to sixty students.

The novel is introduced no earlier than the fourth or fifth week of class. Students are first presented an overview of the human ecology of modern Africa via text and film, followed by an overview of the anthropological enterprise, perhaps via Sally Falk Moore's *Anthropology and Africa* (1994). In-depth analyses of two ethnographic classics—for example, Evans-Pritchard's *The Nuer* (1940) and Jomo Kenyatta's *Facing Mt Kenya* (1938)—occupy a full two weeks of class time as we explore the strengths and, more important, the weaknesses and outright distortions embedded in the structural-functionalist approach to the study of society. In the 1940s structural-functionalism may have represented advances over previous works on Africa by its success in uncovering the contextualized logic of African social organization and political functioning. Much of what had earlier been pointed to as evidence of the primitive and irrational nature of African life was now being revealed as functionally adaptive, effectively integrative, and at times remarkably ingenious. But structural-functionalist approaches are also the central support for an overly essentialized view of Africa, presenting a changeless, timeless Africa, ideally suited to be spoken of in the "ethnographic present." It is a continent of people ill prepared for either conceptualizing or actualizing change. The students are forced to think deeply on issues of cultural change during an additional week of readings on African history from earliest times to the colonial period.

The class next moves from grasping at grand processes to experiencing history and culture more intimately in one particular place through the life of one rather unremarkable individual. Toundi, the young runaway in Ferdinand Oyono's *Houseboy* (1966; see Chapter

19), guides our class through the world of confusing choices and unpredictable consequences created by newly imposed colonial rule in French Cameroon. Mariama Bâ then enters the picture to bear witness to the internalized components of and gendered responses to fully entrenched colonialism. *So Long a Letter*, with its rich repertoire of images, encounters, and inescapable transformations, occasions an opportunity to make explicit what heretofore had been a partially submerged theme of the course—that the legacy of colonialism is best viewed through its lingering imprint on key relationships throughout the African continent. In other words, social transformation, rather than being the modification of things, is best viewed as changes in the relationship between people. Chinua Achebe makes this point exceedingly clear in *Things Fall Apart* (1958; see Chapter 2). The protagonist Okonkwo, in his final moments of despair, begs an answer for the failure of his people to stand united and hold fast to their long-sustaining traditions when confronted with the coercive colonial agenda. His wise old compatriot responds that the white man had come and put a knife on that which held them together, and then things just fell apart. It is instructive that this elder reckons colonialism's most damaging impact not in terms of lives lost, land appropriated, commodities confiscated, or labor exploited. Rather, something about the colonial enterprise has had a deleterious effect on the very things that held African societies together. It is my contention that it is useful to view certain sets of relationships as threads out of which the African social fabric is woven. These relationships bind together individuals in webs of rights and duties, privileges and obligations. They frame local debates over how to interpret and act on historical contingencies. They define what is important enough to fight over.

Thus, with a hesitant nod to the Manchester "conflict resolution" school of thought, I take as my starting point that the natural state of society, if such a thing exists, is one rife with fissures, schisms, and endemic oppositions. Society is an entity precariously balanced on the edge of numerous delicate relationships that have been shown time and again to be notoriously difficult to manage even under conditions of moderate stress. The shock treatment to which Africa has been subjected reverberates still, leaving in its wake the jagged fragments of tradition and modernity with which Africans must construct new mosaics of social life. The pieces do not easily or neatly fit together. Disagreements are saturated with passion because the stakes are so high. The sets of fragile relationships that are continually debated and renegotiated, and that frame our classroom discussion, are heuristically identified as the following:

- Ecological relations (people and their environment).
- Social relations (the individual and the group).
- Intergenerational relations (the old and the young).
- Gender relations (female and male).
- Class relations (rich and poor).
- Intergroup relations (us and them).
- Spiritual relations (this world and the other world).

So Long a Letter serves to animate classroom discussions on the cleavages and the intensity of the emotions associated with each of these relationships.

DISCUSSION THEMES

The early ethnographies addressed traditional environmental ideologies and practices and the existential place of humans within the environment in terms of balance and adaptation. Colonialism, however, brought new forms of environmental management and mismanagement. Nature became less of a partner in production and more of a thing to be conquered, reaped, mined, and transformed with little attention to balance or long-term sustainability. Our images of the majestic Nuer herding their cattle across the landscape in perfect tune to the music of the seasons, and the noble Kikuyu shifting cultivation in balance with the waxing and waning of local soil fertility, are replaced in *So Long a Letter* with images of stultifying urban life, choking on traffic and despair. It is a world where shantytown existence so tramples the human spirit that people are willing to sell body, mind, and soul for their next day's subsistence. It is a world so alienated from nature that a holiday sojourn to the countryside becomes a quasi-religious experience. In *So Long a Letter* we hear lilting descriptions of the intoxicating effects of open spaces and fresh air. We hear of the salutary effects of seaside strolls and picnics in the forest. The ubiquitous nature of the precolonial era is replaced with a nature that is "out there," a nature with the capacity to lift depression and sadness, to stimulate the senses and to restore the soul (p. 21). Yet the novel also shows that colonialism was not an ecological nightmare for all. The profits from new uses of nature propelled some to unimaginable economic heights. But the generator of that wealth was often as fragile as the African soil, as undependable as the African rains. Cash cropping, at the expense of food crop-

ping—such as Senegal's growing reliance on groundnut production—was a dangerous gamble. The new economic bubble could
burst from one season of drought (p. 62). The risks of failure were no
more evenly spread than the profits of success. Ramatoulaye, in her
letter to Aissatou, identifies for us one of the key debates of twentieth-century Africa. How is the environment to be used, for whose
benefit, and at whose expense? Old ideologies will be refurbished;
new ones will continually emerge to passionately justify whatever
position is taken.

In *The Nuer* and *Facing Mt Kenya* the relative weight given
notions of individual autonomy, freedom of choice, and control over
one's own body versus the need of the group to control certain facets
of its members' lives comes down far more heavily on the side of the
latter. Everything from access to the means of production—that is,
land, labor, tools, and knowledge—to protection from the ravages of
wild animals and old age require embeddedness in clearly defined
groups. *So Long a Letter*, however, unveils the new choices that
emerge out of the colonial encounter, the subsequent penetration of
the bureaucratic networks of newly independent nation states, and
the structures set up by mercantile and productive capitalist agents.
These combined forces progressively weaken traditional systems of
rewards and sanctions by which individual behavior has been controlled. Individuals can now float between competing systems,
exploring their own best options, or they can attempt to carve out a
space for themselves in the interstitial region between traditional and
modern coercive systems. In *So Long a Letter* we witness individuals
who have dared to deviate from the well-trodden path of tradition in
favor of blazing new trails. Ramatoulaye, for example, marries the
man she loves despite opposition from her family. It is a marriage
that eschews the usual negotiations over brideprice and that is
entered into without the usual pomp and ceremony (p. 16). Later
Ramatoulaye defies the levirate system that dictates that upon her
husband's death she should marry one of his brothers. She argues
that the social meaning and utility of marriage will not determine her
choices. Marriage to her is an act of faith and of love, the total sur-
render of oneself to the person one has chosen and who has chosen
you (p. 58). Several useful references on questions of women and
gender in Africa are included at the end of this chapter (see, for
example, Abwunza 1997, Davison 1996, Hay and Stichter 1995, or
Terborg-Penn et al. 1987).

So Long a Letter also presages the opening up of caste relations
in West Africa, as we see Ramatoulaye's best friend Aissatou, mem-

ber of a low-caste craft guild, marrying a nobleman who plainly asserts that marriage is a personal thing (p. 17). *So Long a Letter*, however, moves beyond banalities about traditions maintained versus traditions rejected to graphically illustrate that tradition can equally well serve to legitimize change. It can be used to justify the new, to colonize the present with conceptual frameworks and values from the past. At the funeral of Ramatoulaye's husband, for example, we see relatives display their contribution to the cost, not in millet, livestock, rice, flour, oil, sugar, and milk as in former times, but conspicuously and with a great deal of flourish in banknotes. Likewise, relatives who might have waited patiently in the past to receive some small token from the deceased's estate today descend like vultures consuming all that is edible, carrying away all that is transportable. The tradition of receiving is well remembered. The tradition of assuming responsibility for the maintenance of the widow is soon forgotten (p. 4).

So Long a Letter reminds us that people were quite literally texts in precolonial societies that relied on oral traditions. The old were more fully inscribed than the young. Locked within their beings was knowledge of contingencies that youth had yet to experience, nuanced responses to complex issues that only infrequently arise, and remembered solutions to problems lurking just beyond the view of those more junior. The presence of elders had a stabilizing effect on society. They added a sense of security, a sense of stability, perhaps even a bit of majesty to any social grouping. In return, elders were afforded great respect, relieved of as many mundane daily chores as circumstances would permit, and given first choice of the best that local society could generate. Colonialism, however, tended to privilege a different array of talents. It offered its best to those with book learning, those who could labor long and hard in fields, farms, and factories, those with the courage to forsake the familiar in pursuit of the novel. In short, as *So Long a Letter* demonstrates, colonialism heaped its greatest rewards on youth. The commercial interests that accompanied colonialism into Africa targeted youth as the greatest potential consumers of things European. Schools, churches, and the mass media worked in tandem to inculcate an aesthetic that elevated the status of the young at the expense of the elderly. The battle rages in *So Long a Letter* as Ramatoulaye resents but acquiesces to many of the demands of her husband's elderly mother. Ramatoulaye laments the rapidly vanishing respect for the artistic production of the elder generation while pushing her own children to master skills associated with the modern world. She speaks with disdain of her husband's effort to appear youthful to his new wife by dyeing his hair and painfully restraining his expanding waist in trousers far too tight for comfort. But even greater spite is reserved for the young wife who is ignorant of the seductive power of mature age and of silvery temples. Ramatoulaye represents many who are torn between the past and the present, who look back with nostalgia while remaining resolute about the need to introduce modernity (p. 18). Yet some aspects of modernity simply frighten her. At one point she wonders aloud if it is indeed possible to have modernity, understood mostly as technological advances and individual freedoms, without the concomitant lowering of standards. She worries about her daughters' propensity for revealing attire. She can smell cigarette smoke on their breath and fears that they may be drinking and having sex as well. Are the young as trapped within a culture that requires experimentation as the elders are trapped within a culture that requires restraint? *So Long a Letter* provides a wealth of material to stimulate classroom conversations about intergenerational relations in a changing African context.

In reading the classic ethnographies, the class discusses the delicately balanced and complementary relationship between males and females that emanates primarily from their differing positions within the kinship and descent systems, the cultural division of labor by gender, and metaphysical notions of their existential status. *So Long a Letter* illustrates the often perverse continuities and illogical changes in relations between males and females within the new fields of constraints and opportunities of the colonial and postcolonial worlds. Ramatoulaye's husband, for example, has little difficulty secretly taking out a second mortgage on the home the two of them had jointly purchased in order to finance another home for his new wife (p. 10). The husband was apparently able to navigate a path through traditional customs, modern banking procedures, and constitutional provisions that made it unnecessary to receive spousal consent to finalize such a deal. He must also have been able to plot a course through his own consciousness and sense of propriety to convince himself that he need not even inform his wife of his intent. Ramatoulaye comments on the plight of educated women in modern Senegal. "Men would call us scatter-brained," she noted. "Others labeled us devils. But many wanted to possess us" (p. 6).

But not all news from the front of the gender war in *So Long a Letter* is bad. In some quarters, at least, patriarchal attitudes have been among the victims. A successful politician is noted for never accepting any honor without associating his wife with it. He consults her on all his political positions and involves her in all his political actions (p. 67). Ramatoulaye's eldest daughter, likewise, finds a husband who cooks rice as well as she does, shares in the housework, and discusses everything so as to find a compromise (p. 73). Interestingly, Ramatoulaye herself rejects gender inequality in all its various guises. Rather, she believes in the essential unity and existential complementarity of men and women. It is a complementarity that she compares to different musical instruments that nevertheless come together to create a pleasing symphony (p. 88). One of the most provocative statements in the entire novel is when Ramatoulaye notes: "I am one of those who can realize themselves fully and bloom only when they form part of a couple. I have never conceived of happiness outside marriage" (p. 55). This single statement often sets the tone for fascinating classroom discussions about alternative constructions of gender relations and the meaning of gender equality.

The classic ethnographies revealed differences in individual access to certain valued goods (such as land, labor, cash, or commodities). These differences, however, were said to be contained and made palatable by the existence of redistributive leveling mechanisms that hampered the growth of gross inequalities in the precolonial African world. Ideologies of cooperation and mutual responsibility were often underpinned by severe sanctions. New definitions of wealth that arose during colonialism, and new routes for acquiring that wealth, reconfigured notions of duty and obligation, even as the notions of group identity were being redefined. It became increasingly less clear who was responsible for whom, and to whom. More and more individuals would check the flow of personal resources to wider kin networks in favor of capital accumulation or conspicuous consumption for self or, at most, for the nuclear family. *So Long a Letter* pinpoints the obscenity accompanying the new class alignment; the emergence of men with sufficient disposable income to corrupt even the most intimate relationships (p. 35). We find parents so poor they turn a blind eye to the dalliance of wealthy men with their young daughters in exchange for sufficient cash to lift them out of poverty. On the radio we hear the griots singing not of the kings and heroes of yore, but of the men with endless banknotes and the women with heavy gold bracelets (p. 49).

So Long a Letter also richly illustrates the impact of expanding geopolitical boundaries and bureaucratic structures on the processes of identity formation and emerging notions of "Us" and "Them." Colonialism did not so much destroy old identities as it expanded the range of options. In the novel we see identities based on location, class, occupation, and metropolitan association join those based on lineage, clan, chiefdom, and religious affiliation. Among other choices, Ramatoulaye identifies herself as part of a modern West African sisterhood destined for the mission of emancipation; to lift the land out of the bog of tradition, superstition, and custom; to make people appreciate a multitude of civilizations without renouncing their own (p. 15). In other instances we see identity shifting with circumstances or being modified by motives.

So Long a Letter richly details the bricolage of spiritual beliefs and practices that vie for space in urban Senegal. In one scene the fatalism of Islam confronts attempts to revive a dying man in the hospital. Heart massage, mouth-to-mouth resuscitation, ridiculous weapons against the divine will, the author thinks to herself (p. 2). Another scene brings details of Muslim rites for preparing a body for burial. The page comes alive with incense, eau de cologne, cotton wool, miracle water from the holy places of Islam, and meters of white muslin, the only clothing Islam allows for the dead (p. 3). In yet another scene, a person who had only days earlier participated in the Muslim funeral has now returned to her ancestral homeland. Here we find her praying on a mat before the tomb of the ancestors in a place where the living and the dead share space in the family's rural compound. The following day she will make an offering to protect herself from the evil eye, while at the same time attracting the benevolence of the *tours,* or familiar spirits (p. 28).

The characters in *So Long a Letter* rise above the wooden archetypes that often inhabit other novels on the colonial encounter. Neither old nor young, rich nor poor, male nor female, urbanite nor rural dweller is cast as the natural location for pure tradition or pure modernity. Both villains and saints reside within each category and often within the same individual. Life is filled with hard choices. The past offers no lessons for the future.

STUDENT ASSIGNMENTS

Students are asked to read and prepare their thoughts for classroom discussions on the topic of change within key social relations in Africa. While the novel provides a superabundance of images and ideas on all manner of relationships, gender and intergenerational relations invariably excite students the most. Perhaps newfound independence from parents and the coalescing of their own gendered identities make this a natural response. Nevertheless, as the course moves on to more traditional anthropological texts on African kinship, religion, urbanization, and modern ecology, the lessons from *So Long a Letter* are never far away. Students continue to phrase questions and construct answers based on perspectives gained from reading Mariama Bâ. Indeed, at times students need to be reminded that despite its richness of detail and diversity of characters, *So Long a Letter* still only captures one slice of the dynamic African reality.

Students are generally required to complete two writing assignments during the semester, either of which could draw heavily on *So Long a Letter*. Typically topics might include a comparative look at cultural change in two different places or time periods in Africa; the construction of identity in precolonial, colonial, and postcolonial Africa; the ontological status of an "African feminism" and how it might differ from its Western counterpart; religious syncretism; or perhaps Islam and the forces of modernity.

SUGGESTIONS FOR
FURTHER READING AND RESOURCES

Abwunza, Judith. 1997. *Women's Voices, Women's Power: Dialogues of Resistance from East Africa.* Toronto: Broadview Press.

Achebe, Chinua. 1958. *Things Fall Apart.* London: Heinemann. See Chapter 2 in this collection.

Bâ, Mariama. 1981. *So Long a Letter.* Portsmouth, N.H.: Heinemann. First published in French as *Une si longue lettre.* Winner of the 1980 Noma Prize for publishing in Africa.

Conrad, David, and Barbara E. Frank. 1995. *Status and Identity in West Africa: Nyamakalaw of Mande.* Bloomington: Indiana University Press. A solid overview of class and caste in West Africa.

D'Almeida, Irene Assiba. 1986. "The Concept of Choice in Mariama Bâ's Fiction." In *Ngambika: Studies of Women in African Literature*, ed. Carole Boyce Davies and Anne Adams Graves. Trenton, N.J.: Africa World Press.

Davison, Jean. 1996. *Voices from Mutira: Change in the Lives of Rural Gikuyu Women, 1910–1995.* 2nd ed. Boulder: Lynne Rienner.

Evans-Pritchard, E. E. 1940. *The Nuer: A Description of the Modes of Livelihood and Political Institutions of a Nilotic People.* Oxford: Clarendon.

Gellar, Sheldon. 1995. *Senegal: An African Nation Between Islam and the West,* 2nd ed. Boulder: Westview. One of the Nations of Africa series, Gellar's work provides useful background information on Senegalese politics, history, and economy.

Harrell-Bond, Barbara. 1980. "Interview with Mariama Bâ." *African Publishing Record* 6:209–214.

Hay, Margaret Jean, and Sharon Stichter, eds. 1995. *African Women South of the Sahara*, 2nd ed. New York: Longman.

Ibnlfassi, Laila, and Nicki Hitchcott, eds. 1996. *African Francophone Writing: A Critical Introduction*. Oxford: Berg.

Kenyatta, Jomo. 1965. [1938]. *Facing Mt Kenya: The Tribal Life of the Kikuyu*. New York: Vintage.

Manning, Patrick. 1988. *Francophone Sub-Saharan Africa, 1880–1985*. Cambridge: Cambridge University Press.

Moore, Sally Falk. 1994. *Anthropology and Africa: Changing Perspectives on a Changing Scene*. Charlottesville: University Press of Virginia.

Oyono, Ferdinand. 1967. *Houseboy*. Portsmouth, N.H.: Heinemann. First published in French as *Une vie de boy*. See Chapter 19 in this collection.

Terborg-Penn, Rosalyn, Sharon Harley, and Andrea Benton Rushing. 1987. *Women in Africa and the African Diaspora*. Washington, D.C.: Howard University Press.

5 ⌒

Driss Chraïbi's
Mother Comes of Age

Janice Spleth

DRISS CHRAÏBI'S CHARMING TALE OF MOROCCO WOULD
be a welcome addition to any literature class concerned with the
nature and growth of the human spirit. Spanning a period that
extends from colonialism and World War II through the accession to
independence and beyond, the novel introduces a wide variety of
African themes and could easily represent African literature in a survey course on world literatures. The dominant theme of women's
emancipation would also make this an ideal text for a course incorporating feminist theory or the literary representation of women. In my
own case, *Mother Comes of Age* fills a specific geographical place on
my syllabus. In a course for undergraduates that introduces literature
from francophone Africa and the Caribbean, at least one text from the
Maghreb is essential. I was especially interested in finding one that
would allow the class to interrogate women's issues, but had discovered by trial and error that students can deal more effectively with the
subject if the men in the novels are presented more or less sympathet-
ically. Assia Djebar's *Sister to Scheherazade*, a rich and well-constructed narrative that addresses a woman's efforts to escape sequestration and to divest herself of the veil, had proved difficult for
undergraduates to read and relate to. When I encountered Driss
Chraïbi's novel for the first time, I sensed immediately that my students would appreciate the tone and style of the work, and I knew I
had finally found a Maghrebian text that would appeal to them. The

Driss Chraïbi, *Mother Comes of Age*, trans. Hugh Harter (Boulder: Lynne
Rienner, 1998).

subject of the story is, of course, a woman's emancipation, but the male narrators are both delightful characters, and even the patriarch is presented without rancor. The novel has turned out to be extremely popular and is often chosen by students as the subject of one of their analytical papers. It anchors the discussion of African women that is a unifying element in the class and allows me to introduce a variety of themes and motifs that distinguish North African writing from other francophone literatures. I have used the book in French with graduate students, but G. Robert McConnell's French-language edition with vocabulary, notes, and discussion questions would make this work accessible for intermediate or advanced language students. The translation by Hugh Harter is a staple for the undergraduate course I teach titled Francophone Literature in Translation, which fulfills a variety of liberal studies requirements. That edition, currently available through Lynne Rienner Publishers, reads well and contains an excellent introduction by Harter. The enrollment for my course is generally less than forty students, and most of the participants are sophomores, juniors, and seniors.[1]

Originally published in French as *La Civilisation, Ma Mère!* the novel follows the progress of a Moroccan woman who has been sequestered according to custom since the age of thirteen. In the course of the story, she is gradually made aware of her own enormous personal potential and of the scope of the world around her. The work is divided into two distinct parts: "Being" and "Having." In the first part, Mother becomes acquainted with technologies, such as the telephone and radio, that infinitely expand her horizons. With the encouragement and connivance of her sons, she ultimately goes out into the world, tentatively and then with gusto. She learns to read, explores geography and history, discovers the complexity of her own body in science books, and existentially confronts her new-found freedom. In Part 2, she goes even further, assumes the role of subject, and begins to act on her universe, challenging the men who make the laws. She tries to confront the generals responsible for World War II, declares her independence to her husband and her overprotective son, organizes other Moroccan women to help them understand their own situation in a patriarchal society, and channels her criticism of the postcolonial government into political reform.

Each of the two parts is narrated in the first person by one of Mother's sons, and what this means in terms of the story is an excellent subject for class discussion. Junior, the younger son, opens the narrative and appears to be writing a personal diary inasmuch as no intended reader is specified. He is introduced into the text as a schoolboy who must wash his mouth out with soap when he comes home in the afternoon because he has been speaking French all day. He is the more assimilated, academically successful son who achieves within the framework of the colonial education policy and leaves Mother at the end of Part 1 to continue his professional studies in France. He is the one who devises a way to teach Mother to read and shepherds her through her first books.

With Junior abroad, Nagib assumes the narrative role, writing letters to his brother to keep him informed of Mother's progress. He also takes on the responsibility of tutoring Mother, but as she gains more independence, his role changes substantially to that of secretary, confidant, and confederate. Nagib has explicitly rejected the French school system, skipping classes without his father's knowledge and preferring to learn from experience. He is the one who brings new technologies into the house and eventually takes Mother to see a power plant. He has friends at all levels of society, some of whom refer to their group as the antischool. His father calls him a revolutionary at one point. There are suggestions of a socialist affiliation, which Mother may or may not share. When she boards a boat for France at the end of the novel after Morocco has achieved independence, he accompanies her, although he has not paid for his ticket.

Unlike the somber, even tragic tones of much of Chraïbi's previous work, this text is a verbal feast in a much lighter vein. There is some kind of magic on almost every page with each of the narrators bringing his own distinct personality to his part of the tale. Junior is perhaps more poetic, introducing in the preface images of sand, sea, and wild horses that will be developed as the story progresses. His alienation from the culture of his childhood is more complete, and a sense of nostalgia for a simpler past permeates his text. In both parts, humor emanates from the person and discourse of Nagib, a giant of a man with a huge appetite. There is pure physical comedy as he directs the ungainly movers who nearly destroy the house while installing the radio. It is Nagib who clandestinely consumes the food that Mother brings for the man she presumes to be in the box—the elusive, omniscient Mr. Kteu. And there is postmodern irony when Nagib describes the perfect hat for Mother as a chic model that will not come into fashion for decades, or when he anachronistically imputes a Cold War mentality to a Russian soldier of the 1940s. The priceless dialogues in which Mother, so naive but so insightful, tries to bring the incorrigible Nagib to do her bidding or to accept her opinions are narrated with a particular zest. There are warmly touching moments inspired by the sons' love for the mother or by their admiration for her rich imagination and singular personal vision.

While differing in tone and style from much of Chraïbi's previous work, *Mother Comes of Age* develops themes that the writer has already explored elsewhere in narratives that have a similarly autobiographical inspiration. Driss Chraïbi's early years were not unlike those of his fictional character, Junior. Born in 1926 in El Jadida, Morocco, Chraïbi attended the French lycée in Casablanca. At the age of nineteen, he left for France to continue his studies, where he became a naturalized French citizen. In addition to his activity as a novelist, he has adapted works by Chekhov, London, and Hemingway for radio. His first novel, *Le Passé simple* [*The Simple Past*], was extremely controversial in Morocco and attacked both colonialism and the regressive traditions of the Arab-Muslim patriarchy. The main character, Driss Ferdi, who resembles the author in many ways, revolts against a domineering father and pities his submissive, sequestered mother. The protagonist leaves Morocco for France, but the mother's only escape is in suicide. After addressing the situation of the North African immigrant in France in *Les Boucs* [*The Butts*] in 1955, Chraïbi brings his alter ego back to Morocco from Europe on the occasion of his father's funeral in *Succession ouverte* [*Heirs to the Past*], published in 1962. In this variation on his own life history, the mother has not died but ably gives voice to her resentment and pain and meditates on the thirty years of her life spent as a virtual prisoner in her husband's house. The protagonist, realizing that he has lost touch with his roots, boards a plane for France. *Mother Comes of Age* is thus the third novel in which the author works through the patterns of his own childhood and family relationships by means of the catharsis of fiction, and it is the only one in which the son's fulfillment is linked to the mother's emancipation and personal growth. Chraïbi has continued to produce a rich array of novels inspired by his homeland, some of which have been translated into English. My students and I have especially enjoyed Chraïbi's experiments with the postcolonial detective novel, *Une enquête au pays* [*Flutes of Death*] and *L'Inspecteur Ali* [*Inspector Ali*].

I use *Mother Comes of Age* in a unit on the Maghreb in which I devote most of three class periods to Chraïbi's work, followed by three class periods for the viewing and discussion of Gillo Pontecorvo's film about the nationalist movement in Algeria, *The Battle of Algiers*. The unit appears chronologically on the program after the students have read two colonial novels by West African writers, Camara Laye's *The Dark Child* and Ferdinand Oyono's *Houseboy* (see Chapter 19). In addition to highlighting a different region of Africa, the unit treats the subjects of resistance and independence and provides a bridge to the postcolonial period. The first session must make the transition from West Africa to the Maghreb and serves as a general introduction to the geography and culture of North Africa. Clips from a travel video on *Marakesh and Fez*, produced by International Video Network in 1995, are an effective way to make the point that Morocco has a rich historical past and to document the ingenuity of North African artisans, a sort of prelude to Mother's own natural abilities. In this lecture, too, I discuss the role of women in Arab cultures and have found the research of Fatima Mernissi especially useful in presenting the customs of sequestration and veiling (see Mernissi 1988). I also examine the colonial relationship between Morocco and France, the situation of Morocco during World War II, and the movement toward independence, and here I rely heavily on David Gordon's work on the effects of French colonial policy, *North Africa's French Legacy*.

The second and third sessions engage the students in reading the text. I have done this in two ways. The first is a quiz over details of the novel that I give orally in class. The questions are not difficult and can usually be answered with ease by any student who has read the material. Because the answers rarely demand any cultural background, they are chosen specifically to lead into the discussion of major themes. The students exchange papers in class, and the test is graded on the spot. As I ask for answers, students participate actively, from their own reading or from the paper that they are grading. I have learned that this is one way to overcome the students' natural reservations about discussing a text that involves an unfamiliar culture. I build on each question, either when it is asked or when it is answered, to establish major themes and developments in the text, often having students read especially significant passages. The first-person narration and Chraïbi's masterful use of dialogue make this work ideal for oral interpretation, and some of the students bring a great deal of enthusiasm to the task. I may then ask for other students to react to what they have heard as way of carrying the discussion further.

A second way to involve the students is to ask them to select the passages that should be discussed in class as a homework assignment. Again, it may be useful to actually read the passage, or parts of it, aloud in class. When the students write out their reasons for choosing the passages, these responses become the basis for some of the most meaningful class discussions, often drawing on the students' particular areas of interest and expertise. To get discussions started, I may assign one student to react formally to another student's commentary. Some of the students will put more effort and goodwill into the assignment than others, but even a hastily composed paragraph can sometimes lead to an insightful dialogue on the text. I have used this technique with the whole class when there are under fifteen students, and with small groups when the class is large.

During the second part of the unit on the Maghreb, the students watch the Pontecorvo film in class. If there is to be ample time for discussion, the film always has to be cut to fit into three fifty-minute class periods, but I try to include two segments in which women are important: the scenes that show women taking off their veils in order to don Western clothes so they can carry bombs through the checkpoints for the resistance, and the final scenes in which a dancing woman serves to represent the nation of Algeria victoriously celebrating the coming of independence. These scenes have led to some interesting discussions about the real and symbolic roles of women in both works. Winifred Woodhull's analysis of the representation of women in Algerian literature is especially relevant here. Another way to compare the two works is to discuss the different ways in which resistance is expressed in both.

In itself, *Mother Comes of Age* contains a wealth of themes that invite analysis and discussion. Mother's emancipation and self-actualization are paramount, and students need to be able to identify the various stages of her transformation and to understand the significance of each. Feminist theory provides an effective vehicle for analyzing Mother's accession to agency. Education is another major focus in the text, and the author raises questions about the education of women, the politics of education (especially colonial education), and the limits of formal education. It is useful, as well, to identify passages that illustrate cultural hybridity or show how Mother retains her own individuality in the process of assimilating Western culture and modern ways. The text also allows students to reflect on the meaning and value of technology and to recognize the existence of preindustrial technology in Africa.

When students are asked to consider Mother metaphorically as Morocco, or even more broadly as colonized Africa, the discussion goes to another level, and Chraïbi's tale emerges more clearly as social criticism with multiple targets. Referring to another Maghrebian writer, Woodhull has described Abdelkebir Khatibi's

concept of decolonization as "a double critique of Arab-Islamic institutions and culture on the one hand, and of the universalizing, colo-
nizing dynamics of Western metaphysics on the other" (Woodhull
1993: ix). This duality also prevails in *Mother Comes of Age*. There
is a gentle but firm attack in the novel upon those traditional beliefs
and practices that could hamper development and prevent North
Africa from fully enjoying the benefits of modern technologies and
ideas. In this, Mother's release from seclusion is metonymous for the
rejection of various articles of a feudal, patriarchal culture. No one is
perhaps more eloquent in articulating the significance of Mother's
liberation than Father, a successful businessman whose financial pre-
occupations tend to distract him from what is going on in his household. He is at first unaware of Mother's achievements. Eventually
relegated to the sidelines, he struggles to come to grips with her
transformation and is himself transformed in the process. He con-
fides his newfound wisdom to Nagib: "The foundation of every society is the community, and the core of the community is plain and
simply the family. If at the heart of that family the woman is held
prisoner, completely veiled and sequestered as we have kept her for
centuries, if she has no opening onto the outside world, no active
role, society as a whole suffers fatally and closes in on itself with
nothing left to give to itself or to the world" (p. 120).

Further on he affirms that "it isn't just a new woman I see in
front of me but, through her, a new man, a new society and a fresh
new world" (p. 121). As Mother matures, she specifically leaves religion behind, burying it "with the other debris of the past under an
orange tree" (p. 123).

Mother's progress requires her to become educated in Western
terms, and she even goes through a phase in which she gives up her
familiar Moroccan customs, redecorating her home in almost slavish
imitation of European examples. But Chraïbi repeatedly impresses
upon us those qualities that Mother exhibited even before her exposure to the world. She is remarkably resourceful in making clothes
for her son, shearing the sheep, carding and spinning the wool, weav-
ing the cloth, and sewing up the final product from her own design.
Her magnificently durable brazier bears a trademark engraved by
Nagib: "Made in Casablanca, Morocco. By Mummy" (p. 36), and
students may profit from examining Morocco's centuries-old tradition as a center for crafts and commerce. There are several instances,
too, in which Moroccan ingenuity and specifically Western concepts
work together effectively to demonstrate the most positive features

of the cultural hybridity characteristic of both colonial and postcolonial societies. Neither Chraïbi nor Mother remains uncritical of the
West or of modernity. In a variety of ways, the French colonial education system is shown to be repressive or a vehicle of racial and cultural prejudices. The economic consequences of colonialism are also
suggested. Mother's exaggerated desire to purchase everything new
may be intended to evoke the colonial administrative vision of those
like Viollette, who in 1931 could look to the day when "our six million natives acquire needs and become consumers" (quoted in
Woodhull 1993: 18). It is, to a large extent, Father who epitomizes
the capitalist perspective being imposed on a colonized people, a
perspective that could be expected to survive after independence, for
"the wave of future generations will think and act not in terms of civilization or of culture, of humanity or happiness, but in terms of violent and bitter commercial conflict, of efficiency, productivity,
strikes and oppression" (p. 56). The faults of the traditional patriarchy that draw Mother's ire are no less a target than the similarly
presumptuous male-dominated military of the Western powers,
which exposes the globe so completely to its devastation that only
the penguins at the South Pole are left unscathed. She takes her quarrel to General De Gaulle in person: "Those who have suffered the
horrors of this war should be in the forefront of the builders of the
world of tomorrow. And we don't want any more intermediaries or
people who think for us and act for us. We want a world of purity,
goodness, beauty and joy. Men have always made mistakes and committed errors and have always built peace on the ruins of war. We
don't want that world anymore" (pp. 88–89). And in the aftermath of
independence, Mother's fearless pursuit of a people's agenda focuses
on the new politicians of the neocolonial order; in fact, she sees little
to distinguish them from their colonial predecessors.

   Depicting the nation through women characters is a relatively
common device in Maghrebian literature. In this instance, the
defense of women's rights is framed as a criticism of Arab culture
and is easy for a Western reader to accept. Those same arguments,
however, can be turned ever so slightly in order to criticize the prejudices and the abuse of power inherent in the colonial structures or,
more broadly, neocolonialism, racism, and ethnocentrism in general.
This novel follows *The Butts*, Chraïbi's critique of anti-Arab sentiment in France and may reflect his own experiences of prejudice.
The many passages in the novel that deal with discrimination could
serve as an anatomy of discrimination. The dehumanization of

women and colonial subjects is evoked explicitly through comparisons with animals. Nagib argues with Mother when she proclaims a certain fraternity between herself and a mule, but she scores when she maintains that neither the human nor the animal who was born and lived in Morocco was able to freely express an opinion.

Stereotyping is illustrated repeatedly with reference to North Africans: when Mother goes to the movies, for example, she encounters the pejorative Hollywood images of the Arab world, but is relatively successful in replacing the Western narrative with one of her own devising as she retells the story to the audience during the intermission. The geography books she reads are no better and contain errors that are laughable. Paternalism, "the practice of treating or governing people in a fatherly manner, especially by providing for their needs without giving them responsibility," is exceptionally well developed. Mother is perceived as a child not only by Father but also by her sons, who see themselves presiding over her birth. One of the most ingenious scenes in the novel involves a confrontation between Father and Mother in which she finally asserts herself and stands up to her husband. She tells him: "You always paid for everything. From my underwear to my toothpicks and on through the food and clothespins. Everything. Yes, everything. No indeed. My wishes were not fulfilled, they were anticipated. They were your own" (p. 92). As the argument escalates, Nagib feels compelled to step in and separate the combatants, physically ushering Father outside the house. But Mother turns on her son and rejects his protection as well: "I don't need any help. . . . Not from you or anyone else. I am conscious now and entirely responsible for my own life. So you understand that? I haven't just freed myself from the custody of your father in order to come asking for your protection, no matter how big you are" (p. 97). This is a knockout blow in a chapter framed by boxing references. Nagib is, in fact, lured away from a radio broadcast of a Jake LaMotta match by the quarrel between his parents, and students may be familiar with Robert DeNiro's depiction of the boxer in the film *Raging Bull*, a Hollywood classic. It is but a small step to read this entire scene as Morocco's own rejection of protectorate status. And it is no coincidence that when Mother glimpses General De Gaulle in the distance, he looks a lot to her like Father.

Finally, students often want to know if Mother is a real person. In part, this question arises because of the elements in the tale that make Mother seem larger than life, those aspects that are necessary to her symbolic role. It has sometimes been effective in that case to

ask what details of the story lead us to think that she might not be
real, those character traits that seem to be exaggerated for effect, the
events that test our credibility. In part, however, the students ask the
question because they are unfamiliar with women's lives in Arab
countries, and the notion of sequestration is difficult for them to
accept. Mernissi's interviews with Moroccan women in *Doing Daily
Battle* provide a first-person account of life in a harem that corre-
sponds in many respects to Mother's situation; Mernissi also offers
true stories of more educated women that show the diversity of
women's lives in Morocco and offset the possibility that the course
might inadvertently project an outdated stereotype of Moroccan
women.

The work for this unit is evaluated through a short analytical
paper and the essay portion of the midterm exam. Because my course
serves among other things as a component course for our Women's
Studies Certificate, students are nearly always given a choice of
comparative topics that includes at least one question on women in
African literature. Typically, they might be asked to compare the rep-
resentations of women in at least two different works. I have also
given them a quote from the woman novelist Mariama Bâ: "Women
should no longer be decorative accessories, objects to be moved
about, companions to be flattered or calmed with promises. Women
are the nation's primary, fundamental root from which all else grows
and blossoms." I ask them to comment on this passage through references to *Mother Comes of Age* and *So Long a Letter*, Bâ's novel
about a Senegalese woman coping with a polygamous marriage (see
Chapter 4). Relationships between mothers and sons are also an
interesting focus for the readings in the first half of the semester,
especially when I begin with *Sundiata* (see Chapter 17). Another
comparative question that has produced some insightful essays
requires the students to examine the effects of Western education on
the protagonists in Camara Laye's *The Dark Child* and *Mother
Comes of Age*. Because students have a choice of questions, the
exam is a good indication of which works they have found the most
intellectually stimulating, and Chraïbi's novel never fails to find its
partisans, as year after year students demonstrate that, through
Mother's struggle and achievements, they have become more conscious of the whole configuration of ideas relating to women's roles
and women's rights both in African cultures and in their own experience. Like all of Chraïbi's readers, they have reveled in what the
author calls "the triumphal march of the human being towards joy"
(Chraibi's preface to the Aquila edition, p. 8).

NOTE

1. I would like acknowledge the contributions of my students whose discussions and papers on *Mother Comes of Age* were helpful to me in the writing of this essay, especially Susan Cressman and Donnelle Bohnke, who was kind enough to share her fine bibliography and the results of her research.

SUGGESTIONS FOR
FURTHER READING AND RESOURCES

Bâ, Mariama. 1981. *So Long a Letter*. Portsmouth, N.H.: Heinemann.
The Battle of Algiers. 1965. [Battaglia di Algieri]. Directed by Gillo Pontecorvo. Performed by Brahim Haggiag, Jean Martin, Saadi Yacef. Videocassette: Guidance, 1988. Dramatization of the conflict between Algerian nationalists and French colonists that culminated in Algeria's independence in 1962. Especially effective depiction of the role played by women in the resistance movement.
Chraïbi, Driss. 1972. *La Civilisation, ma mère!* ed. G. Robert McConnell. Toronto: Aquila Communications. A pedagogical edition of the novel with glossary, vocabulary exercises, comprehension questions, and composition topics. Jean Dejeux provides a thoughtful introduction to Chraïbi and his work. The text includes some interesting black-and-white photos and selected reviews of the book. A cassette in French is available that includes much of the first part of the novel.
―――. 1972. *Heirs to the Past*. Originally published in French as *La Succession ouverte*. Portsmouth, N.H.: Heinemann.
―――. 1989. *The Butts*. Originally published in French as *Les Boucs*. Boulder: Lynne Rienner. Chraïbi's critique of anti-Arab sentiment in France, perhaps reflecting his own experience.
―――. 1994. *Inspector Ali*. Boulder: Lynne Rienner.
―――. 1997. *Flutes of Death*. Originally published in French as *Une Enquête au pays*. Boulder: Lynner Rienner.
―――. 1998. *Mother Comes of Age*, trans. and introduced by Hugh Harter. Boulder: Lynne Rienner. A very fine translation of the novel with an excellent introduction to Chraïbi as a writer.
Djebar, Assia. 1993. *A Sister to Scheherazade*. Portsmouth, N.H.: Heinemann. A rich and well-constructed narrative that addresses a woman's efforts to escape sequestration and to divest herself of the veil, but somewhat difficult for undergraduates.
"Driss Chraïbi au Maroc: Itinéraire de la mémoire." 1989. Videocassette, in French. Produced by Project for International Communication Studies, Iowa City, Iowa. Driss Chraïbi, a French-speaking writer, returns to his native Morocco and describes his position in francophone literature, halfway between French and Arab.
Gordon, David. 1962. *North Africa's French Legacy: 1954–1962*. Harvard

Middle Eastern Monographs IX. Cambridge: Harvard University Press. A short study of the Maghreb that focuses specifically on subjects treated by Chraïbi—the French civilizing mission, reactions to the policy of assimilation, the ambivalent attitude of Western-educated intellectuals.

Laye, Camara. 1954. *Dark Child*. New York: Noonday Press. First published in French as *L'Enfant Noir*.

"Marakesh and Fez." 1995. A travel video produced by International Video Network; makes the point that Morocco has a rich historical past and documents the ingenuity of North African artisans.

Marx-Scouras, Danielle. 1992. "A Literature of Departure: The Cross Cultural Writing of Driss Chraïbi," *Research in African Literatures* 23, 2: 131–144. A readable, insightful analysis of Chraïbi's works with pertinent observations concerning *Mother Comes of Age*.

Mernissi, Fatima. 1988. *Doing Daily Battle: Interviews with Moroccan Women*, trans. Mary Jo Lakeland. New Brunswick, N.J.: Rutgers University Press. The actual voices of Moroccan women provide a down-to-earth complement for Chraïbi's fictional character.

———. 1991. *The Veil and the Male Elite: A Feminist Interpretation of Women's Rights in Islam*, trans. Mary Jo Lakeland. Reading, Mass.: Addison-Wesley. A scholarly study of the veil in Arab tradition for those students who want to understand the custom in terms of Islamic history.

Niane, Djibril Tamsir. 1995. *Sundiata: An Epic of Old Mali*, trans. G. D. Pickett. Longman African Classics. New York: Addison-Wesley. First published in 1965; see Chapter 17 in this collection.

Oyono, Ferdinand. 1990. [1966] *Houseboy*. Originally published in French as *Une vie de boy*. Translated by John Reed. Portsmouth, N.H.: Heinemann. (See Chapter 19, this volume.)

Woodhull, Winifred. 1993. *Transfigurations of the Maghreb: Feminism, Decolonization, and Literatures*. Minneapolis: University of Minnesota Press. Examines the representation of women in the works of Algerian writers in a way that is highly relevant for the reading of Chraïbi's novel. Excellent bibliography.

6

Lindsey Collen's
The Rape of Sita

Beverly B. Mack

WHO COULD FAIL TO BE INTRIGUED BY A NOVEL THAT
begins, "Please do not read this preface unless you are already a
fanatic novel reader. You will notice that the print is small to dis-
courage everyone except the most persistent reader" (p. 5)? In nineteenth-century literary style the narrative voice conspires,
"Goldswains told me not to talk directly to the reader in my novel.
. . . But I, the undersigned, Iqbal of Surinam, will address you
directly quite often in the course of this novel, reader" (p. 5). The
narrator's publisher had also warned him against diversions, without
which, Iqbal asserts, the reader cannot know who Sita is, or even
who he, Iqbal, is. So he has decided that "Publishers will have to
jump off"—he'll print out the manuscript himself on his home com-
puter, and hawk it in the streets. As it turns out, the narrator was prescient: this 1993 novel was banned in Mauritius, although it won
awards elsewhere.

Before Iqbal the Umpire finishes the first two pages, he has
immersed the reader in a literary carnival, including the Indian
Ramayana epic, Elizabethan literary allusions, and nineteenth-century Islamic theology. In addition, he reminds us that we have already
skipped over his own poem in the preface, presumably because we
had too little of its subject matter: "Time."

Lindsey Collen, *The Rape of Sita* (Portsmouth, N.H.: Heinemann, 1993).

NOVEL AND AUTHOR

Lindsey Collen was born in the South African Transkei in 1948. She began her writing career at the age of six, during a childhood of instability caused by moving frequently with her family whenever her father, an antiapartheid native affairs commissioner, was reassigned in apartheid-wracked South Africa. Collen was interested in the political situation wherever they lived, and her parents encouraged such interest. It is not surprising, therefore, that she studied law and literature at the University of Witwatersrand and was actively involved in the student movement there. Collen has also lived in New York, the Seychelles, and in London, where she studied at the London School of Economics. Collen and her husband, Ram Seegobin, a doctor and trade unionist, live and work in Mauritius. Her first novel, *There Is a Tide,* was published in 1990.

Within hours of the appearance of *The Rape of Sita* in 1993, outraged Hindu fundamentalists barraged Collen with threats of rape and death for having blasphemed the Hindu goddess Sita. Collen was forced to stop the book's publication and distribution, and the Mauritian government succumbed to pressure, confiscating copies already published, banning the book, and establishing a police inquiry. In response, women's groups in Mauritius demanded that the government support the right to free speech and withdraw the ban. Some years later the book was begrudgingly accepted at the local level; internationally it has received accolades, winning the Commonwealth Writers Prize for best African novel of 1994.

COURSE CONTEXT AND DISCUSSION THEMES

The Rape of Sita would be a good choice for a course segment on Mauritian history or politics, but it is best suited to such women's studies and literature courses as African Literature Survey, Southern African Literature, or African Women Writers. I have used it for the last two of these, in which courses it has engendered enthusiastic responses among sophomores and juniors. Its multifaceted style and subject matter force an uninitiated student of Africa to face the complexity that marks the collective nature of the continent and underlines the strengths of African women as a sociopolitical force. Issues of patriarchy, colonialism, and oppressions of many kinds are the novel's central foci. In addition, its intricate integration of epic and oral narrative styles, classic Western literature, and Islamic references requires that it be taught with attention to these features. Beatles' lyrics constitute a contemporary leitmotif connecting major issues throughout the work.

Foremost among issues at the center of this novel is that of rape in its actual and metaphorical contexts. Fervent and immediate opposition to the appearance of the novel confirms its accuracy in criticizing patriarchal control and the silencing of subordinated groups, whether in government or religious contexts. Feminism, trade unionism, colonialism—the work speaks on many levels about a multiplicity of oppressions. These perspectives are certainly the point of departure for discussions, but more specific political allusions, references to ethnicities, religious affiliations, and implications concerning government controls of the individual are important subsets of the larger context. For specific cultural context, students will need to be guided carefully, but being able to teach this work at a multiplicity of levels makes the experience enjoyable as well as educational.

This novel could easily expand to fill a semester, but few teachers have the luxury of spending this much time on one book. I have used Collen's novel in a one-semester, three-credit-hour course that meets for two eighty-minute sessions per week. It is one of nine novels for the course, so I can spend only three or four class meetings on it (stealing time for it from other works). To make best use of so little time I walk students through a close reading of the first sixteen pages in the first class session. Through attention to narrative voice, this approach provides students familiarity with the narrator Iqbal's technique of game playing, introductions to Sita's parents, relevant background information, and Sita's dilemma, all of which are covered by page 15. Page 16 begins "not-chapter three" (the book is divided into sections, not numbered chapters), in which a puzzling verbal exchange between Sita and Dharma propels the reader into the main action by forcing an inquiry into what they are discussing, and requires some background to the current context. Once students have been ushered through this, they feel sufficiently informed to carry on, knowing they can expect only the unexpected. This is one novel students are not required to have read in its entirety prior to the first class discussion of it.

A second class meeting addresses the overall structure of the work; together we create a chart on the board, citing for each chapter points like main characters, main actions, symbolic images, and varieties of oppression, whether gender based, ethnic oriented, religious, or nationalist. This allows students to envision the novel as a whole

piece, seeing interconnections between specific issues in it. This is
an interactive exercise, with appropriately labeled columns on the
board (or students can generate their own categories in the first stage
of a group exercise) for students to fill in from their own perspectives. Its effect is to provide an overview that helps them feel in control of the novel as a whole. In addition, the exercise functions as a
tool for discussing the repetition of images or situations as a means
of creating a certain effect. By examining how circumstances are
metaphorically repeated, students can see how the author layers
meanings as the story unfolds, building image upon image like paint
on a canvas.

The third class meeting addresses oral narrative and its centrality
to this story, pointing out that the inclusion of oral narrative technique allows for reading (recitation) between the lines. Iqbal tells
several stories about Sita's neighbors and relatives, and all these stories prove to be apocryphal. In sorting out their particular relevances,
students learn to make connections between seemingly disparate
images, and follow the intentions of the author in doing so. For
instance, the women who are abducted by policemen face their
potential rapists on a remote mountain and take the offensive, in the
most graphic of ways: they rip off their own clothes and shout,
"Think you can scare us with the threat of rape. You show us, then,
smart alecs. Show us. Give us a demonstration. . . . Come on. Get
going. What's the delay. Goodfornothings" (p. 86). The men retreat
with their tails (!) between their legs, and the legend of strong
women is reified in the townsfolk's constant retelling of this tale,
which carries the explicit message, "From slave days some women
have kept the laughter as a weapon against oppression" (p. 84). The
tale is an appropriate segue into the section describing the exclusive
matriarchal nature of Sita's family.

Indeed, gender issues are central to this work and should be the
focus of another class discussion. Collen's descriptions of matriarchy
and patriarchy help to explain the quirkiness of her main characters.
These descriptions are directly tied to the leitmotif of Iqbal *cum* Jojo
of the Beatles' "Get Back" fame. Sita's father, a union organizer now
wanted by the state, is a gentle man who refuses to marry because he
refuses to own a woman (p. 110). He loves Sita's mother, Doorga,
"because she was independent and strong and had a reputation for
beating people up" (p. 14). She loves him because he has "none of
the traits of a husband" (p. 14). By the time the reader reaches a
description of Doorga's extraordinary family, Iqbal is "a man who'd
rather be a woman" (p. 86). Doorga's family has no males, "just like

neither husbands nor lovers ever settled in in Sita's mother's family, so boy-children were never born to them, either . . . just women and girls. And they kept cows, never a bull, and when the cows calved they were reputed . . . to be she-calves . . . [and the family] always had a bitch with swinging tits and two or three pups gazing up lovingly at her. Their hens produced chicks by immaculate conception. Hen-chicks . . . just women and girls. Not only today. As far back as you could go. . . . So this bit will be a matrilinear story, it will" (p. 90). It is no wonder that by this point, "Iqbal was a man who wished he was a woman" (p. 90).

Another lecture period should involve direct discussion of that old Beatles tune, complete with an in-class playing of "Get Back," to demonstrate that the author has deliberately manipulated the lyrics to suit her theme. It was, after all, not Jojo but "Sweet Loretta Martin" who thought she was a woman, "but she was another man." And so, one needs to ask, why has Collen changed this, and why should Jojo of the song "get back"? To what? To when? Where? How does this reflect what is happening in the novel? What should Mauritian citizens get back to? Students participate most enthusiastically in discussions of politics after hearing pop music, it seems.

An entire lecture can be dedicated to dreams and the relationships among them. Between flying and diving, Freudian extremes are represented in Sita's dreams. Diving becomes live burial, flying represents freedom of individuals as well as nations to overcome oppression and "fly right." In the midst of these are represented the Zimbabwe and Zulu nations, ancient and contemporary, with all they symbolize in terms of independence and oppression. If even fiercely independent Sita, raised to be strong and self-reliant, can be raped, and if even the legendary Sita, wife of Rama in the Ramayana epic, could be carried off (she was not raped in the epic), then what woman could be safe? In that case even the strongest of nations also could be raped, pillaged, and colonized.

Perhaps the most difficult aspect of this novel is that its unusual complexity precludes closure. That may be its intent. Students need to feel comfortable with not understanding every detail about the book, and with knowing they cannot even recognize every detail, unless perhaps they have grown up on Mauritian ground—and even then, perhaps not. This is a richly provocative read, and it provides delight along the way. Students rarely have the chance to find irreverence in a novel. This book thumbs its pages at everything standard and classic (politics, Westernization, classic literature) while simultaneously forcing the reader to understand the infinite number of status quos that life creates. Everyone can find something to elicit laughter and tears in this moving novel.

RELATED MATERIALS

I know of no related materials such as films to use with this novel, but it would be very useful to provide students with a detailed map of Mauritius, showing the town of Surinam, as well as the neighboring region of southern Africa, including South Africa and Zimbabwe. The instructor will need to define the area of Zulu conquest on the map of South Africa.

It would be useful for the instructor to read some portion of (and about) the Indian epic, the Ramayana, to become familiar with Shakespeare's *The Rape of Lucrece*, to be aware of immigration into Mauritius from India, to understand the rudimentary definition of *dharma* in relation to Hinduism, and to know about Iqbal, the Muslim philosopher/scholar whose aim it was to meld politics and religion in his philosophy. Less lofty, but equally important, is a tape of the Beatles' "Get Back."

Shakespeare's *The Rape of Lucrece* involves a perpetrator named Lucius Tarquinius (Sita's rapist is Rowan Tarquin), who rapes Lucrece. Lucrece's resultant suicide leads to her family's vengeance, which in turn results in a change of the government's structure from a kingship to a consulate. Thus in *The Rape of Lucrece* the virtuous, evidently expendable woman is sacrificed for the ultimate transformation of the (patriarchal) political state.

The central myth in Collen's work is the *Ramayana,* the ancient Indian epic with the couple Rama and Sita at its center (speculatively dated between 1500 and 400 B.C.). The story involves the efforts of Rama's father, Dasratha, to vanquish the Ravanas—the evil antagonists who ravage society at every level—and his son Rama's efforts to carry out his intentions. In Collen's story it is Sita who is at the center of the action, while her husband, this time named Dharma, seeks to establish justice and peace. Ironically, Dharma, personifying Divine Truth, cannot effect change because he is unaware of the truth of how Sita has herself been ravished by a contemporary Ravana—Rowan the rapist.

The concept of *dharma* includes the principle of cosmic existence and the idea of an individual's fulfillment of duty in life through the pursuit of cosmic Truth, which is the rationale for human existence. This principle pervades the novel, personified as Sita's husband, Dharma. Collen's intention in pairing characters named after the Hindu goddess Sita, and the Hindu concept of *dharma*, is clearly to unify these Eastern philosophies, as well as to reflect the multiplicity of ethnic and religious backgrounds of the Indian immigrants who populate Mauritius. Iqbal the narrator is careful to clarify the intended meaning: "No one listening to the story asked me who Dharma was. They all knew him already. The older son of Dasratha, the son who was hero of all tales. They knew what his name meant, and that he had *dharma*" (p. 68). Just as Dharma seeks to lead people to the Truth, so *dharma* functions as a mediatory concept connecting Hindu and Muslim beliefs. To the degree that *dharma* conveys the concept of Divine Truth, it is related to the basis of Sufi Muslim philosophy, pursuit of the same cosmic Truth. The character Dharma, whose name suggests a Hindu context, seeks to lead people to Truth; similarly, narrator Iqbal, who bears a name connected to Islam, pursues and broadcasts Truth, and acts as a unifying agent among Mauritian Indians, whether Hindu or Muslim.

The narrator Iqbal is named for Muhammad Iqbal, a Pakistani Muslim polymath (1877–1938) whose best-known work is *The Reconstruction of Religious Thought in Islam*. Iqbal was a poet, philosopher, politician, and lawyer who promoted the principles of independent judgment (*ijtihad*, Ar.) and rule by consensus (*ijma'*, Ar.) in a parliamentary system. As a theologian, Iqbal practiced critical interpretation of the Quran. More important to the aims of this book is the fact that Iqbal was also a renegade, known to possess indefatigable reserves of energy, a propensity for outspokenness, and an activist spirit. One of his first endeavors as a lawyer was to try to defend his brother in a government ministry suit that Iqbal knew could not be successful. Such a dilemma is echoed in Collen's work at its outset, when Sita's father's life is described as a struggle for justice on the part of a unionist who cannot win against a political machine.

Initially a Qadiriyya Sufi, the historical Muhammad Iqbal strove to follow Sufism while eschewing it as a full-time vocation. Eventually he renounced Sufism as an indication of the decline of a nation, criticizing the degree to which Sufis had lost the straight path: "Islam has nothing to do with the discussion of *wahdat* (unity) and *Kathrat* (plurality). The essence of Islam is *Tawhid* [belief in the uniqueness and singleness of God], and the opposite of the latter is not *kathrat* but *shirk* [attribution of partnership to God]" (Malik 1971: 53). Unity and plurality are issues central to Collen's story: they create the sociopolitical chaos that tears society asunder, while *dharma* goes unattended. Just like his historical model, the narrator Iqbal is driven toward a discovery of Truth, maniacal in his efforts to philosophize about Absolutes, and irreverent in the most respectful of ways, constantly holding dualities up to critical examination as opposing sides of the same coin. In his role as Iqbal the Umpire, and in his many other guises, the narrator of *The Rape of Sita* functions as a mouthpiece and mediator who constitutes a central conceit in this work. When Iqbal implores, "Get back to where you once belonged," the reader must give serious consideration to his appeal.

STUDENT ASSIGNMENTS

For a literature course involving *The Rape of Sita*, students choose one feature of two novels for a comparative literary analysis. I do not assign topics, but ask that they select some aspect of the works that strikes them as effective; interest is the only necessary criterion. For example, a student might choose to discuss comparable symbols or metaphors in two novels, addressing the ways in which dreams of flying are used in each, or rape. Sometimes students discuss characters across novels, comparing the husband-wife relationship in each, or the mother-child connection. Whatever the student chooses as a topic must be specific, not general—in other words, in a literature course one cannot write in broad strokes about the novel as an instrument of social change. The points the student makes must be supported by citations from the books, providing evidence for observations throughout the paper.

With these assignments in mind, class discussions seek to discover how the novel has its effect on the reader. Students are quick to master the plot of the work; that is never the prime focus. Instead, class discussions revolve around aspects of the genre: repeated images, metaphorical implications, character development, and the integral functions of these features of the work.

For classes in women's studies, African history, or politics, paper assignments could be quite different. The material in this book would suit studies of gender issues, colonialism, immigration, class struggle, definitions of ethnicity, and historical developments in the region. *The Rape of Sita* lends itself to a wide range of assignments

for a religious studies program, fraught as this work is with multiple
varieties of religious perspectives.

ASSESSMENTS

This novel's range of foci guarantees that it will appeal to everyone
in some way. First and foremost it is a brave novel that forces discussion of the issue of rape in its actual and metaphorical manifesta-
tions. Sita grapples with suppressed memories of the rape that took
place on the nearby, French-colonized island of Reunion. Her rapist
is a probation officer, a friend of the family. The rape occurs as she is
reading T. S. Eliot's *The Wasteland*, and in the historical moment
when the United States begins bombing Iraq. The carefully constructed circumstances and significant details of the situation establish a solid basis for the discussion of patriarchy and feminism,
unionism and parastatals, colonialism and independence.

In addition, the work offers cultural insight from a variety of perspectives, including religious (Hinduism and Islam), ethnic (Indian
immigration and settlement in Mauritius), and global (the effect of an
infusion of popular Western culture). One of the novel's leitmotifs is
some version of "Jojo was a man who thought he was a woman,"
which rapidly turns into a mere "Iqbal was a man" (p. 8). Indeed,
putting oneself into someone else's shoes (or dress) is one of the
main themes of the work. As the story progresses, the leitmotif
"Iqbal was a man" is reduced to "Iqbal was." It resurfaces as the
complement "Iqbal was a man who thought he was a woman" by the
novel's last page.

This novel is filled with an eclectic assortment of quirky characters who seem nevertheless to be remarkably realistic. These characters struggle to come to terms with issues that most North American
students find familiar: conflict over evolving gender roles, ethnic
identities, religion, or class status. Yet some of the central characters
in the novel are distinctly foreign—like the Hindu epic goddess Sita,
Sita's husband Dharma, and the Muslim philosopher Muhammad
Iqbal. These are observed by Iqbal, seeker of Truth, as he identifies
with the Beatles' character Jojo, who was unsure of his own identity.
That this motley assortment of characters coexists in a contemporary
African setting brings students a new perspective on Africa, far from
the stereotype derived from the popularity of kente cloth and Swahili
names in the contemporary United States.

SUGGESTIONS FOR
FURTHER READING AND RESOURCES

Beatles. "Get Back," a song on their "Let It Be" album.

Bennett, Pramila Ramgulan, comp. 1992. *Mauritius*. Santa Barbara: Clio.

Blackburn, Julia. 1995. *Book of Color: A Novel*. New York: Pantheon. Another work of contemporary fiction set in Mauritius.

Bowman, Larry. 1991. *Democracy and Development in the Indian Ocean*. Boulder: Westview.

Collen, Lindsey. 1993. *The Rape of Sita*. Portsmouth, N.H.: Heinemann.

——. 1995. *There Is a Tide*. New York: Macmillan.

——. 1999. *Getting Rid of It*. London: Granta Books. Collen's newest book. Jumila, Sadna, and Goldilox Soo struggle to solve a problem that might send them to prison so that they can move on with their larger struggle against patriarchal oppression in impoverished Mauritius.

"Collen, Lindsey. The Rape of Fiction." 1994. *Index on Censorship* 4–5: 210–212.

"Donna Allen's Comment." 1994. *Media Report to Women*, 22, 1: back page. A discussion of the controversy over publication of *The Rape of Sita*.

Harbage, Alfred. 1970. *William Shakespeare: The Complete Works*. Baltimore: Penguin.

Iqbal, Muhammad. 1934. *The Reconstruction of Religious Thought in Islam*. London: Oxford University Press.

LeClezio, J-M.G. 1993. *Prospector*. Boston: David R. Godine.

Malik, Hafeex, ed. 1971. *Iqbal: Poet-Philosopher of Pakistan*. New York: Columbia University Press.

Moree, P. J. 1998. *Concise History of Dutch Mauritius 1598–1710: A Fruitful and Healthy Land*. New York: Kegan Paul.

Narayan, R. K. 1972. *The Ramayana*. New York: Viking.

Piggot, Jill. 1995. "Rage Deferred," *The Women's Review of Books* 12, 10–11: 28. A review of *The Rape of Sita*.

"*The Rape of Sita*." 1995. *Choice*, 107–108. A book review.

Saint-Pierre, Bernardin. 1989. *Paul and Virginia, 1796*. Oxford: Woodstock Books. Another work of fiction set in historical Mauritius.

Simmons, Adele. 1982. *Modern Mauritius: The Politics of Decolonization*. Bloomington: Indiana University Press.

7

Maryse Condé's *Segu*

Joye Bowman

THE NINETEENTH CENTURY USHERED IN A NEW ERA throughout the African continent. Religious revolutions spread Islam across two-thirds of West Africa, introducing new political and social systems at the same time. Despite laws passed early in the century, the Atlantic slave trade continued to affect local people. Eventually, with the abolition of the slave trade and industrialization in Europe, merchants made new demands for tropical goods from Africa.[1]

Maryse Condé's epic novel, *Segu*, analyzes these changes in West Africa between 1797 and 1860. Segu was a Bambara state, located between Bamako and Timbuctu in contemporary Mali. It was founded about 1712 and continued to exist until it was conquered by the Islamic reformer El-Hadj Omar in the early 1860s. Condé uses the *griot* story-telling tradition of her presumed Bambara ancestors to relay Segu's history through the experiences of Dousika Traore's family. Using four Traore sons, Tiekoro, Siga, Naba, and Malobali, Condé analyzes these three historical themes—the spread of Islam, the abolition of the slave trade, and the development of "legitimate commerce."

Each son and his family illuminate certain dimensions of these themes. Tiekoro, the eldest son, denies his ancestors' religion and converts to Islam. Siga, on the other hand, refuses to convert and holds on to his belief in the Bambara gods. Shortly after Tiekoro's conversion, slave traders capture Naba, his younger brother. Naba is sold to a merchant on Gorée Island, but through a strange turn of

---

Maryse Condé, *Segu*, trans. Barbara Bray (New York: Ballantine Books, 1987).

events, he ends up as a slave on a plantation in Brazil. The fourth brother, Malobali, becomes a mercenary in the Asantehene's army. However, he flees from his post and goes south to the coast, arriving there just as the slave trade is giving way to "legitimate commerce." Malobali eventually becomes a palm oil merchant in Ouidah.

I assign *Segu* in a survey course entitled Africa Since 1500. Although the students find it challenging, the novel is generally well received. Because this course fulfills a general education requirement, some sixty to eighty students from a variety of majors enroll in it each semester. The class meets three times a week, for two lectures and one discussion section. Many students panic when they realize that *Segu* is nearly five hundred pages long. The majority of the students finish the book, however; many even want to read the sequel, *The Children of Segu.* The life stories that Condé tells in this novel capture their attention. I divide the novel into manageable pieces and give students about a month to finish the book. My goal in using *Segu* is to help students understand the consequences of broad historical events for people's lives.

THE NOVEL

Segu captures the spirit of the rapid and dramatic changes that occurred in the nineteenth century in ways that textbooks cannot. By using the Traore brothers and members of their families, Condé paints a picture of daily life in Segu. Read with a basic history textbook, such as Kevin Shillington's *History of Africa,* students can see how life changed for ordinary men and women.

One of the major themes that Condé addresses is the spread of Islam. She uses Tiekoro Traore to illustrate the compelling nature of this religion. Segu is a strong Bambara state, which has resisted conversion to Islam. Muslim merchants, scholars, and advisers are allowed into Segu, but the *mansa* (king) and his court remain steadfast in their belief system. The *mansa*, however, recognizes that the new religion has advantages as well as disadvantages:

> Its cabalistic signs were as effective as many sacrifices. Furthermore, these signs made it possible to maintain and strengthen alliances with other peoples far away, and created a kind of moral community to which it was a good thing to belong. On the other hand, Islam was dangerous: it undermined the power of

kings, according sovereignty to one supreme god who was completely alien to the Bambara universe. How could one fail to be
suspicious of this Allah whose city was somewhere in the east?
(p. 41)

In spite of the *mansa*'s ambivalence, Tiekoro is drawn to Islam.
Living in the thirteenth Islamic century (November 1785–November
1885), Muslims across the Islamic world were preparing for the coming of the Mahdi. Christian Europe was in the process of expanding
overseas. An Islamic revival spread across the Islamic world, and
jihad movements were common. New brotherhoods formed, such as
the Tijaniyya. Condé uses Tiekoro to show how this revival played
itself out. For Tiekoro, "It all began when, out of curiosity, he went
into a mosque. He'd heard the call of the *muezzin* the day before, and
something inexpressible had awakened within him" (p. 20). He is
particularly impressed by the writing process and longs to read and
write.

Tiekoro asks for and receives permission to go to Timbuctu to
study the Quran. But the decision is a difficult one for Tiekoro's
father, Dousika, and for the royal council, of which he is a member.

For Dousika, night had fallen over the world. Forever. In the darkness of his hut, his eyes closed, he lay prostrate on his mat, always
a prey to the same crowding questions. When had he neglected his
gods or his ancestors? When had he failed to offer them a share of
his harvest? When had he forgotten to sprinkle the *boli* [fetishes]
with blood?[2] When had he put food to his lips without first satisfying our mother earth? Rage seized him. It was all because of his
eldest son, Tiekoro, the very one who ought to have been his pride.
(p. 35)

Tiekoro's conversion to Islam illuminates some of the divisions
that existed in West Africa. The majority of the Muslim leaders who
launched the jihads were Fulani. Although there had long been a
symbiotic relationship between the Fulani pastoralists and Bambara
agriculturalists, tensions between the two groups were common. The
herdsmen's poem captures this spirit: "Fulani, keep your flock.
Black, keep your spade, your wearisome spade" (p. 15). Condé uses
Nya, Tiekoro's mother, to explain the situation. She tells Malobali,
Tiekoro's younger brother by a Fulani slave woman, that "for a long
time the Fulani lived alongside us and we didn't pay any attention to
them. Sometimes we even looked down on them because they didn't
build or farm, but just went here and there with their herds. Then one

day everything changed. They all got together and declared war on us. All because of Islam. You see, Islam is a sword that divides" (p. 128).

Condé helps the reader appreciate the complexities of identity. The struggle is not simply a question of Fulani versus Bambara. When Dousika Traore dies, his nephew, Tiefolo, travels to Jenne to tell Tiekoro. Jenne was a major regional trading center located in Masina, an Islamic state just north and east of Segu. By about 1818, Cheikou Amadou's jihad in Masina was well under way. As a Bozo man explains to Tiefolo, "You couldn't have come to a worse place. This is a real nest of pythons. Here, it's fetishist Fulani against Muslim Fulani, Qadriya brotherhood against Tijaniya brotherhood against Kounti brotherhood. Songhay against Fulani, Moroccan against Fulani, and everyone against the Bambara. The place will soon run with blood" (p. 156).

As Condé explains, the Bambara in Jenne began to realize that "if the Fulani were burying their differences it was to join together against an empire that had subjected them for too long" (p. 158). Under Cheikou Amadou, the Fulani had received inspiration and support from Usman dan Fodio, who had established the Sokoto Caliphate with its base in the region of northern Nigeria between 1804 and 1808. One of Cheikou Amadou's goals in Jenne was to purify Islam. Nadie, Tiekoro's concubine and mother of his children, understands Cheikou Amadou's actions: "He says Islam is corrupt here, and the mosques are sinks of inequity" (p. 149).

Siga's story helps the reader see how an unconverted Bambara viewed the spread of Islam. Siga was born on the same day as his brother, Tiekoro. However, his mother was a slave woman who committed suicide by throwing herself down a well. Nya, Dousika's senior wife, raised Siga, but he was never able to overcome his heritage and his mother's death. "Alas, the hazards of birth! If he'd been born of this womb rather than that, his life would have been quite different" (p. 30). Dousika chooses Siga to accompany Tiekoro when the latter travels to Timbuctu to begin his quranic studies. Neither Siga nor Tiekoro are well received in this holy city. Tiekoro immediately turns on his brother, and Siga is forced to fend for himself. Siga has no desire to convert. He also has no way to return to Segu. A young boy, Ismael, befriends him and tells him that to accomplish anything in Timbuctu, he needs to look like a Muslim. Ismael says, "cut off those braids, get rid of those baubles. Hide them. Do what everyone else does. If you knew what those great scholars hid under their caftans! Call yourself Ahmed, don't drink in public, and there you are!"

(pp. 49–50). Ismael promises Siga that he can get him a job as a donkey boy. Siga has few choices without his brother. Thus he changes his name to Ahmed and signs on as a donkey boy. He travels to Fez (Morocco), where he eventually marries a local woman, Fatima, and makes a life for himself. But he never converts to Islam. Siga eventually returns to Segu with his wife. However, he never recovers from his mother's death or his brother's desertion.

Condé uses Naba and his family to suggest the damaging effects the slave trade had on West African communities. Naba, his cousin Tiefolo, and several other young hunters go out to hunt without permission. During this mission, slave raiders capture Naba and carry him to Kankan (Guinea), a major trading center. He ends up on Gorée Island. His owner there is Anne Pépin, a *signare* (a woman of mixed French and Wolof descent), who has become a successful businesswoman through the slave trade. The process of being sold as a slave devastates Naba. When he hears that children are the best catch of all, "Naba wept bitterly still, overwhelmed by the wickedness of a practice he had never thought about before. What reason could there be for parting children from their mothers, men and women from their homes and fellow countrymen? What did those who did it get in return? Material wealth? Was that enough to purchase human souls?" (p. 76). Condé also conveys the pain and suffering felt by relatives of those who have been captured.

On Gorée, Naba becomes a productive gardener for Anne Pépin. Her lover, Isidore Duchâtel, understands that the abolition of the slave trade will soon become a reality. He encourages her to use Naba to begin cultivating agricultural commodities that might then become more valuable than slaves. In the most implausible piece of the story, Naba falls in love with a captive in the slave castle where he often delivers produce. This young girl, Ayodele, captures Naba's heart. When he learns that she is to be shipped off, he decides to stow away on the slave ship. Manoel Ignacio da Cunha, a plantation owner in Pernambuco, Brazil, buys Ayodele. Although a Dutchman purchases Naba, he runs away and somehow finds Ayodele.

In spite of the rather unbelievable nature of these events, the reader can still learn something about the impact of New World slavery from this story: "Ayodele was not sixteen when she was torn away from her family, and even now was only just over twenty. But her heart was that of an old woman, older than that of the woman who bore her, older than her grandmother's. Her heart was bitter, bitter as *cahuchu*, the wood that weeps, which the *seringueiros*, the rubber gatherers, stabbed with their knives in the forests. Without Naba she might have gone mad, or put an end to herself" (pp. 203–204). Her master da Cunha had raped Ayodele, and she gives birth to his child, Abiola. Naba accepts this child as his own. Subsequently, he and Ayodele have three sons together. Naba continues to raise fruits and vegetables. If there is a surplus, Ayodele sells it in Recife's markets. Ayodele uses the money to contribute to a manumission society that helps slaves buy their freedom and return to West Africa, especially to Ouidah and Porto Novo, Benin. The sons of Ayodele and Naba eventually leave Brazil for Ouidah, where they become a leading family in the Agoudah or *retournado* community. Naba, however, is killed before they leave Brazil.

Naba's death is also instructive. During a trip to Recife, a Muslim approaches Naba about a prayer meeting that evening. Naba takes a note written in Arabic from him. When Abiola finds this note, he convinces his father, the slave owner, to search Naba's house. The search party finds the note and Naba is arrested and sentenced to death for involvement in a Muslim plot to foment a slave revolt. As Condé notes, although there were many slave uprisings in Brazil, Naba's character never participates in them. In fact, Naba never accepts either Christianity or Islam. He has been baptized and given the name Jean-Baptiste. But as Ayodele says, "Are we ever really Catholics? We just pretend" (p. 208). At Naba's trial, he says nothing when asked to swear on the Bible. "When asked 'Are you a Muslim?' he only laughs. When told to choose between Catholic rosary and Muslim prayer beads, he stands motionless. The same thing happens when he is asked to choose between a picture of St. Gonçalves of Amarante and a piece of paper with Arabic calligraphy" (p. 215). The judges then decide that Naba is a sorcerer and sentence him to death. Ayodele is crushed. But she manages to use the funds in the manumission society to buy her freedom and that of her sons. They leave for Ouidah, where she hopes to build a new life.

Condé uses Ayodele's story to sketch the transition from the slave trade to "legitimate commerce." After Ayodele becomes a successful businesswoman in Ouidah, she meets Malobali Traore, whose life has been traumatic like that of his brothers. His mother, Sira, is a Fulani woman who left Dousika to return to her own people. When Malobali was ten years old, he learned that Nya, who had raised him, was not his biological mother. His worldview was altered dramatically. Malobali has a difficult relationship with Tiekoro, who has returned to Segu and opened a quranic school there. Tiekoro insists that Malobali be sent to Jenne to study the quran. Malobali cannot fathom this idea and runs away from his family. He lands in the

Asantehene's army, where he serves for several years as a mercenary. On a mission to the coast, Malobali commits a heinous crime, which compels him to continue running. By this time in the 1820s, many of his associates believe that the future for West Africa lies on the coast with the English. "They've got arms, seagoing ships, money—and they know about the new plants" (p. 229). To escape punishment for his crime, Malobali decides to throw his lot in with others on the coast, eventually including those people in Ayodele's *retournado* and Christian community.

Although Christian missionaries take in Malobali, he understands the negative potential of religious conversion: "To be converted! To deny the gods of one's fathers, and through them their whole culture and civilization—this struck Malobali as an unforgivable crime. He would never commit it, even under torture" (p. 230). Yet, because of his desperate circumstances, Malobali nominally converts to Christianity. The missionaries change his name to Samuel and take him to Ouidah, where they hope to build a mission especially for the *retournado* community. After some initial confusion, Ayodele, whose Christian name is Ramona, and Malobali realize their connection. Despite their conversion, Malobali marries Ayodele, Naba's widow, according to Bambara traditions.

The lives of Malobali and Ayodele reflect the new economic realities along the coast. Even before his marriage, Malobali joins forces with Chacha Ajinakou, a slave trader who had responded to the new European demands for palm oil. He helps Malobali establish himself as a trader: "Malobali could be seen taking droves of slaves out of the town to palm groves and supervising their work . . . he was getting rich with the palm nuts Jose Domingos [a planter] let him have in exchange for his services, for he sold them to women who crushed the kernels to make red oil" (p. 272).

Because of his connections in Ouidah, Malobali is given a monopoly over palm oil production from King Guezo of Dahomey. Malobali buys all the red oil produced by the women, pays tax on it to a royal official, and then sells it to merchants. He becomes so rich that he starts his own barrel-making business, employing *retournados* who had learned carpentry in Brazil to produce wooden barrels to hold and transport palm oil. Thus Malobali is a part of the economic revolution in West Africa. Despite his economic success, he struggles with his memories of the past. His life, like those of his brothers, ends tragically.

Condé continues her discussion of major themes in the nineteenth century through Tiekoro's son, Muhammad, and Naba's son,

Babatunde (Eucaristus). These young men represent another generation of people whose lives changed as a result of the spread of Islam
and Christianity. Muhammad is drawn into the conflict between
Cheikou Amadou and El-Hadj Omar against his will. "A quarrel
between two Muslims! Was such a thing possible? . . . People said it
was one of those disagreements between brotherhoods—Tijaniya
against Qadriya. But was it only that? There was a rumor that El-
Hadj Omar had commercial and political designs on the region" (p.
381). Before El-Hadj Omar occupies Segu in 1861, Muhammad realizes that "Islam was a secondary consideration—what it was all really about was the struggle for power and territory" (p. 438). Condé's
discussion enables students to see some of the contradictions that
existed for believers.

Babatunde, the son of Naba and Ayodele, understands the inherent problems with Christianity for West African converts. He studies
at Fourah Bay College in Sierra Leone, where he meets Samuel Adjai
Crowther. But, unlike Crowther, Babatunde questions Christianity:
"Didn't every people have its own civilization, subtended by its
belief in its own gods? What was converting Africa to Christianity
but imposing an alien civilization upon it?" (p. 390). Babatunde's
skepticism continues even after he goes to London in 1840. He realizes that he will go back to West Africa "to Christianize and civilize
Africa—that was his fate. . . . In other words, to pervert it?" (p. 422).
Babatunde questions whether Christianity will really improve people's lives.

CONCLUSION

Using Shillington's *History of Africa* along with the novel *Segu*
seems to work well in the survey course. Students read background
chapters on the trans-Saharan trade and the Islamic states in the
western Sudan, as well as material on the Atlantic slave trade and the
age of empire. In addition, we watch Basil Davidson's film series
Africa to complement *Segu*. The episodes entitled "Caravans of
Gold" and "The King and the City" provide students with a context
for their reading. It takes about four weeks to examine the themes
that Condé develops, but *Segu* covers a wide swath of the nineteenth
century up to the European partition. At least two discussion sections
focus on the novel. Students have an opportunity to talk about the

novel in a small group setting, which helps them articulate their own ideas.

Students then write an essay in which they discuss two of the three major themes previously outlined: the spread of Islam, the Atlantic slave trade, and "legitimate commerce." They must discuss at least two characters in terms of each theme. Because of the nature of any survey course, the papers' quality varies considerably. But students generally have a better understanding of the dramatic changes that took place in West Africa because of Condé's sensitive and eloquent presentation of Traore family history.

THE AUTHOR

Maryse Condé, who was born in Guadeloupe, tells this story of West Africa and the African diaspora in a special way. She left Guadeloupe as a teenager for school in France and has lived there most of her adult life, as well as in West Africa and the United States; Condé herself is a living illustration of the diaspora. *Segu* began as a research project for Condé's doctoral degree in history. It is rooted in historical research but is also part of her heritage. Condé explains that in writing *Segu* she hoped to recreate "A bit of everything: the beauty, the grandeur, the defeats and weaknesses. . . . *Segu* is not a one-sided, dogmatic novel; it is a novel that tries to show Africa in all its complexity" (quoted in Pfaff 1996: 48–49).

Students who have read *Segu* agree that Condé has broadly accomplished her goal. They have come to understand some of the complex social, political, and economic changes that occurred in nineteenth-century West Africa. They also begin to see the interconnectedness of Africa, the New World, and Europe.

NOTES

1. I want to thank Merle Bowen, John Higginson, and Lynda Morgan for taking time out of their hectic schedules to read this essay. I hope that I have done justice to their comments. The mistakes that remain are my own.

2. Condé describes the *boli* as "festishes made of every kind of material: hyenas' and scorpions' tails, bark, tree roots, all regularly sprinkled with animal blood and acting as concentrated symbols of the powers of the uni-

verse, designed to bring the family happiness, prosperity, and fertility" (p. 14).

SUGGESTIONS FOR
FURTHER READING AND RESOURCES

Barry, Boubacar. 1988. *La Sénégambie du XVe au XIXe Siècle—Traite Négrière, Islam et Conquête Coloniale.* Paris: L'Harmattan. This is a revised edition of Barry's original French work. For those who read French, this is in some ways a more detailed account than the following entry.

———. 1998. *Senegambia and the Atlantic Slave Trade.* Cambridge and New York: Cambridge University Press. The most comprehensive analysis in English of the three main themes Condé addresses for the Senegambian region.

Bowman, Joye. 1997. *Ominous Transition: Commerce and Colonial Expansion in the Senegambia and Guinea.* Aldershot: Avebury/Ashgate Publishing.

Brooks, George E. 1980. "Artists' Depictions of Senegalese Signares: Insights Concerning French Racist and Sexist Attitudes in the Nineteenth Century," *Genève-Afrique* 17: 75–89. A discussion of *signares*, Afro-European women illustrated in Anne Pépin's character in the novel.

———. 1983. "A Nhara of the Guinea-Bissau Region: Mãe Aurélia Correia." In *Women and Slavery in Africa,* ed. Claire C. Robertson and Martin A. Klein. Madison: University of Wisconsin Press.

Callaloo. 1995. Summer 1995, Volume 18, 3. This special issue of Callaloo is dedicated to Maryse Condé's work.

Condé, Maryse. 1982. *Heremakhonon,* trans. Richard Philcox. Boulder, Colo.: Lynne Rienner.

———. 1982. *I, Tituba, Black Witch of Salem,* trans. Richard Philcox. Washington, D.C.: Three Continents.

———. 1987. *Segu,* trans. Barbara Bray. New York: Ballantine Books.

———. 1988. *A Season in Rihata,* trans. Richard Philcox. Portsmouth, N.H.: Heinemann.

———. 1989. *The Children of Segu,* trans. Linda Cloverdale. New York: Viking Penguin.

———. 1997. *The Last of the African Kings,* trans. Richard Philcox. Lincoln: University of Nebraska Press.

Gomez, Michael. 1990. "Timbuctu Under Imperial Songhai: A Reconsideration of Autonomy," *Journal of African History* 31, 1: 5–24. Gomez analyzes Timbuctu's connection to Gao.

———. 1992. *Pragmatism in the Age of Jihad: The Precolonial State of Bundu.* Cambridge and New York: Cambridge University Press.

Leynaud, Emile. 1978. *Paysans malinké du Haut Niger: Tradition et développement rural en Afrique soudanaise.* Bamako: Impr. Populaire du Mali.

McIntosh, Roderick J. 1998. *The Peoples of the Middle Niger.* Malden, Mass.: Blackwell.

Niane, D. T. 1965. *Sundiata: An Epic of Old Mali.* London: Longman. A translation of the epic tale told by the *griots* of Mali about the founder of the ancient state. See Chapter 17 in this volume.

Perinbam, B. Marie. 1997. *Family Identity and the State in the Bamako Kafu, c.1800–c.1900.* Boulder: Westview. Interesting analysis of families and lineages in the region stretching from Senegal to Ghana and their relationships with the state.

Pfaff, Françoise. 1996. *Conversations with Maryse Condé.* Lincoln: University of Nebraska Press.

Roberts, Richard L. 1987. *Warriors, Merchants and Slaves: The State and Economy in the Middle Niger Valley, 1700–1914.* Stanford: Stanford University Press. A comprehensive study of the political economy of the Middle Niger Valley over a two-hundred-year period.

———. 1996. *Two Worlds of Cotton: Colonialism and the Regional Economy in French Soudan, 1800–1946.* Stanford: Stanford University Press.

Robinson, David. 1985. *The Holy War of Umar Tal: The Western Sudan in the Mid-Nineteenth Century.* Oxford: Clarendon Press. This is the seminal study of the *jihad* of Umar Tal (El-Hadj Omar).

Rodney, Walter. 1970. *A History of the Upper Guinea Coast: 1545–1800.* Oxford: Clarendon Press, 1970. The classic monograph on the Upper Guinea Coast during the period of the Atlantic slave trade.

Shillington, Kevin. 1995. *History of Africa*, rev. ed. New York: St. Martin's Press.

8

Tsitsi Dangarembga's
Nervous Conditions

Bill Bravman & Mary Montgomery

BETWEEN US, WE'VE USED *NERVOUS CONDITIONS* IN THE classroom for more than ten years, and it's still hard to say whether the novel is more satisfying to read or to teach. A captivatingly told, closely observed story that the vast majority of our students perennially rank among their favorites, it also ranks as a favorite class text of ours for the ways it up-ends a number of standard Western images about Africans and colonialism. Happily, these merits reinforce one another: even as the characters' rich, complicated interactions draw the reader into engrossed sympathy for them, the issues they address reflect larger historical concerns that we want our students to think about as well.

A coming-of-age tale written from the perspective of a young girl navigating her life's rapid changes in late colonial Rhodesia, *Nervous Conditions* lays out how an extended family's already-complex gender and generational relations get further cross-cut when many of its members, in varying ways and degrees, become enmeshed in the colonial African elite's embrace of Western education and values. The novel is packed with frank yet subtle observations about its characters' attempts to survive, thrive, and manage their often difficult relations with one another in this context. Family tensions get played out by recognizably multifaceted people who aren't reduced to cookie-cutter heroines or villains. Their internal and interpersonal trajectories over the course of the novel confound overly stark dichotomizations of urbanity/rurality and traditional-

Tsitsi Dangarembga, *Nervous Conditions: A Novel* (Seattle: Seal Press, 1989).

ism/modernity. Importantly, too, no one character's perspective gets represented as an unproblematic moral high ground.

Our use of the text in class builds on those two interrelated aspects of it: First, we challenge students to rethink staple dichotomies like African/Western and traditional/modern. Second, we use the book's openness about everyone's ambivalences, contradictions, triumphs, and limits to invite students to find more effective ways to grasp the complexities of gender, generation, and Westernization in a mid-twentieth-century African society.

A SKETCH OF THE CLASS AND THE BOOK

We use the book in an introductory survey class on Africa since 1800. It typically has sixty to eighty students, who once a week have small-group discussion sessions of fifteen to twenty. Most are freshmen or sophomores in the humanities and social sciences, but the course also draws advanced undergraduates from across the university who have an interest in Africa. Our school's location near Washington, D.C., ensures a classroom of students from many different backgrounds: Africans, other internationals, and African-Americans together often make up well over half of the survey's enrollment. That mixture becomes a great resource for getting students to discuss one of our major teaching themes for the book: how its characters find their lives and relationships informed by cultural distinctions, cultural hybridity, and cultural change over time.

Nervous Conditions apparently takes place in the late 1950s or early 1960s, and is located in what is now the country of Zimbabwe. Until 1965 Great Britain ruled the territory as Southern Rhodesia, though its European settlers had considerable powers of self-governance. In 1965 the settlers, fearing that Britain would cede control of the state to Africans, declared that they were founding the white-ruled country of Rhodesia. African armed struggle against white control was stepped up, although two major ethnic groups maintained largely separate guerrilla armies. By 1980 the African majority had compelled the white settlers to hand over political power.

Strikingly, *Nervous Conditions* is not specifically contextualized within this political calendar, nor is the ethnic identity of Tambu's family ever discussed. The effect of these authorial choices is to keep the story focused on questions of gender, generation, and cultural change as a distinctly African concern, one that might be complicated by racial oppression and interethnic rivaly, but can also be appreciated as distinct from them. The novel is not apolitical, but its politics are intimate: Europeans' prejudices and vulerabilities, for instance, are represented through a few brief encounters with whites, and have only a marginal place in the overall plotting of the novel.

Tsitsi Dangarembga's novel lays out its banquet of topics by following a young girl, Tambu, through her struggles to gain an education that will allow her to escape her immediate family's impoverishment in 1960s Rhodesia. To do so, she must initially overcome her mother's cautiousness about letting her daughter expect too much of life, her father's laziness and unconcern about their rural poverty, and the wider familial presumption that her older brother's education takes precedence over hers. Soon after the brother suddenly dies, Tambu is pulled into a dizzying new set of opportunities, relationships, and pitfalls: her uncle, Babamukuru, brings her to town, where she can live with his family and attend a good mission school.

Tambu initially idolizes Babamukuru for having gotten an advanced education in England, for being a pillar of the mission elite, for his household's high material standard of living, and for his long-standing benevolence and sense of paternal responsibility for his extended family. In time, Tambu comes to see how his striving has come at a cultural, psychological, and emotional price. Babamukuru has worked hard to create a controlled, orderly world for himself within the mission, but he is high-handed and inflexible whenever his family life falls short of his idea of rectitude. His daughter, Nyasha, having spent much of her childhood in England, is awkward in her homeland. She also feels caught between the inquisitive, questioning ways she acquired in Europe, and her father's expectations that she act like the dutiful African daughter she never learned to be.

Babamukuru's wife, Maiguru, does know how to be dutiful and strives to fulfill that role despite her equal education and her husband's often imperious attitude. But her constant self-abasement and subordination weigh on her, as do her efforts to mediate the tense relations between Babamukuru and Nyasha. Strains between the town-based and rural branches of the extended family increase as well. Tambu witnesses all these tensions and eventually has acculturation problems of her own. But although she comes to recognize the social ambiguities that her extended family members are caught up in and the toll exacted from them, Tambu remains committed to the idea that an advanced Western education can bring her the future she wants.

TSITSI DANGAREMBGA, AUTHOR AND FILMMAKER

Tsitsi Dangarembga was born in 1959 in Mutoko, a small town in colonial Rhodesia. She spent five years in Britain as a child, then returned to Rhodesia with her family. She completed her A-levels in a missionary school in Mutaare, then returned to Britain to attend Cambridge University, where she studied medicine. Homesick and alienated, Dangarembga did not stay at Cambridge or become a doctor. In 1980 she returned to Rhodesia (just before it became Zimbabwe under black majority rule) and studied psychology at the University of Harare. While at the university, she was very involved in student theater productions and explored short-story writing as well. Her first major success came with the 1988 publication of *Nervous Conditions*. She later studied film direction in Berlin and completed several short films, along with *Everyone's Child,* a full-length film focusing on the struggles of four Zimbabwean children left orphaned and homeless by AIDS.

Nervous Conditions is the first novel to be published in English by a black Zimbabwean woman and won the Africa section of the Commonwealth Writers Prize in 1989.

DISCUSSION THEMES

When asked what themes in the novel stand out for them, students are quick to highlight how competing ideas about gender roles shape the experiences of characters. This often leads to some students pointing out which female characters conduct themselves as traditional women (Tambu's mother, Mainini Ma'Shingayi, and, to a lesser extent, Maiguru), and which of the women are modern (Nyasha and, increasingly, Tambu). Central to the these initial assessments are the characters' roles in the home: Mainini toils in the farm fields and runs the rural household. Maiguru has modern conveniences and a servant, but is still first and foremost a homemaker. On the other hand, Nyasha is often described as a protofeminist, for she reads D. H. Lawrence and dares to argue with her father. Tambu, though less rebellious and emotionally tied to the rural homestead, nonetheless aspires to join the urbane ranks of the well-educated.

The discussion of gender roles, however, can quickly take on a great deal more nuance and complexity, gradually undermining the tidy separation between tradition and modernity. Tracing out

Tambu's experience, students often describe her overcoming her father's attempts to curtail her educational opportunities, the general disdain she expresses for him, her excitement about education, and her desire to escape the fetters of homestead life as signs of an ever-modernizing trajectory. But when asked about her conduct at Babamukuru's house, they own that she willingly embraces the part of the good, subservient niece—and maintains that prescribed gender role for the remainder of the book, even embracing the housework that Babamukuru metes out to her as punishment for her one rebellion against his authority. Scales fall from her eyes, but her responses to her broadening knowledge have a complex trajectory that only partially accords with initial student notions of "modernizing."

Although Nyasha's modernness (and Englishness) are immediately apparent to students as the central factor in her tense relationship with her father, many are surprised when we ask whether the tensions might in some degree be generational. However, students soon pick up on the observation, tying it into what they see as a universal truism: children and their parents often have different worldviews. This often leads many students to reconsider the arguments between the two, recognizing that Nyasha often wants to please Babamukuru and to be understood by him. Some point out that the girls' conflict with fathers is a sign that Nyasha represents a generation that has begun to embrace new, Western-influenced roles and possibilities for African women—for Nyasha responds to paternal authority in ways all but unimaginable to earlier generations of women. This observation returns the discussion to the idea of modernity and its relationship to Western and local influences, but in a richer, more cross-culturally nuanced way.

Reciprocally, students' views of Maiguru as bound by "tradition" can easily get rethought. One level of that transition is transparent in the novel: Maiguru initially appears as a paradigm of submissive deference to her husband, fussing over his food while serving herself a meager portion of cold root vegetables, but late in the story she gets so frustrated and angry with Babamukuru's automatic subordination of her that she briefly leaves him. When she returns, she takes up many of her earlier, dutiful roles, but we can see that the relationship has changed: she has shed some subservience and become a more substantive partner in their household. Other aspects of Maiguru that confound the traditional/modern dichotomy are more subtle, though students do respond to them. Many are startled, for instance, when the story eventually reveals that she is as highly educated as her husband. Questions about why she would have gone to the trouble to acquire that education and then not use it for her own advancement lead students to think about Maiguru in terms that give lie to the traditional/modern dichotomy.

Even Mainini, who fears that her children will become alienated from her when they leave the rural homestead and feels a resigned embitterment about her poverty, her hard life with an uncaring husband, and the death of her son, is not unambiguously "traditional." Students recognize how she acts as Tambu's quiet ally in the daughter's initial quest for education. Fearful of elevating the girl's hopes but not scornful of them, she even maneuvers her husband in ways that help. She shows no confidence in Babamukuru's idea that finally having a church wedding will make her husband of nineteen years behave better, but nonetheless enjoys the ceremony and concomitant fuss made over her. While distrustful of the effects of Babamukuru's family on her children, she is nonetheless genuinely pleased when her sister moves there from the rural homestead to work at the mission.

Students are often intrigued by Babamukuru, and discussions of him tie in well with all of these themes. His personal characteristics, in fact, often make for a good lead-in to the overall discussion, because they so readily call up the limitations of the traditional/modern dichotomy. On one hand, some students point out, he is the very epitome of a modernizer: he believes deeply in the Western, Christian, late-colonial vision of how Africans can make themselves ready for a polite, virtuous entry into the modern world. He is comfortable with modern technology, his life's story fairly embodies the Protestant work ethic, and he tries to pull the laggard rural branch of the family into following that same ethos. Yet other students are quick to note that he is a paragon of traditional patriarchy when it comes to ideas about the proper subservience of women and children. African students sometimes defend Babamukuru's character from non-Africans' disapproval by pointing out that his apparent high-handedness only reflects his acceptance of the traditional role of the eldest male of the extended family: to guide the group and accept responsibility for them.

Overall group discussions of how Babamukuru could have both traditional and modern (or African and Western) characteristics open into more careful thinking about what each of those categories might mean and how porous and vaguely defined each might be. For instance, questions about whether Babamukuru's patriarchal attitudes are distinctly Western, African, modern, or traditional quickly dissolve some of the categorical essentialism that student discussions of the book typically begin with. Discussion of the various female characters along such lines has a similar effect. With that level of discussion behind them, students are better equipped to grasp Nyasha's occasional comments about her hybridity—for they can more fully appreciate the cross-cutting cultural reflexes, the sense of partial belonging and partial displacement, and the psychological and emotional turmoil that give her the most pointed nervous conditions of the novel.

Nyasha is by no means the only character for whom the demands of cultural in-betweenness spur an ever-fluctuating combination of exhilaration, tension, creativity, hopefulness, despair, confusion, and pain. Late in the class discussion, we often ask students to apply their accumulated ideas to an analysis of the book's wedding scenes. Babamukuru's decision that Tambu's parents need a proper church wedding can be read in a number of ways, for it speaks at once to the inculcation of Western values and to the possibility that the ceremony puts a Western veneer on a widely felt belief that the family's misfortunes require a cleansing ritual. Tambu grows more and more distressed about the wedding as it approaches and ultimately defies Babamukuru by refusing to attend. When asked about her refusal, students dig into her changing understandings of herself, her immediate family, and Babamukuru. Once she has stood up to him over this inadvertent yet implicit denigration of her birth and upbringing, the question yet remains what ideas, outlooks, and intentions she is standing up for. Student opinions on this have different modulations from year to year, but it is clear that Tambu has embraced a worldview that defies the easy categorizations usually voiced at the beginning of class discussion of the novel.

ASSIGNMENTS

Sometimes we close class discussions of Dangarembga's novel by asking students what it has made them think about the place of Western education in colonial Africa. This question, which often gets turned into a paper or exam essay, revisits once again the complexities the novel has so effectively laid out. The most thoughtful responses generally refrain from declaring Western education a cruel imposition that has eroded holistic African cultures—for the reader who takes seriously Tambu's continued desire for such education and the reasons behind it cannot easily maintain that stance. At the same time, however, the book supports no ardent embrace of Western education, for its impact on many of the characters is clearly problematic. Nor does the novel paint a glowing picture of the missionaries in charge of the educational system, let alone white society in late colonial Rhodesia. The student responses that have resonated longest in our ears show an appreciation that even as cultures are being challenged, the painful, hopeful work of cultural re-creation is going on. Those papers acknowledge that Western education allows some characters to reach for lives they consider better, as well as its tendency to inculcate ideas and values that might disrupt families and—by extension—societies. The moral calculus of valuing improvements and disruptions, then weighing them against one another, varies from student to student. But by the time the best student responses reach that point, they are engaging the material and the issues it raises at the level we are hoping for.

CONCLUSION

Though a number of other novels have been used in this introductory survey course during the past several years, *Nervous Conditions* remains the one we reach for first. It speaks eloquently, richly, and provocatively—but with wide-ranging sympathy—about gender, generation, and the supportiveness and strains of family life. It provides students with insights into how everyday, lived culture is formed, reinforced, challenged, and reshaped over time, and into the multivalent impacts of such cultural reformation. Non-African students reading about the very different world of a young African woman find that that world has not been exoticized. Its differences are recognizable, but Tambu's aspirations, her relationships, and her difficulties are recounted with a nuanced accessibility that draws students in year after year. African students generally appreciate the fullness with which the novel captures situations familiar to them from experiences or stories about their own extended families. We as teachers find that issues raised by the novel dot the remainder of the course. Referring to the book thereafter helps us situate those issues all the more vividly and effectively in students' minds.

SUGGESTIONS FOR
FURTHER READING AND RESOURCES

Dangarembga, Tsitsi. 1996. *Everyone's Child*. Dangarembga directed this film about the crisis faced by four children in rural Zimbabwe whose parents died of AIDS. Despite the tradition that an orphan becomes "everyone's child," villagers shun the children because of the stigma of AIDS. Distributed through California Newsreel (phone: 415/ 621-6196; Web: <www.newsreel.org>).

Everyone's Child soundtrack. Original songs by twelve contemporary Zimbabwean musicians, including the well-known Thomas Mapfumo. Available on CD or cassette from DSR, Inc. (phone: 800-875-0037, 108; Web: <www.catalog.com/dsr>).

Friedrickse, Julie. 1982. *None but Ourselves: Masses vs. Media in the Making of Zimbabwe*. Johannesburg: Ravan Press. A good overview of late colonial history, with striking photographs.

George, Rosemary Marangoly, and Helen Scott. 1993. "An Interview with Tsitsi Dangarembga," *Novel* (Spring): 309–319. An interview conducted at the African Writers Festival, Brown University in November 1991.

Hove, Chenjerai. 1990. *Bones*. Portsmouth, N.H.: Heinemann. A Zimbabwean novel about men's sexual crimes and women's journey from submission to resistance.

Kennedy, Dane. 1987. *Islands of White*. Durham, N.C.: Duke University Press. A comparative study of settler societies in Southern Rhodesia and Kenya that presents a fairly good overview of the African context.

Maraire, J. Nozipo Nkosana. 1996. *Zenzele: A Letter for My Daughter*. New York: Crown Publishers. A Zimbabwean novel of a mother recounting her family's history to her daughter, illuminating the deep roots of gender oppression and encouraging the younger generation to fight against it. (See Chapter 14 in this collection.)

Ranger, Terence O. 1985. *Peasant Consciousness and Guerrilla War in Zimbabwe*. Berkeley: University of California Press. Contains a very good discussion of the tensions confronting African progressives who were torn between cooperating with colonialism and supporting the anticolonial revolt.

———. 1995. *Are We Not Also Men? The Samkange Family and African Politics in Zimbabwe, 1920–64*. Portsmouth, N.H.: Heinemann. A collective biography of the Samkange family that illustrates the lives of the early Christian elite and their sense of obligation toward others.

Schmidt, Elizabeth. 1992. *Peasants, Traders and Wives: Shona Women in the History of Zimbabwe, 1870–1939*. Portsmouth, N.H.: Heinemann.

Veit-Wild, Flora. 1989. "Women Write About Things That Move Them," *Matatu* 3, 6 (1989): 101–108. An interview with Dangarembga.

Wilkinson, Jane. 1992. "Tsitsi Dangarembga." In *Talking with African Writers: Interviews with African Poets, Playwrights and Novelists*. London: James Currey.

9

Modikwe Dikobe's
The Marabi Dance

Iris Berger

SET IN JOHANNESBURG DURING THE 1930s AND EARLY
1940s, *The Marabi Dance* by Modikwe Dikobe vividly conveys not
only the tensions and conflicts of African communities during the era
of segregation, but also their cultural creativity •nd innovation.
Through complex portraits of individuals grappling with how to rec-
oncile older rural values and traditions with the demands of urbanization and how to negotiate intergenerational differences around
these issues, students gain insight into the ways that rural understandings of culture continued to shape city life. The novel portrays
graphically the grim and uncertain conditions in Johannesburg's
slumyards and the dehumanizing aspects of racial domination, focusing on one young woman's struggle to forge her own identity under
these challenging conditions.

Because the book covers so many aspects of both urban and rural
life, from squalid housing, gangs, and the vibrant appeal of *marabi*
music to transitions in religious and marriage ceremonies, it offers
students a window into a broad range of cultural and social issues.
But Dikobe avoids simple dichotomies in representing the choices
open to individuals. The book neither idealizes rural culture nor condemns it absolutely as Ezekiel Mphahlele does in his autobiography
Down Second Avenue.

This rich and complex portrayal of rapid social transformation
makes the book an apt choice for the course Race and Conflict in
South Africa, a one-semester survey of the country's history that

Modikwe Dikobe, *The Marabi Dance* (Portsmouth, N.H.: Heinemann, 1973).

combines a chronological narrative approach with additional readings on issues of gender, culture, and identity that textbooks tend to
slight. Yet, because this novel is not as polished as many works of
fiction, students do not find it as immediately compelling or transparent as a book like *Kaffir Boy*, with which they identify instantly.
But the book's complexity also makes it a rich source of questions
for class discussion.

The course, cross-listed in history and Africana studies, attracts a
range of students, including majors in both departments and other
junior and seniors with no previous relevant background. It usually
draws somewhere between fifty and sixty students, although
Africana studies enrollment has declined somewhat in the last few
years as South African racism has ceased to be a highly publicized
political issue. Adding to the student mixture, a small group takes the
course for writing-intensive credit. For the first time last year, several first-year graduate students also enrolled in a special section. Their
presence contributed to livelier and better-informed class discussions.

THE MARABI DANCE

Dikobe sets the scene of the Johannesburg urban slumyard immediately in his opening paragraph: "The Molefe yard . . . was also home
of more than twenty other people. It served a row of five rooms, each
about fourteen by twelve feet in size. When it rained, the yard was as
muddy as a cattle kraal, and the smell of beer, thrown out by the
police on their raids, combining with the stench of the lavatories,
was nauseating" (p. 1).

In this typical setting lives Martha, a young urban-born woman
who, when the book opens, has just withdrawn from Standard 5 at
the church-sponsored Albert Street School. Her parents made the
decision unilaterally because "she'd been going out with boys, and
they considered the fees to be a waste of money" (p. 1). The boy in
question is George, a popular pianist at *marabi* parties and notorious
for his numerous girlfriends.

These two symbolic settings, school and *marabi*, form the first
contrasts of the book. For Martha, school means using her "round
baritone voice" to star in the award-winning choir. Marabi, by contrast, "a dance party for persons of a low type," is "not favored by
respectable people," including Martha's rural-born parents.

Never a strong student, Martha leaves school without protest, but she will strongly resist her parent's efforts to entrap her in a traditional marriage. Early in the novel, this clash is foreshadowed. When citing her reasons for teaching her daughter to dress like a woman, Mathloare, Martha's mother, explains that she hopes her daughter can attract a man wealthy enough in cattle to pay *bogadi*, bridewealth. Challenging this fate as she struggles successfully to continue her voice lessons, Martha argues, "I won't keep quiet to see myself turned into a country girl who is forced to leave school early and work in the white people's kitchens" (p. 27).

The story unfolds as Martha's father, Mabongo, begins to arrange her wedding to Sephai. This young country-born domestic worker is the son of his cousin Ndala. Through this union Mabongo hopes to reclaim the place in his family that he has lost after his own individualistic marriage choice. His actions set the scene for the novel's major conflict: between urban and rural values and between different generational perceptions of the meaning of marriage and family. To the older generation's claims that marriage is usually arranged by the parents, Martha replies, "How can I love a man I've never seen?" (p. 38). Similarly, Martha's intention to remain in the city contrasts with her prospective husband's lament that town children are ignorant about work in the fields. Eventually, Sephai's father concedes, "My son would have been lost if he had married such a woman. She is pregnant but still moves about like a springbok. What can a farm boy do with a town girl? She would leave him with the children in the night and go to Marabi. I shall tell my child not to be sorry about not marrying her. She is only good for town boys" (p. 97).

This difference between generations and between urban and rural identities is portrayed through complex characters, each of whom has strengths and weaknesses; a complicating aspect of the story is Martha's parents' own nontraditional marriage, which neither family recognized.

Paralleling these differences are those in the city between different forms of popular culture, especially the juxtaposition of the polite society of the Bantu Men's Social Club and a nearby Zulu war dance. Dikobe highlights this contrast: "The one, a shuffling of the feet and the other, a vigorous stamping. The latter a dance of people witnessed by a large crowd and the other of dancers unwitnessed, men and women locked to each other. The free air swept away the perspiration of the Zulus. The closed air polluted the hall and when the music stopped there was coughing" (p. 73).

Intertwined with the main plot are several vividly drawn figures who represent mainstays of township life: Ma-Ndlovu, the Marabi queen; Reverend Ndlovu, the illiterate preacher who absconds with her money while invoking the spirits of Moses, Chaka, and Moshesh; and Ndala, Sephai's father, whose knowledge of magic permeates all aspects of daily life. Dikobe also touches on the reinvention and commercialization of tradition, on support networks among women, and on the urban occupations open to women and men and the social hierarchies they produce. When Martha's teacher comes to the house to discuss her withdrawal from school, Mathloare laments, "Teachers, teachers! They never marry. They just spoil one's child and then go and marry nurses" (p. 26).

In addition to the central conflict over marriage and responsibility to family, the novel's characters all, in different ways, confront the challenges of white domination in their daily lives: in grown men referred to as "boys," in the threat of deportation from the city when Martha's father temporarily loses his job at a white-owned dairy, in wrecked communities being removed from Doornfontein, in the humiliating lack of privacy for domestic workers, and in the background of dispossession and white domination that led her father and uncle to leave their land for the city. Although political organizations and trade unions are mentioned occasionally, they play a minimal role in the story.

In Martha's quest to forge her own identity in this highly charged context, she looks to her son, "who will work for her," as a symbol of hope. Yet Dikobe's "Dedication" undercuts any illusions with his final remarks: "Someone like Martha may still be alive, and her son may be one of those young men now being harassed by the pass laws, endorsed out of the cities and made strangers in the land of their birth" ("Dedication").

MODIKWE DIKOBE

This assessment surely reflects Dikobe's own experiences.[1] Born in 1913 in the northern Transvaal, he moved to Johannesburg when he was ten and lived his early life in the slumyards he describes. His family came first to Sophiatown, but eventually settled in Molefe Yard in Doornfontein, the setting for the novel. Here and in similar areas stretching across the city, the growing African population subsisted in white-owned shanties, usually built around a central courtyard. Despite the high rents, proximity to the city center and the absence of strict controls made these yards popular places to live. Like Martha, Dikobe attended the Albert Street School; indeed, he dedicated the book to his former schoolmates there. Thus, his own personal experience rather than an imagined past form the basis for his fiction.

Dikobe's varied work life also informs the novel, superficially in the brief reference to trade unions, but more profoundly as a person who, like Martha, was faced with choices among competing identities. A self-educated man who loved books, he worked at various times as a newspaper vendor, a self-employed hawker, and a clerk in a furniture factory. Banned for a while in the early 1960s, he lost his job. Before retiring to his birthplace in 1977, where he became boarding master at a local school, he took positions as a domestic worker, a night watchman, and a clerk in the city treasurer's office. He also took part in the bus boycott and sqatters' movements in Alexandra in the 1940s and in later township opposition to high rents.

Although drawn to writing earlier in his life, Dikobe lacked confidence in his English-language skills. His writing career began only when he joined the Shop and Office Workers' Union in the late 1950s and began preparing articles for the union newspaper and other political publications. Encouraged by Norman Levy, a union official, and apparently inspired by the publication of *Down Second Avenue*, Dikobe wrote *The Marabi Dance* in the late 1950s and early 1960s. After being serialized in *South African Outlook* in the early 1970s, the book was published in 1973.

Some controversy surrounded its publication because of the editorial assistance he received from whites, in order, in Dikobe's words, "to make the author's intention clear." He adds, however, that the incidents, setting, characterization, and dialogue were his own and that "the light of that intention showed vividly from the first" ("Thanks"). Africanists will find it interesting, in terms of his own knowledge of the "tradition" he describes, that anthropologist Monica Wilson provided information on bride-seeking practices.

LECTURES, DISCUSSION, AND ASSIGNMENTS

The Marabi Dance is assigned toward the end of the first half of the course, immediately following two lectures on the political economy of segregation between 1900 and 1940. These lectures emphasize the continuing disenfranchisement and dispossession of Africans following Union in 1910 and outline the new strategies of control that white politicians adopted during the interwar years, including new forms of urban segregation. The novel shifts the focus to the internal dynamics of African communities, to how these measures shaped and constricted the lives of ordinary Africans, and to the cultural and generational conflicts of the period.

Earlier readings and lectures have prepared students for understanding the social tensions in rural communities generated by white conquest: Helen Bradford's arguments on the gender dimensions of the Xhosa "cattle killing" in the 1850s, Sandra Burman's article "Fighting a Two-Pronged Attack" on struggles over "customary law" in late-nineteenth-century Basutoland, and Jacklyn Cock's article on domestic service and the incorporation of Xhosa women into colonial society (see Bradford 1966, Burman 1990, Cock 1990). In addition, lectures and discussion on the impact of the mining revolution emphasize the gendered nature of this economic transformation. Thus, students come to the novel with a clear understanding of some of the institutions of earlier rural societies, but also an awareness of early-twentieth-century urbanization as part of an ongoing process of cultural change and controversy.

As with all the non-textbook readings in the course, students are asked to write a brief essay of approximately three pages in response to a question posed in the syllabus. Although these questions change each time I teach the course, they have centered on the concepts of "traditional" and "modern," asking students to reflect on how the novel prods them to see these two constructs not as fixed, easily describable entities, but as flexible notions often interpreted and reconfigured in personal and instrumental ways. Trying to wean students from the notion of "tribal" as something fixed, backward, and nonmodern is a challenge this novel opens for discussion.

Class discussion also focuses on class and gender differences as expressed in the different characters and their choices. Furthermore, because Dikobe shows the strengths and weaknesses of both rural and urban life, students are enabled to discuss the gains and losses of this transformation and to debate how they see Dikobe's position. An unexpected ending in the book's epilogue also leads to consideration of why George and Rev. Ndlovu, both irresponsible rogues earlier in the novel, are transformed. And, of course, the book's central dilemma opens the question of whether they think Martha ought to have married Sephai. Finally, this novel of urban life, in which rural values remain important in so many ways, raises questions about the often-repeated statement that conquest "destroyed" African culture.

One difficulty students have with the novel is the dual names attached to some characters. This, of course, is easily remedied by giving them a list beforehand that identifies people along with both names. Most untranslated African phrases are intelligible in context, although this is a book that could benefit from a glossary.

One possible accompaniment to the book is the account and tape cassette of *marabi* music by Christopher Ballentine, *Marabi Nights: Early South African Jazz and Vaudeville*, which I plan to use for the first time this year. In addition to describing briefly each of the twenty-five songs on the tape, the book succinctly summarizes the history of South African urban music, detailing the controversies over *marabi* culture at the center of the novel's plot. Ballentine's discussion of African American influence on the development of *marabi* music and later of South African jazz may be of particular interest to students. Depicting debates over music in the 1930s that parallel the themes of the novel, he recalls the cautions of an educated writer: "If you wish to keep your wife at home, never teach her how to dance."[2]

NOTES

1. Biographical information on Dikobe's life comes from Sole and Koch 1990.
2. Ballentine 1993: 83, quoting R. R. R. Dhlomo in *Ilange Lase Natal*, March 19, 1936.

SUGGESTIONS FOR
FURTHER READING AND RESOURCES

Ballentine, Christopher. 1993. *Marabi Nights: Early South African Jazz and Vaudeville*. Johannesburg: Ravan. A fascinating book and accompanying audiocassette, interesting among other things for showing connections between South African and North American music.

Beinart, William. 1994. *Twentieth-Century South Africa*. Oxford: Oxford University Press.

Bozzoli, Belinda, ed. 1979. *Labour, Townships and Protest*. Johannesburg: Ravan.

———, ed. 1983. *Town and Countryside in the Transvaal*. Johannesburg: Ravan.

Bradford, Helen. 1966. "Women, Gender, and Colonialism: Rethinking the History of the British Cape Colony in Its Frontier Zones, c.1806–70," *Journal of African History* 37, 3: 351–370.

Burman, Sandra. 1990. "Fighting a Two-Pronged Attack: The Changing Legal Status of Women in Cape-ruled Basutoland." In *Women and Gender in Southern Africa*, ed. Cherryl Walker. London: James Currey.

Cock, Jacklyn. 1990. "Domestic Service and Education for Domesticity: The Incorporation of Xhosa Women into Colonial Society." In *Women and Gender in Southern Africa*, ed. Cherryl Walker. London: James Currey.

Coplan, David B. 1986. *In Township Tonight! South Africa's Black City Music and Theatre*. London and New York: Longman.

Hofmeyr, Isabel. 1977. "The Marabi Dance," *Africa Perspective* 6: 1-12.

Marks, Shula, and Richard Rathbone, eds. 1982. *Industrialisation and Social Change in South Africa*. London and New York: Longman.

Marks, Shula, and Stanley Trapido, eds. 1987. *The Politics of Race, Class and Nationalism in Twentieth-Century South Africa*. London and New York: Longman.

Mphahlele, Ezekiel. 1985 [1959]. *Down Second Avenue*. Boston: Faber and Faber.

Nyamende, Abner. 1996. "Martha Has No Land: The Tragedy of Identity in The Marabi Dance." In *Text, Theory, Space: Land, Literature and History in South Africa and Australia*, ed. Kate Darian-Smith, Liz Gunner, and Sarah Nuttall. London and New York: Routledge.

Sole, Kelwyn, and Eddie Koch. 1990. "The Marabi Dance: A Working Class Novel?" In *Rendering Things Visible: Essays on South African Literary Culture*, ed. Martin Trump. Johannesburg: Ravan.

Walker, Cherryl, ed. 1990. *Women and Gender in Southern Africa*. London: James Currey.

Worden, Nigel. 1994. *The Making of Modern South Africa*. Cambridge, Mass.: Blackwell.

10

Buchi Emecheta's
The Joys of Motherhood

Misty L. Bastian

EMECHETA'S MASTERPIECE, *THE JOYS OF MOTHERHOOD*, begins with its protagonist, Nnu Ego, preparing to jump off a crowded Lagos bridge. The imagery is shocking and immediately catches the reader's interest: Who is this young Nigerian woman? Why is she so distracted, and what has occurred to bring her to such a decision? Many of my students report that they were "hooked" at once by the intensity of Nnu Ego's need to flee from life; the unstated part of that confession, of course, is that North American undergraduates are themselves under a great deal of stress. Their own anxieties about failure catch them and catapult them into sympathy with Nnu Ego's position. The familiarity of Nnu Ego's agitation begins students' engagement with the novel, but it is the strangeness of the rest of the narrative that convinces many to keep reading.

When we talk about "strangeness" in the context of teaching African novels to Western undergraduates, what I mean is that this is a novel about a reality many North American college students no longer see in their own culture: the pursuit of motherhood as the sovereign means for female identity formation. In a society where patriarchal relations are often obscured by media and political/ideological rhetoric about women's "individual choice" of motherhood, Nnu Ego's single-minded devotion to the construction of herself as a mother seems as exotic as any ritual concocted by fertile student imaginations. Indeed, it becomes as great a marker for difference, in

Buchi Emecheta, *The Joys of Motherhood* (Portsmouth, N.H.: Heinemann, 1979).

their discussions of the narratives, as anything more stereotypically "African." Because of this slippage between what students most consciously worry about (future jobs, a date on Friday night, their grades) and Nnu Ego's troubles, *The Joys of Motherhood* serves as a fruitful means for North American undergraduates to grapple with larger meanings in life as well as significant historical and cultural differences between themselves and the West African characters of the novel. While pointing to difference, the novel also requires students to consider their own futures as procreative and socially productive people—issues that we, as teachers, probably should stress more often even while we induct our pupils into the "life of the mind."

Since coming back from fieldwork in the city of Onitsha in southeastern Nigeria in the late 1980s, I have consistently taught *Joys* in African survey classes with an emphasis on anthropological texts (the ubiquitious Peoples and Cultures of Africa) as well as courses on women's lives around the globe, both in large lecture classes and much more intimate seminars. Like all good fiction, it has not dated, and I have always found something new in the novel to discuss with my students. In this chapter, then, we will consider *The Joys of Motherhood* and techniques that have proved successful in teaching it as a text in humanistic social science courses. For those readers with a literary background, I give some information on Igbo social organization that may prove valuable for contextualizing events in the narrative, but I will not comment on its literary merits. Readers who wish to include this text in a course with a social science focus will find suggestions for integrating the novel into a section on gender, African women's working lives under colonialism, or women's position in Igbo and Nigerian society during the twentieth century.

The novel's major themes can be quickly summarized as the importance of motherhood in a West African society, the transformation of gender and social relations under conditions of colonialism and urbanization, West African women's adherence to older religious ideas in the face of missionization, and significant cultural differences between the generations born in the colonized, urban milieu of Nigeria and those raised in rural, largely agricultural villages in the interior. As we examine the narrative, "filling in" sociocultural details that Emecheta as an indigenous Igbo-speaking person takes for granted, these themes will be considered more carefully. The theme of Igbo motherhood, its ideological construction, and sometimes heartbreaking practice dominates the text and frames all other questions, including that of how gender relations were transformed under conditions of high colonialism. As we will see, Nnu Ego's quest for perfection in motherhood (equated by her with perfection in womanhood) distorts her ability to take on other important social roles and to cope with the hardships of life in 1930s and 1940s Lagos. This single-mindedness on the part of the protagonist—along with a constant nostalgia for lost, rural pastimes—both blinds her to opportunities and insulates her from some of the horrors of her pre-carious existence. Nnu Ego is placed at risk spiritually as well as materially by her devotion to motherhood, because she never fully comprehends or addresses her dangerous spiritual inheritance or finds solace in the new Christian religion. And, finally, she learns too late that being a "perfect" Igbo mother does not necessarily guaran-tee raising perfect Igbo children, particularly since her notion of what is appropriate for children is based on a rural ideal and not the urban realities experienced by her sons and daughters.

BASICS OF PLOT AND SOCIAL CONTEXT

Buchi Emecheta sets the action of *The Joys of Motherhood* in south-ern Nigeria, mostly in the former capital, Lagos, during the 1930s, 1940s, and 1950s. This is the period of high, or late, British colonial-ism in the region, and one of the subtexts of the novel has to do with the impact of colonial policy on ordinary Nigerian people's lives. Emecheta is writing here out of her own experience, since she was born in 1944 in the part of Lagos where she sets most of the action. It might be suggested that some of the novel is autobiographical; Emecheta's father was a railway worker (as is Nnaife) and her moth-er a small trader with a growing family during the 1940s and 1950s. Emecheta herself also suffered greatly in her early years as a wife, mother, and immigrant to the United Kingdom because of the pres-sures placed on her both to have a large family and to support her urban household by paid employment. We might, indeed, say that the complexity of Emecheta's feelings about motherhood, which run counter to those expressed to me by women still living in southeast-ern Nigeria itself, are as much a product of her individual history as of her relentlessly inventive authorial imagination.

The protagonist of the narrative is Nnu Ego, a young woman who is forced to move from Ibuza, a small town in the Nigerian inte-rior, to Lagos, on the southwestern coast. Like Emecheta, Nnu Ego comes from the Igbo linguistic/ethnic group—more particularly from a subgroup called the Western Igbo, who live across the River Niger from the majority Igbo populations of the Nigerian southeast. There are clearly echoes here of Emecheta's unhappy early immigration to Europe as well as a co-opting of family stories the novelist heard growing up. Bringing family history into one's storytelling is very much a part of rhetorical style in most Igbo narration, and here we see Emecheta combining Western Igbo sensibilities with recognized, global novelistic practice.

The Igbo-speaking people of Anioma, as Western Igbo call their region, were the focus of intense missionization from the Church Missionary Society (Anglicans) and the Catholic Holy Ghost Fathers during the latter half of the nineteenth century, and they strongly resisted the British administration during the 1880s and 1890s. By 1934, when the novel opens, mission education and the introduction of roads and motorized transport between colonial centers had led a number of young men from the southern interior to try their fortunes in the colonial boom towns of Nigeria. While many Western Igbo went across the Niger River to trade and work in Igbo-speaking towns like Onitsha, some went farther afield, toward the coast. Nnu Ego's second husband, Nnaife, is one of these Anioma pioneers. Using his knowledge of pidgin English and Western domestic skills learned from the colonial or mission presence around Ibuza, Nnaife finds work in Lagos as a washerman for a European couple. Although not a lucrative form of employment, laundry work gives Nnaife a small salary and a place to live, rent free, in the Europeans' compound. The money he saves from several years' labor is transformed into the bridewealth and transport fares that enable him to marry Nnu Ego and bring her to the metropolis. As the reader knows from the first chapter of the novel, the Ibuza man and his new wife quickly conceive a child. It is this son whose death brings Nnu Ego to the suicidal decision of the first few pages of the novel.

Nnu Ego's history before 1934 is told in great detail as a flashback that precedes her birth and brings her to the terrible moment at the beginning of the novel. From the point of view of an ethnographer who has studied Igbo culture intensively, the author sets out to glamorize Western Igbo village life in this section—turning the narrative briefly into the kind of "moonlight tale" that female elders once told young people about the heroic deeds of the ancestors. Here we learn about the romantic struggle between Nnu Ego's parents, the hunter Nwokocha Agbadi and Ona, his proud and "precious jewel." Chief Agbadi had a household full of wives and male children, but he was obsessed by the beautiful Ona. Ona could not marry her lover because she was a "male daughter," a woman who is set aside to produce an heir for her father's lineage (see Amadiume 1987). Ona becomes pregnant and promises Agbadi she will give him her child if it should be a girl. Unfortunately, Agbadi's senior wife becomes ill—some in the village blame this on Ona and her indiscreet sexual activities—and dies before the baby is born. To honor the first wife's funeral, a slave woman from Agbadi's compound is sacrificed. While the slave is being sacrificed, she tells Agbadi that she will return to his house as a legitimate daughter, thus cursing Nnu Ego in the womb to suffer a *chi* (internal spirit) who is displeased with the lineage into which she is born.

At first Nnu Ego appears to live a charmed life as Chief Agbadi's *ada* (eldest daughter, an important person in every Igbo patrilineage) and Ona's only child. However, the slave woman's curse takes effect when first Ona's father, then Ona herself, dies—leaving Nnu Ego motherless and without mother's kin. Although the Western Igbo are patrilineal like the majority of all Igbo-speaking groups—that is, they reckon descent strictly through the paternal line—the kin of the mother offer their daughter's children protection, assistance in times of difficulty, and a great deal of affection. No Igbo person likes to be without mother's kin, but in this case the lack is pronounced. Ona's father had no heirs, besides Ona herself, so Nnu Ego is effectively cut off from her mother's patrilineage and even more dependent on that of her father. (See Achebe 1958 for a view of the importance of mother's kindred among northern Igbo.) Brought up as her father's favorite, Nnu Ego receives little knowledge about women's roles from other women. Her understanding of what constitutes womanly behavior is therefore extremely masculinist, and she grows up thinking, first, of pleasing her father by marrying well, then of pleasing her husband by producing a number of sons for his patrilineage.

Nnu Ego's very name means "twenty bags of cowries," a reference to the standard amount of bridewealth that a young woman would be expected to bring to her father. Emecheta means this as one of the great ironies of the story. Ona was her father's "precious jewel" and valuable beyond bridewealth payments. The slave woman, whose curse will direct Nnu Ego's life, is chattel and never named in the narrative. Nnu Ego is marked linguistically at the beginning of her life as a transaction between men, somewhere between Ona's male daughter freedoms and the *chi*'s former slavery. This naming proves to be prescient, and Nnu Ego embraces her male-directed destiny because she does not wish to subvert it. On the surface she thus appears to be an ideal bride and marries early. However, it becomes clear that, for reasons still unknown, she cannot produce children with Amatokwu. He turns cold toward her and eventually brings a second wife into his household.

Nnu Ego struggles to be a good senior wife, but her husband does not treat her well, particularly after the second wife becomes pregnant and produces a male child. Instead of turning to his senior wife after this event (as Igbo gender ideology would suggest is proper) and allowing his second wife time to breast-feed and bond with their infant, Amatokwu requires the junior wife to sleep with and feed him. Forced to comply with the husband's wishes, the younger wife gives Nnu Ego care of her child in the evenings, thereby tempting her senior into an action that Igbo speakers consider abominable. Starved for affection and weighed down by a sense of her failure at motherhood, Nnu Ego begins to give her breast to the infant and soon is lactating. She takes the baby more frequently and fantasizes that he is truly hers. This feeding is tantamount to stealing another woman's child. When she is discovered acting out this clandestine motherhood, she is beaten and sent to her father's house in disgrace. The sacrificed slave woman is determined to have been the cause for Nnu Ego's bizarre behavior. Agbadi makes ritual reparations to the spirit and returns his daughter's bridewealth, thus freeing her for what is hoped to be a fruitful second marriage.

The second marriage is with Nnaife in Lagos. Nnu Ego's first impressions of her new husband are uniformly negative. He is physically unattractive and involved in work that she considers beneath men. Nonetheless, she goes through with the marriage, allowing Nnaife's sexual advances in hopes that she might become pregnant and a culturally validated woman at last. She also learns quickly that, in Lagos, she is more isolated from her patrilineage and from people who speak the same language than she has ever been; if she has trouble with her husband, there are few people she can turn to for assistance and mediation. Coming from an aristocratic village background, Nnu Ego is used to a certain amount of deference because of her father's position and her romantic personal history. In the city, her heritage counts for very little. For sophisticated Lagosians, she is simply another poor country bumpkin. Pride, poverty, and anxiety transform her from the open, happy *ada* of Agbadi's compound into a secretive matron with few friends. Certainly Nnu Ego has no one to turn to when she suffers the tragedy of the unexpected death of her infant son.

This child is born with supernatural drama, for Nnu Ego's *chi* follows her to Lagos. In the urban area, however, the slave woman shows herself more directly. Nnu Ego has a dream where the *chi* stands on one side of a familiar Ibuza stream and she stands on the other. The slave woman holds out a baby toward Nnu Ego, who tries to stretch her arms over the stream to receive it. The waters begin to rise between them, sweeping away all hope of reaching the infant.[1] This directly foreshadows the sudden demise of Nnu Ego's first baby, as well as the suicidal fate she determines for herself when she becomes, once again, a gender failure. The slave woman, however, is not ready for Nnu Ego to escape into the waters off the Lagos bridge; her revenge on the lineage of Agbadi is to be more subtle than that. An Ibuza compatriot comes upon Nnu Ego as she attempts to leap into the lagoon, and stops her. Brought home to Nnaife, Nnu Ego realizes that her fate lies in Lagos with this unsatisfactory man, and she determines to become a better wife—which she defines in masculine Igbo terms as being a good housekeeper and the mother of his children.

At this point in the narrative, there are intimations of events stirring outside the ken of Nnu Ego and other Lagosians. We hear that the man who saved her from jumping off the Lagos bridge has gone to sea, and there is discussion among Nnu Ego's acquaintances about mysterious European events. This discussion demonstrates an important point for those who would like to use the novel to consider everyday life under colonial domination. Even Nnu Ego and Nnaife, who live in close physical proximity to a European household, have very little idea of what the colonialists are interested in, what their intentions are, and even what they do on a daily basis. As will be seen throughout the novel, even when European actions have dire consequences for the lives of these ordinary Nigerians (for instance, when Nnaife is coerced into military service in Burma), no one seems to comprehend why these things have occurred. Europeans are portrayed throughout as enigmatic, almost whimsical beings—but beings whose whimsy can deliver newly urban Nigerians like Nnu Ego and Nnaife into the gravest physical peril. In this sense Europeans are rather like the slave woman or other spiritual beings in the Igbo cosmos. Their attention is potentially dangerous, so it is best not to attract their notice. Throughout the novel, Nnu Ego, as an African woman, is less likely to be noticed than Nnaife, who becomes almost an exemplar of the ideal colonial subject: obedient, ready to take on menial tasks for cash payment, and accepting whatever the fates (or the British) offer him. It is therefore Nnaife who travels far beyond Lagos and learns more about colonial and military life, while Nnu Ego remains in the city and struggles with foes nearer to home.[2]

One of these foes is the slave woman, although she makes only one more featured appearance in the narrative. Nnu Ego's *chi* appears in another dream to Agbadi's daughter. In this dream, Nnu Ego once more stumbles upon the stream where she last saw the slave woman. This time, there is a filthy baby boy sitting beside the stream unattended. Although Nnu Ego fears her impulse to steal other people's children, she picks up the infant and decides to wash him, realizing that he looks like Nnaife. When Nnu Ego takes hold of the infant, the slave woman appears on the other side of the stream and tells her, "Yes, take the dirty, chubby babies. You can have as many of those as you want. Take them" (p. 77).

Although Nnu Ego is thrilled with this message from her *chi*, she cannot help but notice how "ghostly" the slave woman's laughter sounds as the *chi* turns away from the stream and heads into the bush.[3] She does not immediately recognize the significance of being given "dirty" babies by the spirit in this dream-space. In my reading of the novel, Emecheta means for the audience—and eventually Nnu Ego—to learn that such dirt will not easily wash off. The Igbo word for "dirt" is the same as the term for "pollution" (*alu*; see Metuh 1985), and Igbo speakers say that *alu* sticks not only to the person who has performed an abominable act, but to those around him or her. Nnu Ego receives the "joys" of motherhood several times over in the birth of her children, but she will gain very little emotional joy from them as they grow. Their innate dirtiness/*alu* will stick to her, even if she does not realize it, just as her corporate guilt sticks to them. This is the slave woman's ultimate revenge: Nnu Ego will have every opportunity that her spirit counterpart did not, but she will gain little satisfaction from being a "good" wife and mother.

The second half of the novel, following the slave woman's gift of the dirty babies, is bleak. The European couple suddenly inform their domestic workers that they must return to England. They leave Nnaife and his colleagues with letters of recommendation that they cannot read and an empty compound in which to squat. Because many members of colonial society vacate Lagos at the same time (because World War II is beginning, even if this event is unknown to those who cannot speak, read, or write in English), there is no one to show the letters to. Nnu Ego is forced to engage in small trade to support the growing family, while Nnaife stays at home and unhappily minds his young son, Oshia. Lashed by Nnu Ego's demands that he act more like an appropriately masculine Igbo man and by his own boredom with domesticity, Nnaife finds employment as a laundry worker for three European men who are sailing to Fernando Po. Although he has no idea where Fernando Po is, or under what conditions he will work, Nnaife leaves his pregnant wife with very little money and the burden of keeping her son alive until he returns. Life during wartime brings new hardships to Nnu Ego, since she is displaced from her home by military men and forced to pay a rent that is almost more than she makes in a month. Because of the kindness of her neighbors and of her landlord, Nnu Ego and her children survive long enough for Nnaife to return home, bringing with him most of his Fernando Po wages.

Seduced by his connection to the colonial regime, Nnaife is not willing to look for work immediately and spends most of the money from Fernando Po on a series of festivities celebrating his successful return. He subsequently learns that his brother has died in Ibuza and that Nnaife has thus inherited a number of wives in the levirate (an insitution whereby women's married status is preserved through inheritance from brother to brother, or, in some cases, father to son). These women generally prefer to stay in the village, or to return to their natal patrilineages, but the most junior of the wives decides to escape rural life and journey to Lagos. Realizing that he must decide whether to return to Ibuza and take up his position as a senior man of his lineage or demonstrate his commitment to life in the urban area, Nnaife uses his city connections to secure work as a grass cutter for the Nigerian Railway Department.

Nnu Ego, who secretly hopes to return to her hometown, instead becomes a co-wife to Adaku. Although this is the second time she has shared a husband, polygyny in the city proves even more difficult than it was in the village. Never well versed in the etiquette between women that makes polygyny bearable, now a marginal Christian who is no longer sure about the morals of multiple marriages, and living in too close a proximity to her co-wife, Nnu Ego tries to subvert the new household arrangement—and succeeds only in angering Nnaife and losing Adaku's respect. Rather than working together for the good of the family, Nnaife's wives are in constant turmoil. Adaku bears a daughter for her new marriage, but Nnu Ego, who has sons, makes her feel inferior.

It comes almost as a relief to Nnaife when he is conscripted for military service. Signing over part of his pay to Nnu Ego and his other wives, but without a clear idea of how this money is to be distributed in his absence, Nnaife sails away from Lagos once again— this time to one of the most brutal campaigns in World War II, fighting the Japanese in Burma. (There is a brief account of this campaign in Crowder 1974: 605–606.) Nnu Ego receives a large sum just after Nnaife disappears and places most of it in a post office savings account on the advice of a worldly-wise neighbor, but she does not capitalize her trade or try to enter the booming wartime Lagos economy as does Adaku.

Instead Nnu Ego returns to Ibuza, once again pregnant, with her four children (two sons and female twins) to see her father, who is nearing death. Agbadi praises Nnu Ego as a "full woman, full of children" (p. 153). It would be a proud moment in her life, except for the fact that Agbadi dies before the night is over, after promising that he will return to her house and bring her mother with him. During the mourning period she bears her third son, who is named Nnamdio ("It is my father!") when Nnu Ego's village co-wife announces that the new infant is Agbadi's reincarnation. She lingers in Ibuza as long as possible, but rumors that Adaku is prospering at her expense and advice about the new opportunities available for her sons in the city finally cause Nnu Ego to return to Lagos with her children.

When she arrives in the city, however, things have changed. Adaku has used her time alone—and the proceeds from her burgeoning trade—to establish herself. Unlike Nnu Ego, who feels that sons are everything and must receive the lion's share of her attention and resources, Adaku announces that she will educate her daughters. Without her old streetside trading location, Nnu Ego is more impoverished than ever. When the co-wives fight, men in the community humiliate them both. Typically, Nnu Ego accepts her shame, while Adaku decides to leave Nnaife's house and become a prostitute, supporting herself and her daughters in style. Although Nnu Ego is horrified and the other Lagosian Igbo disgusted, Adaku moves out, becomes wealthy in her new trade, and educates her daughters with the Yoruba elite. (For an account of Lagosian women and education, see Mann 1985; for information on West African "free women" of a slightly later period see Little 1973.) A new era is dawning in urban gender relations as the war grinds on, but Nnu Ego is as uninterested in the possible benefits of Western modernity for her daughters as she is in the global events that have turned her household upside down. However, she seems more meditative about her patriarchal values and refuses to condemn Adaku completely.

Although life is hard in Lagos, Nnu Ego and her family settle in. Fortunately, she is informed that Nnaife's salary, the enormous sum of sixty pounds, has been held for her at the Lagos post office. This time she does not hesitate, but sets herself up in the lucrative *agbada* (wax print cloth) trade, sends her sons to a missionary school, and begins to train the twins in market work. When Nnaife returns home from the war, he finds a prosperous household, even if it contains only one wife. Before long Nnu Ego is pregnant again. Nnaife also brings home a new wife from Ibuza, Okpo, whose bridewealth (thirty pounds) is the highest ever paid in the town. Although his wartime salary is the basis for Nnaife's new wealth, postwar inflation and his own desire to figure as an important person rapidly eat into it.

The realities of life as a co-wife, even though familiar, are not congenial to Nnu Ego. Worse yet, her beloved son Oshia often sides with his father, who seems like a glamorous figure to the young man and who now decides to invest in his eldest son's education. The irony of Nnu Ego's many sacrifices for Igbo patriarchy is not lost on Emecheta, and the final section of the narrative enables her protagonist to see exactly what she has wrought in her determined allegiance to father, husbands, and sons. After the birth of twin daughters, Nnu Ego realizes that she has disappointed the men around her by not adding to their number. Suddenly she is moved to a prayer unlike any other in her life:

> God, when will you create a woman who will be fulfilled in herself, a full human being, not anyone's appendage. . . . After all, I was born alone, and I shall die alone. What have I gained from this? Yes I have many children, but what do I have to feed them on? On my life. I have to work myself to the bone to look after them, I have to give them my all. And if I am lucky enough to die in peace, I even have to give them my soul. They will worship my dead spirit to provide for them. (pp. 186–187)

This realization comes too late. As in all good tragedy, Emecheta's protagonist must suffer the fate she has outlined for herself. However, the author reserves one extraordinary redemption for her creation.

The end of the novel rapidly progresses through the remainder of Nnu Ego's life. Her last pregnancy, at the age of forty, produces only a stillborn daughter. Her children grow up influenced by their urban experience: her eldest son continues in school and eventually leaves Nigeria for the United States. The other children are similarly disconnected from their Ibuza past and less ready to obey or respect their parents. One daughter wants to marry a Yoruba man instead of the Ibuza husband her father has chosen for her. In Nnaife's anger over this cross-ethnic match, he attacks his prospective in-laws and falls afoul of the police. Nnu Ego is forced to testify at his trial, and her evidence—innocently given—helps send him to jail. Knowing that her marriage is effectively over, Nnu Ego finally takes the initiative. She arranges her second daughter's marriage, uses the bridewealth to help pay her second son's school fees, leaves one of her youngest daughters under her married sister's care, then packs her remaining family off to Ibuza.

Even though she has given her life for Nnaife and his lineage, she is branded a bad wife when she arrives and is sent to live with her father's relatives. She never speaks with Nnaife again. Nnu Ego gradually slips into a sad physical and mental state. She receives some support from her Lagosian daughters but nothing from her sons. Nonetheless, when she dies, alone and on the edge of the road, all of her surviving children come home, including the sons living in North America, and give her the largest second burial any Ibuza woman in living memory has received.[4]

Everyone in the village celebrates her, at last, as the ideal Ibuza woman, full of the joys of her motherhood. It is only later, after the second burial, that people begin to wonder about Nnu Ego. No matter how many times people petition her spirit for children, she never bestows this ancestral blessing on them. In death the reader can imagine Nnu Ego sitting on the other side of that stream with her old nemesis, the slave woman, refusing to send any more dirty babies into the world of the living. Never quite able to live up to the strict ideology of proper womanhood in life, Nnu Ego shows no real interest in its communal values after death, when she can no longer be hurt or coerced by popular opinion.

TEACHING *JOYS* IN THE CLASSROOM

This ending, which may seem abrupt, even unfinished, to a Western readership, is startlingly ironic to those raised in West African societies. It should not then surprise us to learn that Emecheta's work has not been well received in Nigeria, and her books are rarely taught there—unlike novels by other Igbo writers, most notably Chinua Achebe. This also has to do with the fact that most of Emecheta's adult fiction has not been published by a major Nigerian publisher, making her novels difficult to find and expensive to purchase. Emecheta herself has taken on the task of publishing her work in Nigeria but has not yet met with great success. She is considered too feminist and even too Western by certain African critics, who point to the fact that she resides permanently in the United Kingdom and suggest that she has lost touch with Nigerian values. Emecheta's greatest audience is and has always been among outsiders seeking insight into Nigerian or, more generally, "African" culture. When teaching *Joys*, therefore, the lecturer should note that it propounds a radical, and even highly individual, message about a universal topic: the role of women as mothers in society. This does not obviate the power of the novel or its usefulness for instruction; quite the contrary: by saying this to students, the teacher reminds them that there is a diversity of opinion possible within an African society, even on a question so central as the proper creation of women's identity.

The undergraduate teacher can also use this novel as a jumping-off point to discuss how "traditions" as deeply engrained as the centrality of motherhood can be transformed under conditions of rapid social change, not only in Nigeria but in our own society. One of my ploys for eliciting this discussion is to ask students how women's roles in the United States changed during World War II. Even though history is not our undergraduates' strong point, usually a few members of the class remember "Rosie the Riveter" and the push to reintegrate women into domestic life after the war. We can then compare Nnu Ego's position as head of a growing urban household during Nnaife's absence with what the class knows about North American women's work at the same period. When using *Joys* in a class on global ideas about gender, I might even assign a reading about women's roles during World War II and tell the students to prepare a one-page memo for a comparative discussion.

In an Africa survey course, I generally use *Joys* for the basis of discussion and essay writing in a section on life in Igbo-speaking areas. It works particularly well after the students have come to grips with Igbo ethnography, preferably something dealing directly with gender. Ifi Amadiume's monograph is invaluable here. If a lecturer does not have time to work through an entire ethnography, however, he or she might pair up Emecheta's novel with the chapter in Amadiume (1987: 69–88) called "The Politics of Motherhood: Women and the Ideology-Making Process." Before we discuss *Joys* in my survey course, I always make sure that students have read at least this chapter and are familiar with the importance of what Amadiume calls "matrifocality" in patriarchal Igbo life. Although Amadiume is writing about Nnobi, a northern Igbo town, there are enough similarities to the social life.

As previously noted, the idea that motherhood defines female identity is a difficult one for North American students, who can be resistant to Nnu Ego's life situation. In past discussions, students have suggested that she should have limited the number of her children in order to prosper in the city. Undergraduates generally know even less about the history of contraception than they do about World War II, but this can lead to a productive discussion about what options were available to ordinary women who wished to practice family planning. Students may also come to a realization that Nnu Ego, and women like her, cannot easily practice abstinence—not only because of the coercive force over their spouses allowed to men in a society like this one, but because women themselves believe that having children will ensure their future livelihood.

Unfortunately, there has been little anthropological work written on Western Igbo groups, although Elizabeth Isichei (1991) has done some oral historical work on gender and myth in Asaba. The older, standard work on Igbo ethnography is Victor Uchendu's *The Igbo of Southeast Nigeria* (1965). This is still useful, but its information relates very specifically to southern Igbo groups whose relationship to Anioma is more distant than towns of the north. However, Uchendu could be used as a background or recommended reading if Amadiume and Isichei are not available. I would also suggest that the teacher read Don Ohadike's (1994) historical survey of Western Igbo in preparation for teaching any of Emecheta's novels.

When constructing questions for student essays on *The Joys of Motherhood*, I take into account what the focus of our class readings and discussion has been. If we have talked about *Joys* as a means to think about changing gender roles in Igbo society, I might ask students to write about what social and historical circumstances led to these transformations, and how we see these transformations expressed in Nnu Ego's and her co-wives' lives. This requires students to go back to the text and give specific examples to buttress their arguments, which is always useful for the development of analytic skills. I also usually offer students an opportunity to write about Nnu Ego's problematic relationships with the important people in her life, including her father, her *chi*, her husbands, and her children. This seems to appeal to many undergraduates, who are also trying to come to some understanding of their most intimate relationships. Perhaps not surprisingly, these essays often judge Nnu Ego harshly and perceive her to be an absolute failure—but they can also be a springboard for interesting final discussions of the novel, generating productive student disagreement about why she has failed. In classes specifically on cross-cultural approaches to gender studies, I may pose the question of whether Emecheta has an overtly feminist agenda or whether she is simply writing a realistic piece of historical fiction. Again, this question can elicit some strong opinions from students, which they must back up with recourse to earlier materials we have read on the meaning of feminist or "womanist" writing.

I have also used Flora Nwapa's classic novel *Efuru* (see Chapter 18 in this volume) in tandem with *Joys*, and, although I have not yet done so, I can see using T. O. Echewa's *I Saw the Sky Catch Fire* or Chinua Achebe's *Things Fall Apart* (Chapter 2 in this volume) together with *Joys* as a way to contrast masculine and feminine styles in Igbo culture. *Efuru* is, in many senses, the "mother" of *Joys*: both novels are written by Igbo women about Igbo women who want motherhood very badly; both have protagonists who have extraordinary personal histories,with strong father figures and missing mothers; those protagonists each have difficult marital situations, including divorce and problems with co-wives; each narrative contains strong elements of women's religious practice; and both novels have endings that question the purpose of motherhood in a patriarchal society. However, where Efuru is able to make peace with her circumstances and grows emotionally and socially through her difficulties, Nnu Ego's struggles are unresolved in life. The contrast between the personalities of the two women can make for very involving class discussions, reminding students that societies with similar ideological constructions of femininity can produce fascinating individual variants on those constructions.

Although I usually use *I Saw the Sky Catch Fire* when teaching about the southeastern Nigerian Women's War of 1929 (half the action of the novel takes place during the war), it might also be used in conjunction with *Joys* as a more sympathetic way to discuss the circumstances and aspirations of Nnu Ego's sons. Half of Echewa's novel revolves around the problems of a young man who, during this same period, wins a scholarship to study in North America. Unlike Nnu Ego's eldest son, however, Echewa's male protagonist is culturally grounded by the narrative of his grandmother's experiences during the anticolonial resistance and is forced to grapple with the consequences of his actions for the women he leaves at home.

Still considering how the idea of maculinity changed during the colonial period, it might also be possible to make an interesting comparison between Achebe's famous *Things Fall Apart* and *Joys*, looking at how gender ideologies in Igbo, taken too far, can be disastrous for both men and women. After all, Okonkwo, that most stereotypically male of Igbo fictional characters, is shown to be as inflexible a prisoner of his masculinity as Nnu Ego is of her femininity. In terms of authorial influence, then, surely Okonkwo is as much Nnu Ego's "father" as Efuru is her "mother."

It may be an important exercise to bring masculinity into a discussion of *Joys*, in order to prevent completely alienating male students in a particular class. Masculine discomfort expressed about motherhood is one more reason why it is important for mixed-gender classes to study and discuss such texts. If students see that male authors are also concerned with questions like motherhood, or that their visions of gender are complementary to those expressed in novels like *Joys*, this may mitigate some of their anxiety.

The Joys of Motherhood is a very approachable book for undergraduate teaching, but it is not (as I hope to have shown) simply a feminist tract or an unexamined description of life in an African city. It is a subtle novel that speaks very eloquently of Western Igbo engagement in the transformative high colonial period of Nigeria, that reminds us that World War II was fought not only in the theaters of Europe and the Pacific, and that tells us something important about how women were integrated into the economies of West African cities during the 1930s and 1940s. Readers also meet a frustrating but compelling African character and experience the important moments of what would otherwise be one of millions of undocumented "third world" women's lives. Along the way, they learn that parenthood may be universal, but its social expression can vary widely from place to place and from one historical period to another. Although Nnu Ego's journey in life may not have "gone well" in Igbo terms, it can provide much food for thought for undergraduates still at the beginning of their own journeys.

NOTES

1. For those who want to look more closely at religious motifs in the novel, the association of the slave woman with water is an important one. We learn earlier in the narrative that the slave woman was an Itsekiri, taken from her home in the (watery) Delta region. She may have been dedicated to the largely female water spirits of that region and she certainly seems to embody and to command such dangerous water spirituality in her dealings with the kin of Agbadi. It is no accident that Emecheta makes drowning Nnu Ego's suicide method of choice or that Nnaife's disappearances later in the novel are all associated with mysterious doings across the ocean. Nnu Ego herself is compared to a *mami wata* (beautiful but perilous water spirit) in the novel (p. 43). There are numerous works on contemporary water spirits in Nigeria and elsewhere; see for example Bastian 1997 and Drewal 1996.

2. For African women's different experiences of colonialism and city life, see, for example, Coquery-Vidrovitch 1997, particularly Chapters 7–9. There are a number of good, contemporary ethnographies on African women in urban settings as well, including Clark 1994.

3. In this case, the bush probably symbolizes the wild place where the dead who are not fully integrated into their own lineages reside. Among present-day Igbo speakers, wildernesses are associated with unsocialized spirits who are jealous of living human beings and who will do them mischief if they can. The slave woman was carried away from her own people, never married, and was murdered in a ritual to honor a woman with a very different life experience. In a complex spiritual transaction arising out of the circumstances of her unusual death, she is both tied to the lineage of her killers through this ritual and empowered to take her revenge on them. The relevant proverb for this transaction might be: "Mmuo adighi egbu onye nadighi ihe omere" (The spirits do not kill an innocent person). See Nwala 1985: 62 for a more serious discussion of the issue of justice between human beings and spiritual forces.

4. Igbo people are accorded two funerals. The first is meant to mark the initial separation of the dead person from his or her lineage, and after it the body is placed in the ground for decomposition. The second burial was literally a redeposition of the remains after decomposition and marked a final severing of the person from human life and a birth into the life of the ancestral world. Today a symbolic second coffin is more often buried in the second burial than a complete redeposition of the corpse. This can take place very soon after the first funeral or up to several years later. In a society where a number of lineage members are likely to be absent at the time of a family death, just as Nnu Ego's emigrant sons were, the second burial has become the funeral that as many relatives as possible will try to attend.

SUGGESTIONS FOR
FURTHER READING AND RESOURCES

Achebe, Chinua. 1958. *Things Fall Apart*. Portsmouth, N.H.: Heinemann.

Amadiume, Ifi. 1987. *Male Daughters, Female Husbands: Gender and Sex in an African Society*. London: Zed Books.

Bastian, Misty L. 1997. "Married in the Water: Spirit Kin and Other Afflictions of Modernity in Southeastern Nigeria," *Journal of Religion in Africa* 27: 116–134.

Clark, Gracia. 1994. *Onions Are My Husband: Survival and Accumulation by West African Market Women*. Chicago: University of Chicago Press.

Coquery-Vidrovitch, Catherine. 1997. *African Women: A Modern History*, trans. Beth Gillian Raps. Boulder, Colo.: Westview.

Crowder, Michael. 1974. "The 1939–45 War and West Africa." In *History of West Africa*, Vol. 2, ed. J. F. Ade Ajayi and Michael Crowder. London: Longman.

Drewal, Henry. 1996. "Mami Wata Shrines: Exotica and the Construction of

Self." In *African Material Culture*, ed. Mary Jo Arnoldi et al. Bloomington: Indiana University Press.

Echewa, T. Obinkaram. 1992. *I Saw the Sky Catch Fire*. New York: Dutton.

Emecheta, Buchi. 1979. *The Joys of Motherhood*. Portsmouth, N.H.: Heinemann.

———. 1989. *Head Above Water: An Autobiography*. Portsmouth, N.H.: Heinemann. Emecheta's autobiography provides information on the author's early years and marital difficulties.

Isichei, Elizabeth. 1991. "Myth, Gender and Society in Pre-Colonial Asaba,"*Africa* 61: 513–529.

Little, Kenneth. 1973. *African Women in Towns: An Aspect of Africa's Social Revolution*. Cambridge: Cambridge University Press.

Mann, Kristin. 1985. *Marrying Well: Marriage, Status and Social Change Among the Educated Elite in Colonial Lagos*. Cambridge: Cambridge University Press.

Metuh, Emefie Ikenga. 1985. "Ritual Dirt and Purification Rites Among the Igbo," *Journal of Religion in Africa* 15: 3–24.

Nwala, T. Uzodinma. 1985. *Igbo Philosophy*. Lagos: Literamed.

Nwapa, Flora. 1966. *Efuru*. Portsmouth, N.H.: Heinemann. See Chapter 18 in this collection.

Ohadike, Don C. 1994. *Anioma: A Social History of the Western Igbo People*. Athens: University of Ohio Press. An excellent general history of the Western Igbo.

Uchendu, Victor C. 1965. *The Igbo of Southeast Nigeria*. New York: Holt, Rinehart and Winston.

11 ⟋

Buchi Emecheta's
The Slave Girl

Kathleen Sheldon

I HAVE TAUGHT BUCHI EMECHETA'S NOVEL *THE SLAVE Girl* several times in upper division courses on African women's history. I have several goals in mind in assigning this story: to provide one example of African women's voices, to present an important historical period through accessible fiction, and to raise a series of questions about women's position in African societies. I have also wanted to make some connections with class discussions about women and slavery in Africa, the advent of colonialism, women's market activities and economic roles, and women's resistance in the 1929 Women's War in Aba, Nigeria, which is mentioned in this novel (pp. 132–135).

THE STORY

The Slave Girl, as Emecheta herself has explained, is based on stories told by her mother about her childhood in Onitsha (James 1990: 44). It takes place in southeastern Nigeria among the Igbo (or Ibo) people of Ibuza and Onitsha, in the early years of the twentieth century. Emecheta begins by setting the village and kin background with a poetic description of the mythic origins of the settlement, portraying the history and ecology of the region in idyllic terms. She then focuses on one couple, a man who works in the colonial courts and

---

Buchi Emecheta, *The Slave Girl* (New York: George Braziller, 1977).

his wife, who cultivates food and occasionally trades at local markets. They have two healthy sons, followed by several female babies who died at birth or at an early age. This is the context for the birth of Ogbanje Ojebeta, a girl who survives and apparently plans to stay with her family rather than die prematurely. To protect her, her parents visit a local diviner who says she must tie charms around her body so that she can tell her "evil friends" (that is, evil spirits), "Go away, I am happy here." The charms include small bells, pieces of tin, and cowry shells, which make noise and frighten away those who would steal her before she can grow up (p. 18). She also is tattooed with spinach-leaf designs on her face and body, another way her parents demonstrate their gratitude for her staying with them and not dying young. The tattoos are also supposed to act as a deterrent to her being sold into slavery, as the distinctive markings will always let people know who she is and where she has been born and raised.

Ojebeta's early years follow the rural agricultural cycle of the seasons, "when her mother used to carry her on her back to the stream and sometimes to the market" (p. 23). Then tragedy strikes in the form of *felenza*, the 1917–1918 international influenza epidemic, which kills her mother and father. Her older brother leaves to find work in Lagos, so only the younger brother, Okolie, remains on the farm to care for the seven-year-old girl. But Okolie is not interested in caring for his sister. He has grown into a vain and selfish young man, who only wants money to buy a special outfit for his coming-of-age celebration. He arranges for a distant relative, Ma Palagada, to take Ojebeta in exchange for money. Ma Palagada is a well-to-do cloth seller in the large market town of Onitsha who already has two grown daughters, a son, two male slaves working her farm, and four other slave girls working in her market stall.

The contrast between rural and urban life is evident from the first glimpse Okolie and Ojebeta have of the Onitsha market. There are many more people, including Hausa and Fulani traders and others from distant lands. There are new clothing styles, a lot of money changing hands, and abundant food of the type that they have eaten only on special occasions in Ibuza. And there is a sewing machine in Ma Palagada's market stall, so that repairs and minor tailoring tasks can be done for customers. All of this is overwhelming to Ojebeta, who is tricked by her brother when he leaves without saying good-bye or explaining that she is not going to return with him to Ibuza but is now a slave in Ma Palagada's household, sold for eight English pounds (p. 65). Although Ma Palagada is distantly related in an unspecified way to Ojebeta's mother's family, providing a kinship idiom, it is clear to the reader, though not to Ojebeta, that she has been sold into slavery.

To compound Ojebeta's misery, the first action Ma Palagada takes is to remove what she refers to as "those stupid bells" and "those cowries [that] make that pagan music." Ojebeta secretly keeps the charms in an attempt to maintain her sense of her self and her connection to her parents and place of origin, and she continues to carry the charms hidden under her clothes throughout her stay with the Palagadas (pp. 71–72).

Ojebeta remains with Ma throughout her girlhood and adolescence and is introduced to a more urban way of life influenced by British colonialism. She attends church, becomes a Christian, and learns to read. The Palagadas believe that the new Christian teaching was not good for "real rich human beings" but is acceptable for the slaves, and that is why the young slaves owned by Ma Palagada attend school on Sundays (p. 93). Ma's son, Clifford, takes an interest in Ojebeta, and Ojebeta does not object, as marriage to Clifford can indicate an end of her slave status and an improvement in her social position.

Despite the degrading aspects of life as a slave, Ojebeta is a character of much inner strength. Clifford does not pursue his interest in her as a potential wife, but Ma's daughter Victoria wants to inherit her after Ma dies. Ojebeta fights back and decides that rather than continue as a slave, she will return to Ibuza and later repay her sale price and make her own way as a free woman. She succeeds in returning to Ibuza, where she lives with her relatives before marrying Jacob, a Christian man who is kind to her. Eventually Clifford collects the eight pounds, and with that exchange Ojebeta ends her slavery status. But the ending of the story is ambiguous, as it has been made clear throughout the narrative that marriage is only another kind of slavery for women. The novel's final sentence is: "So as Britain was emerging from war once more victorious, and claiming to have stopped the slavery which she had helped to spread in all her black colonies, Ojebeta, now a woman of thirty-five, was changing masters" (p. 179).

SLAVERY

The nature of slavery is a central topic in the book. It is introduced as a practice from the past, a business that was carried on with

Europeans, or as a part of the neighboring kingdom of Benin. There is a reference to Ojebeta's grandfather raiding neighboring villages to capture slaves to sell to Europeans, though it is clear that the international slave trade has at least diminished, since "People were not going missing as before" (p. 38). At the same time, the novel provides evidence of the continuation of slavery after its official abolition, although it was much more secretive (p. 70). The novel further corroborates lectures and assigned readings about African women as slave owners and the ability of slaves to better their position (pp. 62–63).

As one successful woman cloth seller in the book comments, "Where would we be without slave labour, and where would some of these unwanted children be without us?" Emecheta then interjects, "It might be evil, but was a necessary evil" (p. 64). Ojebeta's experiences help put a human face on class discussions about the nature of slavery in Africa, in particular the widespread practices of pawning family members and placing children with better-off relatives in time of hardship.

Students in American classrooms are familiar with the plantation form of slavery most common in the American South, and sometimes have difficulty understanding the differences between that history and the wider variety of African forms of control over people, including slavery. I often lecture using information from the introduction to Suzanne Miers and Igor Kopytoff's *Slavery in Africa*. I also assign material from the Claire Robertson and Martin Klein collection on *Women and Slavery in Africa*, such as Edna Bay's article on female slaves in the kingdom of Dahomey and the introduction by Robertson and Klein, so there is a direct connection between class reading and discussion and references in the novel.

One particularly difficult passage concerns the sacrifice of a female slave who has attempted escape. She is buried alive with her mistress when the woman slave owner dies (p. 62; see also Emecheta's *The Joys of Motherhood,* Chapter 10). Many early colonialists and missionaries observed people in the Onitsha region continuing to practice human sacrifice well into the twentieth century, and saw these practices as proof of the savagery of the local people and of the need to proselytize Christian beliefs. Caroline Ifeka discusses this in a context of understanding Igbo ideas about self and community (Ifeka 1982: 404); her article would be useful for an instructor to read before discussing this topic, although it may be too difficult to assign to students. Ifeka is also helpful in conceptualizing women's ideas about themselves and their place in Igbo society at the turn of the century, so her article neatly complements the novel. I have also found it fruitful to place slavery in a broader context of practices that can be considered "culturally challenging," as suggested by Isabelle Gunning (1992). This approach is very effective in helping students step outside their own social assumptions in order to understand (although not necessarily to condone) customs that may be very different from their own.

The ambiguity of Ma's relationship with her slaves is evident when Emecheta comments that Ma "seemed to try as much as possible to treat her girl slaves as her own daughters" but would never allow them to "sleep in the same building as the daughters of 'human beings'" (p. 89). Though Ma is not particularly vicious, her husband, Pa Palagada, regularly beats the slaves for any tiny infraction or lack of attention, and when Ma's married daughter Victoria joins the household to care for Ma when she becomes ill, she also introduces a litany of beatings and scoldings. When Victoria becomes angry with Ojebeta, she comments that "She's only a slave." Clifford responds, "But she is our relation, too," and Victoria retorts, "Who wants a relation like this—a poor one, who had to be sold by her people?" (p. 114).

Emecheta makes an early comparison between slavery and marriage, when she has Okolie initially ask for twenty pounds for Ojebeta because that is the amount that can be commanded as bridewealth when she reaches the age of marrying (p. 67). The slave girls are also expected to acquiesce to the sexual demands of both Pa Palagada and his son, Clifford (pp. 92–94), further suggesting the common position of wives and slave women. When Clifford discusses with Ma the possibility of a marriage between himself and Ojebeta, Ma complains that if she had known of Clifford's interest, she would have spent more on Ojebeta's upbringing, to make her a more suitable wife. Clifford observes that "You can regard what you paid for her as her bride price" (p. 129). And once Ojebeta returns to Ibuza, she discusses marriage possibilities with her aunt, who counsels her, "No woman is ever free. To be owned by a man is a great honour" (p. 158). The concordance of slavery with marriage is repeatedly emphasized.

SOCIAL OBSERVATIONS

In the course of telling the story Emecheta describes many elements of Igbo society, including the organization of the markets, women's work, age groups, burial customs, naming practices and the use of praise names, the food people ate, how *akpu* (a fermented porridge) was made from cassava, and so forth. The detail she provides offers a way of recognizing the contrast between rural and urban life. Emecheta's own ambivalent opinions about the relative value of African and European cultures is also evident in the descriptions of life in Ibuza and Onitsha.

Although Emecheta describes a peaceful childhood for Ojebeta, not all elements of village life are idyllic. Accusations of magic and witchcraft are common occurrences for village residents. One relative by marriage, who happens to meet Okolie and Ojebeta on the road to Onitsha, has been shunned by the family because his eyes are excessively watery. Some believe that his wife has gotten medicine from the local healer to keep him from having eyes for any other woman, and that is the cause of their constant watering (pp. 38–39). Another superstition is the idea among some West African people that twins bring bad luck. One of Ojebeta's fellow slaves is a girl from Calabar who has been sold into slavery by her mother because she is a twin, and if she had not been sent away from her village, she would have been killed (pp. 89, 135).

In contrast, the initial descriptions of Onitsha and Ma Palagada's house are generally positive, as presented through the eyes of Ojebeta. She is pleased with the new smooth cloth that replaces the old cloth woven by her mother, and she marvels at the wide straight road with "trees planted at regular intervals . . . so tidy that she wondered whether it could all possibly have been done by living people. . . . [She] had never seen tamed vegetation before" (pp. 87–88). Many aspects of town life are presented as almost magical from the point of view of a naive village girl.

There are many descriptions of food, which appears with much greater variety and quantity at Onitsha. Meat and other delicacies are available on a regular basis and not just for special occasions. The great difficulty of making and selling *akpu*, which has a distinctive odor, is presented as one of the hardships faced by rural women (pp. 152–153). But in the end, Ojebeta decides that the poorer diet of Ibuza was better than the food offered to her in Onitsha. As she says, eating the mushroom of freedom is better than the meat of slavery.

At the same time, characters in the novel frequently question European colonial assumptions that everything Western and white is more desirable than African customs and beliefs. The efforts of a white woman visitor to the Palagada home to speak Igbo is described as hard to understand because "she speaks through her nose, and pronounces her words in a funny way" (p. 102), a nice inversion of

Westerners' treatment of African languages as "mumbo-jumbo." The woman is also described as very thin, like "a lizard lying flat on its stomach. She must be ill all the time," a suggestion that beauty is a cultural construction. The idea that plump women are admired as healthy and lovely, an ideal of feminine attractiveness, is another useful opening for classroom discussion (p. 102). When Ojebeta returns to Ibuza, she adopts the name Alice, but again Emecheta is somewhat cynical about such Western accoutrements, commenting that after independence, in the future, people again took pride in their African names. Ojebeta's uncle remarks that if she wants to be a Christian, that is all right, but why not go to the "Fathers," who had a lot more magic in their services, so that it would seem more familiar than the poor style of the Christian Missionary Society churches (p. 154).

Although Ma Palagada is generally a figure of strength and power, the source of her wealth is brought into question. It becomes apparent that Ma benefits financially from sending people of her household to Sunday school, because the Church Missionary Society teacher is the wife of the director of the United Africa Company. Due to Ma's compliance with Christianity, she is given advantages in trading and imports. In fact, the reader eventually learns that she has gained her initial foothold in the market because of her earlier relationship with the Portuguese man who was the father of her two daughters. When he returned to Europe, he left marketable goods with Ma that enabled her to begin her career as a trader. Ma's position resonates with the history of eighteenth-century women in Senegal as described in George Brooks's article about women who found advantages in developing relationships in the space between European and African coastal cultures (Brooks 1976).

The education provided to the slave girls, and to Ma's own daughters as well, illustrates classroom discussions about colonialism and domesticity in Africa. Although Ma's daughters have access to Western education, that is because they did not live with her after she married Pa Palagada (p. 93). These racially mixed daughters are disparaged by the Palagada slaves as being "the colour of unripe palm fruits" (p. 102), but they both make successful marriages to men involved in the new colonial economy. The slave girls learn to read and they also have classes in domestic skills such as baking, crocheting, and embroidery (p. 131).

When the girls begin attending Sunday school, they wear Western-style gowns, which they call *gams*. Again the comparison of ideals of decorum and beauty is brought out, as a proper Igbo married woman would always wear two pieces of cloth, and so would still wear an Igbo-style cloth over the dress and wrap an elaborate head scarf as well. From the Igbo point of view the European women are underdressed, though from the European vantage, the Igbo women's insistence on dressing in layers is evidence that they have the "brains of children" (p. 104). Later there is a reference to the girls learning how to lift the hems of their gowns as they walk to church, and this is contrasted with a reference on the same page to people from Ibuza trading along the river at Onitsha, whom Ojebeta observes wearing "tattered clothes patched together in colours that did not match and in various stages of disintegration" (p. 131). Emecheta's ambivalent attitude is evident here. Though there has been open irony in the descriptions of the slave girls' introduction to Western clothing and skills, the description of rural African attire is presented from Ojebeta's point of view as a negative aspect of rural African life.

There is very little direct comment on the politics of colonialism. The final sentence, which obliquely suggests that colonialism is another kind of slavery, is never elaborated. The only exception is the brief description of the Aba women's war of 1929 (pp. 132–135). Ma Palagada, though initially resistant to becoming involved in the planning, was convinced that her financial interests were at stake, and that she should protest the taxes being imposed by the new colonial power. The students also have read about this in Judith Van Allen (1976), and sometimes Caroline Ifeka-Moller (1975) and a chapter from Marjorie Perham (1937) as well. In this case, the novel provides very little context for the incident, so that wider reading about the Aba women's war is necessary.

ANALYSIS

Emecheta's writings have been the focus of a great deal of attention and analysis, some of it quite contentious. Her motives and ideas are not self-evident in her fiction, allowing readers to make a number of arguments about what her position is on various topics concerning women, politics, and history. The fact that Ojebeta took action to end her own slavery is cited by Helen Chukwuma as evidence of Emecheta's feminist and positivist point of view (1989: 4). Other readers have felt that Emecheta is essentially a pessimist, presenting African women as victims and constantly subject to the oppressions of men and society (Emenyonu 1988: 141). This ambiguity makes Emecheta especially suited as an opening for students to think through the issues for themselves. As another commentator has noted, Emecheta's "viewpoint shifts between shame and pride in her people. . . . Her ambivalence reveals an English strain in her attitude towards life, a strain in constant conflict with her innate Africanness" (Ogunyemi 1983: 65). In *The Slave Girl,* in particular, scholars have focused on Ojebeta's attempt to keep her own sense of being an African, while separating herself from the oppressive aspects of African society (Frank 1982: 478). But the answers are not clearly found in the novel. It is fairly easy to select references from the novel that indicate Emecheta's disillusion with Igbo society and women's place in it, but it is equally easy to find text that demonstrates how she values African society and the strength of African women.

Emecheta's analysis is perhaps too obvious, but it works well for discussion purposes: women are like slaves, whether they are called slaves or not. For Ojebeta there was scant difference between her girlhood enslavement to Ma and her marriage as an adult. As Emecheta comments, "Every woman, whether slave or free, must marry. All her life a woman always belonged to some male" (p. 112).

Katherine Fishburn has addressed some of the more vexing issues confronting readers of this particularly ambivalent novel. In her study of Emecheta's work she focuses on two aspects of the book that can be difficult for Western readers. The first is the variability of the narrator's voice, which sometimes seems omniscient in describing international events and apparently reflecting a Western perspective. At other times the voice is clearly African. She describes a frustration that readers might have, as it appears that Western and African cultures are being set up in a kind of opposition, yet the narrator refuses to take sides. (For discussions of Emecheta's authorial "voice" and literary technique, see Spencer-Walters 1996 and Emenyonu 1996.)

This ambivalence is most evident at the end when Ojebeta seems to be happily settled in a marriage of her own choosing—but that marriage includes the exchange of bridewealth, so that the narrator in Ojebeta's voice describes the marriage as another form of slavery: "I feel free in belonging to a new master from my very own town Ibuza; my mind is now at rest" (p. 178). Fishburn believes that this paradox and lack of a "happy ending" are deliberate, and that Emecheta presents the story in this framework to reflect the very real ambivalence of the clash of cultures. Whatever Emecheta's motives (and these may be impossible to discover for this novel), this dual vision makes it possible to have some very interesting discussions, especially in feminist classrooms (see Haraway 1990). If marriage is simply another form of slavery, it is easy for feminist readers to take this as a tragic ending to Ojebeta's story. But if Ojebeta is truly happy in a marriage to a man she has chosen for herself, it appears to be a more traditional happy ending. In actuality, it is both. It is a happy ending for Ojebeta, but one in which she herself recognizes the limitations of her choices. This can lead to many interesting discussions about cultural understandings of marriage and of slavery, about what kinds of choices women face in different cultures, and about how we interpret novels such as *The Slave Girl* from our own perspective. My students ask whether there is not a universal idea about human rights that we can apply to condemn slavery and oppressive marriages across cultures. Obviously, there is no easy answer to this, but there is a lot of material for discussion.

CLASSROOM ASSIGNMENTS

I have usually had the students read Emecheta's novel in the first half of a ten-week class, and sometimes have assigned Tsitsi Dangarembga's *Nervous Conditions* in the second half (see Chapter 8). Dangarembga's novel provides a contrast in its cultural setting and time period, but addresses many of the same themes: the push and pull of African and Western cultures, the experience of African girls with Western schooling, and the place of girls in their families and their societies. I always include an exam or essay question about at least one of the novels, sometimes asking for a comparison of the two. One year I asked for a comparison of women's status and opportunities in the different regions and historical eras depicted in the two novels and whether these fictional accounts were consistent with historical research.

Depending on the background and abilities of the class, I might ask a question as general as "What is the central theme in Emecheta's *The Slave Girl*? Explain your answer." For a longer essay written at home, I have asked students to "Discuss slavery and women in an African context," with a focus on the historical content of *The Slave Girl* as one of several options. I include an admonishment to make the connections to other materials we have read on slavery.

I have also referred to the issue of evidence with this question from a final exam: "Using either Buchi Emecheta's *The Slave Girl* or Emma Mashinini's *Strikes Have Followed Me All of My Life* (or both if you want to compare them), discuss the importance of fiction and/or autobiography as evidence in African women's history. What does such an account offer, and what are the problems?" I sought to provoke some thinking about the nature of the evidence (or lack of it) that we have for African women's history.

CONCLUSION

Buchi Emecheta has written many books portraying African women's experiences in a variety of settings. In *The Slave Girl*, one of her earlier novels and the one that depicts the earliest time period, she has defined a heroine who lives through the terrible childhood event of being sold into slavery. Although she grows into a forthright adolescent, by the end of the story she has become a beaten-down shadow of her former self, who has accepted the "master" she chose in marriage. Students find her predicament compelling and come to class ready to debate the many ideas that Emecheta raises and to discuss how the events of the novel correspond to other class assignments and discussions.

SUGGESTIONS FOR
FURTHER READING AND RESOURCES

Bay, Edna G. 1983. "Servitude and Worldly Success in the Palace of Dahomey." In *Women and Slavery in Africa*, ed. Claire C. Robertson and Martin A. Klein. Madison: University of Wisconsin Press.

Brooks, George E., Jr. 1976. "The Signares of Saint-Louis and Gorée: Women Entrepreneurs in Eighteenth-Century Senegal." In *Women in Africa: Studies in Social and Economic Change*, ed. Nancy J. Hafkin and Edna G. Bay. Stanford: Stanford University Press.

Chukwuma, Helen. 1989. "Positivism and the Female Crisis: The Novels of Buchi Emecheta." In *Nigerian Female Writers: A Critical Perspective*, ed. Henrietta C. Otokunefor and Obiageli C. Nwodo. Nigeria: Malthouse Press.

Dangarembga, Tsitsi. 1988. *Nervous Conditions*. Seattle: Seal Press.

Emecheta, Buchi. 1977. *The Slave Girl*. New York: George Braziller.

Emenyonu, Ernest N. 1988. "Technique and Language in Buchi Emecheta's *The Bride Price, The Slave Girl*, and *The Joys of Motherhood*," *Journal of Commonwealth Literature* 23, 1: 130–141. This essay also appears in

Emerging Perspectives on Buchi Emecheta, ed. Marie Umeh (Trenton, N.J.: Africa World Press, 1996).

Fishburn, Katherine. 1995. *Reading Buchi Emecheta: Cross-Cultural Conversations*. Westport, Conn.: Greenwood. See especially pp. 92–103.

Frank, Katherine. 1982. "The Death of the Slave Girl: African Womanhood in the Novels of Buchi Emecheta," *World Literature Written in English* 21, 3: 476–497.

Gunning, Isabelle R. 1992. "Arrogant Perception, World-Travelling and Multicultural Feminism: The Case of Female Genital Surgeries," *Columbia Human Rights Law Review* 23: 189–248.

Haraway, Donna. 1990. "Reading Buchi Emecheta: Contests for Women's Experience in Women's Studies," *Women: A Cultural Review* 1, 3: 240–255.

Ifeka, Caroline. 1982. "The Self Viewed from 'Within' or 'Without': Twists and Turns in Gender Identity in a Patrilineal Society," *Mankind* 13, 5: 401–415.

Ifeka-Moller, Caroline. 1975. "Female Militancy and Colonial Revolt: The Women's War of 1929, Eastern Nigeria." In *Perceiving Women*, ed. Shirley Ardener. New York: John Wiley.

James, Adeola. 1990. "Buchi Emecheta." In *In Their Own Voices: African Women Writers Talk*, ed. Adeola James. Portsmouth, N.H.: Heinemann.

Kopytoff, Igor, and Suzanne Miers. 1977. "African 'Slavery' as an Institution of Marginality." In *Slavery in Africa: Historical and Anthropological Perspectives*, ed. Suzanne Miers and Igor Kopytoff. Madison: University of Wisconsin Press.

Mashinini, Emma. 1991. *Strikes Have Followed Me All My Life: A South African Autobiography*. New York: Routledge.

Ogunyemi, Chikwenye Okonjo. 1983. "Buchi Emecheta: The Shaping of a Self," *Komparatistische Hefte* 8: 65–77.

Perham, Margery. 1937. "The South-East: The Aba Riots." In Perham, *Native Administration in Nigeria*. London: Oxford University Press.

Robertson, Claire C., and Martin A. Klein. 1983. *Women and Slavery in Africa*. Madison: University of Wisconsin Press.

Spencer-Walters, Tom. 1996. "Orality and Patriarchal Dominance in Buchi Emecheta's *The Slave Girl*." In *Emerging Perspectives on Buchi Emecheta*, ed. Marie Umeh. Trenton, N.J.: Africa World Press.

Van Allen, Judith. 1976. "'Aba Riots' or Igbo 'Women's War'? Ideology, Stratification, and the Invisibility of Women." In *Women in Africa: Studies in Social and Economic Change*, ed. Nancy J. Hafkin and Edna G. Bay. Stanford: Stanford University Press.

12

Nuruddin Farah's *Gifts*

Lidwien Kapteijns

IN THE CONTEXT OF MY UNDERGRADUATE AFRICAN history classes, Nuruddin Farah's beautiful novel *Gifts* fulfills two pedagogical objectives. First, it introduces my students to the mind of Somali novelist Nuruddin Farah (here at his most accessible) as he imagines, describes, and provides a progressive social commentary upon Somalia in the late 1980s. Familiarizing students with contemporary African intellectuals, whether they write fiction or social science analyses, is one of the objectives of my teaching; the African novel is a crucial site of exploration in this endeavor. Second, Farah's novel allows my students to experience a particular African context through particular fictional individuals, in this case a young, middle-class Somali nurse in Mogadishu, the Somali capital, about four or five years before the disintegration of the Somali state in January 1991. Both goals are of pedagogical value to me. Given the garbage often propagated by this country's media, an encounter with Africa's own thinkers and commentators is indispensable if students are to be pushed beyond sympathy and pity for the continent toward an analysis of wider historical and contemporary contexts. Empathy and identification with individuals (even fictional ones) will help students understand that Africa's "difference" does not lie primarily in the qualities of individuals (who, novels often show, are not so different from us) but must be sought in history. Social history begins when students try to understand that in Africa, as elsewhere, the social institutions of the present are the crystallization of social

Nuruddin Farah, *Gifts* (London: Serif, 1993).

145

struggles of the past, and that these institutions are maintained or changed by people as much like themselves as unlike themselves, facing circumstances not of their own making.

At the undergraduate level, the novel is accessible both for students of the small upper-level seminar on African women's history (consisting of fifteen students, mostly seniors), and for those of the 200-level survey on colonial and postindependence African history (who usually number twenty-five to thirty and represent all years). I would not hesitate to teach the novel at the graduate level as well.

The protagonist of *Gifts* is Duniya (whose name means "world" both in Somali and Arabic), a young woman of thirty-five who works as a senior nurse in one of Mogadishu's best maternity hospitals. Duniya is a single parent, with three children from two marriages, neither of which was a love match. The main story line involves Duniya falling in love and shaping this relationship in such a way that she remains mistress of her own narrative and does not have to sacrifice her sense of autonomy, individuality, and personal choice. In this sense, this is an optimistic, happy story set in Mogadishu of the 1980s. A second narrative theme, however, embedded in and interwoven with Duniya's story, deals with international development aid, here criticized in numerous creative and culturally grounded ways. Duniya resents gifts in her personal life, as she believes that there are no innocent gifts and that "unasked-for-generosity has a way of making one feel obliged, trapped in a labyrinth of dependence" (p. 20). Similarly, Duniya and other characters in the novel diagnose international development aid as a cause of national dependence in the international arena, and of dictatorship in the domestic one.

The book begins with Duniya reluctantly admitting to herself that she is in love with Bosaaso, an educated and sensitive man who gave up a job with a United Nations agency in the United States in order to serve his own country. Duniya realizes that she is in love when she begins to drop and knock things over in the hospital in which she works: Love throws "the world" off balance. There is a shortage of gas (and lots of other things) in Mogadishu, paralyzing almost all transportation. However, Bosaaso keeps showing up to give Duniya rides. Duniya is both delighted, as she is interested in Bosaaso, and reluctant, for she jealously guards her autonomy and is suspicious of gifts. The story of Duniya's two marriages gives this reluctance a deeper meaning. Duniya was seventeen when her father, on his deathbed, gave her hand to his best friend, Zubayr, a blind man of almost sixty, who lived in Galcayo (the capital of central Somalia). Duniya abided by her father's wish. Perhaps her half brother, Shiriye, could have prevented the marriage, but when offered part of the bridewealth as a gift, he concurred. During this first marriage (which lasted only a year or so), Duniya bore Zubayr twins, a daughter, Nasiiba, and a son, Mataan, both about seventeen when the novel opens. After Zubayr's death, Duniya and her children moved to Mogadishu, where Shiriye provided her with housing. Her second husband, Taariq, a highly intelligent and politically progressive journalist, first became her landlord and then, partly because he was so kind to her and her twins, her husband. She had a daughter by him, Yarey, nine years old at the time the book opens. It is Taariq's alcoholism, related to his depression, that made Duniya leave him, at least in part for the sake of her children. As part of the divorce settlement, Taariq's brother Qaasim (whose current wife had not borne him children) gives Duniya and her twins an apartment, while she allows him to raise her youngest daughter.

Duniya's emerging relationship with Bosaaso becomes more intimate when her daughter Nasiiba brings home an orphan, in reality the illegitimate child of Qaasim and Nasiiba's friend, Fariida. The foundling, a boy who lives only a few days—and is also a gift of sorts—becomes a catalyst for change in Duniya's personal relationships. When her half brother, Shiriye, uses the foundling's presence in her house to come and insult her, she throws him out of her apartment. When Qaasim's wife visits to jeer at Duniya for not being able to match all the gifts she is able to buy Yarey, the youngest child, Duniya not only tells her that she will raise her daughter herself but also that she will move out of Qaasim's apartment. Because Nasiiba dealt with her friend's pregnancy and difficult birth without initially consulting her mother, Duniya must begin to relate to her as an adult who is capable of making her own decisions and is free to do so. Moreover, in the frenzy of activities surrounding the foundling, Bosaaso becomes an intimate member of her family. The foundling becomes a symbol of their togetherness as a couple (p. 94), changing even their way of speaking, Duniya realizes, "producing a *we* that had not been there before, a *we* of hybrid necessities, half real, half invented" (p. 132). Duniya decides to make Bosaaso a recipient more than a giver of gifts by giving him the gift of her body in lovemaking. The climax of the story is the visit of Duniya's older brother Abshir, who lives, works, and has a family in Italy. Abshir is the only person in the world whose gifts Duniya does not distrust, and his wealth and generosity (and his commitment to her children's education) make it possible for her to accept Bosaaso's marriage proposal without fear of dependence.

As this story develops, the theme of international aid and the dependence it creates in Somalia, as in other parts of Africa, is developed in a number of ways. The most important vehicle for this political commentary consists of editorials published in the local newspaper by Taariq, Duniya's ex-husband. These pieces are well crafted and very critical, going so far as to accuse international aid of protecting economically incompetent and politically tyrannical rulers (such as Somalia's Siyaad Barre, r. 1969–1991) against being overthrown by their own people. Given the disintegration of the Somali state after the overthrow of the Somali dictator in January 1991, this is an analysis worth pursuing with one's students. The Somali or Arab folktales told in the novel by Duniya's son or in Taariq's newspaper articles constitute another, less direct, but culturally grounded form of commentary upon international aid. However, although Duniya's story has a happy ending, with Duniya confident that her decision to marry Bosaaso will not compromise her autonomy, there is no closure with regard to Somalia's story of dependence. The novel offers no solutions here, but it constitutes an excellent basis for further discussion with students (see Samatar and Samatar 1987).

THE NOVEL IN THE CONTEXT OF SOMALI HISTORY

The late 1980s are an interesting time period in Somali history. Colonialism (which lasted from 1885 to 1960) had been particularly divisive, as Somali territories were divided up between the French, British, Italians, and Ethiopians. This gave birth to French Somaliland, now the Republic of Djibouti; British Somaliland, now with a secessionist agenda; British Kenya's Northern Frontier District, now part of Kenya; Italian Somaliland, currently contested by different warlords and clan organizations; and the currently Ethiopian-dominated Ogaden and Haud regions, which accrued to Ethiopia as a result of Italian and British colonial boundary demarcations.

At political independence in 1960, British and Italian Somaliland joined to form the united Republic of Somalia. Independence caused an outpouring of popular joy and enthusiasm and gave rise to a rich legacy of poetry and songs, some of which are available in translation (Johnson 1996, Kapteijns 1999). Like many other newly independent African states, however, the young Somali state had serious problems, ranging from economic dependence to political corruption. When the military intervened and proclaimed scientific socialism in 1969, the initial response of the Somali people was again enthusiastic and full of hope. However, the regime of the new military ruler, Siyaad Barre, with its divisive manipulation of clan loyalties and its suppression of generation after generation of resistance, proved disastrous. Nevertheless, as long as the Cold War raged, Western powers (including the United States and the European Community) kept bolstering Barre's power with both economic and military aid. When Barre was overthrown in January 1991, this legacy expressed itself in clannist bloodletting and a power struggle between a number of warlords, each with his own clan militia, many of whom had held power in the Barre regime (Samatar 1988, 1991, 1992; Lyons and Samatar 1995).

This novel is situated toward the end of the Barre regime, when power cuts and shortages of sugar, rice, gas, and other necessities were the order of the day; when inflation had made a joke out of the salaries of civil servants; when highly trained Somalis (like Abshir and, before he volunteers his services to his country, Bosaaso) often preferred to work and live abroad; when politically aware intellectuals who had remained behind were often depressed and drinking heavily (like Taariq at the beginning of the novel); when only the privileged, with access to "hard currency" (like Duniya, who received Abshir's remittances), still had ways to make ends meet or even to enjoy luxury; and when public law and order had begun to break down.

ABOUT THE AUTHOR

Nuruddin Farah was born in 1945 in what was then Italian Somalia and received his secondary education in Ethiopia and then in Mogadishu. After working briefly in the Somali Ministry of Education, he traveled to India, where he studied philosophy and literature at the University of the Punjab. After completing his studies in India, Farah returned to Somalia and taught at secondary schools in Mogadishu and then at the National University of Somalia for four years. From 1974 on, he has spent much of his life abroad, living, researching, and writing in Britain, Italy, the United States, Germany, Uganda, Sudan, South Africa, and Nigeria. Although all of his works are situated in Somalia, they have not been widely available in his own country, even before the chaos and destruction of the early 1990s.

Farah was already under the scrutiny of the military regime when he left Somalia in 1974, after publishing his first novel, *From a Crooked Rib*. Among his other works, Farah has published two trilogies. One, consisting of *Sweet and Sour Milk, Sardines,* and *Close Sesame*, had dictatorship as its major theme. The second trilogy, consisting of *Maps*, probably his most masterful and difficult novel, *Gifts,* and *Secrets,* appears to have a common thread in the theme of the orphan and the construction of identities—but the verdict of literary analysts is still being constructed. The search for individual and national identity and autonomy are powerful themes in all of Farah's work. As Ngugi wa Thiong'o expressed it in 1998, "Nuruddin Farah questions all the oppressive stabilities, whether rooted in the family, the clan, the nation, or in the supernatural claims of religion and political systems" (Ngugi 1998: 716). Women's emancipation is part of Farah's vision of freedom, and his feminist consciousness, so present in *Gifts,* has received much praise. Farah won the prestigious Neustadt prize for world literature in 1998. The Neustadt is sometimes considered a stepping stone to the Nobel prize. (See *World Literature Today* 1998.)

GIFTS IN THE CLASSROOM:
WRITING ASSIGNMENTS AND DISCUSSION THEMES

I use African novels in my classes mostly to generate discussion about contemporary Africa and about the historical roots of Africa's present. I usually spend only one class period on the discussion of the novel, but I ask the students to write one of two types of paper. One type is what I call a "reaction paper." A reaction paper, usually graded on a credit/noncredit basis, is a four-to-five-page paper in which students write about what they learned from the book, what moved them or struck them most, and what questions the book raised in their minds. Sometimes a reaction paper is organized around one or more quotations from the novel, but in any case, it is usually not a comprehensive book report. The second type of paper is a book report or book review; in this case, students are expected to write a more formal essay, which reports on the story line and major themes and articulates a personal evaluation of the novel as a conclusion.

The themes I have found worthwhile pursuing in *Gifts* are:

• The position of women; in particular how Duniya attempts to find autonomy without being forced to sacrifice family, male companionship, and other forms of community. What are explicit examples of Duniya's feminist thought?

• The issue of international development aid. Does it always create dependence? Are there alternatives? If so, what are they?

• How are gifts discussed and analyzed in this novel? Are there, according to this novel, any gifts that do not bind and subject?

• The role stories and storytelling play in this book. What themes are addressed through storytelling?

• Duniya's feminist principles and Somali customs. Duniya is neither representative nor unrepresentative of Somali womanhood. However, her feminist consciousness and her acceptance of individual freedom (in others as well as herself) are remarkable. Give examples of this (e.g., when her son speaks of homosexuality). Also, while Duniya articulates her principles throughout the novel, her mind and body register initial hesitation and discomfort (e.g., when she first sees her daughter smoke; when she hears her son is seeing an older woman; when she goes out with her hair uncovered for the first time since her first marriage; when she eats food that she does not know and prays that it will not be pork, and so forth). Describe some instances of this hesitation and discomfort that are very informative about Somali women's sense of conventional propriety.

• Mogadishu in the 1980s as a fascinating cultural mélange of old and new. What are some examples of this? (For example, people call their children Aaspro, Omo, and Layluun—a bastardization of nylon—but also believe that there are naughty spirits in their way when they stumble.)

• The obvious class privilege enjoyed by Duniya and her friends. What are some of the elements you notice? What are the limitations of this privilege?

• Whether the praise Nuruddin Farah has received for his feminist consciousness is justified. What can you say about Duniya's ambitions and horizon beyond her principled insistence on autonomy in personal relationships? Does the author show the limitations of his own feminist vision here, or is he true to the character in her particular context?

• The effectiveness of Nuruddin Farah as teacher. Although this book's audience does not exclude Somalis, his writing makes Somali culture accessible to non-Somali and non-Muslim readers. Give examples of such didactic passages on Somali and Islamic culture.

SUGGESTIONS FOR
FURTHER READING AND RESOURCES

Alden, Patricia, and Louis Tremaine. 1998. "Reinventing Family in the Second Trilogy of Nuruddin Farah," *World Literature Today* 72, 4: 759–766.

Farah, Nuruddin. 1970. *From a Crooked Rib*. Portsmouth, N.H.: Heinemann.

———. 1980. *Sweet and Sour Milk*. Portsmouth, N.H.: Heinemann.

———. 1982. *Sardines*. St. Paul, Minn.: Graywolf.

———. 1983. *Close Sesame*. London: Allison and Busby.

———. 1986. *Maps*. New York: Pantheon. Probably Farah's most masterful and difficult novel.

———. 1993. *Gifts*. London: Serif.

———. 1998. *Secrets*. New York: Arcade.

Johnson, J.W. 1996. *Heelloy, Heelleelloy: The Development of the Genre Heello in Modern Somali Poetry*. New edition. Bloomington: Indiana University Press.

Kapteijns, Lidwien. 1994. "Women and the Crisis of Communal Identity: The Cultural Construction of Gender in Somali History." In *The Somali Challenge*, ed. A. I. Samatar.

Kapteijns, Lidwien. 1999. *Women's Voices in a Man's World: Women and the Pastoral Tradition in Northern Somali Orature, c. 1899–1980*. Portsmouth, N.H.: Heinemann.

Lyons, Terrence, and Ahmed I. Samatar. 1995. *Somalia: State Collapse, Multilateral Intervention, and Strategies for Political Reconstruction*. Washington: Brookings Institution, 1995.

Ngugi wa Thiong'o. 1998. "Nuruddin Farah: A Statement of Nomination," *World Literature Today* 72, 4: 716.

Samatar, Abdi. 1992. "Destruction of State and Society: Beyond the Tribal Convention," *Journal of Modern African Studies* 30, 4 (1992): 625–641.

Samatar, A., and A. I. Samatar. 1987. "The Material Roots of the Suspended African State: Arguments from Somalia," *Journal of Modern African Studies* 25, 4: 669–690.

Samatar, Ahmed I. 1988. *Socialist Somalia: Rhetoric and Reality*. London: Zed Books.

Samatar, Ahmed I., ed. 1994. *The Somali Challenge: From Catastrophe to Renewal?* Boulder: Lynne Rienner.

Samatar, Said S. 1991. *Somalia: A Nation in Turmoil*. A Minority Rights Report. London: Minority Rights Group.

World Literature Today. 1998. Special Issue: *Focus on Nuruddin Farah: The 1998 Neustadt Prize*, 72, 4.

Wright, Derek. 1994. *The Novels of Nuruddin Farah*. Bayreuth: Bayreuth University.

13

Elsa Joubert's *Poppie Nongena*

Jeanne Penvenne

I BECAME INTERESTED IN THE HISTORY OF AFRICAN PEO-
ples through the characters and stories of the continent's writers.
African writers continue to draw me into new areas of the continent,
rekindle my curiosity, and challenge me to rethink my interpretations. I combine literature, music, and visual texts with scholarly
essays in my history classes because they so enrich the classroom.
Furthermore, to the extent that they draw out the experience of ordinary women, men, and youth, such texts compensate to some extent
for the elitism and androcentricity that, despite some marked
improvement, still characterize much of the historical literature.
Novels and short stories bring students much closer to the populations discussed in the scholarly essays and, in combination with
African faces, voices, and landscapes carried on video- and audio-
tape, help them grasp conditions and relationships that may be otherwise quite unfamiliar.

I often tell my students that our first task is to reformat their
disks so that they can more easily receive and interpret information about Africa. Not only are Africa and things African generally unfamiliar to North American students, most come to the
classroom heavily burdened with deeply embedded misinforma-
tion. If African texts, African authors, and the sights and sounds
of Africa are brought into the classroom, students engage them
directly and very often experience and enjoy their power and
authority. Obviously some texts are more accessible to students

Elsa Joubert, *Poppie Nongena* (New York: W.W. Norton, 1985).

153

than others. I try to introduce several texts that require students to reach.

Within the ever-growing and changing repertory of literature and film I use to teach history, Elsa Joubert's *Poppie Nongena* has become a staple favorite. I like to teach it, and it is very popular with my students, although for reasons I explore in this chapter, it may resonate more with women than with men. Many women have told me that they bought copies to give to friends. Bill Freund mentioned one of the earliest English translations of *Poppie Nongena* in 1984, when he noted: "Elsa Joubert's *Poppie* . . . powerfully expresses the impact of labour control / Bantustan policy on the lives of black working-class women in particular" (Freund 1984: 337). He was right on the mark. *Poppie Nongena* is a fine vehicle for pedagogy at several levels: it raises issues of authorship, form, and history and memory; power and agency; gender, day-to-day choices; and the insidious ability of the apartheid system to encourage self-oppression.

I regularly assign *Poppie Nongena* in two courses: an introductory course on southern African history from the late nineteenth century to the present, and a colloquium entitled "Seeking Gendered Perspectives." The first course usually enrolls between fifty and seventy-five students. Although a slim majority of students who take the course are international relations or history majors, the course draws students from all majors and classes, in part because it fulfills the university's world civilization requirement. The southern Africa course is designed to introduce major historical themes and relationships of the twentieth century through case studies in the southern African region

The second course is a high-demand course, specifically limited to fifteen students. Despite efforts to target sophomores in our colloquia courses, the class is often top-heavy with seniors who must take a colloquium to complete their history major. When I first taught the colloquium, my challenge to students was to read African history exclusively through women's texts. I now include several explicitly male texts, but the course retains its emphasis on women. The colloquium is intended to introduce beginning history majors or potential majors to historiography, methodology, and theory. In each class *Poppie Nongena* helped students understand how historical experience is recorded, ordered, interpreted, and filtered; how historical agency is gendered and shaped by life cycle and shifting hegemonies; and, most important, how major eras and historical phenomenona shape and are shaped by ordinary people.

FORM AND PLOT

The work was first published in 1978 in Afrikaans. The W. W. Norton edition published in 1985 with the title *Poppie Nongena* is the edition I use and shall refer to in this essay.

Poppie Nongena is the pseudonym of a black South African woman, Ntombizodumo, "girl born from a line of great women" (p. 13). Poppie is her nickname, from Poppietjie (little doll), an endearment coined by her grandmother, Hannie, who raised her. Poppie conveyed her life story to another South African woman, a white woman named Elsa Joubert. Joubert, a professional writer, collaborated closely with the woman they together decide to call Poppie Nongena. Joubert experimented with several strategies to convey Poppie Nongena's life story effectively and truthfully. What emerges is a true story written as a novel, not a personal narrative or autobiography. Joubert intended her novel to be true to Poppie Nongena's original narrative in idiom and key (Schalkwyk 1989: 255). The idiom is Afrikaans and Xhosa, and the reader is easily and quickly swept into the company of Poppie's *oompies* and *ouma*, her uncles and grandmother, and the languages of the many peoples of Poppie's world. Sometimes Joubert defines terms in the course of the narrative, and the U.S. edition has a glossary (pp. 357–359), but often an Afrikaans or Xhosa word's meaning quickly becomes evident in the context of the conversation. To some extent Joubert's approach to language or "idiom" is similar to that developed by Theodore Rosegarten in the classic book, *All God's Dangers: The Life of Nate Shaw*. Rosegarten argues that he "compiled" the biography of U.S. sharecropper Ned Cobb, under the pseudonym Nate Shaw. His goal was loyalty to Cobb's language and interpretations, but he reworked the many hours of conversations to achieve a chronological narrative. Authorship issues remain important in both works.

Poppie Nongena conveys the life of an ordinary South African woman born in the eastern Cape in the late 1930s. Through the combination of an anonymous third-person narrator and Poppie Nongena speaking in the first person, readers follow Poppie and her family through forty years' experience: her childhood memories of early life in Upington and Lamberts Bay in the Northern and Western Cape, her schooling (cut short by the need to care for her mother's youngest children), her first paid job at age thirteen in the Lambert's Bay fish packing factories, her playful adolescence, her arranged marriage, and her efforts and those of her husband to keep their family together and to raise and educate their children under the changing conditions of apartheid South Africa. The incremental constraints that progressively narrow the family's possible choices; the difficulties, demands, tensions, and loving support of large intergenerational families; and the life cycle expectations of men and women emerge episode by episode in this story.

Poppie Nongena is a poor woman with very limited formal education, who consequently has limited opportunities and few options. Urban influx controls, popular dispossession, and exile to the remote "homelands" as part of the implementation of apartheid in the 1950s and 1960s increasingly intrude upon her daily life. The overlay of the Christian, Xhosa patrilineal, and apartheid expectations make conflicting claims on Poppie Nongena's life and identity after her marriage to Stone Mqwati, a Xhosa speaker and migrant to the Cape. Although Poppie's grandmother spoke Xhosa and Afrikaans, and scolded her grandchildren for speaking Afrikaans at the expense of their knowledge of Xhosa, Poppie and her brothers were raised speaking Afrikaans in Blikkiesdorp location in Upington in the northwestern Cape. As township children, they were as unfamiliar with Xhosa language as they were with Xhosa culture. Indeed, tensions between Poppie, her extended urban family, and her rural in-laws figure centrally in the narrative framed by the challenges of raising and educating the extended family—siblings, children, and grandchildren. For example, Poppie is torn between satisfying her husband's desire to send their daughter to care for his aging parents in their rural home and allowing her to stay in town and attend school, knowing she will probably have less schooling than her brothers in either case.

Apartheid policies, such as Cape area hiring preferences for people considered "coloured" by apartheid eugenics, complicate the family's ability to live and work. In order to remain in Cape Town with her family, for example, Poppie Nongena runs a chronic battle to retain a valid residence and work pass. She eventually relents in her struggle to resist the apartheid policy that assigns her and the children to their supposed Xhosa "homeland," the Ciskei. There, isolated from family and friends, and uncomfortable with Xhosa language, custom, and ritual, their son Bonsile completes his initiation ritual, and all their children are assigned to schools. Poppie eventually forges a new support network among the local Christian community in the Ciskei, but she, Stone, and the children all experience the strain of separation and its resultant isolation.

Stone, who was never robust, becomes increasingly ill and eventually dies in Cape Town. Without Stone's limited financial contribution, Poppie finds it increasingly difficult to support her family. She returns to the townships outside Cape Town to find work, leaving her older children in schools in the Ciskei. When the black townships throughout South Africa erupt into the consuming violence of the "children's war" of the late 1970s, Poppie experiences the uprising as a middle-aged mother and grandmother. She soon realizes that she cannot protect her children from the violence and uncertainty that engulfs South Africa. Indeed, throughout the book Poppie wrestles with the limits of her agency: "When one trouble is solved, the next one is on its heels. . . . But you can't sit and wait for the day you die, it's now you have to do what you think best" (p. 343). She does what she must, sometimes with resignation: "If it must be so, then it is well" (p. 268) and more often takes comfort in the will of the Lord: "If the Lord wants you to go, you will go; if the Lord wants you to stay, you will stay" (pp. 244, 355). The story thus begins with a girl's happy youth in a socially secure if impoverished extended family and ends with a parent's heartbreak, fear, and grief in the midst of social upheaval and family dissolution.

Although Poppie is the central figure, she is a woman amidst family members. Through her we are introduced to the extended family. The textures of familyhood are deftly wrought in this book. Tensions between sisters and their brother's wife or girlfriend; tensions between a politically active youth, his fearful and somewhat bumbling uncle, and hapless, ill father around whether or not to show up at a rally or to honor a boycott; the complexity and tenderness of living with alcohol abuse and abusive alcoholics emerge in simple but compelling detail. The mundane becomes both convincing and penetrating. Character portraits and development are as important to this book as the sequence of events.

ANALYSIS AND PEDAGOGY

In both courses the book is introduced in the second third of the course, when students are already familiar with the geography, ecology, and peoples of the southern African region. Important theoretical debates and methodological issues have been introduced, but are then specifically reintroduced in conjunction with the case study readings. The formation, mechanisms, implementation, and reproduction of apartheid's core components are central to the introductory survey. Revealing and interpreting the strategies and options ordinary men and women develop to secure and promote their sometimes contrasting interests is a major theme in the colloquium. I shall discuss the colloquium first and then turn to a more detailed consideration of the survey course.

Students in the colloquium read a series of core texts written by and/or about women. These include scholarly essays, autobiographies, personal narratives, prison diaries, memoirs, and novels. The core texts are read in conjunction with critical essays that address specific theoretical and methodological problems. For example, Poppie Nongena might be combined as a core text with Emma Mashinini's *Strikes Have Followed Me All My Life*, Tsitsi Dangarembga's *Nervous Conditions* (see Chapter 8), Ruth First's *117 Days*, Phyllis Ntantala's *A Life's Mosaic*, and essays from Cherryl Walker's *Women in Southern Africa*. In conjunction students read Sondra Hale's 1998 essay on women and gender in Africa; Personal Narratives Groups' *Interpreting Women's Lives;* and a range of theoretical and overview essays from journals and edited collections such as Rosalyn Terborg-Penn and Andrea Benton Rushing's *Women in Africa and the African Diaspora* and Margaret Jean Hay and Sharon Stichter's *African Women South of the Sahara*.

Poppie Nongena implicitly and explicitly suggests many important questions and issues, but in my experience students are most intrigued with the questions of methodology and authorship. Poppie Nongena's "voice" reaches students through a series of filters: a pseudonym, an author/interpreter, and translations through at least two languages. How do those filters shape and change Poppie's words and their meaning? To what extent is the published book *Poppie Nongena* really "Poppie's" story? To what extent is it Elsa Joubert's? Can a privileged, educated white South African women serve as a vehicle for the voice of a poor black South African woman with very limited formal education? Was "close collaboration" between two such parties possible in the period this work was accomplished, and (assuming it was) what did it mean? Several scholarly essays specifically address these questions. I assign those as required readings for the colloquium course. Those issues are raised in less detail in the survey course, but the critical essays make fine recommended readings. Alternatively they can be developed as part of a historical essay written as an option in lieu of the in-class hour exams.

In the southern Africa survey course *Poppie Nongena* provides an excellent companion piece for two specific sets of readings and films, the first focusing on leadership and the second on public policy for social change. The leadership unit includes Steve Biko's collected essays, *I Write What I Like*, and two documentary films, *You Have Struck a Rock* and *Generations of Resistance*. The films, produced in 1981 and 1980 respectively, address the period from the late nineteenth century through the "Children's War" of the late 1970s. Both emphasize the period of widespread political confrontation in the decade from the mid-1950s to the mid-1960s.

Generations emphasizes male leadership, particularly within the African National Congress, and *Struck a Rock* focuses on women in political, labor, and community leadership roles, in particular the Federation of South African Women and the Women's March on Pretoria in 1956. This set of texts features women like Lillian Ngoyi, Frances Baard, and Helen Joseph, and men like Nelson Mandela, Robert Sobukwe, and Steven Biko, all of whom served prison time, house arrest, and "banning" for their political struggles. Biko clearly paid with his life. The use of these films with *Poppie Nongena* explicitly juxtaposes the costs of confrontation and the costs of accommodation. Life in the apartheid era was a costly and contested affair for black South Africans regardless of the strategy elected.

I Write What I Like includes a brief biographical essay, so students can compare the details and perspectives of two South Africans, a strongly political man and a seemingly apolitical woman, and the range of political postures revealed by Poppie's male relatives. Biko argued that if people did not purposely confront apartheid, it could reproduce its oppressive impact almost on automatic pilot. Black South Africans were self-policing agents of their own oppression through their compliance with the outrageously unjust apartheid laws and relationships. Poppie might be "Exhibit A" in Biko's case, but she also provides a window into the challenges and costs of resistance and compliance. Biko, Ngoyi, and the rest suffer imprisonment and even death for their political commitment. Poppie's brother narrowly escapes being beaten to death during a labor action. Hundreds of black South Africans, regardless of their political commitment, died simply because they were poor and lived in communities that exploded in violence as part of apartheid's horrific toll. Poppie's neighbors include the innocent as well as the enemy, but both die in the township violence.

The second set of texts analyzes South Africa's socioeconomic and political dilemmas and grapples with policy development to effect social change. It includes Mamphela Ramphele and Francis Wilson's *Uprooting Poverty* and Omar Badsha's *South Africa: The*

Cordoned Heart, a collection of photographs and essays. Both books were completed in collaboration with the Carnegie Study of Poverty in Southern Africa, and they are indeed complementary.

The photographic collection highlights sets of images: apartheid commuters between Pretoria and the Kwandebele "closer settlements," squatters at Crossroads, drunks at a flop house, residents of migrant worker hostels. The latter photographs convey powerful prints of pervasive, grinding poverty. The photographs, like *Poppie Nongena*'s written text, convey the dignity of the poor embedded in their exhausting and harrowing plight. Wilson and Ramphele's measured discussion of South Africa's essential cultural, structural, and endemic problems and conflicts, and their basic outline of key measures that South Africa must consider in order to begin to move toward socioeconomic and political equality, are complemented and enriched by the photographs. Students who have read *Poppie Nongena* prior to reading Ramphele and Wilson get much more from the text because Poppie's broad range of family and life experiences resonates so clearly with the sets of issues raised by the two scholars. Poppie and Stone's specific experience with Coloured privilege in the Eastern Cape, for example, lends insight into apartheid-engineered tensions and into the "creation" and reinforcement of "tribal" identities.

SPECIAL ISSUES

Gender, family bonds, faith, and political activism emerge strongly in student discussions around *Poppie Nongena*. The reader experiences much of the narrative from Poppie's perspective, and to a large extent it is a woman-centered narrative—the women in Poppie's extended family, her friends from church, the women with whom and for whom she works. Any temptation to essentialize South African black womanhood in the person of Poppie is blunted, however, by the many contrasting portraits and personalities of women in her family, church, and community. Furthermore, by following Poppie from childhood to middle age, and from her own extended family to that of her in-laws, the story helps students gain insight into the kinds of power women exert over other women and the extent to which gender subordination is shaped by age, life cycle, and family placement.

One never gets a very strong sense of Stone Mqwati, but

Poppie's brother Jakkie, for example, develops as a strong male character. Her uncles, whom she dearly loves, occasionally emerge as totally irresponsible and violent. They cause her endless expense, headache, and heartache, but she loves them no less. The narrative introduces contrasting and contending concerns from both men and women. On the whole men emerge as more politically focused than women. The Black Sash, a group founded and run by white South African women, used white privilege within the apartheid system to stem or at least to blunt the abuse of black women, but it did not directly challenge the system. The frustrations, if not the utter futility of their tactics and the particular vulnerabilities of African women emerge when Poppie seeks Black Sash assistance to renew her pass in order to remain as a family in the Cape: "but those people couldn't do nothing for me because my husband did not qualify for the Cape, that's why I had to go away. So they said to me I must tell my husband he mustn't leave that job before he's worked ten years in the Cape. That's the only chance for me" (pp. 162–163).

Such examples clarify the gendered impact of apartheid paternalism. The book also reveals the privileges young males expect and receive from older people and most women. The narrative juxtaposes Poppie's revulsion and confusion in the face of township violence in the late 1970s with the explicitly politicized views and actions of her brothers and son. Students discuss why this might be the case. Young males enjoy a certain license to take costly risks, because they have learned that their elders and womenfolk will pick up after them and hold the fort. An ordinary woman whose politics land her in jail does not expect her family simply to pick up her workload and care for her children without raising an eyebrow.

Students immediately notice Poppie's explicit statements of despair and fear of confrontation, but through discussion they come to appreciate not only the courage and persistence of her actions (regardless of her words) but also the difference between her attitude toward activism and those of the other actors. Poppie Nongena looks to a strong Christian faith to reinforce her energy and focus, to ensure that her will does not flag. She needs energy and focus to consistently negotiate and mediate the burdens that the pass system and her poverty place upon her ability to make a life and a livelihood. The multiple and diffuse techniques developed by the majority of ordinary black South African women to promote and defend their self-interests are often devalued by privileged youthful students. Although students initially perceive Poppie Nongena as an apathetic, apolitical character, eventually they come to appreciate the courage and strength necessary to sustain day-to-day resistance. For some students, Poppie Nongena's faith and prayer are as foreign as her poverty. Ethnic tensions and name calling among black South Africans also provide an opportunity to unpack any unrealistic or romantic notions of black solidarity, just as the tensions among the many women characters provide some perspective on solidarity among women. As with all fine texts, this one leaves students asking more sophisticated questions and complicates as many issues as it clarifies.

CONCLUSION

Apartheid sits like the two-thousand-pound gorilla in the middle of any southern African history class. Although most students appreciate the particularly cruel and ingenious forms of oppression embedded in apartheid, the extraordinarily privileged young people who generally occupy North American college classrooms typically wonder why anyone would put up with that level of oppression. They ask again and again: "Why did people put up with those conditions? Why didn't they resist?"

These are only slightly more naive versions of the questions I asked as a graduate student doing field research a generation ago. I can still recall the patient smiles of old Mozambican men who had agreed to introduce this hopelessly dim young foreigner to reality as experienced by ordinary black folks in colonial Mozambique. Eventually I came to know Mozambicans as people with first and last names, personalities, families, jobs, and strategies for making ends meet. When I reached that point, of course, my questions changed. Instead of asking "Why didn't you resist?" I asked, "Why would you risk your life, your health, your family, and your very limited property to challenge a colonial official, an employer, or a settler, who—like most whites in a colonial setting—would have his own way in the end anyway? What was worth that?"

People, whether real or fictive, are both the hook that draws students to ask the deeper questions and the glue that holds their interest long enough to wrestle through the multiple complexities of historical relationships. Students get to know Poppie Nongena, her family, her personality, her jobs, and her goals for herself and her children. Because they come to know her, through her words, her attitudes, her decisions, and her actions, to some extent she becomes their window into South Africa. The textbooks, films, short stories, and scholarly articles obviously introduce them to some of the more famous and generally more privileged black South Africans of the twentieth century. Poppie's experiences and attitudes help students appreciate the many peoples of South Africa and to understand the subtle and persistent mechanisms of apartheid. They begin, perhaps most important for many privileged students, to see the daily assaults on people's dignity and personhood, to appreciate how very hard poor people work, and how much courage and stamina it takes simply to persevere from one day to the next. That is a lot to ask from a single book. In my experience *Poppie Nongena* delivers all that and more.

POPPIE NONGENA DISCUSSION MEMO

Poppie Nongena is a "true story" of daily struggles of race, class, and power in South Africa. Poppie is poor, black, and female. In many ways her daily struggles are overwhelmingly difficult, but her humble, simple daily endeavors are also cumulatively powerful, and for long periods of time they are also effective.

Characters and Terms

Upington (Blikkiesdorp location)	Cape Town
Lambert's Bay	Ouma (Duma) Hannie
Ciskei	Oompie Sam
Oompie Pengi	Lena
Grootma	Abakwetha
Buti	Ntombizoduma (Poppietjie,
Skollies	Poppie, Rachel, Regina)
Machine Matiti	Oompie Japie
"It's the law."	Tataka Bonsile (Stone Nongena)
Tip material	Mdantsane
Nombula	Fezi
Kindjie	Bonsile
Thandi	Mosi
Wilson	Comrades
Doring Baai	

Issues

We are mainly concerned with two key sets of questions. The first set considers "Poppie's story" itself and what it tells us about race, class, and power in twentieth-century South Africa:

1. What are Poppie's main concerns? What are her goals?
2. What is the value of this book as a source for South African history?
3. Poppie begins with her recollection of girlhood. She eventually assumes the perspective of a youth and then a parent. By the time she introduces us to the "Revolt of the Children" (p. 313), she has adopted a parent-centered view. What was the "Revolt of the Children"? How has childhood changed for black South Africans in Poppie's lifetime?
4. Contrast Poppie's children's view of the "Revolt of the Children" with her own.
5. What were the key components of Poppie's experience of poverty?
6. What are the occupations of the poorest of South Africa's poor?

The second set of questions considers the telling of "Poppie's story"—questions of authorship, methodology, interpretation, and perspective. Journalist Elsa Joubert recorded her extended conversations with the woman she calls Poppie Nongena, and after much experimentation with ways she might convey them to a larger audience, she decided to shape Poppie's words into a "novel-like" format—with the goal of remaining true to Poppie's "idiom" and perspective. The work was first published in 1978 in the Afrikaans language as *Die Swerfjare van Poppie Nongena*. Joubert subsequently translated it into English and published it in South Africa and the United Kingdom in 1980 as *The Long Journey of Poppie Nongena*. The version you read is the U.S. edition published in 1985 by W. W. Norton as part of a group of texts published around the report of the Second Carnegie Inquiry into Poverty in South Africa. The other two publications are also on reserve: Francis Wilson and Mampela Ramphele, *Uprooting Poverty*, and Omar Badsha, ed., *South Africa: A Cordoned Heart*.

1. What are the implications of a white Afrikaner woman conveying the "story" of a black Xhosa woman in apartheid-era South Africa?

2. What do we as historians "need to know" about Joubert's methodology in the production of the book *Poppie Nongena?*

SUGGESTIONS FOR
FURTHER READING AND RESOURCES

Badsha, Omar, ed. 1986. *South Africa: The Cordoned Heart.* Introduction and text by Francis Wilson. New York: W. W. Norton. A collection of photographs and essays. The photographs in this powerful collection combine perfectly with Poppie's narrative and Ramphele and Wilson's analysis, historical background, and policy statements. W. W. Norton published all three. They are as important today as they were in the late 1980s.

Biko, Steve. 1988. *I Write What I Like.* Selected and edited by Aelred Stubbs; introduction by N. Barney Pityana. London: Penguin.

Biko: Breaking the Silence. 1988. Producers: O. Maruma, E. Spicer, R. Wickstead, and M. Caplan. 52 minutes. Distributed through Southern Africa Video Library with Filmmakers Library.

Collins, Patricia Hill. 1998. "It's All in the Family: Intersections of Gender, Race, and Nation," *Hypatia* 13, 3: 62–82.

Coullie, Judith Lütge. 1997. "The Power to Name the Real: The Politics of Worker Testimony in South Africa," *Research in African Literatures* 28, 2: 132–144.

Dangarembga, Tsitsi. 1988. *Nervous Conditions.* Seattle: Seal. See Chapter 8 in this collection.

First, Ruth. 1988. *117 Days.* Forward by Albie Sachs; afterword by Tom Lodge. New York: Monthly Review.

Freund, Bill. 1984. *The Making of Contemporary Africa: The Development of African Society Since 1800.* Bloomington: Indiana University Press. A revised edition of Freund's text has recently been published by Lynne Rienner.

Generations of Resistance. 1980. Produced by the United Nations, directed by Peter Davis. 52 minutes. Distributed through California Newsreel's Southern Africa Media Center.

Hale, Sondra. 1998. "Some Thoughts on Women and Gender in Africa: Listening to the Whispers of African Women," *Journal of African Studies* 16, 1: 21–30.

Hay, Margaret Jean, and Sharon Stichter, eds. 1995. *African Women South of the Sahara,* 2nd ed. New York: Longman.

Joubert, Elsa. 1980. *The Long Journey of Poppie Nongena.* Johannesburg: Hodder and Stoughton. Originally published in 1978 as *Die Swerfjare van Poppie Nongena.*

———. 1985. *Poppie Nongena.* New York: W. W. Norton.

Mashinini, Emma. 1989. *Strikes Have Followed Me All My Life.* London: Women's Press.

Nfah-Abbenyi, Juliana Makuchi. 1997. *Gender in African Women's Writing: Identity, Sexuality, and Difference.* Bloomington: Indiana University

Press. I found Chapter 1—"Gender, Feminist Theory, and Post-colonial (Women's) Writing"—most useful.

Ntantala, Phyllis. 1992. *A Life's Mosaic*. Berkeley: University of California Press.

Personal Narratives Group. 1988. *Interpreting Women's Lives: Feminist Theory*. Bloomington: Indiana University Press.

Ramphele, Mamphela, and Francis Wilson. 1985. *Uprooting Poverty: The South African Challenge*. New York: W. W. Norton.

Rosengarten, Theodore, comp. [1974] 1989. *All God's Dangers: The Life of Nate Shaw*. New York: Vintage.

Sached Trust. 1985. *Working Women: A Portrait of South Africa's Black Women Workers*. Braamfontein: Ravan.

Schalkwyk, David. 1986. "The Flight from Politics: An Analysis of the South African Reception of *Poppie Nongena*," *Journal of Southern African Studies* 12, 2: 183–195.

———. 1989. "Domestic Struggle in *Poppie Nongena*." In *Women and Writing in South Africa: A Critical Anthology*, ed. Cherry Clayden. Marshalltown [South Africa]: Heinemann Southern Africa.

Terborg-Penn, Rosalyn, and Andrea Benton Rushing, eds. 1996. *Women in Africa and the African Diaspora: A Reader*. Washington, D.C.: Howard University Press.

Walker, Cherryl, ed. 1990. *Women and Gender in Southern Africa to 1945*. Oxford: James Currey.

You Have Struck a Rock. 1981. Film, produced by Deborah May with the United Nations, 28 minutes. Distributed through California Newsreel's Southern Africa Media Center.

14

J. Nozipo Maraire's
Zenzele: Letters to My Daughter

Karen R. Keim

SELECTED AS A *NEW YORK TIMES* NOTABLE BOOK OF THE
Year, J. Nozipo Maraire's debut novel *Zenzele* offers the reader a
highly accessible introduction to upper-middle-class life in
Zimbabwe. In the form of a letter from an African mother in Harare
to her undergraduate daughter at Harvard University, Maraire's text
portrays Africans as people whose lives are full of opportunity and
whose values can be appreciated, if not embraced: self-dignity based
on one's heritage, respect for family, the wise use of education, the
building of long-lasting relationships, and the promotion of global
and racial understanding.

Zenzele works well with American students, whether taught as a
single example of contemporary African literature or as one of several African novels. I have used it in an introductory undergraduate
course, The Experience of Literature, and in a midlevel special topics
course, Contemporary African Women's Writing, with as many as
thirty and as few as four students. The novel stimulated the best discussions when it was taught with other examples of African writing.

The structure of Maraire's novel does not rely on plot but on the
device of a letter, organized somewhat thematically into twelve chapters, in which the narrator Shiri shares her thoughts and stories.
While Zenzele, the recipient of the letter, is described as energetic,
intelligent, and able to define her own world, her part in the narration
is limited to providing prompts for Shiri's observations. The memories and perceptions of "Mai Zenzele" (Mother of Zenzele) serve as a

J. Nozipo Maraire, *Zenzele: Letters to My Daughter* (New York: Delta, 1996).

legacy for her daughter but also as a means of self-definition. The themes that emerge include the generation gap, the diverse roles of African women, dilemmas brought about by Westernization and racism, the richness of ancestors and traditions, the value of lasting love, the struggle for freedom, the need for a syncretic black-oriented religion, and the meaning of death.

Chapters 1 and 2 establish the relationship between the middle-aged narrator and her daughter, the one belonging to what Maraire terms a peri-independent generation and the other to a generation with seemingly unlimited opportunities. The mother has lived through colonialism and the struggle for freedom, whereas her daughter has experienced only the results of that struggle, such as material wealth, education, and Western ways of thinking. Mai Zenzele depicts how damaging wealth and Westernization can be by describing another urban family's problems. She believes, however, that old-fashioned values arising from contact with the village and the solidarity of the extended family have made a positive impact on her children. She is glad that she insisted on regular visits to the village and that, by implication, her daughter is a Harvard student and not an unwed mother.

In Chapter 3 the narrator recalls Zenzele's impatience with the extended African family and customs such as *lobola*, or brideprice. She tells a story about the visit of her husband's mother on the eve of their wedding, thereby eliciting respect for African women who have given their lives to caring for their husbands and children. The woman's aging body becomes a symbol of creating and sustaining life.

Chapters 4 and 5 focus on the dangers that might lure Zenzele away from her African environment and heritage. In a graphic and touching story, the narrator describes the behavior of a cousin, Byron Mukoma, who was sent to be educated in England but dropped out of medical school and became so British that he neglected his mother and forgot his mother tongue. Shiri wants Zenzele to be alert to the problem of "brain drain" and the pressures of Western ethnocentrism and racism. Chapter 6 continues the discussion of racism, using anecdotes from the narrator's travels to Warsaw and Geneva with her lawyer husband.

The next chapters of the novel offer positive role models and examples of right decision making. In Chapter 7 an African American sister joins the struggle for freedom in Africa. In Chapter 8 the narrator describes a sad love story that occurred prior to her meeting Zenzele's father, whom she knows to have been the better choice of husband. A lengthy Chapter 9 is devoted to the narrator's sister Linda and her cousin Tinawo, who were freedom fighters in the struggle for independence. Tinawo's account provides the greatest suspense in the novel, as it details risky intelligence activities carried out by a young nanny in the home of the chief of the Rhodesian air force.

Chapter 10 is devoted to Shiri's praise of Zenzele for her "special gift . . . of the third eye." Mai Zenzele sees in her daughter the revolutionary mind-set needed to "create the world that you wish to live in" (p. 174). This gift of vision is contrasted with the hopelessness of an abused African wife who continually returns to her husband. Unlike that woman, Zenzele has the ability to dream and to use those dreams to bring about a better life in Africa and in the world.

Chapters 11 and 12 are reflections on religion and death. Shiri is struggling with a cancerlike illness and realizes that she may not see her daughter again. The depiction of visits to the family graves is especially moving, as the narrator explores her belief in a continuity between life and afterlife based on commitment and love.

HISTORICAL CONTEXT

This novel reflects the lives of the members of a black elite urban family, who participate fully in the economic and social structures of their country as a result of Zimbabwe's hard-won independence. Historically, the land that is now Zimbabwe was claimed by white pioneers from South Africa in 1890. Africans were displaced and ruled first by the British South Africa Company as a British protectorate, then as the British colony of Southern Rhodesia with internal self-government from 1923 until 1964. After a Unilateral Declaration of Independence in 1965, the white-ruled Rhodesia was cut off from all outside affiliations and suffered sanctions imposed by Western countries and the United Nations. It soon declared a state of emergency, due to the increasing activity of African freedom fighters. The guerrilla war escalated in the 1970s (the setting for the wartime activities of Maraire's characters, sister Linda and cousin Tinawo). Zimbabwe eventually gained independence with majority rule by black Africans in 1980. Two black political parties with histories going back to the 1960s joined to form leadership for the new government: the Zimbabwe African National Union–Patriotic Front (ZANU–PF) and the Zimbabwe African People's Union (ZAPU), which had fought for socialist doctrine. Under President Robert Mugabe, however, independent Zimbabwe followed a policy of reconciliation between the former white rulers and the black majority, a policy that has resulted in a capitalist rather than a socialist society. Today most of the black population of Zimbabwe still lives in poverty, a situation that is not obvious in Maraire's novel, although the narrator's husband is explained to be an internationally known lawyer who has fought for the rights of the unemployed and the homeless.

Maraire's novel describes the lives of people who belong to the patrilineal Shona society, one of two major ethnic groups in Zimbabwe, the other being the Ndebele. Some qualities of the novel reflect traditions in Shona oral and written literature, such as its moral tone, storytelling, idealism, and the celebration of wartime feats. Maraire contributes a new literary perspective in that the heroes of her stories are women. (For further discussion of Zimbabwean literatures, see Chiwome 1998.)

The strong voice of women in *Zenzele* has some historical basis. Under colonialism African women in Rhodesia/Zimbabwe were both laborers and reproducers, whose multiple roles allowed them to exert influence in areas of society other than domestic. Although women had little access to education, a situation that has not changed significantly since independence, that did not prevent them from exerting political and economic leadership. Maraire's novel showcases the heroic actions and potential of women in characters like Linda, Tinawo, and Zenzele, to whom the narrator attributes the gift of the third eye.

J. Nozipo Maraire was born in 1966 in what is today Harare, Zimbabwe. Many of the stories in her novel are based on those told by family members who were engaged in the struggle against the British and the white elite of her country. However, her novel is not completely autobiographical. Her parents divorced when she was young, and she left Zimbabwe during the war to live in Canada, the United States, and Jamaica. In the late 1970s she returned to Zimbabwe, where she experienced the intense racism of the guerrilla war as a student in an all-white school. She went to Harvard University for undergraduate study at age eighteen, then completed training for neurosurgery at Columbia Medical School and Yale University. Maraire was a medical student when she wrote *Zenzele*, and had no intention of publishing it. She values the ideals expressed in her novel and would like to return to Zimbabwe to give something back to her people (see Wohl 1997).

HANDOUTS AND DISCUSSION THEMES

I teach two or three classes on this novel, introducing it with a handout on Zimbabwe's colonial history and some facts about the country, such as population and average life expectancy. I point out the usefulness of the glossary of terms at the front of the novel and ask students to consider some questions for journal writing and discussion, such as the following:

- What kind of person is the narrator? What class of society does she belong to, and what seem to be her values?
- In what form is the novel written, and how does that affect your reading or understanding of it?
- How does Maraire view the roles of women?
- What does the extended family mean to the narrator? Is there anything comparable in your own society?
- What problems are associated with assimilating another culture under colonialism?
- Explain the terms "brain drain" and "postcolonial dilemma." Should or can Westerners be involved in solutions to such problems?
- How is the African belief in ancestors different from North American views of life and death?
- How would you describe this novel to someone who has not read it?

The themes in *Zenzele* that are easy to teach are those that deal with life experiences related to love, death, and individuality. In class discussions, women students are especially interested in the narrator's views on the roles of women and on love and marriage. They appreciate the intimacy of the narrator as she recounts events on the eve of her wedding and later tells about her first love, which ended tragically before she met Zenzele's father. They also notice the narrator's unquestioning acceptance of her daughter and her multigenerational view of the African woman as having the faces of the village grandmother, the urban middle-class wife, and the international student. I ask them to focus on the prenuptial scene in Chapter 3 to draw attention to Maraire's emphasis on the wisdom of the elder and the symbolic beauty of aging, something that many young Americans rarely think about.

Many students notice the ways in which the narrator and her

people deal with death, including the likelihood that the narrator will die before she sees her daughter again. The funeral of the narrator's first love (Chapter 8) and scenes of the living talking to the dead at family graves (Chapter 12) provide an opportunity to discuss differences between African and Western views of life after death, such as the accessibility of ancestors. Maraire gives African views a modern twist with the narrator's belief that love may be what ultimately creates bonds between the living and the dead.

Students enjoy discussing the story of Byron Mukoma (Chapter 4), the errant son who was unable to heal his mother or speak with her on her deathbed. Some students have difficulty understanding the problem Byron presents and argue that Byron has a right to a better way of life in England. I focus on the implications of learning the colonial language and culture, as well as measuring success according to Western materialism. I also draw attention to the situation of the writer, who has used English to get her medical education and to publish a novel in the United States. I point out that her intention to stay connected to her roots may not be as much linguistically based (although she uses thirty Shona words or phrases in the novel), as it is kinship based. Students are also told that the writer—like Zenzele's mother—would rely on English in upper-middle-class Harare and would indeed have to make an effort to remain connected to her Shona heritage through family in the village.

Racism is a theme that most students want to talk about because of their surprise at the extreme behavior of the white Rhodesians, 1970s Americans, and contemporary Europeans depicted in the novel. The Rhodesian examples, such as the actions of Commander Pelleday, enable students to understand African commitment to the resistance and to preserving African identity. With the inclusion of heroes like Sister and Baba Africa, as well as Zimbabwean freedom fighters, Maraire suggests that the issue of freedom in Africa should be one of international dimensions and of concern to both men and women. I urge students to think about contemporary American attitudes toward Africans and people of African descent as part of the discussion.

Zenzele can be taught as a feminist novel that explores the sensitivity of a mother to her grown daughter, illustrates that women can bring about change, and celebrates the awareness of the female self in relation to family, history, and contemporary issues. The cosmopolitan views of the narrator are leavened with her disclosure of self, love of storytelling, and desire to share wisdom and values from a humble past. Students are drawn to her emphasis on family and human relationships.

If there is anything disconcerting to students about this novel, it is the almost flawless sincerity with which the narrator speaks of the innocence and goodwill attributed to her daughter and husband. One student wrote that *Zenzele* "was not a consistently believable reading experience." Questions like "Mama, what do you think it means to be an African woman?" struck this student as being "asked so that the answer can be eloquently entered into the text of the novel." Although some of the narrative may seem too good to be true, I point out that African societies are more formal than American society and that, culturally, Americans tend to expect a more troubled relationship between parent and child. I also emphasize that the narrator's life is one of privilege, regardless of her ideals and sentiments about the past. Shiri enjoys freedom from poverty and a socioeconomic status still not accessible to the black majority in Zimbabwe. This reality is missed by readers who focus on the similarities between the narrator's values and their own. Ultimately, *Zenzele* is a book about the importance of relationships in the context of Westernization and opportunity.

If *Zenzele* is taught with other novels from Zimbabwe, I recommend Shimmer Chinodya's *Harvest of Thorns* or Tsitsi Dangarembga's *Nervous Conditions*, novels that portray life during the years of resistance to white rule in Rhodesia. Chinodya's novel tells the story of a young man who joins the freedom fighters, whereas Dangarembga's novel follows a rural girl's struggle to gain access to education, and to understand the implications of becoming Westernized. In the course on African women's writing, I teach *Zenzele* immediately after *Nervous Conditions* and find that students are more alert to the implications of the two novels taken together (see *Nervous Conditions,* Chapter 8).

As part of teaching *Zenzele*, I find it useful to show a film (video) that helps students visualize life in Zimbabwe. In the past I have shown *Jit*, a 1990 comedy made in Harare to entertain a popular African audience. However, students are not easily engaged in the plot and characters of *Jit*, which has little thematic correspondence to the focus of *Zenzele*. Two films more appropriate for teaching *Zenzele* are *Neria* (1993) and *More Time* (1993). These films portray the educated middle class of Harare and address social issues important to women. *Neria*, directed by Godwin Mawuru, is based on a short story by Tsitsi Dangarembga that deals with the conflict between tradition and modern law regarding women's inheritance rights. *More Time*, directed by Isaac Mabhikwa, presents the problem of AIDS among teenagers of Harare by focusing on a young woman from a middle-class family. The acting is better in *More Time*, but *Neria* has features that make it especially relevant to *Zenzele* readers: it portrays three generations of women, takes the viewer on trips to the village, and shows an empowered woman finding justice in the court system of contemporary Zimbabwe.

SUGGESTIONS FOR
FURTHER READING AND RESOURCES

Chinodya, Shimmer. 1990. *Harvest of Thorns*. Portsmouth, N.H.: Heinemann. A portrait of life during the years of resistance to white rule in Rhodesia, Chinodya's novel tells the story of a young man who joins the freedom fighters.

Chiwome, Emmanuel Mudhiwa. 1998. "The Interface of Orality and Literacy in the Zimbabwean Novel," *Research in African Literatures* 29, 2: 1–22. Interesting for providing a broader discussion of Zimbabwean literature.

Dangarembga, Tsitsi. 1989. *Nervous Conditions*. Seattle: Seal. Dangarembga's novel follows a rural girl's struggle to gain access to education and to understand the implications of becoming Westernized in colonial Rhodesia. See Chapter 8 in this volume.

Gordon, Rosemary. 1994. "Education Policy and Gender in Zimbabwe." *Gender and Education* 6, 2: 131–139. Argues that since independence, black women have continued to be exploited by patriarchal governmental structures that restrict educational opportunities and promote gendered poverty.

Jit. 1990. A romantic comedy directed by Michael Raeburn and made in Harare to entertain a popular African audience. A village youth seeks his fortune in the city and manages against great odds to produce the brideprice and win the heart of a middle-class city girl. Afro-pop star Oliver Mtukudzi plays the protagonist's uncle.

Kahari, George P. 1993. "New Literatures in Zimbabwe: A Key-Note Address." In *Imagination and the Creative Impulse in the New Literatures in English*, ed. M.-T. Bindella and G. B. Davis. Amsterdam/Atlanta: Rodopi. Gives an overview of the growth of the contemporary novel in Shona, Ndebele, and English since the establishment of the Southern Rhodesia Literature Bureau in 1954.

Kriger, Norma J. 1992. *Zimbabwe's Guerrilla War: Peasant Voices*. African Studies Series. Cambridge/New York: Cambridge University Press. Examines the ZANU guerrilla war from the point of view of the rural population in a Shona-speaking area of Zimbabwe, based on extensive field research.

Maraire, J. Nozipo. 1996. *Zenzele: Letters to My Daughter.* New York: Delta. First published in the United States by Crown Publishers, now available in a Delta paperback.

More Time. 1993. A film directed by Isaac Mabhikwa, produced by Media Development Trust. This film presents the problem of AIDS among teenagers of Harare by focusing on a young woman from a middle-class family. See next entry.

Neria. 1993. A film directed by Godwin Mawuru, produced by Media Development Trust. Based on a short story by Tsitsi Dangarembga, *Neria* deals with the conflict between tradition and modern law regarding women's inheritance rights. Both *Neria* and *More Time* are award-winning films distributed by DSR, Inc. (phone 800-875-0037, x108).

Schmidt, Elizabeth. 1992. *Peasants, Traders, and Wives: Shona Women in the History of Zimbabwe, 1870–1939.* Portsmouth, N.H.: Heinemann. Demonstrates in a study based on archival research and oral interviews that, despite control of African women's sexuality under colonialism, Shona women were agents in creating new opportunities for themselves, bringing about social, economic, and political change.

Weiss, Ruth. 1994. *Zimbabwe and the New Elite.* London/New York: British Academic Press. Outlines the development of a new, equal, black and white elite as a result of independent Zimbabwe's policy of reconciliation with Rhodesia. Argues that the black majority continue to experience social and economic deprivation.

Wohl, Melissa E. 1997. "J. Nozipo Maraire." Web site: http://www. emory.edu/ENGLISH/ Bahri/Maraire.html (19 June 1999). This Emory University Web page includes bibliography and gives biographical information based on an e-mail interview with the writer.

15 ⌐‾‾‾‾

Meja Mwangi's
Going Down River Road

Charles Ambler

IN THE MID-1970s NAIROBI'S RIVER ROAD WAS A CROWD-
ed, peeling commercial street crammed with wholesalers, retailers,
tea rooms, and restaurants. A few blocks from the major thorough-
fare Government Road (now Moi Avenue), River Road represented a
boundary zone between the stores and offices of the modern and ster-
ile city center that lay to the south and the dense warren of bars,
hotels, storefront shops, petty manufacturers, country bus stations,
and decrepit flats to the north. Behind these crowded streets illegal
shantytowns multiplied along the Nairobi River—a continual challenge to authorities determined to torch them or plow them under.
Beyond the valley, Nairobi's burgeoning workforce lived in massive
housing estates and shantytowns. The figures who inhabit *Going
Down River Road* move through these zones daily: they sleep in the
housing estates or shantytowns, they drink and shop in the streets
near River Road, and they work in the offices and construction sites
of the city center. When Ben, the novel's main character, leaves the
block of flats where he lives, he follows "the general exodus toward
the city centre."

> The whole field was swarming with path-finders. . . . They walked
> slowly, quietly, their slow tortured boots kneading the mud and shit
> on the path. . . . In the city center two miles away the giant Africa
> Hotel dominated the grey skyline. Smoke, thick and black rose
> from the chimney above the twentieth floor. From this far the little
> stub of the rising Development House [where Ben worked as an

Meja Mwangi, *Going Down River Road* (Portsmouth, N.H.: Heinemann, 1976).

unskilled construction worker] looked rough and rugged in its
early life. (p. 6)

Going Down River Road works well in general courses on modern Africa because it can be read both as a gritty depiction of urban
life during the first decade of independence and as a document of its
time. The rapid expansion of secondary education in Kenya during
the 1960s and 1970s coupled with the growth of urban populations
had created a substantial and youthful reading public in the market
for books that spoke to their own experience—in the colloquial
English that Mwangi employs to great effect. In the streets that
crossed River Road, booksellers spread their odd assortments of
magazines and books on the pavement. Increasingly, local publishers
turned out racy and formulaic potboilers to feed the tastes of young
readers. In contrast to the conscientiously political and artistic work
of Ngugi wa Thiong'o, Meja Mwangi's novels (and especially *Going
Down River Road*) responded to this demand for action and sex. The
imprimatur of the African Writers Series made clear the author's tal-
ent and signaled the importance of the novel's themes, but high
school students and office clerks still circulated copies of the book
with corners turned down and passages marked. *Going Down River
Road* both documents and was the product of an urban popular culture sensibility that embraced sexual freedom, soul music, and kung
fu movies in ways that intrigue American college students. With
notable detachment, the novel recounts violence, extreme alcohol
and drug abuse, and passionate and (for Kenya at that time) graphic
sexuality. For what was probably a largely male readership, *Going
Down River Road* may well have reinforced stereotypes of avaricious
female duplicity, sexual infidelity, and arrogance. Yet it is doubtful
that these male readers could take much heart from Mwangi's portrayal of seemingly dissolute, spendthrift, and corrupt men.

Going Down River Road is a pessimistic work and, in that
regard, very much reflects its times. By 1976 a sense of decay and
decline had begun to undermine the optimism and confidence of the
immediate postindependence years in Kenya. Increasing numbers of
secondary-school leavers found themselves jobless, and even university graduates were by no means guaranteed satisfactory positions. In
the Nairobi bookshops and sidewalk bookstalls, copies of Walter
Rodney's *How Europe Underdeveloped Africa* and the Kenya
Council of Churches' volume *Who Controls Industry in Kenya?* testi-
fied to a persistent neocolonialism. Scholars turned decisively
toward the radical pessimism exemplified by Rodney's work, docu-

menting the historical development of underdevelopment and dependency. Yet in marked contrast to Ngugi's *Petals of Blood*, which was published about the same time, *Going Down River Road* makes no explicit attack on the forces of international capital. The perspective is street level. The situation is complex. Humans are frail. The novel thus works well in class as a complement to a lecture or reading assignment (for example, an article by Colin Leys) presenting the broad arguments regarding neocolonialism and underdevelopment. Writing assignments and discussion can then focus on identifying in the novel the ways the broad forces of change impact ordinary lives and how people resist those forces or attempt to profit from them.

Going Down River Road has the quality of a postcolonial novel and in that respect bears comparison to the more overtly political and philosophical *The Beautyful Ones Are Not Yet Born* (see Chapter 3 in this volume). Both of these books convey an almost tangible stench in the offhand yet vivid descriptions of rotting garbage, mold, and excrement that surround tales of corruption. The first pages of *Going Down River Road*, describing Ben's morning, portray a stinking shower room covered in slimy green mold and, on the long walk to the construction site, "paths . . . scattered with human excrement. One of these mounds of shit was still steaming in the middle of the path. . . . The cold wet wind that blew . . . carried, in the same medium with the smell of shit and urine, the occasional murmur, the rare expression of misery, uncertainty, and resignation" (p. 6).

In his choice of title, Meja Mwangi suggests comparison, as well, to Ezekiel Mphahlele's classic *Down Second Avenue*. Although *Going Down River Road* eschews the exuberance that the child's perspective gives *Down Second Avenue*, it is similar in the ways that it richly depicts the lives of ordinary urban women and men. In the absence of any significant body of scholarly or journalistic work that reconstructs the social history of Nairobi, *Going Down River Road* gives shape to the lives of ordinary people in ways that both convey the texture of day-to-day life and raise critical historical issues. *Going Down River Road* tracks the existence of Ben, a down-on-his-luck construction worker. He had once been an army officer but was kicked out when a plot he was involved in to steal military property was uncovered. He managed to find a good office job but was fired from that position when his enemies told his employers about his criminal past. On the day of his firing he wanders into a bar and meets up with Wini, a secretarial student and quasi-professional bar denizen.

The two find something above the ordinary in each other and connect. The facts of their lives are often absent or only vaguely sketched in, and much of the story surfaces in flashbacks. Neither seems to have any family, although Wini has a child, "Baby." By the time of the present in the novel, Wini has finished her course and found a good job; Ben is working as a menial laborer for an Asian-owned construction company on the site of a new office building in central Nairobi. With a taste for espresso coffee, museums, and restaurants, Ben is a cut above the typical construction worker. This situation provides Mwangi a neat but not always convincing narrative device: Ben is a character in the events that transpire, but he is also able to interpret and reflect on them. By delivering a steady supply of drugs and rotgut to the Indian foreman, Ben manages to edge his way up in the job hierarchy and allows himself to imagine a better life. But a pregnant Wini coldly abandons both Ben and her son and runs off with an executive; Ben and Baby are evicted from her flat and end up living with Ben's mate from work, Ocholla, in his squatter shack. The shack is razed by the police, but once they get it thrown back together, they are descended upon by Ocholla's two wives and children. Ocholla bends to the wishes of his wives, and Ben and Baby are once again left homeless. In a final drunken confrontation Ben denounces Ocholla: "You let women rule you," he charges. The bar no longer seems to offer an escape or respite from daily life; "this is not the Karara Centre that used to be. . . . There is nothing to sing about, nothing to laugh at, nothing to fight for and nothing to vomit. . . . They just sit like dead fish; hardly drunk, cold and lonely, each lost in his own dark small world. Bleak, contagious loneliness surrounds each." Ben chases after his friend and out in River Road shouts, "Wait for me; don't leave me here alone" (pp. 214–215). Ocholla first ignores him, then pauses to wait.

For the most part the plot is muted; basic facts are easily missed in the novel's concentration on quotidian events that surface irrationally along the axis of Ben's life: construction site, home, and bar. On the site of the future twenty-five-story Development House, Ben and his fellow workers jockey relentlessly to avoid the most unpleasant tasks, to extend rest periods, and to garner the small perks that the supervisor can distribute. It is rare in either fiction or scholarship to find such full descriptions of the workplace. Readers observe the confused disorder of the construction site, the nature of management control of workers, and especially the flavor of life for the workers themselves—how their interaction contains the long hours of drudg-

ery and how that interaction becomes in itself the basis for comrade-
ship, in this case between Ben and Ocholla. Here, the name of the
building represents an ironic counterpoint to the backward character
of industrial relations and industrial process. The tower gradually
materializes, floor by floor, as the result of work that seems as well
suited to the construction of a rural house as a skyscraper. All of this
is overseen by an incompetent and drug-addicted foreman, Yussuf,
an Indian who owes his position to family connections. African hos-
tility to the Asian presence in Kenya surfaces repeatedly in the relations between the "skilled" Indian workers and their unskilled
African counterparts. Although the Africans reserve an amused contempt for the individual Indians they work closely with, they are well
aware that the Asian-owned construction company that is building
Development House reserves the best jobs for Indians, using bribery
to obtain or renew work permits for Indian staff who are not Kenyan
citizens. In the end Ben obtains a minimal promotion only because
the company is being forced to show some progress toward
Africanization of management, while all the key positions remain in
the hands of expatriates. Such circumstances voiced eloquently the
anxieties of readers who faced increasingly tough obstacles in
obtaining good jobs, notwithstanding substantial education.

Mwangi also effectively draws attention to the huge disparity
between managers and the ordinary workers like Ben, who barely
manage to survive on meager salaries. Payday, what Mwangi calls
"the greatest day of the month," sets in motion a monthly cycle of
boom and bust (p. 164). At the beginning of the month, workers
avoid the cheap canteens that operate illegally adjacent to work sites
and splurge at chips shops for lunch. As the month wears on,
employees return to the canteens, establishing a credit relationship
that allows them to make it through the month. Negotiating lunch is a
continual theme of conversation in the workplace, and Mwangi
describes in vivid detail both the hunger pangs experienced by those
who by the end of the month can no longer afford three meals and
the gastrointestinal upsets of those who resort to unsanitary kiosks.
On payday the canteen owners are present to collect what they are
owed for lunches obtained on credit, preparing to renew the cycle for
another month. These petty traders are themselves revealed to be
pathetically vulnerable when a cholera scare leads the city to bull-
doze their makeshift establishments and put them out of business.
When one of these victimized canteen owners hysterically invades
the building site in the middle of the month, demanding money for

the lunches he had advanced on credit, the workers coolly dismiss this recently "powerful" man as an irritating lunatic. After all, who could possibly have money so long after payday?

Also present on payday are a scattering of wives. These women know that the workers, as they collect their money, are debating among themselves whether to go to the Eden or the New Garden or Majengo nightclubs. "Now begins the real trouble," in Ben's account. "Where will it be, the bars, movies, night clubs or the brothels? It's easier when one has five shillings; there is only one place to go, the Capricorn or Karara Centre [downscale bars]. But with fifty times that much money one is even expected to send some of it back home to one wife or wives. It gets to be blackmail. Send it before they decide to come fetch it themselves and find you with your Eden wives" (p. 164).

Ben and Wini are prototypical figures in an atomized future urban society. Each lives in a bare one-room flat with minimal services, seemingly cut off from family or friends. Wini is described as a devoted mother, but her small three- or four-year-old child is barely attended to. The stench of his urine-soaked bedclothes open the novel, and the news that he had drunk too much coffee. He lives a life of uncertain meals, of sexual encounters on the other side of the room, of strange men, and of long hours unsupervised either locked away or allowed to run wild in a dangerous and anonymous urban world—scarcely a romanticized African childhood. Just how dangerous is illustrated when Ben rescues Baby from the hoodlums who live next door, who have reduced Baby to a drugged stupor. We have already been introduced to this group as the noise of their radio and the screams of victimized girls disturb sleep. Now, when Ben finds Baby, he immediately pulls down the child's shorts to be sure he has not been sexually abused. Mwangi's urban vision, however true to the intellectual concerns of the time, demands some "correction" as an objective account. Notwithstanding rapid population expansion and persistent impoverishment, Nairobi's people have tenaciously maintained networks based in kinship and common origin through which connections to rural home areas have thrived.

Like everyone else, Ben and Wini are engaged in the monthly struggle for survival. They are in constant battle against the urban vices that surround them and the filth that pervades. Repeated cleaning can't contain the stench of Baby's bed or invasions of brazen cockroaches. The odors of excrement, urine, garbage, and vomit mix in showers, toilets, streets, eating establishments, and the workplace. It is a predictable surprise that Ben detects no odor when he enters the men's room at the white-run office where Wini had worked. On the job, Ocholla repeatedly philosophizes that "germs don't kill Africans." After all "if germs did kill Africans, Development House would never have got off the ground. What with all those green latrine flies swimming in the pot, shitting in the porridge and dying all over, even drowning in the tea. . . . Only hunger will kill an African—tough beast" (p. 38). If the residents of Mwangi's Nairobi escape outright starvation, cyclical hunger is their regular plight. Over and over, readers encounter the stiff porridge (*ugali* or *sima*) or gruel (*uji*) that sates appetites and *sukuma wiki* (literally, "to push the week"), the cheap greens from which bitter stews are made at the end of the month when there is no money left to buy the occasional bit of meat or better vegetables. Although Ben lives with Wini and Baby, a model family life is scarcely possible in their squalid living arrangements or when Wini continues to "go out" after work to pursue her trade on the boundaries between secretary and prostitute. Marginal as their lives are, much worse is possible. Whether at the hands of Asian employers or African landlords, ordinary working men like Ben are powerless against the forces of accumulation. A padlocked flat is retribution from a landlord, angry at tenants who failed to vote for him in recent elections and anxious to increase rents. Eviction sends Ben and Baby to Ocholla's shack in the squatter camp, only to be bulldozed out of their home by municipal fathers anxious to make the city healthy, safe, and attractive for the middle classes, expatriates, and tourists. Whether in South Africa or Nairobi, however, such "cleanup" campaigns are Sisyphean endeavors. Within hours the shacks are reconstructed and the drug dealers, beer brewers, and *chang'aa* distillers are back in business. Grim as their circumstances are, they are descended upon by Ocholla's two wives and numerous children, refugees from the even greater poverty of a drought-stricken countryside. If there is hope to be found in *Going Down River Road,* it is in the persistence of Ocholla's family. The typical Kenyan migrant urban dweller, with wives and children left behind and sometimes forgotten in his home area, still succumbs to the lure of family life when they turn up on his doorstep, a seduction that costs Ben his shelter and emphasizes again his individual isolation and vulnerability.

This second notice of eviction takes place in an alcoholic haze in the protective atmosphere of the working man's bar, the Karara Centre. Like so many accounts of modern urban Africa, *Going Down River Road* floats along on a river of booze, a reflection of the fact that drinking is the single most important "leisure" activity for a large proportion of male city dwellers. No author conveys the power of drink in urban culture or the rituals and practice of drinking better than Mwangi. There is a pleasure and joy in drinking, but there is also despair and violence. Drinking is an escape; it anesthetizes men plagued by poverty, hunger, and loneliness; it provides an opportunity for socializing and meeting women in a harsh urban environment. Drinking also forces into relief the powerful divisions in society. Mwangi describes the dreaming that gets workers through the day on the construction site: "Think of the day you will be rich and won't have to burrow in the mess of the low-incomed underprivileged. Think of heaven, think of a bottle of *Karara*, or of a full stomach and a woman. Discouraging thoughts, if you don't then have them, but by the time you get over the disappointment you will be on the next floor and going up" (p. 55). At night in the desolate city center, a theater marquee advertises a film "to keep you awake through the night," with pictures of nude white women, but men hurry by, "the price of a cinema ticket could be more realistically squandered on the more effective *Karara*" (p. 55). In papers or discussion, students might be asked to reflect on the meanings of "leisure" in a radically different culture and in the desperate circumstances of modern African cities.

Drinking, like everything else, adheres to a monthly cycle. On payday workers flock to the nightclubs and drink bottled Pilsner, but as the month stretches on, they return to the Karara Centre, where *Karara,* the mass-produced "traditional" grain brew, can be had for a fraction of the cost of European-type beers. Of course, people with well-paying jobs never turn up at the Karara Centre at all. When Ben gets fired from his office job, he repairs to his then-favorite hangout, the New Garden Hotel, the "liveliest joint in town," where young men and tourists come to meet available women (p. 13). In his description of Ben's first encounter with Wini, Mwangi portrays in detail the ambience of the New Garden and the complicated interaction between men and the semiprofessional party girls who frequent the establishment. Soon the wages of a construction worker banish Ben from the New Garden and confine him to bars like the Karara Centre. In numerous passages Mwangi evokes the sordid pleasures of the Karara Centre, where "distorted music, rowdy talk and the smell of beer, cigarettes and vomit spill out into the dimly lit street. . . . As usual there are a lot more people in Karara Centre than there will ever be anywhere. A crowd of ragged, emaciated low-income drinkers, pathetic and not giving a shit about it. . . . They are simply a lot of happy, drunk people . . . and no one pretends to be decently

drunk" (pp. 57–58). On one visit Ben finds himself at the bar with
James, a self-proclaimed "big man." James claims to have attended
Kenya's most prestigious secondary school and to have a good job
and a lot of money. As he downs the beers, he continues to assert his
wealth and status—claims that Ben refutes with a simple question,
"What the hell are you doing *here*?" (p. 105).

In the negotiations between men and women at the New Garden,
in a loud fistfight between a husband and wife at the Karara Centre,
and in desperate and drunken conversations between Ben and
Ocholla, Mwangi draws our attention to the shifting tensions and
conflicts between Nairobi's women and men. Women like Wini are
bitterly resentful of men: they are "bastards," "brutes," and "animals" who mislead and mistreat young women (pp. 4, 24, 26). But
for many men, Nairobi's new women are dangerous and threatening.
They are "bitches," "like animals," and "no good for anyone" (pp.
62, 208, 211). The relationship between Wini and Ben is instructive
and can serve as the beginning point for analysis of Mwangi's portrayal of gender definition and roles in a novel in which women
emerge less as fully realized characters than as individuals who prey
on men. Wini has the better job and picks up extra money in casual
liaisons; Ben lives in her flat and brings in a minimal salary, most of
which he throws away on drink. He assumes his right to visit bars as
he pleases, but is shocked when she walks out on him and her own
son. Yet Wini, of all the characters, seems to have the most promising future. Ocholla bemoans the burden that his wives and children
represent; but when they turn up on his doorstep, he lacks the will or
authority to resist their wishes. Yet if *Going Down River Road*
reveals bitter gender conflict and deeply held racial antipathy, it is
interesting that Mwangi avoids the ethnic labeling central to much
popular and political discourse in Kenya. Urban residence, employment, and political affiliation often strongly reflected rural roots or
ethnicity, but Mwangi is deliberately silent in what must have been a
conscious nationalist gesture. Certainly, this silence does not reflect
the intense sensitivity to "tribal" favoritism, and in particular to
Kikuyu favoritism, that characterized Jomo Kenyatta's Kenya in the
1970s. Ben and Wini appear to have no rural or kinship connections,
whereas Ocholla's remain undefined; Kenyan readers doubtless
made and make implicit ethnic assignments.

Going Down River Road is in some respects an intensely political novel. Certainly, the story flows from hard-won understandings
of the inequities that are intrinsic elements of capitalist development
in Kenya. But the expression of these politics is fragmented and

incomplete, in characteristic postcolonial fashion. Like many work places, the construction site has a political voice, Machore, and an audience or "congress" of workers on lunch break looking for entertainment. When Machore denounces the presence in Parliament of a man who collaborated with the colonial rulers during Mau Mau, listeners challenge his facts and his right to speak. "The truth of the labourers' conference is that no-one believes in it. Nobody takes Machore seriously. They only listen to him because it is the lunch break and there is nothing better to do" (p. 54). In the neighborhoods of River Road, there is no point to politics and no sense of possibility. The most one can hope for is to negotiate those small and incremental improvements that make life tolerable. But the future offers little hope. Ben was prepared to build a family, but Wini abandoned him. His small success on the job is the product of corruption, as was his fall from prosperity. At the end of the novel, Ben plans to dump Wini's son but cannot bring himself to break the attachment the boy feels for him. But if the Nairobi-born "Baby" is the hope of the future, that future is bleak. He despises and avoids school; running wild, terrorizing and raping Ocholla's children, he manages to get Ben and himself kicked out of their shack. Still, from the vantage point of twenty-five years later, a certain nostalgia colors Meja Mwangi's Nairobi. In the aftermath of the attempted coup in 1981, the corruption and violent political repression of the Moi regime coupled with the larger forces of structural adjustment have made Nairobi in many respects a nightmare city—where tens of thousands of homeless children roam streets that are alive with gangs of violent thugs who operate in the shadows of luxurious tourist hotels. Time has only accentuated the dire circumstances, vividly depicted in *Going Down River Road*, of the vast majority of an exploding population.

MWANGI'S LIFE AND WORK

Meja Mwangi was born in 1948 and grew up in central Kenya, in Kikuyuland, amid the Mau Mau rebellion and its brutal suppression. He is part of a second generation of Eastern African writers and is distinguished from most of them by the fact that he has pursued a career outside the academy. He did not even begin work toward an undergraduate degree until the 1990s. Following on the remarkable success of his first novels in the 1970s, Mwangi focused most of his attention on self-consciously "popular" writing, particularly thrillers. In addition, he began a career in film that involved him in script writing and production, notably in features filmed in Kenya. In the early 1980s he was involved in production of the movie *Bushtrackers*, which raised a furor in Kenya because of its graphic depiction of violence linked to poaching. Like other African writers, Mwangi has had to contend with the "African book famine"—the collapse of the market for books (whose price is now out of reach of most consumers) in Kenya and other African countries and the concomitant absence of opportunities for writers. Thus during the 1990s his publications have focused much more on works aimed at adoption for use in schools, and in particular children's literature.

I assign *Going Down River Road* in a general survey of modern African history, in which I typically require several novels, including notably Achebe's *Things Fall Apart*, Sembene's *God's Bits of Wood*, Dangarembga's *Nervous Conditions*, and Armah's *The Beautyful Ones Are Not Yet Born*. (There is a chapter devoted to each of these novels in the current collection.) The course is organized around a series of issues, arranged chronologically and explored in depth for a single region. No effort is made to achieve comprehensive coverage, and the textbook is optional. I typically place a variety of textbooks on reserve, but generally recommend Kevin Shillington's *History of Africa*. Lectures are used to provide the chronological thread and context and to cover certain subjects that I or the students regard as essential. The first part of the course concentrates on West Africa; the second on settler capitalism, resistance, and decolonization in Eastern Africa; the third explores the history of South Africa from the late nineteenth century and involves a student research project. The final, and briefer, section of the course explores contemporary issues, notably the crisis in central Africa, debates about "development" and aid, AIDS, and—picking up a theme I introduce at the beginning of the course—the interrelationship between Western ideas about Africa and relations between African countries and peoples and the Western countries. In connection with this last topic, there is a danger that a work like *Going Down River Road* will serve to reinforce American students' perceptions of the hopelessness and intractability of Africa's problems. But I have found that students are impressed more by the novel's portrayal of complex characters in many ways flawed but also creative and persistent in their determination to make the best of life. In addition to the novels, students read one or two monographs and a series of short pieces made available in photocopy form. Most recently I used Emmanuel Akyeampong's

Drink, Power, and Cultural Change and Tabitha Kanogo's *Squatters and the Roots of Mau Mau*. Akyeampong's book explores a range of issues related to alcohol use in Ghana that can be explored further in discussions based on the descriptions of drinking that are so prominent an element of *Going Down River Road*. Kanogo's study is the takeoff point for analysis of colonialism in Kenya and the Mau Mau rebellion. Kanogo explicitly extends her analysis into the postcolonial period, where the issues that she raises can be picked up in *Going Down River Road* and in a brief piece by Colin Leys that I assign in conjunction with it (see suggested readings). There are writing assignments for all readings, which in turn form the basis for class discussion. These assignments take the form of one- or two-page responses to provocative statements or questions. Generally, there will be two writing assignments for each monograph, but novels and shorter assignments are covered in one. The assignments change, of course (and sometimes I provide choice), but for *Going Down River Road* I might ask students to apply some of Akyeampong's ideas about alcohol use in Ghana to the descriptions of drinking practices described by Mwangi; or to consider the implications of urbanization and capitalism on "African life"; or to explain how (drawing on class lectures or a reading) the global processes of underdevelopment and dependency play out in the lives of ordinary people; I might also ask students to explore gender roles as they emerge in the novel. The papers are meant to be focused, with a clear point of view presented and backed up with specific references to the text. Discussion would elaborate on the topic chosen, but would also delve into Mwangi's depiction of everyday work and leisure lives. In my experience, questions such as, What are the conditions of work for ordinary residents of Nairobi? or, How do people spend their "leisure" hours? easily provoke extended interchange. Of course, almost all of my students have extensive knowledge of life in a "third world" urban area, Ciudad Juárez, Mexico, directly adjacent to the campus of the University of Texas at El Paso.

SUGGESTIONS FOR
FURTHER READING AND RESOURCES

Novels by Meja Mwangi

Mwangi, Meja. 1973. *Kill Me Quick*. Portsmouth, N.H.: Heinemann.
———. 1974. *Carcase for Hounds*. Portsmouth, N.H.: Heinemann.

―――. 1976. *Going Down River Road.* Portsmouth, N.H.: Heinemann.
―――. 1979. *The Cockroach Dance.* Nairobi: Longman Kenya.
―――. 1980. *The Bushtrackers.* Nairobi: Longman Kenya.
―――. 1987. *Bread of Sorrow.* Nairobi: Longman Kenya.
―――. 1989. *Weapon for Hunger.* Nairobi: Heinemann Kenya.
―――. 1990. *The Return of Shaka.* Nairobi: Heinemann Kenya.
―――. 1990. *Striving for the Wind.* Nairobi: Heinemann Kenya.

About Meja Mwangi

Gikandi, Simon. 1993. "Meja Mwangi." In *Twentieth-Century Caribbean and Black African Writers*, Second Series (Dictionary of Literary Biography, vol. 125), ed. Bernth Lindfors and Reinhard Sander.
Johansson, Lars. 1992. *In the Shadow of Neocolonialism: A Study of Meja Mwangi's Novels, 1973–1990.* Umeå, Sweden: Umeå Studies in the Humanities. Johansson's published dissertation includes both a detailed literary analysis of Mwangi's novels and a comprehensive bibliography.
Kurtz, J. Roger. 1997. "Meja Mwangi." In *African Writers*, vol. 2, ed. C. Brian Cox. New York: Charles Scribner's Sons.
Lindfors, Bernth, ed. 1980. *Mazungumzo: Interviews with East African Writers, Publishers, Editors, and Scholars.* Athens, Ohio: Ohio University Press. Includes an interview from the 1970s with Mwangi.
Otieno, Frederick. 1990. "Meja Mwangi Is a Merchant of Trash," *Sunday Nation*, 17 June: 14. Provides a hostile view of Mwangi's more recent work.

On Nairobi and Postcolonial Urbanization More Broadly

Akyeampong, Emmanuel. 1997. *Drink, Power, and Cultural Change: A Social History of Alcohol in Ghana, c. 1800 to Recent Times.* Portsmouth, N.H.: Heinemann.
Bujra, Janet. 1979. "Women Entrepreneurs of Early Nairobi," *Canadian Journal of African Studies* 9: 220–249. Information on women's lives in squatter communities in Mathare Valley, outside Nairobi.
Crush, Jonathan, and Charles Ambler, eds. 1993. *Liquor and Labor in Southern Africa.* Athens: Ohio University Press. In thematic terms, students might connect Mwangi's novel to studies on alcohol use, like this one.
Kanogo, Tabitha. 1987. *Squatters and the Roots of Mau Mau, 1905–1963.* Athens: Ohio University Press, and Oxford: James Currey.
Leys, Colin. 1975. *Underdevelopment in Kenya: The Political Economy of Neo-colonialism, 1964–1971.* Berkeley: University of California Press. Read together with Mwangi's novel, might give resonance to the scholarly debates about Kenyan political economy.
Martin, Phyllis P. 1995. *Leisure and Society in Colonial Brazzaville.* Cambridge: Cambridge University Press. In thematic terms, students

might connect Mwangi's novel to studies on work and leisure in colonial cities, like this one.

Miller, Norman, and Rodger Yeager. 1994. *Kenya: The Quest for Prosperity*, 2nd ed. Boulder, Colo.: Westview. A broad and useful introduction to history, society, and politics in contemporary Kenya.

Mphahlele, Ezekiel. 1971 [1959]. *Down Second Avenue*. New York: Anchor Books. A classic South African parallel to *Going Down River Road*.

National Christian Council of Kenya. 1968. *Who Controls Industry in Kenya?* Nairobi: East African Publishing House.

Nelson, Nici. 1979. "'Women Must Help Each Other': The Operation of Personal Networks Among Buzaa Brewers in Mathare Valley, Kenya." In *Women United, Women Divided*, ed. Patricia Caplan and Janet Bujra. Bloomington: Indiana University Press. Information on women's lives in squatter communities in Mathare Valley, outside Nairobi.

Robertson, Claire. 1998. *Trouble Showed the Way: Women, Men, and Trade in the Nairobi Area, 1890–1990*. Bloomington: Indiana University Press. Documents in great detail the historical experience of Nairobi's female petty traders.

Rodney, Walter. 1982. *How Europe Underdeveloped Africa*, rev. ed. Washington, D.C.: Howard University Press.

Shillington, Kevin. *History of Africa*, 2nd ed. New York: St. Martin's. One of the most accessible general history texts.

White, Luise. 1990. *The Comforts of Home: Prostitution in Colonial Nairobi*. Chicago: University of Chicago Press. Focusing on the changing social and economic experiences of prostitutes, this is the single best book on Nairobi's urban history.

16

Ngugi wa Thiong'o's
A Grain of Wheat

Margaret Jean Hay

A GRAIN OF WHEAT IS THE GREATEST HISTORICAL NOVEL
set in East Africa and is one of Ngugi's richest and most textured
works. Every time I read it, I find more to appreciate. The novel
focuses on the experiences of five friends, ordinary men and women
who come of age during the late 1940s and early 1950s, in the cru-
cible of that wide-ranging movement of anticolonial resistance and
civil war we call Mau Mau. With its focus on the Kikuyu (or Gikuyu)
rural areas, the novel provides a useful balance to most political histories of Kenya, which focus on the more formal organized politics
centered on Nairobi. Of Ngugi's novels, I find *Grain of Wheat* hits a
happy medium for my students—halfway between the limiting sim-
plicities of *Weep Not, Child* and *The River Between* and the much
longer, more complex plots of *Petals of Blood* and *Devil on the
Cross*. I also find it more useful as a portrayal of Mau Mau and the
late colonial period than Ngugi's more recent novels, which devote
greater attention to postcolonial Kenya and to the betrayal of the
people's struggle for independence.

Although the five principal characters all grew up in the village
of Thabai and were roughly the same age, they respond to the political crisis of the 1950s in quite different ways. Kihika, the self-educated revolutionary, flees to the forest and organizes guerrilla attacks
against British colonial infrastructure; he is eventually captured by
British forces and hanged. Gikonyo, the poor carpenter, is arrested
shortly after the declaration of emergency and spends six years in

Ngugi wa Thiong'o, *A Grain of Wheat* (Portsmouth, N.H.: Heinemann, 1968).

191

detention. Mumbi, "the most beautiful maiden in the valley," who marries Gikonyo, has romantic notions of her own heroism yet is apparently not involved in the struggle; she stays behind in the village with Gikonyo's mother and keeps their homestead intact. Karanja stuns his friends by joining the "loyalists," ultimately becoming the government-appointed chief of the area; his betrayal stems both from his assessment of British power and his desire to remain near Mumbi, whom he hopes to win for himself. The most problematic character is Mugo, a landless orphan who has grown up antisocial and paralyzed by insecurity; in spite of his desperate attempts to remain neutral and to stay out of trouble, he is jailed and tortured by the British and is ultimately executed by a secret Mau Mau court. (This critical aspect of the ending is often missed by students, who are probably racing through the last pages.)

Most of the action of *Grain of Wheat* takes place over the five days immediately preceding Kenya's independence ceremony in December 1963. Local representatives from the party invite Mugo to be the keynote speaker at the upcoming independence ceremonies. They view him with awe and respect because he withstood beatings in detention and never confessed to having taken the oath. They don't realize that he had never joined the movement, had never taken an oath, and so had nothing to confess. In fact, the great irony of the plot is that Mugo, lionized by the villagers for his courage, is in fact the man who betrayed Kihika to the British. In the end, Mugo summons his courage to admit that betrayal, a confession that will cost him his life.

An interesting aspect of the novel's range of characters is that neither white colonialists nor Kikuyu Loyalists are demonized. The Christian teacher who drives Kihika from the mission school when the boy dares to challenge the teacher's biblical interpretation of circumcision is in fact a Kikuyu, not a European. Even the shallow cruelty and racism of the principal white characters are offset to some degree by Ngugi's account of John Thompson's earlier idealism about the uplifting potential of British colonial rule. Reverend Jackson and Teacher Muniu were devout (if rigid) Kikuyu Christians killed for their faith, whereas the Western education originally brought by missionaries represents salvation for many, and Kihika's radical political philosophy is firmly based on his interpretation of the Bible.

A Grain of Wheat shows there is no socially recognized position of neutrality in a time of civil war. From the colonial perspective, any Kikuyu who are not "loyalists" (formally acknowledged British sympathizers) are presumed to be Mau Mau. From a community standpoint, those individual Kikuyu who fail to support the Land and Freedom Army or who refuse to take the oath are presumed to be loyalists. In this sense, it works very well to assign both *Grain of Wheat* and Ousmane Sembene's *God's Bits of Wood* (see Chapter 21), which the students read earlier in the semester. There are striking parallels between these two political novels—the importance of the railway line as a symbol of both colonialism and technological change is just one small example—and those interesting junctures really animate class discussions. In other ways the two novels are quite different. Whereas the Senegalese railway workers' strike is over in a matter of months and illustrates the potential strength of workers and peasants as a collective force, the political crisis in Kenya lasts for most of a decade and highlights individual frailty more than collective strength.

Ngugi's novel muddies the waters of resistance and collaboration to some extent and makes clear the high costs for everyone involved; courage and personal sacrifice for the greater good are prominent themes, but so is betrayal. At the highest levels, the self-interest and greed of the newly elected Kenyan government are a betrayal of those who fought and sacrificed for independence. In that sense, what should be a joyous celebration of national independence is muted by the villagers' awareness of that betrayal. Britain's ultimate decision to grant independence to her colony seems like betrayal to John Thompson, the British district officer whose zeal in persecuting presumed Mau Mau activists later becomes an official embarrassment. Mugo betrays Kihika to the British out of fear for his own safety. Karanja betrays his friends and comrades when he chooses the role of British collaborator; he in turn feels betrayed when he realizes Thompson, his boss, is returning to England without having even informed him. Gikonyo betrays the solidarity of Mau Mau detainees when he confesses the oath in order to be released from detention. And Mumbi herself betrays her vow of fidelity when she submits to Karanja's seduction immediately after she hears the stunning news of Gikonyo's release from detention. Even Ngugi's presumed hero, Kihika, suffers from some very human failings—very much like Bakayoko in *God's Bits of Wood*, his commitment to the struggle keeps him from close involvement with friends, family, or lovers, and he is off stage for most of the novel. The real hero, if there is one, is Mumbi, who shows compassion toward all and maintains a quiet dignity while she does whatever needs to be done. In fact, the names of Gikonyo and Mumbi, nearly identical to Gikuyu and Mumbi, the putative ancestors of all Kikuyu (like Adam and Eve) suggest they represent Everyman and Everywoman to some extent and that we should consider their experience as central.

Ultimately, however, Mugo's courageous confession is the final sacrifice needed to restore a sense of healing and reconnection, both personally and within the community. Gikonyo and Mumbi begin to open their hearts together and begin the process of reconciliation, although it is clear that the marital relationship is being renegotiated and that Mumbi will become an equal partner. The final chapter leaves us with the hope of rebirth, reflected in Gikonyo's determination to carve a beautiful stool for Mumbi that would include the images of a man, a pregnant woman, and a child, along with the agricultural symbols of a field, a hoe, and a bean flower.

NGUGI WA THIONG'O

Ngugi is the best-known and most prolific of East African writers. He has published six major novels as well as several plays, collections of short stories, and works of intellectual and political criticism. Several of his novels and plays have appeared in both English and Kikuyu, and he is a passionate advocate of the need for African writers to write and publish in indigenous languages. Ngugi is sometimes described as a political writer, and it is fascinating to see the development of his political philosophy and critique of Kenyan society in his writings over time. Many of his works involve themes of the shattering impact of colonial rule on Kikuyu society, the traumatic experiences of the Mau Mau resistance, the hopes raised for dramatic change following independence, and the cruel disappointments caused by greedy and corrupt Kenyan politicians.

Born in 1938, Ngugi was a teenager at the time of Mau Mau, and many story elements in *Grain of Wheat* seem to draw on his own family's experiences. His father was a squatter, and the family had been forced off their land. Ngugi attended a mission school for two years but was forced to drop out, presumably for difficulty in paying school fees; later he attended one of the Kikuyu independent schools. A very bright student, he ultimately did well enough on his exams to receive full scholarship support and was admitted to Alliance High

School just outside Nairobi, the best African school in Kenya. Thus, like Mumbi's younger brother, Kariuki, in the novel, he was relatively safe during the Mau Mau years, attending boarding school away from home.

Meanwhile, both of his parents were arrested and detained at various points during the Emergency, and his own village of Kamriithu (like the fictional Thabai) was destroyed and then forcibly rebuilt. He had a half brother who could not hear or speak properly and who was shot during a British roundup of suspected Mau Mau, like the character of Gitogo in the novel.

After Alliance High School, Ngugi was fortunate to go on to Makerere University College in Uganda to earn a bachelor's degree, and then spent several years as a graduate student at the University of Leeds in England. One story, which might be apocryphal, is that while he was supposed to be drafting his M.A. thesis at Leeds, he was in fact writing *A Grain of Wheat* instead.

When Ngugi finished his education abroad, he came home to teach in the Department of English at the University of Nairobi from 1968 to 1977, where he worked very hard to change the focus of the department to African languages and literature. He also became convinced of the need for African writers to address nonelite African audiences more broadly. One of his most innovative projects involved developing a community center and community theater in Kamiriithu, near his home in Limuru. Volunteers offered adult literacy classes, and participants were encouraged to go beyond literacy to take part in writing and then producing a play in Kikuyu. Ngugi came under increasing fire from the government for the implicit critique of Kenyan society in his writings and was detained in 1977 after the publication of *Petals of Blood* and, perhaps most tellingly, after the Kikuyu-language performance of his play *Ngaahika Ndeenda* (*I Will Marry When I Want*) by a cast of peasants and workers. Ngugi was imprisoned for a year without charges and was never reinstated in his position as head of the Department of Literature at the University of Nairobi. After his release from prison, he went into voluntary exile with his family and taught at various universities in the United States and Britain. In recent years he has settled with his family in New York, where he holds an endowed chair in literature at New York University and continues an active writing and speaking career. One of his most recent books is a revised edition of *Writers in Politics* (1997), which demonstrates Ngugi's passion as a politically engaged third-world writer.

COURSE CONTEXT AND DISCUSSION THEMES

I assign Ngugi's novel in a one-semester history course on Colonialism in Africa: Impact and Aftermath. Enrollment varies from sixty to one hundred and includes a range of students from sophomores to seniors.

When I teach about twentieth-century African history, I usually focus on five or six African countries (perhaps Senegal, Nigeria, Kenya, Tanzania, Mozambique, and South Africa, for example) and use those case studies repeatedly to explore a variety of historical themes. The particular countries and themes may change from year to year, but I always include Kenya and Mau Mau, because Mau Mau is consistently a great focal point for teaching about both socioeconomic change and anticolonial resistance. One reason is that there is such a vast and impressive literature available to students, including both accessible secondary sources and numerous novels and autobiographical accounts.

Students read one novel or autobiography for each of the African countries, along with shorter articles or excerpts on history and society in that area. Thus I might assign Sembene, *God's Bits of Wood* (see Chapter 21), Emecheta's *Joys of Motherhood* (see Chapter 10), and Tim Couzens's *Facing the Storm* in addition to *Grain of Wheat*. The four lectures pertaining to Kenya usually include (1) "The Settler Economy and the Demand for African Labor"; (2) "Labor Migration, Urbanization, and Social Change"; (3) "Mau Mau and the African Response to Colonial Rule"; and (4) "Kenya After Mau Mau: The Politics of Ethnicity." A separate class period is entirely devoted to a discussion of *Grain of Wheat*.

From the students' perspective, the most difficult aspects of *A Grain of Wheat* involve its internal architecture and the names and identities of numerous characters. Formally taking place over just a few days leading up to Kenyan independence, the novel relies heavily on flashbacks to earlier times to give us a better sense of what these individual characters have suffered, how their relationships evolved, and what critical choices they each had to make. In a number of cases the same scene is depicted at different points in the novel, but each time from the perspective of a different character—a technique that is richly rewarding for those rereading the novel a second or third time, but one that sometimes adds to the confusion of undergraduates if they are not forewarned. I distribute a handout identifying the five principal Kikuyu characters and suggest the students focus on them. I also explain the time frame of the novel and the frequency of flashbacks, and give them a short glossary of terms. I suggest they keep these handouts tucked in the novel itself for easy reference when they're reading (the handout is reproduced at the end of this chapter).

Some of the major questions we consider in class discussion include these:

- What is your overall reaction to the book? What particular elements of the story really struck you?
- In some of the assigned readings we encountered the suggestion that Mau Mau had elements of a civil war as well as a nationalist movement. Are there any signs of that latter aspect here?
- Is there a hero in this novel? Who is he (or she)? Who displays the greatest courage?
- Let's try to compare *A Grain of Wheat* and *God's Bits of Wood* as novels about colonialism and African reactions to colonialism. What similarities do you see? What are some of the differences? How is Western education presented in the two novels? Why do you think the railway is presented as an important element in both cases?
- One of the primary themes we talked about with regard to *God's Bits of Wood* involved the way the Senegalese railway strike altered the relations between men and women, and between old and young. Do you see any parallels here?
- Let's talk about each of the primary characters: what do they seem to represent?
- Why do you think so many white characters are included? Do they distract you from "the main story," or do you think they advance that story in some ways? Do you think Ngugi is drawing our attention to the parallels between the marriage of Gikonyo and Mumbi and that of John and Margery Thompson?
- Some critics have suggested that in this novel Ngugi is consciously explaining and defending the Mau Mau movement to those outsiders who initially portrayed it as atavistic and primitive. If you wanted to make that argument, what elements from the story could you use to back it up?
- How do you think Ngugi feels about Christianity? Why does it play such a prominent role in the novel? How has it influenced Kihika's life and his political thought?

- What do you think the character of Mugo stands for? Why would the main action of the novel in many ways begin and end with him? What happens to him in the end?
- Do you think Ngugi feels optimistic about the newly elected African government in Nairobi? What clues might there be in the story about what they stand for?
- If we assume that the title chosen by the author is an important clue as to its ultimate meaning, how would you explain what this title means and how that idea is developed throughout the story?

STUDENT ASSIGNMENTS

Students are required to write a two-to-three-page essay on *A Grain of Wheat*. I sometimes ask them to discuss the major theme of the novel as reflected in the title, using specific references from the book to illustrate their argument. This essay is due at the beginning of class on the day we're going to discuss the novel. Having a written assignment due (or having a brief quiz) on the novel guarantees that students will have done the reading and have thought about it before they come to class, and that as a group we will have a spirited and informed discussion.

The novel comes up again as part of the final paper assignment, when students are asked to choose one major aspect of economic or social change in twentieth-century Africa, to do some library research and report briefly on the broad parameters of the chosen theme, and then to discuss that topic further in terms of evidence from five novels or life histories read during the course of the semester. (Students are allowed to omit one or more of the novels from discussion whenever there is insufficient material for the theme they've chosen, but they must obtain the instructor's blessing before doing so.) The final paper should be twelve to fifteen pages long, with a bibliography indicating all the sources consulted. (The topics can range widely, including changes in religion, the nature of leadership, the position of women, the role of the elders, advantages and disadvantages of Western-style education, and so on. I do require students to submit a brief paper proposal beforehand, so I can steer them away from any choices that might prove particularly difficult.) Structuring the paper in this particular way also makes it extremely unlikely that I'll have to worry about plagiarism or purchased papers.

A *Grain of Wheat* is never the students' favorite book—they prefer the unity of purpose and ultimate strikers' victory in *God's Bits of Wood*—yet Ngugi's novel works extremely well year after year in suggesting the complexities and contradictions of an anticolonial war from the perspective of individual villagers.

CLASS HANDOUT:
A GRAIN OF WHEAT, BY NGUGI WA THIONG'O

This is a novel about Mau Mau, armed resistance against British colonial rule, a period that lasted roughly from 1952 through 1960 in the Kikuyu areas of Kenya. Mau Mau was extremely difficult for all Kikuyu to live through, and they had to make critical choices of how to respond: to join the resistance forces outright, to try to support the fighters indirectly, to join the Loyalists (the group publicly supporting the British), or to try somehow to stay neutral.

The novel recounts the story of a small group of men and women and the individual choices they made. The story is set in the week before independence celebrations in Kenya (December 12, 1963), although there are many flashbacks to the Mau Mau period and to the earlier lives of the main characters. As you read the novel, think about the consequences of their different choices. Who is the hero of the story? Which character do you admire most? Who made the greatest sacrifice, and why? Why do you think Ngugi chose this particular title? As you read through the various chapters, keep that question in mind. Hint: the title has a symbolic meaning and does not concern agriculture.

These are the principal characters; try to keep them in focus:

Gikonyo: a carpenter, arrested and detained for his political involvement.

Mumbi: his wife, who remains in the village and tries to keep the family together during the years of his detention.

Kihika: the political activist and theoretician, a freedom fighter who leads the resistance movement from the forest; also Mumbi's brother. Secondary characters include Wambuku, his long-term girlfriend who stays behind, and Njeri, who follows him to the forest.

Karanja: a Loyalist (appointed chief of Thabai during Mau Mau) who now has a semiskilled job at the British forestry research station at Githima.

Mugo: the loner, the man without a family, who spends much of
               the novel in a state of panic. Generally trying to stay neu-
               tral, he is arrested during Mau Mau when he tries to save
               a pregnant woman from a soldier's beating.
Also note: *Warui* (male) and *Wambui* (female), elderly commenta-
               tors on the action, who are active in planning the inde-
               pendence day celebrations; *John Thompson*, a British
               civil servant, who had been a district officer and was in
               charge of several detention camps during Mau Mau and is
               now head of the Githima Research Station, and *Margery*,
               John Thompson's wife, who can't get her husband's
               attention and becomes involved with other men.

The action of the novel takes place in several locations, including:

Thabai: the name of both the old ridge (where people live in scat-
               tered settlements), and also the new village constructed
               by force.
Rungei: the market center where the people of Thabai go for tea,
               sugar, tailoring, and so on, or to watch the train from
               Nairobi come through the station.
Githima: the Forest and Agricultural Research Station where
               Karanja and Thompson both work.

TRANSLATION OF KIKUYU AND SWAHILI PHRASES

A number of Kikuyu and Swahili words and phrases appear in the
novel without explanation and may be frustrating. The more common
terms are listed here:

Agikuyu	the Kikuyu (Gikuyu) people
Fenna Brokowi	Fenner Brockway, a Labour M.P. in Britain who actively supported East African political aspirations
gikoi (or *kikoi*)	a length of printed cloth
heifer boma	young women's corral (used in irony)
"Hodi"	"Anyone home? May I come in?"
jembe	hoe
mithuru and *miengu*	long skirts and aprons, traditional Kikuyu women's dress
muthuo	young men's dance

Ngai	(also Mwenenyaga) God, the High God
panga	machete
rika (often *riika*)	age grade, the group of men or women circumcised at the same time
shamba	farm plot
shauri	matter or problem
sufuria	metal cooking pot
Toboa!	literally "Bring it out," (i.e., Tell the truth!)
Uhuru bado	not yet independence (i.e., let's wait)
Uhuru na kazi	independence [goes together with] hard work (i.e., no handouts)

Nikihiu ngwatiro (Kikuyu, pp. 78, 106) "Things are hot," i.e., coming to a head.

Kamwene kabagio ira (Kikuyu, p. 172) "One's own child gets the chalk first," i.e., people look out for themselves first.

Kikulacho kiko nguoni mwako (Swahili, pp. 15, 152) "What eats you is in your clothes" [lice?], i.e., the enemy is within.

Aspro ni dawa ya kweli (Swahili, p. 176) "Aspro is true medicine" (ad slogan).

Usiogope Mzee (Swahili, p. 187) "Don't be afraid, old man."

Chege Githiora of Boston University's African Language Program has kindly provided the translations of the more complex phrases.

SUGGESTIONS FOR
FURTHER READING AND RESOURCES

Bjorkman, Ingrid. 1989. *Mother, Sing for Me: People's Theater in Kenya.* London: Zed. Popular, journalistic account of the "people's theater" Ngugi launched in his home area; includes a number of photographs.

Cantalupo, Charles, ed. 1995. *The World of Ngugi wa Thiong'o.* Trenton, N.J.: Africa World Press. Includes interviews with Ngugi.

Clough, Marshall. 1998. *Mau Mau Memoirs.* Boulder, Colo.: Lynne Rienner. A very accessible analysis of some thirteen first-person accounts of Mau Mau participants; ultimately gives us a good sense of what daily life was like in the resistance.

Cook, David, and Michael Okenimkpe. 1997. *Ngugi wa Thiong'o: An Exploration of His Writings.* Revised edition. London: Heinemann. Separate chapters on five Ngugi novels, including one on *Grain of Wheat*, along with broader discussions of his life, career, and role as social/political critic.

Furedi, Frank. 1974. "The Social Composition of the Mau Mau Movement in the White Highlands," *Journal of Peasant Studies* 1, 4: 485–505.

Gugelberger, Georg, ed. 1985. *Marxism and African Literature*. Oxford: James Currey. Two separate chapters provide Marxist analysis of *Petals of Blood*, the Ngugi novel that follows *A Grain of Wheat* chronological-ly.

Kanogo, Tabitha. 1987. *Squatters and the Roots of Mau Mau*. Oxford: James Currey. A very accessible account of Mau Mau and its relationship to the increasingly difficult situation Kikuyu squatters found themselves in from the 1920s onward. I usually assign it together with the Ngugi novel.

Kidd, Ross. 1983. "Popular Theater and Popular Struggle in Kenya," *Race and Class* 24, 3: 287–304. A compelling account of Ngugi's experi-ments with popular theater and Kikuyu-language productions, as well as government repression. A special issue on "Kenya: The Politics of Repression," using the government's response to the failed coup attempt of 1982 as a prism to interpret Kenyan politics.

Killam, George D. 1984. *Critical Perspectives on Ngugi wa Thiong'o*. A collection of previously published articles about Ngugi's work, includ-ing five articles specifically on *A Grain of Wheat*.

Maloba, Wunyabari O. 1994. *Mau Mau and Kenya: Analysis of a Peasant Revolt*. Bloomington: Indiana University Press.

Maughan-Brown, David. 1985. *Land, Freedom, and Fiction in Kenya*. London: Zed. A provocative analysis of the ways the Mau Mau struggle was used (and sometimes distorted) by British novelists in the 1950s and more recently by indigenous Kenyan writers. Includes an interest-ing discussion of Ngugi's "ambivalence" toward Mau Mau in *A Grain of Wheat*, pp. 247–251.

Miller, Norman, and Rodger Yeager. 1994. *Kenya: The Quest for Prosperity*, 2nd ed. Boulder, Colo.: Westview. A broad and useful introduction to history, society, and politics in contemporary Kenya.

Ngugi wa Thiong'o. 1964. *Weep Not, Child*. Portsmouth, N.H.: Heinemann. A simpler and shorter fictional account of Mau Mau from a village per-spective.

———. 1965. *The River Between*. Portsmouth, N.H.: Heinemann. Novel focuses on the ways local society is torn apart as a result of Christianity and other aspects of the British colonial presence.

———. 1967. *A Grain of Wheat*. Portsmouth, N.H.: Heinemann.

———. 1977. *Petals of Blood*. Portsmouth, N.H.: Heinemann.

———. 1982. *Devil on the Cross*. Portsmouth, N.H.: Heinemann.

———. 1997. *Writers in Politics*, rev. ed. Portsmouth, N.H.: Heinemann. Gives a clear sense of how Ngugi sees himself as a politically engaged third world writer.

Otieno, Wambui. 1998. *Mau Mau's Daughter: The Life History of Wambui Waiyaki Otieno*. Boulder: Lynne Rienner. A useful and engaging overview of Mau Mau activities and several decades of African politics in Kenya from a woman's point of view.

Robertson, Claire. 1998. *Trouble Showed the Way: Women, Men, and Trade in the Nairobi Area, 1890–1990*. Bloomington: Indiana University Press. Documents the experience of Nairobi's petty traders, most of them Kikuyu women, through the twentieth century.

Sicherman, Carol. 1990. *Ngugi wa Thiong'o, The Making of a Rebel: A Source Book in Kenyan Literature and Resistance*. London: Hans Zell.

17

Djibril Tamsir Niane's
Sundiata: An Epic of Old Mali

Curtis A. Keim

THE SUNJATA EPIC RECOUNTS THE STORY OF THE
thirteenth-century foundation of the Mali empire by the culture hero
Sunjata (or Sundiata, r. 1235–1255). The epic is short and engaging,
so students read it relatively easily, but teachers need to prepare carefully because the work poses a number of problems related to historical accuracy, literary form, and cultural context. The epic is suitable
for classes in literature and history as well as for general introductions to African culture. I use the epic in two classes of an introductory course in history and culture, but it would also work in a unit of
several weeks and upper-level courses because there are many questions to ask of the text and because there are sufficient secondary
materials for illustration and exploration.

In outline, the story has three sections:

1. Sunjata's mother, Sogolon, is a powerful sorceress from the
kingdom of Do who marries the king of Niani. Diviners predict that
her son will be a great ruler, but he is born a cripple. Both mother
and child suffer insults for a decade until Sunjata miraculously walks
and becomes a strong and attractive prince. When the king dies, his
kingdom is claimed by Sogolon's greedy co-wife and her weak son,
Sunjata's half brother.

Djibril Tamsir Niane, *Sundiata: An Epic of Old Mali*, trans. G. D. Pickett,
Longman African Classics (New York: Addison-Wesley, 1995). In this chapter, I
use the more modern spelling of Sunjata for the historical figure and *Sundiata*
when referring to the Longman text.

2. Sogolon goes into exile with Sunjata, his sister, and a half brother. They travel to other kingdoms, where they receive hospitality and Sunjata grows up. In Mema, Sunjata, still in his late teens, becomes governor, general of the army, and heir to the throne. Meanwhile, Sumanguru, the king of Soso, begins to conquer the kingdoms of Mali. He invades Niani and chases away the king, Sunjata's weak half brother. The Niani people search for the long-lost Sunjata so he can save the land.

3. After burying Sogolon in Mema, Sunjata returns with cavalry and leads the enemies of Sumanguru. The Soso king is defeated at the Battle of Krina (c. A.D. 1235), and Sunjata becomes emperor of the kingdoms of Mali plus the lands of many neighbors.

Like all epics, the Sunjata epic was orginally transmitted orally. In the Mande region of the West African grasslands, lineages of specialists called *jeli*, or, in French, *griots* (gree-oh), have preserved the epic for nearly eight hundred years. Niane's version, the one I use in my classes, was recorded from the griot Mamoudou Kouyaté and translated into French prose in 1960 and then into English in 1965. There are nearly thirty other transcribed versions of the epic, but Niane's has become the most widely used in the classroom because it is the most accessible in terms of cost, availability, and readability.

Historian D. T. Niane was born in 1932 in Conakry, Guinea, and studied at the Institut des Hautes Etudes, Dakar, and the University of Bordeaux. Most of his scholarly career has been spent at the Institut Fondamental d'Afrique Noire in Dakar. He has authored a number of works on the premodern history of West Africa and edited *Africa from the Twelfth to the Sixteenth Centuries*, the fourth volume in the *UNESCO General History of Africa*.

Niane's prose version is excellent for giving students access to the meaning and excitement of the story. It is limited, however, because it does not use up-to-date Mande names and does not convey the poetic or musical forms of the epic. To address the first problem, teachers should explain that many African words have multiple spellings and pronunciations both because of local African variants and because of the ear and system of the person who recorded the word. Modern variants are preferred because they reflect current usage and more accurate methods of transcription. Students should understand that in this case we continue to use Niane's version because it is widely available and accessible to nonspecialists.

The second major problem with Niane's version of the epic is that unlike the original, it is neither oral nor in verse. If you teach the epic as literature or in upper-level classes, you might consider substituting another version such as that provided by John Johnson in *The Epic of Son-Jara.* Many teachers, however, use the epic in introductory courses, where access is an important concern. For those of us in this category, a partial remedy for Niane's deficits is to provide students with excerpts of the original Mande text, a linear translation, and an audiorecording of a *griot* performance. Excerpts of a Mande text and a linear translation are available in Johnson, Hale, and Belcher's *Oral Epics from Africa.* A Bambara version is provided by Youssouf Cissé in *La Grande Geste du Mali.* Other Mande versions are reproduced in Gordon Innes's *Sunjata: Three Mandinka Versions.* An audiorecording of the version translated by John Johnson is available from the Archives of Traditional Music at Indiana University. Commercial versions exist but are relatively difficult to locate; it's worth checking the "Afro-Caribbean Musics" Web site. All of these references are given in fuller detail at the end of this chapter.

As I have mentioned, I teach the epic in a one-semester introductory course on sub-Saharan African history and culture. For most of my students, this is the only non-Western course they will ever take. The first half of the semester we focus on the nature of culture and the variety, complexity, and dignity of traditional African cultures. I lecture on geography, human evolution, culture, and history, and students read introductory essays, such as those included in Martin and O'Meara's *Africa.* Because I want students to approach Africa in several ways, I assign Achebe's *Things Fall Apart* and Niane's *Sundiata* (see Chapters 2 and 17), to represent, respectively, village and kingdom societies. Both of these works present the problem of "fiction as history," but I incorporate the problem into our class discussions as a way to help students become more aware of how people construct the past and present. Let me address that problem before I describe how I teach the epic.

FICTION AND HISTORY

Many students do not immediately recognize that historical fiction is a *story* about the past and *evidence* for the time it was written. *Things Fall Apart* can help us *imagine* what late-nineteenth-century Igbo society was like, and it can help us *document* the history of Nigeria in the 1950s. It would certainly have been a different work had it not been written by a young, Western-educated Igbo on the eve of Nigerian independence. The epic is similar to the novel because, although it presents itself as factual history, we know that it is not the

same story that was told a century ago, let alone nearly eight centuries ago. We can prove this to ourselves by the fact that there are
significant discrepancies between different versions collected in different parts of West Africa. For example, in some versions Sunjata is
the rightful heir to the throne of Niani, while in others he is not.

On the other hand, the epic is not a wholly contemporary creative work that is useless as history. Epics evolve over hundreds of
years and thus reflect the creativity and facts of many generations.
Thus teachers should treat the Sunjata epic as part of a "tradition"
and present examples of other versions. They should also situate the
epic within contemporary Mande society and discuss how the epic
both represents mainstream culture and fails to include the often-
conflicting perspectives of Islam and modernism that are part of
today's Mande culture. And teachers should help students understand
that although the epic is not the kind of history we undertake in the
academy, it is nonetheless deeply rooted in events and images of the
past because of the way it has been transmitted over centuries.

The critical work that has been done on the Sunjata epic reflects
these concerns. For example, John Johnson's excellent short introduction to the epic in his *Epic of Son-Jara* includes discussions of
the profession of the *griot* (or *jeli*), modern Mande village society,
and the literary characteristics of the Mande epic. Johnson argues
that the epic is folklore, not history, and that it is a key to contemporary, not historical, African culture. Charles Bird and Bonnie Kendall
examine the Mande heroic ideal, which requires that young men
leave their villages and succeed in the wider world. They compare
the exile of Sunjata to today's exile of young Mande men who must
go to cities in Africa or France to find work. Thomas Hale's *Scribe,
Griot, and Novelist* contrasts the interpretations of history and society provided by a West African epic (the Songhai epic in this case)
with those provided by Muslim documents. We will see that the
Sunjata epic contrasts with Muslim documents in similar ways.
Nehemia Levtzion employs the Sunjata epic as a guide to the history
of ancient Mali. He assumes that specific facts from the epic can help
calculate the genealogies of kings and illustrate the nature of the
ancient civilization. Levtzion emphasizes the emperor and his court,
the political economy, staple products and regional trade, towns, and
Islam. He is constrained, however, by the literary nature of the epic
and uses the epic only as a way to question or corroborate other
sources.

One of the more interesting approaches to the epic is a film,
Keita: Heritage of the Griot, which raises the question of the place of

the story in modern Africa. The film opens with a village *griot*, a Kouyaté, arriving at the city compound of a Keita family. (The Kouyatés are the traditional *griots* of Sunjata's family, the Keitas.) The old *griot* takes it as his responsibility to teach the Sunjata story to the Keitas' son, a lad who is being educated in a Western, French-language school. A conflict ensues because the boy prefers the Sunjata story to studying for his school examinations. His mother and schoolteacher insist that the modern world should come first. But his father, himself a prosperous and Western-oriented man, recognizes the value of the epic and does not intervene. As the story unfolds, the audience sees scenes of urban African life as well as the Sunjata story to the point where the hero stands up. The film interests most students, but lasts an hour and a half, too long for most survey courses, and the action is slow for American students. Unfortunately, because it is a low-budget film, the scenes at the Niani court do not do justice to the splendor of West African kingdoms.

Depending on the purpose of your course, you might want to focus on a specific aspect of the epic such as literary form; Mande culture; interactions of modernity, Islam, and Mande culture; ancient history; or reader reaction. Those who teach Sunjata or other West African epics should also consult Patricia Alden's useful essay about teaching the African epic. Whatever the focus, it seems that teachers ought to help students understand that this epic is not creative writing of the same genre as a novel, that it is not history, and that it is not a stabilized artifact of the past like other non-African epics they might have read. Rather, it is a complex mixture of ongoing creative expression, myth, and history that is intended to entertain, inform, and define reality for a living society. At the same time, it is not without challenges from other versions of reality such as Islam and modernity.

SUNDIATA IN THE CLASSROOM

In my class, my main efforts are to help students appreciate African diversity, complexity, and dignity and to provide background for understanding contemporary Africa. From this perspective the epic is not used uniquely as either literal history or contemporary literature, but as a guide to a way of thinking about the world that has both historical and contemporary relevance. I am interested in points frequently made by historians such as those concerning the organization

of ancient Sudanic states and economies, as well as those emphasized by ethnographers, such as the roles of the family, ideals of masculinity and femininity, and notions of fate and magic. Because students in my classes have already read *Things Fall Apart,* we are able
to compare and contrast the village society depicted there with the
kingdom societies portrayed in *Sundiata* and with the nation-state of
our own country. I emphasize *compare* and contrast because it is
important for students to see that different societies attempt to solve
many of the same problems.

Before we begin our class discussion of *Sundiata*, I give at least
one lecture on the nature of ancient Sudanic states and empires. Here
I discuss names and dates of kingdoms and empires, the roles of
environment and technology, and the growth of political centralization and trade networks. I provide handouts of travelers' accounts
from Ghana, Mali, and Songhai (see the references to Leo Africanus,
Murphy, and Hamdun and King in the resource list at the end of this
chapter.) When time permits, I show portions or all of the video
Keita: Heritage of the Griot. Later in the course we briefly consider
other kingdoms, empires, and city-states in precolonial Africa.

On the day of our discussion I give a ten-minute reading quiz or
collect a two-page paper to make sure that all students have read
Sundiata. Paper topics vary to reduce plagiarism, but frequently the
subject is the treatment of women, men, government, fate, or a similar theme in the epic. If the schedule permits, I give a quiz before the
discussion and ᵗʰᵉ � ask students to write papers based on the more
complete understanding of the epic they gain from the discussion.

For me the best way to begin our class discussion is to ask students to talk about *griots* and their roles. Students can usually list the
functions of a *griot,* such as historian and diplomat, and the various
relationships of the *griot* to kings, such as friend, counselor, cheerleader, and spokesperson. I add information about professions
reserved for specific lineages, female *griots*, the fact that the epic is
sung in poetry, and the existence of other epics and other versions of
this epic. I provide an example of a linear translation and a brief
audio excerpt of a *griot* performance. In the linear translation I
include an episode that describes events differently from Mamoudou
Kouyaté's version in Niane, such as the moment when Sunjata's birth
is announced to his father or when Sunjata stands up. This provides a
good point to ask whether the epic is history, literature, folklore, or
something else.

From a discussion of the nature of the epic, I move to the question of specialization. Here students can begin to sort out similarities and differences between village societies, kingdoms, and industrialized nation-states. The society depicted in the epic has more full-time specialists (e.g., *griots*, kings, horsemen, witches, hunters, and traders) than the less centralized society of *Things Fall Apart*, but fewer than our own. Students frequently want to see this increasing specialization as progress. Fortunately, *Things Fall Apart* is such a sympathetic portrayal of village society that it is possible to engage students in a discussion of the problems as well as the benefits of increasing specialization and centralization. By this time in the term we have already talked extensively about ways to look at culture in relativist and adaptive terms.

We next consider questions of leadership and power. I let students take the lead while providing prompts so that they list most of the relevant topics, including beliefs in fate, magic, the concept of *nyama*, the jinn, charisma, inheritance, sibling support and rivalry, Islam, alliances, physical prowess, and intelligence. While Sunjata might have been a great warrior, the *griots* present his coming to power as a function of his ability to use the tools offered by Mande culture. Most important, however, Sunjata is presented as a magician king. A simple question that can focus the discussion of leadership is, What factors allow Sunjata to defeat Sumanguru?

Sunjata descends on his father's side from kings who trace their lineage back to a companion of Muhammad, and on his mother's side from the renowned magicians of Do. He is fated to be emperor even before his birth, but fate is something that is completed through action and can be delayed by opponents. Indeed, many opponents attempt to harm Sunjata and his mother, but the two are great magicians who can divine what is really going on and take measures to protect themselves.

Mande heros like Sunjata must be great magicians because they can succeed only if they accumulate and control *nyama*, a kind of mystical power. This power is released in all actions, but within the context of normal village life the power is manageable. More potent and dangerous *nyama* is released in actions that do not fit into ordinary village life. In Mande, this is conceived of as a tension between individualism and community, between *fadenya* and *badenya*, between father orientation and mother orientation. Thus, for example, hunters must be magicians because they hunt alone outside the village, kill powerful animals that have strong *nyama*, and then deal with the *nyama* that is released. Sumanguru, the terrible king of Soso, is also a magician, and he rules because of his ability to release, accumulate, and control *nyama*.

Sunjata is portrayed as a weak child to emphasize the importance of magic and fate. He does not succeed by strength or even wit so much as by his ability to manage *nyama*. Indeed, he is not even a "good" Mande because he fails to follow the rules of the village. Early in life, for example, he dishonors his mother by not collecting baobab leaves. But Sunjata's frequent individualistic actions release *nyama*, and his superior fate allows him to control it. Up to the point of the Battle of Krina, the story can be read as one of his accumulating this mystical power. He cannot triumph, however, until he discovers the key to Sumanguru's control of *nyama*. This is delivered to him by Sumanguru's unmanly stupidity. Every wise man keeps secret the key to his ability to control *nyama*, but the vain Sumanguru cannot resist telling his secret to a lover—Sunjata's half sister, who feigns hatred of the hero. Once the tyrant is grazed by an arrow tipped with countermagic, his *nyama* escapes and he is finished.

Other elements of Sunjata's power are presented in less mystical terms. Students can note that Sunjata is supported by childhood companions, a half brother and half sister, a full sister, his *griot*, the people of Niani, neighbors who are also enemies of the Soso, kings who recognize Sunjata as a fellow noble, and a key defector from Sumanguru's army. Likewise, there are references to the importance of trade, cavalry, and blacksmiths in warfare. The fact that Sunjata became a leader first in Mema, a land to the north with better access to good horses and to trade than Niani, seems significant.

Sunjata's Islamic pedigree might be puzzling in an epic that relies almost entirely on fate and magic for justification of the hero's actions. Historical documents confirm that Islam was present in Sunjata's Mali, yet they also indicate that it had not taken a deep hold. Therefore, the epic is essentially correct in portraying Sunjata as a magician king who also happened to be Muslim. It is also correct in depicting Ghana as more Muslim than Mali in Sunjata's era. It is not until several generations after Sunjara that the *mansas* of Mali define themselves as Muslim emperors (despite evidence that several of Sunjata's predecessors might have made the pilgrimage to Mecca). Thus Mansa Musa (r. 1312–1337), who is famous for his support of Islam, becomes the hero of Muslim texts, while Sunjata reflects different aspects of Mande culture.

The nature of Mande government organization is displayed here and there throughout the work. This is a hierarchical system with the dispersed power of feudalism. Its clearest expression is in the final scenes of the epic, where Sunjata's generals pledge their allegiance to him and give him their kingdoms. Then Sunjata returns the kingdoms and asks his subkings to meet regularly to reconfirm their unity. This general organization was common throughout the Sudanic region and a function of the possibilities and limits of Sudanic technology. While the details lie outside the scope of this discussion, in general one can say that Sudanic agricultural production and trade were large enough and of such a nature that they fostered centralization. At the same time, transportation, communication, and the means of warfare were limited enough that they made direct control of the imperial periphery expensive and difficult. Thus Sunjata and other Sudanic emperors ruled much of their empires indirectly and had to be constantly on guard against usurpers and breakaways.

The epic also contains illustrations of the economies and technologies of ancient Sudanic empires. Students can find examples of agriculture, local trade, long-distance trade in gold, markets, the use of caravans and boats, the importance of iron and horses, and the protection of cities through the use of walls and gates. Cities that depend on rural agricultural surplus and trade play an important role in the economic and political systems. The epic is not very helpful, however, in demonstrating how technology and economy shaped the events depicted. For example, infantrymen in the story were really ordinary farmers who volunteered or were drafted for service, so warfare was ultimately limited by food supplies. Likewise, the struggle for control of material resources played a larger role in events than the epic suggests.

One topic that students are eager to discuss is the role of men and women. In an age of gender awareness, many students note the misogynist tone of the epic, and they often find it difficult to believe that women have any dignity or power at all in African cultures. My students have also read *Things Fall Apart*, which seems even less appreciative of women than the Sunjata epic. We take time to describe women's roles in different societies and discuss ways that women might exert power as well as reasons why literature created by men might not emphasize those ways. At several points in the semester we also read secondary and other creative material on women in African history and culture so that by the end of the course students can discuss roles of African women with some subtlety.

I always look forward to teaching *Sundiata* because I know that my students will enjoy the epic and the classes. I also know that we will have interesting discussions that can lead us to many important topics.

SUGGESTIONS FOR
FURTHER READING AND RESOURCES

Achebe, Chinua. 1998. *Things Fall Apart*. Portsmouth, N.H.: Heinemann. A classic novel of the colonial impact on an Igbo village, which I like to teach along with *Sundiata*. This Heinemann edition contains notes and additional background information useful for students and nonspecialist teachers. See also Chapter 2 in this volume.

"Afro-Caribbean Musics" is a noncommercial site that provides a complete list of commercial African music recordings: <http://web.ina.fr/ cp/Music/index.en.html>.

Alden, Patricia. 1997. "Notes from the Roundtable on Teaching the African Epic," *African Literature Association Bulletin* 23, 3 (Summer): 33–35. A compilation of remarks presented at a panel on teaching the African epic at the 1997 African Literature Association annual meeting. Alden's excellent piece points to more resources for turning study of African epics generally into an extended unit on African literature and culture.

Austen, Ralph A., ed. 1999. *In Search of Sunjata: The Mande Oral Epic as History, Literature, and Peformance*. Bloomington: Indiana University Press. A recent collection of articles on the Sunjata epic, from a wide range of disciplines.

Bird, Charles S., and Martha B. Kendall. 1980. "The Mande Hero: Text and Context." In *Explorations in African Systems of Thought*, ed. Ivan Karp and Charles S. Bird. Washington, D.C.: Smithsonian Institution Press. Examines the Mande heroic ideal that young men leave their villages to succeed in the wider world.

Cissé, Youssouf. 1988. *La Grande Geste du Mali*. Paris: Editions Karthala: Association Arsan. A Bambara version of the epic, useful for comparison.

Connah, Graham. 1987. *African Civilizations: Precolonial Cities and States in Tropical Africa: an Archaeological Perspective*. Cambridge: Cambridge University Press. An accessible history text useful for undergraduates.

Curtin, Philip, et al., eds. 1995. *African History: From Earliest Times to Independence*, 2nd ed. New York: Longman. A detailed history text useful for undergraduates.

L'Épopée du Mandingue. 1970. A full version of the Sunjata epic by Kouyaté Sory Kandia was published in 1970 as (2 vols: CD76037-2; CD 76038-2) by Editions Bolibana (23, Rue des Tulipes, 94240 L'Hayles-Roses, France).

Fage, John D. 1979. *Cambridge History of Africa*, vol. 3: *From c. 1050 to c. 1600*. Cambridge: Cambridge University Press. A solid history text useful for undergraduates.

Hale, Thomas A. 1990. *Scribe, Griot, and Novelist: Narrative Interpreters of the Songhay Empire*. Gainesville: University of Florida Press. This work was reprinted in an amended edition in 1996 by Indiana University Press.

Hamdun, Said, and Noël King. 1975. *Ibn Battuta in Black Africa*. London:

Rex Collings. Contains Ibn Battuta's description of fourteenth-century Mali.

Innes, Gordon. 1974. *Sunjata: Three Mandinka Versions.* London: School of Oriental and African Studies, University of London. Includes other Mande versions of the Sunjata epic.

Johnson, John William, Thomas A. Hale, and Stephen Belcher, eds. 1997. *Oral Epics from Africa: Vibrant Voices from a Vast Continent.* Bloomington: Indiana University Press. Contains excerpts of a Mande text and a linear translation useful in teaching.

Johnson, John William. 1986. *The Epic of Son-Jara: A West African Tradition.* Bloomington: Indiana University Press, 1986.

July, Robert W. 1997. *A History of the African People,* 5th ed. Prospect Heights, Ill.: Waveland Press. A basic history text useful for undergraduates.

Keita: Heritage of the Griot. Directed by Kani Kouyae in Dyula with English subtitles. A film that raises the question of the place of the Sunjata epic in modern West Africa. Distributed by California Newsreels, 149 Ninth Street, Suite 420, San Francisco, CA 94103, tel. 415-621-6196.

Leo Africanus. 1994. *Geographical Histories of Africa Written in Arabic and Italian by John Leo, a Moor Born in Granada Brought up in Barbarie.* Pittsburgh, Pa.: Jones' Research and Publishing. Contains one version of Leo Africanus's portrayal of the early sixteenth-century Sudanic region.

Levtzion, Nehemia. 1973. *Ancient Ghana and Mali.* London: Methuen. An early discussion of the history of the best-known kingdoms of the Western Sudan.

Martin, Phyllis M., and Patrick O'Meara, eds. 1995. *Africa,* 2nd ed. Bloomington: Indiana University Press, 1995. Contains useful broad chapters on various aspects of contemporary African life.

Miller, Joseph C., ed. 1980. *The African Past Speaks: Essays on Oral Tradition and History.* Folkestone: William Dawson. An introduction to the literature on the question of whether and how African oral sources can be used as historical sources.

Murphy, E. Jefferson. 1972. *History of African Civilization.* New York: Dell. A well-known excerpt from Al-Bakri's eleventh-century account of Ghana is quoted on pp. 110–111.

Niane, Djibril Tamsir. 1995. *Sundiata: An Epic of Old Mali,* trans. G. D. Pickett. Longman African Classics. New York: Addison-Wesley.

———, ed. 1997. *Africa from the Twelfth to the Sixteenth Centuries,* vol. 4 of the *UNESCO General History of Africa.* Berkeley: University of California Press, and Oxford: James Currey.

Niane, Djibril Tamsir, Parker James, and Lynda Shaffer. Forthcoming. *The Sundiata Epic.* A CD-ROM version of the epic intended for classroom use, with background essays, glossaries, maps, photos, and a bibliography, and an interview with Niane. Includes interactive features. For further information about availability, call 617-267-8024.

Sunjata Epic: Audiorecording of the version translated by John Johnson, available from the Archives of Traditional Music at Indiana University.

Tel: 812-855-4679; fax: 812-855-6673; web site: <http://www.
indiana.edu:80/~libarchm/home2.html>. The complete collection on
cassette was around $45.00, a one-hour demonstration excerpt around
$15.00 at the time of writing. Copies are also available at higher prices
in reel-to-reel, DAT, or CD format.
Vansina, Jan. 1985. *Oral Tradition as History*. Madison: University of
Wisconsin Press. An introduction to the literature on the question of
whether and how African oral sources can be used as historical sources.

18

Flora Nwapa's *Efuru*

Sandra E. Greene

WHEN I FIRST DECIDED TO INCLUDE *EFURU* AMONG
the texts assigned for my freshman writing seminar, African
Imaginations in History and Literature, I wasn't quite sure how
the students would respond. I had scheduled the novel to be read
and discussed after we had explored several other texts, all written by men who used the classic trope of exile and triumphant
return to illustrate gripping and often exhilarating scenes of male
bravado. *Efuru*, in contrast, was a quieter, more contemplative
novel. It relied less on surrealistic imagery and glorious depictions of war and bravery, and emphasized instead the maternal
and the social, the quiet triumphs and tragedies associated with
marriage and motherhood. Would my students view this text
as "tame" and even dull by comparison with their earlier readings?

To my delight, the response to *Efuru* was tremendously positive. The students loved it. On reflection, I can attribute their
response to a number of factors. Perhaps the most significant, however, was the context in which I presented the novel. Prior to reading and discussing *Efuru*, we had read D. T. Niane's *Sundiata* (see
Chapter 17), Thomas Mofolo's *Chaka,* and Chinua Achebe's *Things
Fall Apart* (see Chapter 2). My students found that our discussion
and analyses of these texts gave them an excellent introduction to
particular African histories and cultures. They gained a better
understanding of how Africans understand and write about their

Flora Nwapa, *Efuru* (Portsmouth, N.H.: Heinemann, 1966).

own societies. They also obtained the skills needed to approach a text as one intentionally shaped by the author to convey certain messages. When we read *Efuru,* the students brought these skills to their readings, but they also hungered for additional knowledge about African women. In reading Nwapa's novel, they began to understand the full extent to which the previous texts were gendered in very specific ways. All had included women, but most often they were described in flat, one-dimensional terms. In contrast, Flora Nwapa presented women with complete identities and histories of their own. Some she depicted as assertive and very independent, others as more passive, and still others as mean-spirited and spiteful. Although she focuses on such traditional themes as marriage and motherhood, Nwapa also presents very powerful images of sisterhood and female solidarity, in stark contrast to the images of women in our earlier readings. Both male and female students were ready to obtain a fuller picture of African women and their lives.

As an instructor concerned with using African novels to introduce first-year students to a gendered understanding of African history and culture, I found Nwapa's text does just that. But there are other reasons I return to *Efuru* time and again. As the first novel authored by an African woman, *Efuru* was written in response to one of the most widely read texts in African literature, Chinua Achebe's *Things Fall Apart. Efuru* is also a text to which many other authors in turn have responded. This situation is ideal for giving students a particularly accessible set of readings that they can use to explore African history and culture as well as the intertexual conversations that have taken place between African men and women, and among African women writers, about how one can/should/must represent the historic lives of African women to a reading public. Perhaps as important is the fact that Nwapa's particular presentation of the world of Igbo women in early colonial Nigeria provides an additional forum to discuss some of the most recent controversies that have become central to the way American students understand certain African cultural practices and the status and roles of African women. I am referring specifically to the issues of female circumcision, bridewealth, and polygyny, all of which are often shrouded in misconceptions and stereotypes. Because Nwapa's novel addresses these issues and others pertaining to women, it is an ideal novel to use as an introductory text on African understandings of their own cultures and histories.

SUMMARY OF THE TEXT

Efuru focuses on the life of an Igbo-speaking woman living in eastern Nigeria in the early twentieth century whose name also serves as the title of the novel. Exceptionally beautiful, intelligent, generous, hardworking, and possessing a knack for effortlessly making money, Efuru is a woman envied and admired by both women and men. She is self-confident but not arrogant, knowledgeable about the social norms that dictate appropriate behavior, but willing to use this knowledge both to conform to, and to defy, those norms. She participates willingly and successfully in the female circumcision rite that prepares her for marriage, yet in making the transition from young unmarried woman to wife, she breaks with tradition by arranging her own marriage, paying her own bridewealth to her father, and declining to follow her husband to his fields to work on his farm. This portrayal of Efuru sets the stage for subsequent developments in her life. She has difficulty conceiving, and then when success comes on the heels of consulting a diviner/herbalist, first her husband leaves her to live with another woman, and then her child dies after less than two years of life. After waiting more than the accepted period of time to move on with her life, Efuru marries again, but this marriage too is plagued by childlessness. Recognizing that her husband would want children, she willingly accepts into her household a son her husband had conceived with another woman in a different village. She also accepts a young woman as her co-wife, and when this marriage fails, she arranges for her husband to take a third woman in marriage. These acts of selflessness and magnanimity, however, do not prevent Efuru from suffering the effects of childlessness in a society that believes children are more valuable than money. As Efuru's friends ask her rhetorically: "What is money? Can a bag of money go for an errand for you? Can a bag of money look after you in your old age? Can a bag of money mourn when you are dead?" (p. 37). Throughout her struggles, Efuru lives up to her reputation as an extraordinary woman. She refuses to sink into bitterness, rarely shows anger, and remains incredibly generous with her friends and neighbors, her in-laws, and those who are dependent upon her for financial, emotional, and material support.

By the end of the novel, however, Efuru decides to eschew motherhood and marriage, and to devote herself instead to the worship of the Woman of the Lake, a goddess who has been appearing in her dreams throughout much of her life (see Drewal 1988a, 1988b). This

deity is beautiful and generous, and just as prosperous as Efuru; like
Efuru, she also lacks both husband and children. Efuru worships her,
nevertheless, because she has come to realize that a woman can
indeed be happy even though she might be incomplete by society's
standards. One needs only financial independence and the generosity
of spirit that gives Efuru and the Woman of the Lake their legendary
beauty.

Of course, *Efuru* is concerned with more than the novel's name-
sake. Nwapa uses the novel to reveal the full range of personalities
and possibilities that influence how Efuru chooses to live her life.
The most strongly developed female characters include Efuru's
mother-in-law (who is usually referred to by this relational title or as
"old woman") and Ajanupu, the sister of Efuru's mother-in-law. Both
represent personalities different from Efuru's, women who nevertheless also make their own choices in life. Nwapa portrays Efuru's
mother-in-law, for example, as a rather meek woman, very patient,
willing to wait years in hopes that her husband will return for good
after long, unexplained absences. In the end, however, he returns to
his wife only to die. In counseling Efuru, the mother-in-law still
advises her to be patient with her own husband, for the satisfaction of
knowing that she had "stayed the course" in her own marriage,
unlike her husband and so many others. Nwapa presents Ajanupu, on
the other hand, in a very different light. Exceedingly independent, an
awe-inspiring businesswoman, unconcerned about what other people
think as she acts with determination to defend her interests and her
friends, and certainly not dependent on any man, Ajanupu's personality is in striking contrast to both her sister's and Efuru's. By including these two well-developed portraits (and other more tangential
characters), the novel emphasizes the extent to which African and
Igbo women cannot be lumped into a single category in which men
dominate the lives of women. Women are of all personalities and
backgrounds, and all make decisions about their own lives even if
sometimes a woman's decision places her at the mercy of an uncaring man.

In teaching *Efuru* as a gendered text, I also encourage my students to examine the way Nwapa portrays the male characters. As a
female author, does she stereotype men, just as some accuse Achebe
of stereotyping his female characters in *Things Fall Apart*? The two
most prominent men in Efuru's life are her father and her husband.
The father is portrayed as respected but indulgent. He does not raise
serious objections to Efuru's contracting her own marriage; when she
leaves that union, Efuru is accepted without difficulty back into her

father's home. Efuru's husband also indulges his wife and does not attempt to exercise a great deal of control over her. When Efuru objects to engaging in farmwork, he allows her to return to town to pursue trading instead. He also seems little bothered that Efuru proves far more adept at trading than he. In the end, however, he leaves Efuru to pursue another woman. Are these portrayals generally negative or positive? Why did Nwapa portray the men this way? These questions always generate a lively discussion and form an important element of our analysis of the novel, for they encourage the students to examine in much more detail the larger question of why Nwapa wrote as she did.

A third aspect of the novel concerns its setting. *Efuru* takes place in the town of Oguta—located on a major riverain trade artery—during the period just before and after World War I. Nwapa gives only glimpses of how colonial influence affect Efuru and the other characters in the novel. She does, however, provide a fuller picture of community economic life. Town life is centered on trade, conducted by both men and women; the market is a site not only for economic exchanges but also for social exchange and ritual displays. People move in and out, buying and selling, bringing farm produce and fish catches, trading in goods, both locally manufactured and imported. Smaller markets are connected to much larger ones like Onitsha, which is mentioned frequently in the text as a bustling market where one can buy virtually anything. Nwapa portrays Efuru (and Ajanupu) as excelling at trade, traveling widely, and winning the respect of their friends and neighbors because, in part, of their sharp business acumen.

THE TEXT AS A POSITIVE
STATEMENT FOR AND ABOUT WOMEN

Yet *Efuru* is a novel first and foremost about women and women's experiences. This is how most literary critics view the book. It is how my students also see *Efuru*, because for many this is the first African novel they have read that portrays the main female character in such a feminine yet independent and assertive way. I would even venture to say that many of my female students enjoy this book so much because they would like to see themselves in these same terms: feminine yet strong, assertive, and independent. Does this portrayal make this text a feminist text, as claimed by so many literary critics?

I have never posed this particular question directly to my students, for I believe it would lead to a discussion of feminism that
could be more distracting than useful. The questions we do address
are those I believe will guide the students to understand the book as
both a story and a statement by the author. What was Nwapa trying
to say about women in her society? To whom was she directing her
message? And how are we to understand a novel that so resolutely
challenges a culture yet also takes for granted certain practices—
female circumcision, bridewealth, and polygyny—that most of my
students understand as degrading to women and therefore antife-
male? In addressing these questions, *Efuru* is a novel around which
one can easily weave both literary and cultural discussions about the
author and her intent, the place of women in early-colonial Igbo culture, the cultural practices that affect women's lives and bodies, the
students' own definitions of how women should conduct themselves
and how society should treat women, and how the students situate
themselves in Western debates about the issues of female circumcision, polygyny, and bridewealth.

To guide these discussions, I present a series of informal lectures
and assign related readings about these themes. With regard to
Nwapa as an author, for example, I read from several interviews with
Nwapa that literary scholars have published. These interviews reveal
much about how this recently deceased author viewed her own role
as a writer, why she chose to write *Efuru* in a conversational or
seemingly oral style, and why she wrote in English. Nwapa's comments also reveal much about how she viewed herself as a female
writer, as indicated in the following excerpts from interviews with
literary critics Marie Umeh (1995: 27) and Christine Loflin (1995:
80):

> The male [Nigerian] writers have disappointed us a great deal by
> not painting the female character as they should paint them.
> 　　[Women] are not only mothers; they are not only palm collec-
> tors; they are not only traders; but they are also wealthy people.
> 　　I happened to know Chinua Achebe very well, and I read
> *Things Fall Apart.*
> 　　I attempted to correct our menfolks when they started writing,
> when they wrote little or less about women, where their female
> characters are prostitutes and ne-er do wells. I started writing to
> tell them that this is not so. When I do write about women in
> Nigeria, in Africa, I try to paint a positive picture about women
> because there are many women who are very, very positive in their
> thinking, who are very, very independent, and very, very industri-
> ous.

That she was devoted to the goal of trying "to project the image of women positively" (Umeh 1995: 27) throughout her writing career is evident in the tribute Gay Wilentz wrote after Nwapa's death in 1993:

> Nwapa always invested her female protagonists with the strength she saw in women who influenced her as she grew up. For those in her own culture, she presented a view of traditional and modern African society that focused on the place of women, unlike the portrayals proffered by her male contemporaries like Chinua Achebe and Wole Soyinka. For those outside her culture, she brought us into a matrifocal world, close to its precolonial roots, where women suffered from the constraints of society and their men, but where women were also the lifeblood of the community. (Wilentz 1994: 8)

In 1975, twelve years after she published *Efuru*, Nwapa extended her interests in writing and women's issues into the publishing industry. She began her own publishing company, Tana Press, and although she published books by both male and female Nigerian authors, she gave special attention to women authors and children's books.

After highlighting these facets of Nwapa's writing and publishing careers, I then return to Nwapa's own definition of what she was attempting to do, and I ask my students whether Nwapa has been really successful in projecting a positive image of women:

- How should we understand Efuru's paying her own bridewealth to her father?
- Can we read this as her defiance of the whole concept of bridewealth, interpreted in this context as a system that treats women as commodities to be passed from father to husband on payment of a certain amount of goods or money?
- Or should we understand the bridewealth system as one in which the movement of goods from husband to father is rather a symbol of the husband's recognition of the bride's value to her family, with whom she will no longer be primarily resident, and an indication as well to the bride's father that the husband is capable of economically maintaining his bride?
- Does she provide the bridewealth herself not only because her fiancé is too poor to do so, but because she also wants to gain control over her own body?

- Or do we understand Efuru's action as one that is designed to accomplish many goals at the same time?
- Does she provide her own bridewealth both to compensate for her partner's poverty and to maintain good relations with her own family—to whom she can turn if the marriage does not go well—by upholding their reputation in the community as a family that is not prepared to give their daughter away without material recognition of her worth?
- Similarly, how should one understand her positive presentation of polygyny and female circumcision? Both of these practices have been widely condemned in the West as examples of the sexual oppression of women. Yet Nwapa presents these practices as unquestioned norms that Efuru willingly supports. They are neither condemned nor glorified; they are simply part of Igbo society.
- Given the way Nwapa presents these particular cultural practices, can one really say that this is a novel that portrays women and their cultural practices in a positive light?

To help the students address these questions, I separate the issue of Nwapa writing to provide positive images from the discussion of the cultural practices themselves. I then have the students discuss these topics separately. In focusing on bridewealth, female circumcision, and polygyny, I ascertain the students' readings of these practices and then present alternative ways of viewing them. Such alternative views are found in the supplementary readings I assign (for example, Tambiah et al. 1989, Megafu 1983, and Case Western 1997), but I also present them in class to make sure my students understand the arguments presented and that they have an opportunity to respond to them in class discussion.

Again, my purpose is to force students to take different perspectives into consideration when thinking, discussing, and writing about the text. After what are often very lively discussions, we then return to the issue of how we are to understand Nwapa's purpose in writing *Efuru,* given their expanded understandings of how one might view her presentation of polygyny, bridewealth, and female circumcision.

A significant element in our discussions is a continual return to Achebe's *Things Fall Apart,* which they had read previously. On the issue of polygyny, my students find it revealing that Chinua Achebe portrays polygyny in the same positive terms as does Nwapa. In both novels, co-wives are presented as being respectful and supportive of one another. Our subsequent reading of Buchi Emecheta's *Joys of*

Motherhood—a novel written by another Igbo woman at least partly in response to Nwapa's *Efuru*—eventually disrupts this notion of a unified Igbo perspective on polygyny; but during the period when the students have read only *Things Fall Apart* and *Efuru*, this seemingly shared view serves very well the purpose of upsetting their notions that polygyny can be viewed as an institution exploitative of women in all places, at all times, under all circumstances (see the discussion of *The Joys of Motherhood* in Chapter 10).

These discussions of bridewealth, female circumcision, and polygyny rarely change my students' views. That is not the purpose. Focusing on these particular institutions does, however, force the students to contend with the fact that there is no one legitimate perspective on these issues. Nwapa presents a novel about one woman as someone who resists the sexist character of her own culture without losing her femininity. Yet Nwapa also presents Efuru as a woman who willingly engages in practices my students consider sexist. In a course that focuses on a gendered and culturally informed reading of African novels, I encourage the students to confront these seeming contradictions so they will then be able to challenge their own stereotypes of Africa, African culture, and African women.

THE TEXT AS HISTORICAL LITERATURE

As a historian, I find *Efuru* difficult to use as a vehicle for introducing students to African history and culture through literature. Scattered throughout the text are references to the slave trade, missionary education, conscription into the colonial military, and Western medicine. Yet none of these topics are foregrounded in a way that competes with her overall message that women can find happiness with or without a husband and children. In commenting on the slave trade, for example, Nwapa notes that the cannons being used to commemorate the life of Efuru's recently deceased father were obtained in exchange for slaves and then used in war to produce even more slaves. She then uses the fact that few people in Efuru's community remember the historical origins of these cannons to emphasize the point that although certain things have changed (the slave trade and intercommunity warfare have come to an end), much has remained the same. Belief in the goddess of the lake, Umahiri, continues, as does the society's insistence that a woman without children is incomplete. Thus, while the slave trade is introduced as a topic, it is framed in a way that provides minimal opportunities for further discussion. Nwapa does not address the issue of what impact the slave trade had on the socioeconomic hierarchy in Efuru's community. Nor does she discuss the indigenous institution of slavery or how this institution was or was not connected to the Atlantic slave trade.

I compensate for Nwapa's minimalist treatment of these historical topics by giving informal lectures about a whole range of subjects. These include presentations on the particular form that slavery and the slave trade took in the Igbo-speaking areas of Nigeria, Igbo naming practices, how Efuru and her community might have interpreted the missionary imposition of a European name on Eneberi, Efuru's second husband, and why the missionaries found it necessary to rename the students they educated in the first place. I draw their attention to the few references that Nwapa makes to the forced recruitment of soldiers for World War I and then discuss the historical literature about the ways the British used their colonies and the soldiers they recruited in the war (for example, Page 1987 and Barrett 1977). I point out that Nwapa portrays Efuru using both the indigenous medical system and the Western medical system and then explain how these different systems operated and discuss the often-conflicted relationship that developed between them. I also address issues that are not even discussed in the novel, including the existence of titled women among the Igbo and the decline of such titles during the colonial period, clashes among Christians and between Christians and traditional believers, the changes brought about by the inclusion of the area into a colonial economy, and Igbo resistance (including women's resistance) to colonial rule.

USING THE TEXT TO TEACH WRITING

Teaching *Efuru* in a course that focuses on writing skills has influenced the way I use the text. I divide the novel into two separate sections, with a division at Chapter 6. To this point Efuru has combined an independence of spirit with respect for and ready compliance with most of her society's values concerning appropriate behavior for a respectful wife and daughter-in-law. In this section I lead the students through a discussion of bridewealth and female circumcision. After Chapter 6 Efuru breaks with her first husband, marries her second husband, and assumes an even more compliant wifely role while also taking on the problems of her neighbors and friends. By the end of this second section, Efuru realizes that without children, she cannot satisfy the demands of her society. Coming to terms with this, she leaves her second husband and devotes herself even more completely to the worship of Umahiri. In the discussion about this segment of the novel, I introduce the topics of polygyny, the historical elements included or ignored, and whether as a whole the novel can be viewed as both about and supportive of the interests of women. Organizing the reading and discussion of the text in this way allows the class to focus much more closely on the specific content in each section.

Students in the small writing seminar have an opportunity to develop their ideas through a series of writing assignments. Each student, for example, writes a three-page paper on each section. Most often I encourage them to write about their reactions/responses to the text and to the suggestions I offer as the areas they may want to give particular attention. They then share their responses in a series of class discussions. During these exchanges the students become aware of alternate ways of reading the text based on their fellow students' responses. In these discussions I respond to their questions and provide information about the culture and history of eastern Nigeria that they should use to inform a final, longer essay on the text. I intentionally do not provide specific cultural information *before* we discuss their reactions to the text because I want to hear what students are thinking, how they are responding to the text and the cultural practices described therein. I want to create an atmosphere in which the students do not know what I am thinking, where they have little clue as to what a more informed reaction should be. After two or three class periods devoted to formal discussion, students begin working on their final five-to-seven-page essay, in which they analyze the novel as informed by their own reading, class discussion, my informal lectures, and outside readings.

The essays that students write on *Efuru* invariably reveal that studying the novel provides them with insight into African and more particularly Igbo history and culture. They gain a more nuanced understanding of how African women writers see and understand their own cultures, how Nwapa's perspective on women may differ from those of other Igbo writers. This becomes most apparent in the comparative discussions I lead after we have read and analyzed individually *Efuru, Things Fall Apart*, and *Joys of Motherhood*. Their essays also reveal the extent to which they do, indeed, come away with a very different understanding of African women. This is a particularly valuable lesson given the overwhelmingly negative imagery of African women in the West and the absence of their voices in the Western media.

SUGGESTIONS FOR
FURTHER READING AND RESOURCES

Achebe, Chinua. 1959. *Things Fall Apart*. Portsmouth, N.H.: Heinemann. A novel in dialogue with *Efuru*. (See Chapter 2 in this volume.)

Afigbo, A. E. 1981. *Ropes of Sand: Studies in Igbo History and Culture*. Ibadan: Ibadan University Press. A general study of Igbo precolonial and colonial history and culture.

Amadiume, Ifi. 1987. *Male Daughters, Female Husbands*. London: Zed Books. A text that contains information on marital relations between women among the Igbo, as well as historical accounts about Igbo female roles in general and the changes wrought by colonialism not discussed in *Efuru*.

Andrade, Susan Z. 1990. "Rewriting History, Motherhood and Rebellion: Naming an African Women's Literary Tradition," *Research in African Literature* 21, 1: 91–110. A literary study that addresses the issue of feminism and Nwapa's writing.

Badsden, George Thomas. 1966 [1938]. *Niger Ibos*. Frank Cass: London. An early anthropological study that contains many of the racist and ethnocentric tendencies found in such early studies; nevertheless, it does contain a useful discussion of female circumcision among the Igbo in the early 1920s.

Barrett, John. 1977. "The Rank and File of the Colonial Army in Nigeria, 1915–1918," *Journal of Modern African Studies* 15: 105–115.

Berrian, Brenda. 1995. "Flora Nwapa (1931–1993): A Bibliography," *Research in African Literatures* 26: 124–129. This article is in a special issue of the journal devoted to Nwapa's life and work.

Case Western. 1997. "Colloquium: Bridging Society, Culture and Law: The Issue of Female Circumcision," *Case Western Reserve Law Review* 47, 2. A comprehensive and outstanding review of the sometimes contentious literature on this subject, which presents various cultural, political, historical, and legal perspectives.

Davies, Carole Boyce. 1986. "Motherhood in the Works of Male and Female Igbo Writers: Achebe, Emecheta, Nwapa and Nzekwu." In *Ngambika: Studies of Women in African Literature*, ed. Carole Boyce Davies and Anne Adams Graves. Trenton, N.J.: Africa World Press. A literary study that addresses issues of feminism and motherhood in Nwapa's writing in comparison with other Igbo writers.

Drewal, Henry John. 1988a. "Mermaids, Mirrors and Snake Charmers: Igbo Mami Wata Shrines," *African Arts* 21, 2: 35–45, 96.

———. 1988b. "Performing the Other: Mami Wata Worship in Africa," in *Drama Review* 32, 2: 160–185. Both articles provide a useful context for the religious culture mentioned in *Efuru,* and specifically her worship of the Woman of the Lake.

Ekwensi, Cyprian. 1979. *Jagua Nana.* Portsmouth, N.H.: Heinemann. A novel in dialogue with *Efuru.*

Emecheta, Buchi. 1979. *The Joys of Motherhood.* New York: George Braziller, and Portsmouth, N.H.: Heinemann. A novel in dialogue with *Efuru.* (See Chapter 10 in this volume.)

Frank, Katherine. 1984. "Feminist Criticism and the African Novel," *African Literature Today* 14: 34–47.

———. 1987. "Women Without Men: The Feminist Novel in Africa," *African Literature Today* 15: 14–34. Both articles by Katherine Frank are useful literary studies that address Nwapa's writing in the context of feminism.

Isichei, Elizabeth. 1976. *A History of the Igbo People.* London: Macmillan.

Isiugo-Abanihe, Uche. 1994. "Consequences of Bridewealth Changes on Nuptiality Patterns Among the Ibo of Nigeria." In *Nuptiality in Sub-Saharan Africa: Contemporary Anthropological and Demographic Perspectives,* ed. Caroline Bledsoe and Gilles Pison. Oxford: Clarendon. A discussion of historic changes in the Igbo bridewealth system alluded to in *Efuru.*

Jell-Bahlsen, Sabine. 1995. "The Concept of Mammywater in Flora Nwapa's Novels," *Research in African Literatures* 26: 30–41. Contains information on the religious culture mentioned in *Efuru.*

Loflin, Christine. 1995. "An Interview with Flora Nwapa," *Sage* 9, 2: 80–81.

Megafu, U. 1983. "Female Ritual Circumcision in Africa: An Investigation of the Presumed Benefits Among the Ibos of Nigeria," *East African Medical Journal* 60, 11: 793–800. A very accessible account of female ritual circumcision among the Igbo by a medical doctor.

Mugambi, Helen Nabasua. 1991–92. "Re-Creating a Discourse: The Scriptable Novels of Nwapa and Emecheta," *Papers in Comparative Studies* 7: 167–179. An examination of the dialogue between *Efuru* and *Joys of Motherhood.*

Nnaemeka, Obioma. 1995. "Feminism, Rebellious Women and Cultural Boundaries: Rereading Flora Nwapa and Her Compatriots," *Research in African Literatures* 25: 80–113. A literary study that addresses the issue of feminism and Nwapa's writing.

Ogundipe-Leslie, Molara. 1984. "The Female Writer and Her Commitment," *African Literature Today* 14: 5–13. A literary study that addresses Nwapa's writing and its relationship to feminism.

Ohadike, Don C. 1991. *The Ekumeku Movement: Western Igbo Resistance to the British Conquest of Nigeria, 1883–1914.* Athens: Ohio University Press. A text on Igbo resistance to British conquest, an important historical issue never raised in *Efuru.*

Page, Melvin E. 1987. *Africa and the First World War.* New York: St. Martin's.

Tambiah, Stanley J., et al. 1989. "Bridewealth and Dowry Revisited— Comment/Reply," *Current Anthropology* 30, 4: 413–435. This article makes important distinctions between the terms "brideprice" and "bridewealth." It is most useful for instructors familiar with anthropological terminology.

Uchendu, Victor. 1965. *The Igbo of Southeast Nigeria.* New York: Holt, Rinehart, and Winston. A useful if somewhat dated general study of precolonial and colonial Igbo culture, including information on polygyny.

Umeh, Marie. 1995. "The Poetics of Economic Independence for Female Empowerment: An Interview with Flora Nwapa," *Research in African Literatures* 26: 22–29.

Vaughn, James H. 1986. "Population and Social Oganization." In *Africa,* 2nd ed., ed. Phyllis M. Martin and Patrick O'Meara. Bloomington: Indiana University Press. An accessible reading on bridewealth.

Wilentz, Gay. 1994. "Flora Nwapa, 1931–93," *The Women's Review of Books* 9, 6 (1994): 8.

19

Ferdinand Oyono's *Houseboy*

Barbara M. Cooper

FERDINAND OYONO'S BRIEF BUT VIVID NOVEL, FIRST
published in 1956, provides a glimpse into the world of a young man
in French colonial Cameroun whose mission education earns him a
place as "boy" to the new French colonial officer, the Commandant.
Written as the journal of a young man named Toundi whose literacy
has ambiguous implications, the novel helps bring to life a particularly fraught moment in colonial history: the period immediately following World War II, when the edifice of French authority was beginning
to crumble partly as a result of the experiences of African soldiers
fighting to liberate France. The novel presents us with Toundi's
emerging consciousness as it develops in and through the medium of
writing. It captures a colonial moment imbued with tremendous sexual tension: African males, simultaneously infantilized and feminized
in domination, were becoming more and more threatening as their
intimate knowledge of the hypocrisy of colonial power began to call
the very moral grounds of domination into question.

BIOGRAPHICAL BACKGROUND

Oyono's works clearly draw from his own experiences. He was born
in a village in southeastern Cameroon amid the cocoa plantations

---

Ferdinand Oyono, *Houseboy* (Portsmouth, N.H.: Heinemann, 1990).
Translated from the French by John Reed. The original English translation
was first published in 1966.

that serve as the backdrop for his novels. His father, Oyono Etoa Jean, was a respected indigenous leader who served as a secretary-interpreter for the colonial regime. Conflicts between his "traditional" polygynous father and his devout Catholic mother, Mvodo Belinga Agnès, caused the couple to break up. His mother worked as a seamstress in Ebolowa, where she raised Oyono and his sister, Mfoumou Elisabeth. As a child Oyono was a chorister and houseboy at the Catholic mission (Everson 1998). After completing his Primary School Certificate, Oyono was sent to France to complete his secondary education and to study law and political science at the Sorbonne. He obtained a *licence* in law in 1959. He wrote his two most famous novels, both published in 1956, during this period of study in France.

While critical of French colonialism, Oyono himself never became a militant in the anticolonial struggle of the Union des Populations de Cameroun (UPC), the nationalist movement that was active at the time he was writing. Indeed, with the defeat of the UPC and the French orchestration of independence, Oyono immediately embarked upon a diplomatic career within the conservative neocolonial regime of Ahmadou Ahidjo. He was appointed ambassador to France and held a series of prestigious diplomatic postings (the European Economic Community, the United States, UNICEF) and served as ambassador in a host of European (Italy, Benelux) and North African (Liberia, Tunisia, Morocco, and Algeria) countries. With the retirement of Ahidjo in 1982 and the succession of Paul Biya, Oyono went on to occupy a series of ministerial positions within Cameroon.

Oyono's most famous work, *The Old Man and the Medal,* could be seen as a rather bitter reflection upon the meaninglessness of Oyono's father's accomplishments and upon the deluded naïveté of African villagers. It is the story of an old peasant who receives a medal for his exceptional service and devotion to France, only to discover through police violence the hollowness of his sacrifices. *Houseboy*, by contrast, draws upon Oyono's own life and experiences as a fresh and vulnerable young man in close proximity to white colonial life. These complementary novels, both set in the immediate postwar period, were written and published simultaneously. Unlike earlier Cameroonian writers, Oyono is not nostalgic for a romanticized traditional past. While Oyono's writings are not simple derivatives of the European novelistic tradition—he, for example, deploys proverbs, images from oral folktales, and oral culture subtly but to great effect—it is not clear that Oyono's writings could be said to have contributed to the radicalization of Africans within Cameroon. Composed in French and directed largely at a European audience, the novels received wide publicity in the metropole and probably contributed to France's realization that independence for her African colonies was inevitable and that the dream of assimilation had been shattered. They were incendiary enough that Oyono's father lost his job subsequent to their publication.

Once Oyono entered into the service of the Cameroonian state, his critical voice seems to have dried up. In 1960 he published his most bleak and experimental novel, *Chemin d'Europe*, in which the protagonist (unlike those of his first two novels) is cynical rather than naive. The novel continues his critique of racism, the Catholic Church, and French colonialism by recounting the autobiography of an unsympathetic educated man, Aki Barnabas, who is consumed by his fixation with France. However, it offers neither a vision for the future nor an assessment of the contemporary predicaments facing postcolonial Cameroon. After 1960 Oyono fell silent, and as far as I can tell never published a novel he evidently began under the title *Le Pandemonium*. It is possible that it proved far more difficult to sustain a critical voice from within postcolonial bureaucratic structures than it had been to do so from without. Many Cameroonian authors have written about Cameroonian political life from exile, and those who have written from within Cameroon have often been forced to leave. Oyono's choice to be active within government may have eliminated his ability to use literature as a form of critique. He seems to have taken up other political modalities, arguing forcefully against apartheid in his role as a diplomat, for example.

Oyono's close connection with the Ahidjo regime undoubtedly also strained his credibility as an outsider to the abuses he describes in his earlier novels. The contrast with his contemporary, Mongo Beti, is instructive. Beti supported the UPC resistance movement and retired to exile in France with its defeat rather than remain in Cameroon under Ahidjo. He went on to write a number of fictional works on the resistance movement and a nonfiction critique of the Ahidjo regime. Christopher Dunton (1997a) observes that one of the deep ironies of Oyono's career is that as ambassador to France in 1972 he prevailed upon the French government to seize all the copies of Mongo Beti's open critique of the Ahidjo regime, *Main Basse sur Cameroun,* and attempted to have Beti deported to Cameroon. Not surprisingly, under the circumstances, critical work on Oyono has been slim in comparison with work on the less compromised and more prolific Mongo Beti.

Nevertheless, whenever I teach *Houseboy,* I wish Oyono had
continued to write because he has an acute eye for the nuances of
social interactions, for the subtle violence of daily life, and for the
tragicomic dimensions of the hollow spectacle of power. I particularly enjoy the verbal interchanges he manages to capture with simple
elegance and, in his best writing, tremendous sympathy and humor.
From the vantage point from which I teach *Houseboy,* Oyono's compromised position serves to exemplify the complexities of consciousness, postcolonial Africa, and resistance to domination.

HISTORICAL AND LITERARY CONTEXT

The appeal of *Houseboy* for me as a historian rests in its evocation of
a moment in time. If I were teaching a conventional African history
survey, I would probably place this novel alongside a chapter from
Myron Echenberg's *Colonial Conscripts,* or after a chapter from
Elizabeth Schmidt's *Peasants, Traders, and Wives.* It would also resonate nicely with Ousmane Sembene's lovely short film, *Black Girl,*
which could come later in the course in a segment on international
labor migration. The novel would also make a nice element in a
course on gender in Africa—one reason I like to use it is that it confronts students with a clear case in which the construction of gender
affects men as well as women.

The novel is characteristic of the writings of postwar, preindependence West African writers who moved beyond the celebratory
self-confidence of Negritude to denounce the violence of colonial
relations and to condemn colonialism as the source of a profound crisis in identity for educated Africans (Lee 1997). This crisis was perhaps particularly acute for Cameroonians, as the territory's history of
multiple and shifting colonialisms had left it with a legacy of even
more profound linguistic and judicial confusion and territorial fragmentation than is common in much of Africa. As Richard Bjornson
argues, the task of the Cameroonian author has been to simultaneously generate the groundwork for a shared Cameroonian identity and to
debate what freedom might mean in this complex and contingent
context (1991).

Cameroon came into being originally as German Kamerum,
established in 1884. With the defeat of Germany at the close of
World War I, the western and northern portions of the country bor-
dering the British colony of Nigeria were placed under British rule
(British Cameroons), while the bulk of the country fell under French

rule (French Cameroun) as League of Nation mandate territories (later known as "trusts" under the United Nations). This messy patchwork of territories, each with its own distinctive history, economy, and culture, was riven with linguistic, religious, ethnic, and economic divides that presented particularly acute difficulties as decolonization approached. Africans who wanted to push for independence faced the predicament of determining what form of national government and national identity they might pursue as an alternative to French colonial rule and assimilation to French culture. Different portions of the country could elect to affiliate with French or British territories, reject any ongoing postcolonial affiliation altogether, or propose some third alternative. In this ferment the Cameroonian nationalist movement under the Union des Populations du Cameroun (UPC) emerged to demand a break with France and to forward a socialist form of government. With the French suppression of the UPC, civil war broke out as other factions crystallized with the backing of the French. France engineered independence under a northerner, Ahmadou Ahidjo, who was less threatening to France's economic and political interests than the leaders of the UPC. At independence in 1961 the southern Anglophone portion opted to remain with the francophone territory Cameroun to become the Federal Republic of Cameroon, while the smaller northern anglophone portion became part of Nigeria. Since 1984 the nation has been known as the Republic of Cameroon. The nation is thus flanked to the west by English-speaking Nigeria, to the north and east by French-speaking Chad, Central African Republic, and Congo, and to the south by French-speaking Gabon and Spanish-speaking Equitorial Guinea.

This history of linguistic and territorial multiplicity frames the novel. The bulk of the work consists of Toundi's journals of his life as a houseboy (the French title, *Une Vie de boy*, captures this quotidian quality of the novel). However, we as readers are given access to these private reflections through the device of a first-person narrator who is another educated African on vacation in Guinea from Cameroun. The narrator comes upon Toundi as he is dying, having escaped from imprisonment in French Cameroun into the imagined promised land of Spanish Guinea. The novel opens with the dying Toundi's question to his compatriot, "Brother, what are we? What are we black men who are called French?" The narrator tells us he has translated the diaries from Ewondo (a major dialect in Cameroon) into French for us. The opening, then, casts the entire subsequent work in tragic terms; we know from the outset that Toundi will be destroyed by the action that follows, and that his death emerges somehow out of his fractured and contradictory identity.

The linguistic thread of the novel is one of its most enjoyable elements. Toundi is renamed several times as the novel progresses. By the end he has become "Monsieur Toundi," an ironic title deployed by the Commandant's wife that captures his contempt for and contamination by the French. To Toundi's compatriots the appellation is a clear indication that it is time for him to seek safety elsewhere. Woven into the novel are many irreverent conversations among the Africans in local dialects unintelligible to the French which are hilarious. Nevertheless, there is a poignancy to the Commandant's complaint to his sexually alluring, but unfaithful, wife that he is known in Ewondo as "The Commandant whose wife opens her legs in ditches and in cars." The novel turns on Toundi's fatal access to both of these worlds: he knows the intimate details of French colonial life, and he can hear and understand the commentary of the Africans about their masters. Toundi is seduced by the world of the French, embodied in the figure of the Commandant's wife, yet at the same time he experiences fascinated revulsion at the immorality and dishonesty of that world. Toundi becomes the scapegoat who must be eliminated if the system of domination, with all its masks and hypocrisy, is to continue.

There are three issues the novel raises particularly forcefully:

- Education in colonial Africa was highly contradictory, because it was through education that colonial bureaucratic and ideological control could in principle be expanded, but it was equally possible that "the tools of the master" would provide Africans with the means to articulate an alternative resistant consciousness.
- Colonial racism was bound up with gender constructs leading to deep sexual tensions that were likely to play themselves out with particular ferocity in encounters in the intimate spaces of colonial domestic service.
- Africans responded to the indignities of domination through a broad array of resistant strategies from theft to gossip, not the least of which was humor.

HOUSEBOY IN THE SYLLABUS AND IN CLASS DISCUSSION

I actually teach this novel in the context of an interdisciplinary "great books" seminar on resistance and agency. The course tends to attract relatively advanced undergraduates, but not necessarily students specifically interested in Africa. Students may, for example, have done prior work on gender, imperialism, or political theory. We open the course by playing Robert Darnton's classic essay, "Workers Revolt: The Great Cat Massacre of the Rue Saint-Séverin," off Marx's *German Ideology* in order to raise questions of class, the meaning of "consciousness," and the relations between work, domestic spaces, masculinity, and power. We go on to consider Frantz Fanon's subtle analysis on colonialism, the complexities of resistance, and the psychological dynamics of the relations between dominants and subordinates in *A Dying Colonialism*. Fanon's work provides us with the Algerian liberation movement as an example of successful militant resistance. Because outright rebellion is so appealing to undergraduates, we then take the time to consider João Jose Reis's *Slave Rebellion in Brazil* as a cautionary example of the risks of revolution and as an occasion to think about the multilayered cultural dimensions at play in moments of conflict. Having begun to appreciate the limitations of direct confrontation, we take up James Scott's *Domination and the Arts of Resistance* to think more carefully about strategies of resistance.

Scott insists that we as readers of history cannot deduce from records of public encounters anything about the real feelings, attitudes, or consciousness of those who are subordinated. He proposes that we attend to the "hidden" or private transcripts of those who are dominated. His insight, for many students, shakes a dismissive conviction that anyone who doesn't rebel in situations of domination suffers from a "slave mentality." However, some bright student inevitably points out that Scott's examples for the contents of such "transcripts" come heavily from fictional works, particularly novels. We then take some time to talk about where we look for historical evidence, its fragmentary and accidental quality, and the kinds of interactions that generate documents or recoverable "texts." Having begun to notice the difficulty of actually finding the "hidden" transcript of either the dominant or the subordinate, we are in a position both to appreciate the power and novelty of fictional works and to note some of the problems with Scott's hermeneutic assumption of a hidden transcript.

It is at this point that *Houseboy* enters the syllabus: it is full of interactions between colonists and Africans in which the kind of masking performance Scott describes is enacted. These charades are then set off by scenes in which Africans in the employ of the Europeans speak openly to one another about how they feel about the French, joking with one another, teasing and gossiping, scheming and satirizing. The students always enjoy this novel a great deal and are torn between their frustration with the naïveté of the main character, Toundi, and their admiration for his seemingly suicidal directness in his encounters with the French. For my purposes it helps them to begin to make fuller sense of some of Scott's claims, particularly his important observation that once the mask of the dominant has been taken off, the relations of domination have been forever compromised. It also offers a moment to revisit some of Fanon's observations about the psychic effects of colonialsm.

The novel helps students begin to get a sense for both the range of subtle forms of resistance and the limitations celebrating resistance as an end in itself. After all, Toundi dies and Oyono, the author, falls silent. In the course we go on to complicate the notion of resistance considerably with, among other things, Paul Willis's *Learning to Labour: How Working Class Kids Get Working Class Jobs* and Janice Boddy's *Wombs and Alien Spirits: Women, Men, and the Zar Cult in Northern Sudan.*

STUDENT RESPONSE TO THE NOVEL

This is not a difficult novel for undergraduates to grasp, and it has the added virtue of being very short. The story breaks tidily into two segments (The First and Second Exercise Books) that can be read in two class periods. I generally spend fifteen to twenty minutes setting out the historical and linguistic context before the students read the book, and elucidate other details as they become relevant to the developing discussion. A map of the region is a useful handout. In short, I find this a reasonably easy novel to teach, and I try as much as possible to let the novel speak for itself rather than overburden the students with detailed background information.

Nevertheless, there are a few pitfalls to teaching this book. I don't tell the students very much about Oyono himself until they have read the book and have made some headway in thinking about it. It is too easy for students to dismiss the author and the book unreflectively, particularly given their predilection for more dramatic forms of resistance. The details of Oyono's life become a great deal more interesting if one takes the novel seriously first. One way of interpreting Oyono's silence as an author is that he has learned the lesson of Toundi's dangerous outspokenness. Another way, I suppose, would be to say that he has become his father, "the old man and the medal"—a pathetic creature of the state he serves. The UPC movement, the novel, and Oyono's life then all become different modes of response to power and domination, all important and all in one way or another limited. The dangers of co-optation and complicity become far more poignant when embodied in someone who can so clearly articulate the psychic and physical abuses of the colonial era.

The force of the novel is that Oyono understands so acutely the consequences of unmasking the facade of power. But having understood the consequences of "raising the curtain," he seems to have been unable to imagine any further option beyond silence. This is odd because some of the minor characters in *Houseboy* are far more resourceful and resilient than the protagonist. The novel presents students with the tremendous challenge of imagining for themselves some alternatives beyond dangerous ineffectual critique, complicity, and utter silence. Toundi, the central character in the novel, rejects religion in his disillusionment with French hypocrisy. But other alternatives, such as seizing upon the moral high ground in order to motivate collective action, are also available and have been important in Cameroonian political discourse. Given the context in which I teach, I tend to use a public speech by Dr. Martin Luther King Jr., to give students a feel for the power of this form of unmasking, one that also, obviously, is not without risk or human cost. A speech by Nelson Mandela would work equally well.

Students may also need some help appreciating the humor of the novel and understanding its importance. I have yet to have a classroom of students respond to the humor of the novel as fully as I do. I suppose that for them the immediacy and perhaps unfamiliarity of the conditions of domination Toundi faces make them feel that laughter is an inappropriate response. But the novel is funny! The blurb on my paperback from *Punch* magazine, which reads "very funny and inexpressibly sad," is apt. But the students seem to see the sadness without always seizing on the laughter and its rehumanizing power. The only time my students have ever taken the humor seriously, so to speak, was one time when I inadvertently failed to assign the opening framing prologue. Because the students didn't know that Toundi had to die, they actually found the first part of the novel funny. I probably couldn't teach this book over and over again if it didn't make me laugh as well as cry.

Another pitfall of the novel from my perspective as a feminist is that the wife of the Commandant is such a despicable creature that it is possible to conclude that French women in colonial settings had unlimited power indeed, and that white women more generally are the secret rulers of the universe. Tempting as it may be to play up the unrecognized power of women, I have begun to be troubled by the easy attribution of all the sins of the racist domination to white women. The possibility that the novel may play into this unthinking prejudice disturbs me. I address this fairly directly in my class by asking the students to compare the Commandant's wife to the wife of the Bourgeois in Darnton's "Cat Massacre" (a figure who can be attacked with impunity when the object of resentment is the male bourgeois in power). And, fortunately, the novel is full of wonderful African female characters to play off against the Commandant's wife.

The main reason I like teaching this novel is that it is clear to me that the students use it to continue thinking later about race, gender dynamics, the masquerade of power, and the subtle modes of resistance we all engage in. They identify with Toundi and his predicament—something about him resonates with their own experiences of action under conditions of constraint. I don't instruct the students to write on this novel in their final writing assignment; I simply tell them that they have to write on at least three texts from the course. But many of them do choose to include the novel, and many of them use the book later in their senior colloquium (which is an oral exam on a list of books selected by the student). I would venture that it is one book I teach that students take with them and make their own long after the course is over.

SUGGESTIONS FOR
FURTHER READING AND RESOURCES

Bayart, Jean-François. 1989. "Cameroon." In *Contemporary West African States,* ed. Donal B. Cruise O-Brien, John Dunn, and Richard Rathbone. Cambridge: Cambridge University Press. For an overview of postcolonial politics in Cameroon.

Bjornson, Richard. 1991. *The African Quest for Freedom and Identity: Cameroonian Writing and the National Experience.* Bloomington: Indiana University Press. For a perceptive overview of Cameroonian literature and politics.

Boddy, Janice. 1989. *Wombs and Alien Spirits: Women, Men, and the Zar Cult in Northern Sudan.* Madison: University of Wisconsin Press.

Chocolat. 1988. Directed by Claire Denis. Distributed by Movies Unlimited, Philadelphia. A feature-length film on themes that resonate eerily with Oyono's novel, but told from the vantage point of a young white woman revisiting her childhood in Africa as the daughter of a colonial administrator. I would not use it on the same syllabus as the novel, but it might be interesting to invite students to watch the film on their own and to write a comparison with the novel.

Cohen, William B. 1971. *Rulers of Empire: The French Colonial Service in Africa.* Stanford: Hoover Institution Press. The classic study of the French colonial service.

Darnton, Robert. 1984. "Workers' Revolt: The Great Cat Massacre of the Rue Saint-Séverin." In *The Great Cat Massacre and Other Episodes in French Cultural History.* New York: Vintage Books.

DeLancey, Mark W. 1989. *Cameroon: Dependence and Independence.* Boulder: Westview. For a good overview of Cameroonian politics.

Destination Cameroon. 1993. Directed by Sandra D. Radtke. Washington, D.C.: Peace Corps of the United States of America, World Wise Schools. One videocassette (20 min.). A short video to give some students some visual images of Cameroon and to raise issues of development.

Dunton, Christopher. 1997a. "Ferdinand Oyono." In *African Writers*, vol. 2, ed. C. Brian Cox. New York: Charles Scribner's Sons.

———. 1997b. *The Novels of Ferdinand Oyono.* Boulder: Lynne Rienner.

Echenberg, Myron. 1991. *Colonial Conscripts: The Tirailleurs Sénégalais in French West Africa, 1857–1960.* Portsmouth, N.H.: Heinemann.

"Entretien avec Ferdinand Oyono," *Cameroon Tribune,* 23 February 1976.

Everson, Vanessa. 1998. "Ferdinand Oyono." In *Postcolonial African Writers: A Bio- Bibliographical Critical Sourcebook,* ed. Pushpa Naidu Parekh and Siga Fatima Jagne. Westport: Greenwood. A useful biographical overview with notes on critical work on Oyono. This is a wonderful resource for background on other African authors well.

Eyongetah, Tambi, and Robert Brain. 1974. *A History of Cameroon.* London: Longman. For a broad historical study of Cameroon as a whole.

Fanon, Frantz. 1990. *A Dying Colonialism*, trans. Haakon Chevalier. New York: Grove Press.

Keim, Karen Ruth King. 1986. "Trickery and Social Values in the Oral and Written Literature of Cameroon." Ph.D dissertation, Indiana University. Useful for her consideration of the oral and written taken together.

Kibera, Leonard. 1983. "Colonial Context and Language in Ferdinand Oyono's *Houseboy,*" *African Literature Today*, 13: 79–97.

Lee, Sonia. 1997. "Francophone Literature in Western Africa." In *Encyclopedia of Africa South of the Sahara,* vol. 3. New York: Charles Scribners.

Linnemann, Russell. 1976. "The Anticolonialism of Ferdinand Oyono," *Yale French Studies* 53, Traditional and Contemporary African Literature. A classic assessment of Oyono's critique of colonialism.

Manning, Patrick. 1988. *Francophone Sub-Saharan Africa: 1880–1985.* Cambridge: Cambridge University Press. A useful overview of the francophone context that bridges the occasionally artificial divide between West and Equatorial Africa and between French and Belgian territories.

Marx, Karl. 1978 [1932]. "The German Ideology: Part I." In *The Marx-*

Engels Reader, 2nd ed., ed. Robert C. Tucker. New York: Norton. I use this for his classic discussion of consciousness and an intriguing but fleeting vision of what a socialist utopia might be like.

Moore, Gerald. 1963. "Ferdinand Oyono and the Colonial Tragi-comedy," *Présence Africaine* 18, 46: 221–233.

Ogunsanwo, Olatubosun. 1986. "The Narrative Voice in Two Novels of Ferdinand Oyono," *English Studies in Africa* (Johannesburg) 29, 2: 97–120.

Okirike, Boniface Ifere. 1987. "Blancs et noirs dans l'oeuvre d'Oyono: une approche sociologique." Ph.D. dissertation, University of Cincinnati. A rare recent assessment of Oyono's work.

Oyono, Ferdinand. 1956. *Le Vieux Nègre et la médaille*. Paris: Julliard.

———. 1956. *Une Vie de boy*. Paris: Julliard.

———. 1960. *Chemin d'Europe*. Paris: Juillard.

———. [1966] 1990. *Houseboy*. Translated from the French by John Reed. Portsmouth, N.H.: Heinemann.

———. 1969. *The Old Man and the Medal*. Translated from the French by John Reed. Portsmouth, N.H.: Heinemann.

———. 1989. *Road to Europe*. Translated from the French by Richard Bjornson. Washington, D.C.: Three Continents Press.

Reis, João Jose. 1993. *Slave Rebellion in Brazil: The Muslim Uprising of 1835 in Bahia*. Translated by Arthur Brakel. Baltimore: Johns Hopkins University Press.

Sarvan, Charles Ponnuthurai. 1985. "French Colonialism in Africa: The Early Novels of Ferdinand Oyono," *World Literature Today: A Literary Quarterly of the University of Oklahoma* 59, 3: 333–337.

Schmidt, Elizabeth. 1992. *Peasants, Traders, and Wives: Shona Women in the History of Zimbabwe, 1870–1939*. Portsmouth, N.H.: Heinemann.

Scott, James. 1990. *Domination and the Arts of Resistance: Hidden Transcripts*. New Haven: Yale University Press.

Willis, Paul. [1977] 1981. *Learning to Labour: How Working Class Kids Get Working Class Jobs*. New York: Columbia University Press.

Yetiv, Isaac. 1985. "Le Rire, arme de combat contre le colonialisme, dans les romans de Ferdinand Oyono," *Griot: Official Journal of the Southern Conference on Afro-American Studies* 4, 1–2: 8–17. Houston, Texas.

20

Tayeb Salih's
Season of Migration to the North

Farouk Topan

SALIH'S *SEASON OF MIGRATION TO THE NORTH* WAS ORIGI-
nally written in Arabic and translated into English by Denys Johnson
Davies in a way that captures poetically the nuances and moods of
the original. I teach it as part of a trilogy of novels in which Islam
features as an influencing factor; the other two are Hamidou Kane's
Ambiguous Adventure and Ousmane Sembene's *God's Bits of Wood*
(see Chapter 21). Inherent in the selection of these novels is thus
scope for comparison, whose ingredients include self-discovery and
(or even through) the colonial experience. Any of the three novels
could have been selected for this paper, but I have two reasons for
choosing *Season*. Part of the story is set in London and, although the
period is the 1920s and 1930s, the setting is more familiar to students
than those of the other two novels (set in France and West Africa).
Second, the colonial engagement Salih attempts to explore in the
novel is personally meaningful to me, as the two main characters are
intellectuals from an anglophone country, the Sudan, who study and
reside in England for a while. Having come to England from
Zanzibar (where the population is also mainly Muslim), and having
lived here intermittently for close to four decades, I appreciate the
tensions involved in the cross-cultural negotiations of the self and the
other, both in Britain and subsequently in Africa.

Tayeb Salih was born in 1929 in a village in Sudan's Northern
Province of the Sudan. His earliest education was in the quranic

Tayeb Salih, *Season of Migration to the North*, trans. Denys Johnson-Davies
(Boulder: Lynne Rienner, 1997).

school of the village. The first part of his secular education was
undertaken at Gordon College in the capital, Khartoum; he proceeded to England to complete his higher studies in the 1950s and then
joined the Arabic Service of the British Broadcasting Services. It was
following this period that he wrote *Season of Migration to the North*,
his first novel. In a speech to students at the American University of
Beirut in 1980, Salih elaborated:

> I started *Season* in the summer of 1960, when on holiday in a little
> village near Cannes. I had just arrived from Beirut where I had
> spent three months in hospital. I nearly died then. I don't know if
> there are links here, but this was my most fertile period. . . . I want-
> ed first to write a straightforward thriller, a thriller about a crime of
> passion. . . . I also got interested in English characters like
> Lawrence of Arabia, Sir Richard Burton and such people who
> showed a strange attraction to the Arab world, the type of romanti-
> cism which I started to challenge in the novel. I fell under the
> influence of Freud as well and read more than once *Civilization
> and its Discontents*. What fascinated me then and would seem sim-
> plistic now, is Freud's theory of man as divided up between Eros
> and Death. (quoted in Amyuni 1985:15)

The speech informs us of the provenance and message of the novel
from the novelist's viewpoint; in order to appreciate the points made,
and to place the discussion in perspective, it is appropriate to give a
summary of the plot.

THE PLOT

The story is told in the first person by a narrator who remains name-
less throughout the novel. He has returned to the Sudan after spending seven years studying in England. He visits his village, which is
situated at a bend in the Nile in Sudan's Northern Province (identified as Wad Hamid by Nasr 1980: 88). In his answers to many questions that assail him regarding the people among whom he had lived
abroad for so long, he surprises the villagers when he tells them that
Europeans "were, with minor differences, exactly like them, marrying and bringing up their children in accordance with principles and
traditions, that they had good morals and were in general good people" (p. 3).

Among the people present there to meet the narrator is a man of
about fifty who does not seem to be a local man. When the narrator

asks about him, he is informed that Mustafa Sa'eed had come to live in the village five years ago, that he had built a house and married a local woman, Hosna, by whom he had two children. Not much is known about him. The narrator's curiosity is aroused, for he can see that Sa'eed has gained the respect of the villagers through his quiet authority and presence of personality. The narrator feels instinctively that there is much more to Sa'eed than he or any villager can see or be permitted to see. One day, during a drinking session, Sa'eed quite unexpectedly recites an English poem in "an impeccable accent," leaving no doubt in the narrator's mind that the man is a Western-educated intellectual of high caliber. Having thus inadvertently revealed himself, Sa'eed then relates his tale to the narrator ("lest your imagination run away with you").

Mustafa Sa'eed was born in Khartoum, where he grew up as an independent child: his father had died before Sa'eed was born, and his mother rather let the child grow up almost by himself. It was Sa'eed who agreed to be taken to school, and, later, to go to Cairo for further studies. There was not much communication between the boy and his mother; one wonders whether there was even much love. When they parted company for the last time, neither shed any tears. In Cairo, an English couple—Mr. and Mrs. Robinson—looked after the twelve-year-old boy; Mrs. Robinson's hug aroused in him his first sexual feelings. From Cairo, he proceeded to England for further education, where he became a lecturer in economics and wrote books expounding his economic theory. Throughout his childhood and then into his manhood, Sa'eed was aware of himself as someone different from others. He attributed that difference to his intelligence. "My mind was like a sharp knife, cutting with cold effectiveness. . . . I was cold as a field of ice, nothing in the world would shake me" (p. 22).

The most striking aspect of Sa'eed's thirty-year stay in London that emerges through the novel is his sexual exploitation of English women. His seduction was built on lies: he told them what they wanted to hear from a member of an exotic race. "What race are you?" one of them asks him. "Are you African or Asian?" He replies: "I'm like Othello—Arab-African" (p. 38). Three of the women kill themselves because of him, but he meets his match in Jean Morris, who is intelligent, and like him, cold yet impulsive and calculating. They get married and lead a tempestuous life. In the end, Sa'eed kills her while making love. This, in a sense, is the climax of the meeting of Death and Eros that Salih mentions in his speech. As Abbas points out, Jean Morris turns out to be Iago, not Desdemona, to Mustafa

Sa'eed's Othello (Abbas 1985: 34). Sa'eed is tried and imprisoned
for seven years for the murder. When he is released, he returns to the
Sudan and settles in the village on the bank of the Nile. A short while
after telling his story, Mustafa Sa'eed disappears and is presumed
drowned. He leaves a note to the narrator, appointing him trustee and
executor of his estate, and the guardian of his children. Sa'eed also
leaves him a key to a room in the house he had built—a room that no
one besides himself had entered before.

Over the next two years, the narrator gradually falls in love with
Hosna, Sa'eed's widow, but does nothing about it, even when her
hand is sought in marriage by Wad Rayyes, a lecherous old man
almost twice her age. When she is forced to marry him—having
failed to get the narrator himself to marry her—she avoids consum-
mating the marriage for two weeks. When Wad Rayyes forces himself upon her, she kills him and then herself.

The news and manner of Hosna's death plunge the narrator into
deep gloom. He now enters Sa'eed's private room to find out more
about his "adversary." The room is, to all intents and purposes, an
English room: there are an English hearth, books, paintings, manu-
scripts—even the Quran is in English. And there are portraits of
Sa'eed's women and photographs of Sa'eed himself in England. It is
a part of the North carefully constructed in the South for Sa'eed's
pleasure or pain alone. There is also a mirror, one of the first objects
that the narrator sees in the room:

> I struck a match. The light exploded on my eyes and out of the
> darkness there emerged a frowning face with pursed lips that I
> knew but could not place. I moved towards it with hate in my
> heart. It was my adversary Mustafa Sa'eed. The face grew a neck,
> the neck two shoulders and a chest, then a trunk and two legs, and I
> found myself standing face to face with myself. This is not Mustafa
> Sa'eed—it's a picture of me frowning at my face from a mirror. (p.
> 135)

Nazareth draws our attention to the narrator's earlier remarks about a
mirror. When the narrator had first returned to the village from
England, he had basked in the warmth of the homecoming: "I was
happy during those days, like the child that sees its face in the mirror
for the first time" (p. 4; Nazareth 1985: 125). But now the mirror in
this dark room reflects a troubled being, one who decides to put an
end to his life. Like Sa'eed (who is presumed drowned) the narrator
goes into the river to drown himself but, in that very attempt, there
arises in him a new strength and determination: "All my life I had

not chosen, had not decided. Now I am making a decision. I choose life. I shall live because there are a few people I want to stay with for the longest possible time and because I have duties to discharge" (p. 168).

CONTEXT AND ISSUES

I teach the three novels at the School of Oriental and African Studies in a new course convened by Louis Brenner, Islamic Religious Culture in Sub-Saharan Africa. It is a multidisciplinary team-taught course whose aim is to explore selected social, political, and cultural aspects of both past and contemporary Muslim societies in Africa. The three novels exhibit a perception of Islam on a continuum that portrays it in different ways. At one end is Hamidou Kane's almost esoteric story, whose focus is the journey of Samba Diallo through phases of doubt and uncertainties when his Islamic beliefs are tested in Paris, a country and culture far from his own. He finds it difficult to integrate into the French culture and gradually feels alienated. When he returns to Senegal, his self-assessment at his teacher's grave is almost final: "I do not believe—I do not believe very much any more, of what you had taught me" (Kane 1971: 173). Not quite at the other end of the scale, but certainly further down the continuum, is Sembene's narrative of the strike in Senegal in 1948. Islam is not the focus of the novel: the people act as they do because they are human beings in search of their rights, not *because* they are Muslims. Some of Sembene's characters would like to keep the two separate: "Don't mix religion in this," as Sounkare tells Bakary (Sembene 1995: 18). But it is hard not to, as Islam permeates action and thought, sometimes for better and sometimes for worse—as in the case of the hypocritical leader at Dakar, Mabigué. Thus Islam forms the backdrop to the strike but not its driving force.

Unlike Kane, Salih does not set out to "portray" Islam as such, but its values and teachings are interwoven in the plot, perhaps more intrinsically than in Sembene's work. And yet it is in the breach of the accepted norms, with varying degrees of seriousness, that the plot unfolds: Sa'eed's lies, womanizing, and his murder of Jean Morris in England; drinking alcohol in the village (when his guard is lowered and his hidden self reveals itself in a recitation of poetry); the sexual greed of Wad Rayyes and his abuse of marriage; Hosna's refusal to give her consent to marry Wad Rayyes and her proposal—unthinkably forward in that society—for the narrator to marry her; the burial of Hosna and Wad Rayyes without a funeral ceremony; and, finally, suicide.

For Sa'eed, the breach is at its widest in England; it is there that he loses part of himself in the consciousness of the other, and the other's consciousness becomes part of his. Hence the creation of his "English" room in a village in Sudan: "my private room where you will perhaps find what you are looking for," as Sa'eed tells the narrator in his final letter (p. 65). The existence of the room is important to Sa'eed's well-being. For it is in that room, as Nasr suggests (1980: 98), that Sa'eed finds his peace of mind, which in turn suggests his alienation from the people around him. And yet, in the letter to the narrator, Sa'eed entrusts the care of his children to him, hoping that in the future they will not only come to know "what sort of a person their father was—if that is at all possible" but, more important, that the children will grow up "imbued with the air of this village, its smells and colours and history, the faces of its inhabitants and the memories of its floods and harvestings and sowings" (p. 65). What is at stake here, as we discuss in class, are the issues of identity, belonging, and peace of mind. Sa'eed does not wish to transmit to his children the cultural schizophrenia that afflicts him and that eventually destroys him. "The black Englishman" is the nickname given to him by his classmates at Gordon College, even before his departure for England; once in England, he takes in his stride the behavior, attitudes, and even the prejudices around him. He settles well in London as a lecturer in economics, and he seems to enjoy his exploitation of English women. Even his relationship with Jean Morris has moments of pleasure and ecstasy, albeit sometimes from pain and longing. Why, then, does he return to the Sudan and settle in an obscure village?

The answer is not straightforward, and in its complexity lies one of the important messages of the novel. It may be that feelings of shame prevent Sa'eed from continuing to live in England after his imprisonment. Or—what is more probable—he longs for his roots and the cultural comfort of living among his people. It appears paradoxical at first sight that Sa'eed should decide to return to live among his own people in Africa and still retreat into his private "English" room for his peace of mind. The implication of this act, and its underlying attitude, give rise to an interesting discussion in class on the issues of identity, self-perception, and personal happiness. Some students find this puzzling: how can an African yearn for Britain in the midst of Africa—"mother" Africa? (a debate of the

1960s revisited by another generation). To others, Sa'eed's act is an outcome of the corrosive effects of colonial education, which broadens the mind but alienates it and the soul from its cultural origins. This is a point from Davidson (1989: 385–400), who considers Salih's concern with the role of education in the former colonies. A distinction is made between knowledge, a positive asset, and (as Davidson puts it) "the education one receives from an oppressor, especially in the language of oppression, and the potential sabotage of native culture it entails" (p. 386). One sees its effects on the two main characters of the novel, the narrator and Sa'eed: "both have allowed their minds and souls to be separated, and they fight feelings of betrayal of self and community" (p. 387).

It is to assuage such feelings that Sa'eed, however he might feel alienated within himself, returns to settle in the Sudan. He chooses to live not in the urban environment of Khartoum (which he knew well), but in a small, quiet village whose people lead a simple life. The narrator is not very different from Sa'eed in *this* respect (except that he does not have to carry the burden of English justice on his shoulders, nor presumably the guilt of the events that led to imprisonment). The narrator has his family in the village, and it is interesting that, for both these intellectuals, the narrator's grandfather, Hajj Ahmed, is a symbol of the life of the village. Despite his age, he is still physically fit; the villagers look up to him and come to him for advice, and his devotion and piety are exemplary. He is untouched by Western education and he is considered a good Muslim. But, as Nasr points out, the villagers follow popular Islam, a mixture of both orthodox teachings and indigenous beliefs (Nasr 1980: 89). The result is a society in which certain Western stereotypes of how Muslims should behave are shown to falter. I quote from the essay of a student:

> But the contrast of European and Islamic values . . . is not the theme of the book; rather it contains some challenges to a stereotyped image of Islam that the West overwhelmingly holds. For example, among several old people in the Sudanese village there is an extensive discussion about sex in which a woman also participates very actively. Bint Majzoub has had eight husbands, she smokes a lot and talks to other men about her sexual experiences. This is certainly not the way Islamic women are supposed to behave.

It needs be said, though, that Bint Majzoub is a forceful individual whose status and freedom are partly due to her wealth, amassed through inheritance from her late husbands. She is also portrayed as traditional in other respects, as when she jokes with the narrator (perhaps a little sarcastically) at the beginning of the novel: "We were afraid . . . you'd bring back with you an uncircumcised infidel for a wife" (p. 4). In fact, the issue of female circumcision forms a topic of discussion among Bint Majzoub's group later in the novel when a significant message on tolerance is portrayed by Salih. The discussion is on the pleasures of sex, and Wad Rayyes's assertion that foreign uncircumcised girls offer greater enjoyment than local, circumcised ones. The response from one member of the group is that "circumcision is one of the conditions of Islam." "What Islam are you talking about?" retorts Wad Rayyes. "It's your Islam and Hajj Ahmed's Islam. . . . The Nigerians, the Egyptians, and the Arabs of Syria, aren't they Moslems like us? But they're people who know what's what and leave their women as God created them. As for us, we dock them like you do animals" (p. 81). Thus, quite uncharacteristically, Wad Rayyes transcends the narrow confines of custom and pleads for a broader outlook, albeit on a matter—sensuous delights—that most occupies his mind. Salih conveys the message that such a custom, like many others that have evolved locally, is not a requirement of the religion.

The status and position of women, both Western and African, is another area addressed by the novel. The patriarchy that prevails in the village is challenged by the behavior and attitude of Hosna; she not only withholds herself from the husband imposed upon her but kills him when he tries to take her forcefully. The fact that both are buried without proper services indicates the conservativeness of the elders: they are not yet ready to consider, much less sympathize with, Hosna's wishes. For all her talk, Bint Majzoub is not prepared to grant equal status to one of her gender. As Davidson points out, her group "maintains 'the old ways' which show the 'colonized oppression' already inherent in their culture—not of Britain but of Islam and patriarchy" (1989: 387). These two facets are reflected in Sa'eed's attitude to women in England. He seduces English women for pleasure as well as for a psychopolitical goal: to liberate Africa, as he says. He thus sees them as women *of* the colonizers who had dominated Africa. But, like Wad Rayyes with Hosna, Sa'eed meets his match in Jean Morris. Today, such an attitude is clearly perceived as outdated. Colonialism is over, at least de jure if not entirely de facto; and the interracial society that Britain is becoming, particularly in the big cities, makes Sa'eed's actions less comprehensible to the younger generation. On the other hand, the dynamics of interracial gender relationships make Sa'eed's references to Othello still relevant, even in the new millenium. (For thoughts in a similar vein, see Ben Okri's 1997 essay.)

DIFFICULTIES FOR STUDENTS

There have not been major difficulties in the teaching of *Season of Migration to the North*. Three minor aspects may be cited. The first is the need to have a general knowledge of Islam, sufficient to follow the nuances and messages discussed in this chapter. Rahman's book on Islam (Rahman 1979) is a good starting point. The second aspect relates to an understanding of English culture—a general knowledge that enables one, for instance, to appreciate the contents of Sa'eed's private room and their significance in the story. The final aspect has to do with the author's style. It should be noted that the novel has a double narration with two main characters—Mustafa Sa'eed and the narrator: two locations, two points of view, two chronologies, and two styles. An excellent aid to understanding this dimension of the novel is the article by Peter Nazareth (1985) in Amyuni's *Casebook*.

Teaching *Season* as part of a trio of novels with an overarching theme has been both enjoyable and challenging. The challenge lies mainly in exploring a meaningful continuum of relationships between the three novels in terms of their narratives, characters, and messages. This had to be done within the framework of a new course, which was itself in a process of development. The three novels are different in their styles and orientations, yet—at a deeper level—the concerns of Salih, Kane, and Sembene are similar. The focus is on the engagement of the human dimension in the colonial cauldron through the impact of education, denial of workers' rights, and imposition (perhaps even erosion) of identity. The mold, the authors suggest, is ready for breaking. The question now is whether the postindependence period in Africa has aided the process.

SUGGESTIONS FOR
FURTHER READING AND RESOURCES

Abbas, Ali Abdallah. 1985. "The Father of Lies: The Role Mustafa Sa'eed as Second Self in Season of Migration to the North." In *Season of*

Migration to the North: *A Casebook,* ed. Mona Takieddine Amyuni. Beirut: American University of Beirut.

Amyuni, Mona Takieddine. 1985. *Tayeb Salih's Season of Migration to the North: A Casebook.* Beirut: American University of Beirut. A very helpful companion to the novel. Twelve essays discuss various aspects of Salih's work. Amyuni's introduction places the novel in context. Also contains an extensive bibliography on Salih and his works.

Davidson, John E. 1989. "In Search of a Middle Point: The Origins of Oppression in Tayeb Salih's *Season of Migration to the North*," *Research in African Literatures* 20, 3: 385–400.

Kane, Hamidou. [1962] 1971. *Ambiguous Adventure*, trans. Katherine Woods. Portsmouth, N.H., and Oxford: Heinemann.

Nasr, Ahmad A. 1980. "Popular Islam in Al-Tayyib Salih," *Journal of Arabic Literature* 11: 88–104.

Nazareth, Peter. 1985. "The Narrator as Artist and the Reader as Critic in Season of Migration to the North." In *Season: A Casebook*, ed. Mona Takieddine Amyuni. Beirut: American University of Beirut.

Okri, Ben. 1997. "Leaping Out of Shakespeare's Terror: Five Meditations on Othello." In *A Way of Being Free*. London: Phoenix House.

Peled, M. 1977. "Portrait of an Intellectual," *Journal of Middle Eastern Studies* 13, 2: 218–228.

Rahman, Fazlur. 1979. *Islam.* Chicago: University of Chicago Press. A good general introduction to Islam.

Salih, Tayeb. 1991. *Season of Migration to the North*, trans. Denys Johnson-Davies. Boulder: Lynne Rienner.

Sembene, Ousmane. 1995. *God's Bits of Wood*, trans. Francis Price. Portsmouth, N.H., and Oxford: Heinemann. (See Chapter 21 in this volume.)

21

Ousmane Sembene's
God's Bits of Wood

Dennis D. Cordell

GOD'S BITS OF WOOD IS A WONDERFUL NOVEL FOR
teaching about the complexity of social movements and social
change, ranging from labor organizing and gender relations to
race relations and nationalism. But if it is a novel about change, it
is at the same time a novel about "tradition." The book is also
very useful as a tool to teach students about the nature of history
and the "truth" of the historian, the nature of creative writing and,
if you will, the "truth" of the novelist. Moreover, the pages of
God's Bits of Wood are populated by an extraordinary array of
memorable African characters who reflect the many ways that
women and men reacted to French colonial rule in West Africa
and its impact on their societies. Students identify readily with
many of the characters and seem to feel the passion and pathos of
their individual situations and collective struggles. The novel is
long, some 250 pages, and when composing my book list, I
always ask myself if it is a good idea to ask students to read so
much. When it shows up on the syllabus, however, the engaged
student response immediately persuades me of the wisdom of my
choice.

Ousmane Sembene, *God's Bits of Wood*, trans. Francis Price (Portsmouth, N.H.:
Heinemann, 1970). First published in French as *Les Bouts de bois de Dieu* in
1960. Note that in much of francophone West Africa, he would more commonly
be referred to as Sembene Ousmane, and readers will find both variations in the
literature.

COURSE CONTEXT

I use *God's Bits of Wood* in two courses that I teach regularly. The first and most obvious is a course entitled Modern Africa, which explores major themes in the history of the continent from the abolition of the Atlantic slave trade to the present. I teach the course annually to a class of about thirty-five students. I also ask students to read the novel in a second course, Négritudes: The Literatures and Histories of the Struggle for Black Liberation. This course deals in a comparative and interdisciplinary way with themes of colonialism, racial oppression, liberation, identity, and self-expression in the Caribbean, West Africa, the United States, France, and Britain. Taught usually with a colleague from the Department of Foreign Languages and Literature, the class enrolls about forty students.

THE NOVEL AND ITS AUTHOR

The Historical Context

God's Bits of Wood is a historical novel that builds its story around the strike by African workers on the Dakar-Niger railroad between October 10, 1947, and March 19, 1948. It was a time of enormous change in Europe and Africa. During the "high tide" of colonialism between World Wars I and II, colonial policies and the colonial economy began to influence the inner workings of African societies more than ever before, a process accelerated by the Depression of the 1930s and the mobilization that accompanied World War II. Following the war, winds of change blew from several directions. First, at a conference in Brazzaville in 1944, Charles De Gaulle, the war hero who later founded the Fifth Republic, proposed recasting the French empire to permit greater participation by "overseas Frenchmen" in the institutions that governed them. In addition, the independence of India in 1947 and the continuing struggle of the Indonesian people against efforts by the Dutch to reimpose their rule following the Japanese defeat called colonialism itself into question. Finally, France and Great Britain, the greatest of the colonial powers, were eclipsed by the emergence of the United States and the Soviet Union as major players on the world stage following the war. Neither nascent superpower looked favorably upon colonial empires, the United States for historical reasons and the USSR for ideological ones. Although blowing from afar, these winds undoubtedly had some impact in French West Africa in the years and months preceding the 1947 strike—even though historical writing about the conflict is in disagreement about just how much (see Cooper 1996 and Suret-Canale 1978).

It seems obvious that Sembene's thinking about the 1947 conflict would have been influenced by the rapid steps that France's West African colonies took toward independence in the late 1950s. Indeed, 1960, the year the novel was published, witnessed the independence of virtually all of France's African possessions and was thus a culmination of sorts in the drive toward greater self-determination in European colonial empires worldwide. In this sense, then, Sembene's view of the strike, recounted nearly a decade and a half after it occurred, undoubtedly differed in important ways from that of the *cheminots,* or railroad workers, in 1947, who acted within a climate that promoted challenges to European rule but could not have predicted the itinerary of the march toward independence. Indeed, Frederick Cooper, in a recent article on the strike, records that some strikers today accuse Sembene of having stolen "our strike." Whether he stole it or not, it is apparent that the *cheminots* had their strike and Sembene has his, which was somewhat different. But rather than undermining the usefulness of the novel for the classroom, the discrepancies between the "real" strike of 1947 and that recounted in *God's Bits of Wood* create opportunities to help students ask questions about the nature of history, historical sources, historical research, and historical writing. For a timely discussion of these issues, see Atwood (1998), Demos (1998), Hunt (1998), and Spence (1998), whose articles are part of an *American Historical Review* forum on "Histories and Historical Fictions."

A Sketch of the Author and His Work

Ousmane Sembene is, without a doubt, one of francophone Africa's greatest living authors. And the translation of most of his major, and many of his minor, works into English has made him a well-known writer in the English-speaking world as well. Self-educated, and at one time or another a fisherman, a plumber, a mason, a soldier, a longshoreman, and an avid union organizer, he began his literary career in the 1950s with short stories and short novels such as *Le Docker noir* [*Black Docker*] (1956), *O Pays, Mon Beau People!* (1957), *Voltaïque* (1962), and "Le Mandat" ["The Money Order"]

(1965). *God's Bits of Wood*, published in 1960, was his first major
novel. With the independence of nearly all of France's African
colonies that same year, Sembene moved on to examine postcolonial
government and society in his native Senegal. His piercing observations produced the scathing satirical novels *Xala* (1973),
L'Harmattan (1964), and *The Last of the Empire* (1981). They also
provoked decided disapproval and censorship by the regime of
Léopold Senghor, Senegal's first president, the only African member
of the Académie Française, and a major literary figure in his own
right.

   Along with being a major writer, Sembene is also a celebrated
filmmaker. Indeed, he is hailed throughout the world as the founder
of African cinema. Many of his films are available with subtitles in
English, although they are less readily available than the films of
other African filmmakers because he is reluctant to circulate them in
videotape format for fear of piracy. For Sembene, writing and film-
making have gone hand in hand. Many of his films are visual versions of his short stories and novels. Others, such as *Ceddo* (1976)
and *Camp de Thiaroye* (1989), are original celluloid creations—not
film versions of earlier literary works. Sembene's films deliver their
messages in local languages, depend neither on literacy nor on
knowledge of French, and have therefore had wide appeal. But
Sembene has not chosen to make *God's Bits of Wood* into a film.
Asking why this might be often provokes animated class discussion.

GOD'S BITS OF WOOD

The book opens in Bamako with a chapter that quickly underscores
three of the novel's major themes—the social changes wrought by
colonialism and its accompanying technology and institutions in the
first half of the twentieth century, efforts by African men and women
to take control of this new world, and the way that the ensuing struggle transforms women as well as men. Sembene presents these
themes very concretely. The "story" begins with an encounter
between Niakoro, a Malian Bambara woman of an older generation
who tries her best to ignore the changes wrought by French colonial
rule, and Ad'jibid'ji, her young granddaughter, who understands
French and participates in public life in a way erstwhile forbidden to
women and the young. Action then rapidly moves to a meeting of
railroad workers to decide whether or not they should strike to force

their company, the Régie Dakar-Niger, to pay wages and provide benefits on a par with those granted European workers. Apart from the momentous decision at hand, the men are also called upon to act in a new context, that of the Western-inspired union meeting where young and old speak with equal authority. Niakoro's husband, Mamadou Keïta (called Fa Keïta or "the Old One"), who attended the meeting, reports this shift to his wife: "Niakoro, . . . even we old people must learn, and recognize that the things people know today were not born with us. No, knowledge is not a hereditary thing. For months I have been learning that—and with regret, believe me" (p. 11). This chapter also brings news of one of the novel's two major characters, committed union leader and militant Ibrahim Bakayoko—Ad'jibid'ji's father, and son of Niakoro and the Old One. Chief strategist behind the strike, Bakayoko is more allegory than mortal man, representing the Worker, the People, and the Union, but also the great Keïta founders of the empire of Old Mali. Always absent but always talked about—he appears for the first time two-thirds of the way through the novel (p. 171)—he is nonetheless the apparent life force of the movement.

From Bamako the story moves east and west along the Dakar-Niger line—through nineteen more chapters from Bamako to Thiès and Dakar, and back and forth again, reflecting both the new geography created by the railroad in French West Africa and the movements of the trains themselves. The second and third chapters take us to Thiès, the heart of the rail network, where the line to Saint-Louis branches off from the Bamako-Dakar route, and where the union makes its headquarters. We meet Maïmouna, a blind woman with twins who "sees," a remarkable character who speaks with the voice of an oracle of yore. Maïmouna urges compassion, but also displays great strength in the face of the first major clash provoked by the strike, a police attack on workers at the market just outside the rail-yard that leaves one of her own children dead. We also meet the principal European protagonists, Dejean, Leblanc (which translates ironically as "the white"), and Isnard—each a colonial caricature from central casting. But the real story here is the women, and the omniscient narrator brings our sojourn in Thiès to a close by observing that "if the times were bringing forth a new breed of men, they were also bringing forth a new breed of women " (p. 34).

The novel's fourth, fifth, and sixth chapters unfold in Dakar, the western terminus of the railroad. Here too live a host of memorable characters, many of them women: Ramatoulaye, the grandmother, who, out of initial concern for finding food for her family, attacks and indeed "sacrifices" her brother's ram Vendredi (named "Friday," presumably for the Muslim day of prayer). The brother, El Hadji Mabigué, is a prominent Muslim leader who supports the French authorities who run the colony and the railroad. Another determined woman in Ramatoulaye's household in Dakar is Mame Sofi, who deceives a Tukolor water carrier into filling her water jars and then drives him away when he demands payment. Finally come two characters who are far more ambiguous in their behavior: N'Deye Touti, Sofi's niece, who has been to school and is terribly enamored of all things French, although she daydreams about Bakayoko; and her male counterpart and would-be suitor Beaugosse ("Handsome Guy"), whom we first see at the union offices, but whose Parisian attire, demeanor, and use of French suggests that his vote to strike was perhaps less "decided" than those of his compatriots. He too is focused on Bakayoko, the absent rival: "'Bakayoko, Bakayoko!' Beaugosse exclaimed. 'All day long I hear nothing but that name— as if he were some kind of prophet!'" (p. 39). Near the end of this stopover in Dakar, the police appear in order to arrest Ramatoulaye; a dramatic fight ensues, and the women carry their opposition from the compound to the community. The chapters close betwixt tradition and modernity. The strikers and their families revive ceremonies "that went back to time immemorial . . . and pageants that had long been forgotten" (p. 75). But they are also weighed down by "the loss of the machine," the train they call "the smoke of the savanna" (pp. 75–76).

Chapters 7 and 8 jump to the other end of the line—to Bamako. Here attention focuses on the men who are also venturing into new arenas of action. They set about to mount a trial of Diara, a strike-breaker. But if Western in inspiration, the trial nonetheless evokes elements of African institutions and history. Diara is, after all, charged with *dynfa*, betrayal of one's own people. And as Tiémoko makes plans for the tribunal, he begins singing hymns associated with Sunjata, founder of the empire of Old Mali (p. 90). But for Sembene, this insertion of a Western trial in an African context is not enough. Women are invited and women speak. Fa Keïta, the "Old One," is sufficiently upset to make a religious retreat "to address his troubled thought to the Almighty" (p. 96). In the meantime, militiamen come to arrest him. His wife Niakoro and granddaughter Ad'jibid'ji resist, he is dragged off, and Niakoro collapses, striking her head fatally against the "beaten earth" (pp. 102–103). The old order seems to be dead; and yet, just before her death Niakoro calls the new order into question with a riddle to her granddaughter: "Well then, since you are such a little miss-know-it-all, tell me this—what is it that washes the water?" (p. 101). Moreover, Sembene chooses to end this Bamako segment by introducing Bakayoko's wife, Assitan, whom he had inherited, according to custom, upon the death of his elder brother: "By the ancient standards of Africa, Assitan was a perfect wife: docile, submissive, and hard-working, she never spoke one word louder than another" (p. 106).

The next chapter returns to Dakar, where we pick up the story of grandmother Ramatoulaye. Following the earlier battle, Mame Sofi accosts a servant of El Hadji Mabigué, who has tried to calm her and her fellow women, denounces Mabigué for requesting police intervention simply to avenge his ram Vendredi, and then hits the servant "squarely in the forehead" with a bottle (p. 110). Then word comes that the forces of the law are returning, this time in the guise of *spahis*, or mounted militiamen. The women respond with a rain of burning straw that spooks the horses, but in so doing they set a fire that gets out of control and soon devours many of the houses in the neighborhood, including that of Mabigué. In the aftermath of the conflagration, Mame Sofi's niece N'Deye Touti is ashamed and then outraged by the comments of French officials who survey the disaster and talk about her in degrading anatomical terms, not knowing that she understands French: "'Did you see those eyes?' the officer said. 'And those breasts? A real little filly—just the way I like them!'" (p. 117). By this time, the police have returned yet again to arrest Ramatoulaye, who decides instead to go freely to the police station. Conversant in French, N'Deye Touti accompanys the old woman, who, in fact, needs no escort, "standing defiantly in the middle of the room" (p. 120) facing the chief of police. Outside, the women surround the building to prevent the authorities from sneaking Ramatoulaye out a back door. Another confrontation with the police follows. In the melée, Houdia M'Baye, another of the women's leaders, is struck down and killed by the power of water from firehoses unleashed on the assembly. In an effort to defuse the situation, the authorities call El Hadji Mabigué, Ramatoulaye's brother, who arrives, predictably ingratiates himself with the police chief, and tries to control his sister. Pushed to ask for pardon, Ramatoulaye denounces her brother and the interpreter: "People like those two are neither relatives nor friends. They would kiss the behind of the *toubabs* [Europeans] for a string of medals and everyone knows it" (p. 126). She turns on her heel, takes N'Deye Touti by the shoulder, and marches out the door. Seeing her fallen friend, Houdia M'Baye, Ramatoulaye is overcome with grief. For the first time, the continuing violence and mounting casualties overwhelm her, and she appeals to Alioune, a railway worker who accompanies the cart bearing the body of Houdia, to end the strike. Lowering his head, he replies, "We must wait for the results of the meeting at Thiès. . . . Perhaps tomorrow" (p. 126).

Chapters 10 through 15 take place in Thiès, which is fitting. For just as this Senegalese city sits at the nexus of the two major lines of the railroad, so does the action of these chapters bind together *God's Bits of Wood*. Chapter 10 tells the sad tale of Sounkaré, the night watchman at the railyards in Thiès, who remains a company man. We are first privy to his thoughts while he wanders through the surreal landscape of the abandoned yard in search of something to eat. Rat that he is, he hunts other rats for food, all the while justifying his loyalty to the company by intoning earlier failures to oppose the French—the feckless resistance of the Muslim leader Mour Dial, who opposed the initial construction of the railroad through his territory, and the failed strike of 1938, which left only death in its wake. After attempting in vain to beg grain from the women, Sounkaré returns to the railyard to chase his last rat. Enticed by a large rodent, he is overcome by dizziness, falls into a grease pit, and strikes his head against the cement. Alone and lifeless, it is Sounkaré who is ultimately eaten by the rats.

The next chapter belongs to Penda, another of Sembene's strong women, whose practice of "the world's oldest profession" has afforded her an independence denied her peers. Worldly and aware and not at all "traditional," she ultimately teams up with the blind seer Maïmouna. At the invitation of the union leader Lahbib, she assumes the task of distributing rations to the wives of strikers. But her authority grows out of inner commitment and strength, not from a husband's status, a fact illustrated in a confrontation with Awa, a foreman's wife, who calls her a whore and refuses to accept grain from her: "Awa shouted, and then, before the men had had a chance to intervene, she was screaming like a sow in a slaughterhouse. Penda had reached across the table, seized her by the neck, and spat full in her face" (p. 142).

If Chapter 11 is a testimony to Penda, Chapter 12 provides us a male hero in the guise of Doudou, the union's secretary general. Six weeks into the strike, the French director of the repair shop offers Doudou his old position back and three million francs to betray the strike. Doudou rejects the bribe. The refusal signals for Director Isnard the crumbling of his colonial world, a collapse underscored in the drunken musings of his assistant Leblanc ("the white").

This general mobilization of the women and the men in Thiès grows to include the youth in the following chapter. Led by Magatte, Doudou's apprentice, a dozen young men fan out across town in search of food. From their hideout in a huge hollow baobab, the supernatural sanctuary of sorcerers and *griots* of bygone days, the apprentices raid the chicken coops of the *toubab,* and steal rice from the Syrian merchant Aziz as well as an inner tube from his truck to make slingshots. Thus armed, they terrorize the "Vatican" (or European quarter), shooting out lights and breaking windows. Their organized band is mirrored by the women, who, led by Penda, formalize their association in a "Committee of Women" in this chapter. Tragedy strikes with the death of two of the boys at the hands of Isnard, but in a sense triumph follows with their funeral and a huge demonstration that threatens to spin out of control: "It was not until almost nightfall, when the mass of this human river was already indistinguishable from the shadows, that the funeral procession ended and the remains of the two children returned at last to their homes" (p. 161). Frightened, officials of the Régie Dakar-Niger announce that they will receive representatives of the union. A short chapter 14 sketches life in the Vatican, where the Europeans now feel not only under siege, but divided among themselves. At the conclusion of a torrent of stereotypically racist characterizations of "the Africans," we learn from a still drunk Leblanc that he twice sent the railroad workers a ten-thousand-franc note to support the strike!

The Thiès episodes climax in the next two chapters. Although subtitled "The Return of Bakayoko," Chapter 15, in fact, introduces the always-elusive-yet-ever-evoked strike leader for the first time. Bakayoko appears at his Uncle Bakary's house in clothes that meld the garb of the major ethnic groups of French West Africa. In town for the meeting with railroad management, Bakayoko attends a difficult meeting with Edouard, a railway company representative, during which Bakayoko responds to the Frenchman's condescension by noting that he and his comrades deign to speak French only because Edouard does not understand Wolof. Negotiations then begin in earnest at the company offices where the regional director Dejean make its clear that, although the French will entertain the workers' demands for salaries equal to those of their European counterparts, family allowances are out of the question: "it would amount to a recognition of a racial aberrance, a ratification of the customs of inferior beings" (p. 181). Bakayoko, in turn, rejects the company proposal to invite the several Senegalese deputies to the French parliament to serve as mediators, charging that "their mandate is simply a license to profiteer" (p. 182). Bakayoko and Dejean come to blows, the negotiations collapse, and the strikers call for a mass demonstration.

Chapter 16, "The March of the Women," opens with the gathering of the people, and the union leaders recount the events of the meeting with French officials. Bakayoko pledges that the men will hold out, but the women steal the stage. In the discussion that follows, a woman joins in—"the first time in living memory that a woman had spoken in public" (p. 185)—and the day's drama is capped off by the women's announcement that they will march to Dakar. In yet another gesture to the complexity that is twentieth-century Africa, Sembene festoons Bakayoko's Uncle Bakary with amulets and fetishes, ancient sources of supernatural power, in order to protect the women on their tradition-breaking odyssey (p. 187). A description of trials and tribulations follows, as the women brave the hottest season of the year to cross the barren land between Thiès and Dakar. At the entrance to the city, they meet a wall of soldiers. The armed men fire, and Penda and Samba N'Doulougou, a strike leader and the undeclared father of Maïmouna's twins, fall before the gates of Dakar. The march across this parched "desert" evokes the wanderings of the Jews in the wilderness before they reach Canaan. In a twist on gender and leadership characteristic of Sembene, Penda the woman, like Moses the man, dies just as her people reach the Promised Land. But despite her death, the women march on to greatness, a "great river . . . rolling on to the sea" (p. 202).

The "March of the Women" also recalls the famous march of working women to Versailles in October 1789 during the French Revolution, after which the king and the national assembly were removed to Paris, where they could be more closely watched. Sembene would undoubtedly have been aware of this event and its revolutionary nature. Hence, the women's march in the novel may also be Sembene's way of underscoring the contradiction between the French Revolution and its ideals, and the oppressive actions of the French colonial administration in West Africa during the railroad strike.

The penultimate two chapters take place in Dakar, in a time out of time, where gender roles are topsy-turvy. In Chapter 17 men, rather than women, collect water (p. 203), and the triumphant women, rather than men, stride on cloths spread on the ground before them where warriors tread in times past (p. 210). But a great meeting at the racetrack between the workers, the women and their supporters, and the French colonial administrators, railroad management, and their local African subordinates portends impasse. Islamic leaders, local African leaders, and officials of other unions fail to support the strikers. Finally, in desperation, Bakayoko addresses the multitude with a rousing speech that turns the tide. The next day, bowing to the demands of the people, a general strike is called; after ten days company officials agree to resume negotiations. The future looks bright and victory at hand. The chapter closes with Maïmouna nursing her surviving twin, who has been called "Strike" to commemorate the momentous struggle for control of "modern" Africa just concluded. But Strike's mother also locates her son in the heroic past of Sahelian Africa, echoing generations of *griots* who have described the childhood of Sunjata, founder of the ancient empire of Mali: "I am nourishing one of the great trees of tomorrow" (p. 219).

Chapter 18, the last Dakar stop, launches the denouement of *God's Bits of Wood*. In the wake of the strike, N'Deye Touti embraces her African heritage—so much so that she begins doing domestic chores. Her European clothes and pretensions left behind, Sembene tells us that she looks like a bronze head from Ife, an African icon. Moreover, she offers to become Bakayoko's second wife, a proposition that he rejects. But never at rest, and certainly very unpopular with the authorities in Dakar following his oration against them, Bakayoko takes his leave of Ramatoulaye and Maïmouna and makes his way back to Bamako. The chapter closes with a letter from Lahbib in Thiès to Bakayoko, letting him know that the women had returned safely, but that "they wanted to start running everything! . . . In future, though, we will have to reckon with them in whatever we do" (pp. 225–226). Stretched out under a tree along a little-used road between Kati and Bamako, Bakayoko reflects on the martyred Penda—how "she, like himself, was a traveler from one station to another" (p. 226).

The next chapter wraps up the story in Bamako at the other end of the railroad line. The first half recounts the sordid tale of Fa Keïta in prison, where the light of his piety contrasts dramatically with the darkness and filth of his surroundings. Unlike the self-serving faith of El-Hadji Mabigué in Dakar, the Old One's faith is pure: "His eyes were lifted toward a meeting with the only thing truly worthy of any form of suffering—a faith in God" (p. 232). Shortly thereafter, a telegram arrives in Bamako announcing the end of the strike. Prisoners are released. The Old One returns home, bathes, and invites the men of the union to an audience with him. And then, in the presence of the men, his wives, his son Bakayoko, Assitan, and Ad'jibid'ji, he counsels them to claim their "right to live" but emphasizes that "hatred must not dwell with you." His granddaughter bolts upright with the answer to the riddle Niakoro had posed to her: "Grandfather, I know now what it is that washes the water. It is the spirit. The water is clear and pure, but the spirit is purer still" (p. 237). Bakayoko wonders if such advice is really true: "But how could a man take arms against injustice without hating the unjust? To fight well, it was necessary to hate" (pp. 238–239).

The final chapter, "Epilogue," brings us back to the center—to Thiès. By this time, the women have all but set up a separate community. The men return to the railyard but refuse to work until Isnard is removed, a task that calls forth another women's march to the Vatican, the European quarter. Faced with removal, Isnard's wife, Beatrice, commits suicide, and the shots echo over the crowd "as if they had written a brutal ending to a long, long story" (p. 244). The crowd scatters, and in the "rapidly descending night" the seer Maïmouna's voice is heard intoning an ancient ballad, "The Legend of Goumba" (p. 245):

> From one sun to another,
> The combat lasted,
> And fighting together, blood-covered,
> They transfixed their enemies.
> But happy is the man who does battle without hatred.

THEMES RAISED IN CLASS DISCUSSION

In Modern Africa students read a novel in each section of the course. *God's Bits of Wood* is included in a section that I variously label "The Making of Contemporary Africa" or "The Rise of Nationalism." Given the novel's length, I suggest to students that they begin reading *God's Bits of Wood* early in the semester. I encourage them by assigning readings from the novel a month before we begin discussing it.

Sembene's novel is preceded by three or four classes that begin with a survey of European rule between World Wars I and II, followed by periods devoted to specific case studies of how colonial administrations attempted to reengineer the inner workings of African societies, African resistance to such interference, and rising African demands for participation in government. Following our reading of *God's Bits of Wood,* I usually conclude this section of the course with three classes on the rise of nationalism in Kenya and the armed resistance of the Land Freedom Army. In the Négritudes course, the novel is one reading among several in a unit on the increasing self-consciousness of black communities in the Caribbean, North America, Europe, and Africa. Other texts include Aimé Césaire's *Return to My Native Land* (1983) and prose and poetry by writers of the Harlem Renaissance.

The major themes that usually arise from discussion of the novel are as follows (also see the text of a handout included at the end of this chapter):

• The geography of the novel as a reflection of the colonial geography imposed by France in the form of the railroad.
• The relationship between new technology and new social constructs introduced by colonial rule and earlier African technology and paradigms of social action. The novel is not a romantic rejection of things European, but a much more complex tale of the struggle to control and reinterpret new technology. This is illustrated by the fact that the workers miss "the smoke of the savanna."
• The contrast in the ways that African men and women in the novel react to the challenges posed by the strike. Whereas the men tend to adopt European institutions (such as the union and the trial) and patterns of action (such as the strike), usually in confined spaces created by European rule (such as the union hall or railyard), the new social and political consciousness of the women grows out of their domestic gender roles through a process of trial and error—usually in open, undefined spaces.
• The depiction of leadership among men and women in the novel, and the relationship between individual responsibility and collective action. Comparison between Bakayoko and Penda is often fruitful. Whereas the men remain dependent on Bakayoko to the end, women first take initiative as individuals, are then unified under the leadership of Penda, freed by her death at the doors of Dakar, and finally march to collective victory.
• The different ways in which the old and the young respond to the strike. Niakaro, for example, announces that "our world is falling apart" (p. 88), in sharp contrast to her son Bakayoko, reported by his father to have said that "our world is opening up" (p. 88).
• The place of religion in the novel. While Sembene clearly condemns the way that Islamic leaders collaborate with the colonial

authorities—as illustrated by Mabigué and the Imam—he apparently respects genuine faith such as that exhibited by Fa Keïta during his imprisonment.

• The "truth" of the novelist as illustrated by the novel, compared with the "truth" of the historian as illustrated by the essays of Suret-Canale (1978) and Cooper (1986). What does Sembene want to teach us about the strike, and how does he know it? What do the historians reveal, and how do they know it?

• A consideration of the ways that *God's Bits of Wood* reflects the social realist tradition of the great novels of French authors such as Emile Zola and Honoré de Balzac.

• A consideration of the ways that *God's Bits of Wood* reflects the oral traditions of West African historiography. Discussion of the novel as a "circular journey that results in self-understanding" and whose encounters have didactic purpose (Mortimer 1990:72).

• The narrator as social commentator and *griot*. Bakayoko as sometime union activist and sometime *griot* with the gift of speech who exhibits the creative value of the word (Mortimer 1990, 76).

RELATED MATERIALS AND STUDENT ASSIGNMENTS

In my African history survey course, I ask students to read the survey chapters on the twentieth century included in Kevin Shillington's text *History of Africa*. In order to assure that students understand some of the specific contexts in which resistance to European rule and nationalism arise, I supplement this broad coverage with selected chapters on colonial policies of forced labor, military recruitment, and taxation from *African Population and Capitalism: Historical Perspectives* (Cordell and Gregory 1994). In the course Négritudes: The Literatures and Histories of Black Liberation, students will already have read René Maran's *Batouala*, which provides a context in which to discuss the imposition of European colonial rule in francophone Africa. Therefore, rather than assigning chapters from Shillington's text as background reading in that course, I present the broader continental overview as a lecture, augmented, again, by chapters from *African Population and Capitalism*.

In addition to the supplementary readings just mentioned, I find that the video "The Rise of Nationalism," produced and narrated by Basil Davidson as part of the series *Africa* (1984), is extremely useful. It allows me to place *God's Bits of Wood* in the broader context of increasing African demands for participation in government in the postwar era. At the time Sembene wrote his novel, activists in both anglophone and francophone Africa limited their goals to a greater role in the colonial regimes that governed them. By and large, independence was not on their agenda. The reticence of the colonial powers to grant such requests, however, led to greater militancy. Davidson's video provides an orderly geographical survey of the rise of nationalism in each of the European colonial empires in Africa, and in apartheid South Africa. At the same time, he is attentive to present the chronology of such demands in a comprehensible way.

Over the years, I have usually asked students to write a paper on *God's Bits of Wood*, although topics have varied. Sometimes I simply assigned a critical review of the novel in which I asked students to identify one or two themes, show how Sembene treated them, and then compare his vision of events with versions found in conventional historical narratives assigned in the course.

In recent years, I have framed topics on *God's Bits of Wood* that require students to compare the "truth" of the novelist with "historical truth" as exemplified by Suret-Canale and Cooper. In 1978, Suret-Canale, a French Marxist historian and postwar activist in French West Africa who was eventually thrown out of the colonies by the French administration, published an account of the same railroad strike. Apparently neither the French nor the Senegalese archives were open to him, for he based his account on his own documentary record of the period. Nearly a decade later, Cooper published another account of the strike. His access to a much more complete archival record allowed a much more detailed analysis of events that led up to the conflict, the strike itself, and its aftermath. Cooper's agenda also included efforts to show just how Sembene had distorted the historical record in *God's Bits of Wood*; his research, for example, suggests that women did not play as vital a force in the real strike as they did in Sembene's strike. Assignments that require the students to compare the historical materials to which they have access (the textbook, focused essay, and video) with each other, and with the novel, have produced great interest and good work. Students have had to master the chronology of the events surrounding the rise of nationalism, union movements, and the strike itself. In addition, they have had to grapple with what constitutes historical truth, as well as how literary portrayals of historical events influence historical memory.

Were I to carry this assignment further in a course where I had more time to focus both on Sembene and the immediate preindependence era, I would add his historical films to the materials covered in class. I would, for example, show Sembene's film *Camp de Thiaroye,* which explores the fate of a group of Senegalese veterans who served in World War II, were taken prisoner by the Germans, and then rebelled following their release in 1944 when the French denied them their back pay. I would also assign Echenberg's excellent historical essay on the incident, and then ask students to compare the two versions of events. I realize that I stray here from African novels in the classroom, but in this era of epic films on both the big and little screens, people's visions of the past are as much, if not more, likely to come from films as from the printed page— whether historical monograph, textbook, or historical novel. Therefore, it is also of vital importance to teach students how to view historical films carefully and critically, as well as how to read historical novels. Cognizant of this duty, the American Historical Association now routinely includes reviews of historical films in its major publications, the *American Historical Review* and *Perspectives.*

A HANDOUT: READING
OUSMANE SEMBENE'S *GOD'S BITS OF WOOD,*
BY WILLIAM BEAUCHAMP AND DENNIS D. CORDELL

Ousmane Sembene is from Africa, born in Ziguenchor, a town in the Casamance region of southern Senegal, in 1923. Unlike many of the authors whose works we have read this term, Sembene is not of middle-class origins. In the earlier part of his life he worked as a fisherman, a plumber, and a mason. He served in the French forces in World War II, and after that was a dockworker in Marseilles on the Mediterranean coast of France. During these years he became involved in union activity. Self-educated, he was an avid participant in workers' study groups. In the 1950s, he went on to become a writer and a filmmaker. Today he is emeritus professor at the Université Cheikh Anta Diop in Dakar, Senegal, and is hailed throughout the continent as the founder of African cinema.

God's Bits of Wood is one of the masterpieces of contemporary African literature. Jacques Chevrier places it in a class of novels he calls "the novels of contestation," works conceived toward the end of the colonial era that "reflect the uneasiness or anger of men [*sic*] dominated by a western culture that they reject and whose consequences affect the group as well as the individual" (Chevrier 1984: 99).

This novel is based on a true historical event, the strike of workers on the Dakar-Niger railroad in 1947–1948. Sembene uses this conflict as a vehicle for denouncing evils linked to the colonial administration. These include racism, the corruption of traditional chiefs, and the recourse to force against the strikers. At the same time, Sembene makes profound observations about the impact of colonialism on African people and societies along the railroad. And unlike many of the male authors whom we have read this semester, he also examines gender roles—the relations between men and women and the roles of each in society.

With the above paragraphs as background, here are some comments and guidelines to help you with your reading of the novel:

• Think about the kinds of changes that French rule imposed on African societies in the novel. How has the nature of work changed? How has the organization of work altered? To what degree do the African workers themselves adopt European means to demand higher wages and better working conditions?

• How has Western technology affected local people and societies? How has the railroad "reorganized" the mental space of the workers and their families? To what degree have the Africans in the towns along the railroad become dependent on European technology? Is the strike action about the rejection of European technology or about more complex issues?

• What is the relationship of the individual to the group in *God's Bits of Wood*?

• Think about the events leading up to the strike itself. How do the meetings and discussions that preceded the strike represent a "mediation" between African institutions and ways of doing things and new European forms of organization? Were strikes part of African tradition? If not, how do the workers come to accept using a European form of protest? Does everyone agree that a strike is the best course of action?

• Look at the relationships across generations in the novel. How many generations are represented? Do people respond differently to the notion of a strike depending on their age?

• How is the strike a "transforming" event for men in the novel? How does it affect the awareness of men? What do they learn about themselves, their society, and European authority as a result of the protest? To what degree do men act individually and independently;

to what degree do they depend on external institutions and/or the group to make decisions?

• How is the strike a "transforming" event for women in the novel? How does the men's strike affect them? Do the women arrive at decisions and take action in the same ways as the men? To what degree do they "invent" their own forms of protest? How do these forms relate to "traditional" women's roles? What do they come to learn about their potential influence on events outside the household—their customary arena of action?

• Look at leadership in the novel. Who are the leaders among the men? How are they different? How are they similar? What is the role of Bakayoko in the novel? Who are the leaders among the women? How are they similar? How are they different? What is the role of Penda? Of Ramatoulaye? Are the men and women in the novel capable of acting autonomously, or do they depend entirely on their leaders?

• Examine the theme of assimilation in God's Bits of Wood. Who are the most Europeanized among the Africans? How do they relate to their "two worlds," that of Africa and that of France? What does N'Deye Touti represent in the novel, and why do you think that Sembene created such a character? What about Beaugosse (whose name means "handsome guy" in French)?

• Does religion play an important part in the book? How does Sembene represent Islam and Muslim leaders? What is the significance of the slaughter of the sheep Vendredi ("Friday") by Ramatoulaye? How does Sembene present the faith of Fa Keïta?

• Look at the entire novel. How does the emphasis shift as the narrative moves along? Certainly one of the major events in the last part of the book is the women's march. Where were they going? Why? What is the significance of this gesture? What was Penda's role in it? Why does she die before the end of the march? What other famous marches are evoked by the incident? Why do you think Sembene includes it?

SUGGESTIONS FOR
FURTHER READING AND RESOURCES

Novels by Sembene

Sembene, Ousmane. 1957. *O Pays, Mon Beau People!* Not available in translation. Paris: Amiot-Dumont.

———. 1964. *L'Harmattan.* Not available in translation. Paris: Presence Africaine.

———. 1970. *God's Bits of Wood,* trans. Francis Price. Portsmouth, N.H.: Heinemann. Originally published (1960) in French as *Les Bouts de bois de Dieu.*

———. 1971. *The Money Order, with White Genesis.* Portsmouth, N.H.: Heinemann. Originally published (1965) in French as *Le Mandat et Vehi Ciosane.*

———. 1974. *Voltaïque.* English translation. Portsmouth, N.H.: Heinemann. Originally published (1962) in French.

———. 1976. *Xala.* English translation. Portsmouth, N.H.: Heinemann. Originally published (1973) in French.

———. 1983. *The Last of the Empire.* Portsmouth, N.H.: Heinemann. Originally published (1981) in French as *Le dernier de l'empire.*

———. 1987. *The Black Docker.* Portsmouth, N.H.: Heinemann. Originally published (1956) in French as *Le Docker noir.*

Films by Sembene

Sembene, Ousmane. 1976. *Ceddo.* Available from New Yorker Films, phone: (877) 247-6200, X213; Web site: www.newyorkerfilms.com. A newly remastered video version of Mandabi is also available through them.

———. 1989. *Camp de Thiaroye.* Available from New Yorker Films, phone: (877) 247-6200, X213; Web site: www.newyorkerfilms.com.

Other Reading

"*AHR* Forum: Histories and Historical Fictions." 1998. A special issue of *The American Historical Review* 103, 5.

Atwood, Margaret. 1998. "In Search of *Alias Grace*: On Writing Canadian Historical Fiction," *The American Historical Review* 103, 5: 1503–1516.

Boahen, A. Adu. 1970. "Introduction." In Ousmane Sembene, *God's Bits of Wood,* trans. Francis Price. New York: Doubleday.

Case, Frank. 1981. "Workers' Movements: Revolution and Women's Consciousness in *God's Bits of Wood,*" *Canadian Journal of African Studies/Revue canadienne des études africaines* 15, 2: 277–292.

Césaire, Aimé. 1983. "Notebook of a Return to the Native Land." In *The Collected Poetry of Aimé Césaire,* ed. and trans. Clayton Eshleman and Annette Smith. Berkeley and Los Angeles: University of California Press. Also available as a separate Penguin paperback. Originally published in French as *Cahiers d'un retour au pays natal.*

Chevrier, Jacques. 1984. *Littérature nègre.* Paris: Armand Colin.

Cooper, Frederick. 1986. "'Our Strike': Equality, Anticolonial Politics and the 1947–48 Railway Strike in French West Africa," *Journal of African History* 37: 81–118.

Cordell, Dennis D., and Joel W. Gregory, eds. 1994. *African Population and Capitalism: Historical Perspectives.* Madison: University of Wisconsin Press.

Davidson, Basil. 1984. "The Rise of Nationalism," part of the video series *Africa.*

Demos, John. 1998. "In Search of Reasons for Historians to Read Novels. . . ." *The American Historical Review* 103, 5: 1526–1529. Part of "*AHR* Forum: Histories and Historical Fictions."

Diawara, Manthia. 1992. *African Cinema: Politics and Culture.* Bloomington: Indiana University Press.

Echenberg, Myron J. 1978. "Tragedy at Thiaroye: The Senegalese Soldiers' Uprising of 1944." In *African Labor History,* ed. Peter C. W. Gutkind, Robin Cohen, and Jean Copans. Beverly Hills: Sage.

Hunt, Lynn. 1998. "'No Longer an Evenly Flowing River': Time, History, and the Novel," *The American Historical Review* 103, 5: 1517–1521. Part of "*AHR* Forum: Histories and Historical Fictions."

Klein, Leonard S., ed. 1986. *African Literatures in the Twentieth Century: A Guide,* rev. ed. New York: Ungar.

Makward, Edris. 1991. "Women, Tradition, and Religion in Ousmane Sembene's Work." In *Faces of Islam in African Literature,* ed. Kenneth W. Harrow. Portsmouth, N. H.: Heinemann.

Mortimer, Mildred. 1990. *Journeys Through the French African Novel.* Portsmouth, N.H.: Heinemann.

Riddell, Barry. 1990. "Let There Be Light: The Voices of West African Novels," *Journal of Modern African Studies* 28, 3: 473–486.

Shillington, Kevin. 1995. *History of Africa,* rev. ed. New York: St. Martin's.

Spence, Jonathan. 1998. "Margaret Atwood and the Edges of History," *American Historical Review* 103, 5: 1522–1525.

Suret-Canale, Jean. 1978. "The French West African Railway Workers' Strike, 1947–1948." In *African Labor History,* ed. Peter C. W. Gutkind, Robin Cohen, and Jean Copans. Beverly Hills: Sage.

22

Wole Soyinka's
Ake: The Years of Childhood

Tamara Giles-Vernick

I FIRST PICKED UP WOLE SOYINKA'S CHILDHOOD MEMOIR, *Ake: The Years of Childhood*, in the mid-1980s, before I even considered studying African history. I was in the Central African Republic at the time, recovering from a bout of malaria, and I needed something to transport me from this tedious process. A memoir of a childhood—one that ostensibly bore no resemblance to my own early years—seemed an appropriate choice. Soyinka's first lines both disoriented and seduced me into the world of an unusually precocious two-year-old, who, in his childhood narcissism, interwove fantasy and reality. His first lines pondered the great puzzle of the Ake parsonage, his childhood home: why God himself had to look down the "profane" hill of Itoko, where the chief resided, to see His "own pious station," the Ake parsonage in southwestern Nigeria. Each week, Soyinka mused, God "took his one gigantic stride over those babbling markets [on Itoko]—which dared to sell on Sundays—into St. Peter's Church, afterwards visiting the parsonage for tea with the Canon. There was the small consolation that . . . he never stopped first at the Chief's, who was known to be a pagan" (p. 5). Soyinka set up this monumental conflict between a Christian God and "pagan" chiefly authority, only to muddy it relentlessly in the following pages. He recalled the Ake parsonage where he grew up as a vanished Eden. There, luxuriant orchards and faithful Christians had once flourished, and the ghost of the long-dead Bishop Crowther, who had lived in the parsonage,[1] now lurked in the hydrangeas and

---

Wole Soyinka, *Ake: The Years of Childhood* [1981] (London: Minerva, 1994).

bougainvillaea, terrifying a young Soyinka. In that parsonage, too, his devoutly Christian mother recounted stories of her brother Sanya, a widely acknowledged tree demon who felt at ease in the forest. Stumbling over remembrances that skipped from Soyinka's present to his childhood past, his mother's past, then back to his present, I soon found myself transported by the captivating narrative of a young child as he suffered the tribulations of sibling rivalry and bed-wetting, his eviction from his father's room at night, his younger sister's tragic death, and his education. The memoir buffeted me between familiar and strikingly different worlds, and my disorientation gave way to insight into the people, events, and processes that had shaped Soyinka as he grew up. At the very least, Soyinka's absorbing, moving, and at times riotously funny memoir was a good way to forget about postmalaria depression.

Several years later, I encountered *Ake* in graduate school and began to think about how it fit into the broader historical and social contexts of colonial and contemporary Nigeria and Africa. His memoir, I realized, elaborated insights that extended well beyond the personal: it allowed readers to interpret one African's perspective on what it was like to grow up in an elite, educated Christian family in colonial Nigeria. It provided a particular glimpse into the direct and indirect ways that British colonialism could shape education and families, and the varied ways in which African women and men could negotiate and reshape these influences.

Ake makes for an engaging, fast undergraduate read. Students relish reading history from a child's perspective, and the memoir's witty, merciless insights into the peculiarities of adult behavior, and its exquisite descriptions of the traumas of birth, death, and discipline, are reassuringly familiar for students. It doesn't surprise me that most students enjoy *Ake* enough to finish its 220-odd pages. For instructors of African history, *Ake*'s exploration of 1940s British colonialism in Nigeria and its influences on African childhood, family, education, and Christianity also make it an effective illustration of colonial rule's complexities. *Ake* explores how the men and women in Soyinka's family and town, and ultimately Soyinka himself, embrace Western education and Christianity, yet remain fiercely critical of British rule. His charismatic, articulate, Western-educated Aunt Beere exemplifies this apparent contradiction, as she castigates the district officer for the Allied bombing of Hiroshima: "I know you, the white mentality: Japanese, Chinese, Africans, we are all sub-human. You would drop an atom bomb on Abeokuta or any of the colonies if it suited you!" (p. 215). Soyinka's exploration of his childhood and family, education, and Christianity under British colonialism thus interrogates a web of misleading assumptions to which undergraduates cling: that "traditional" Africans, mired in their static, ancient ways of life, rejected outright European "modern" beliefs and practices; or that they unquestioningly accepted Western education, Christianity, and consumer goods and degenerated into shriveled nuclear families of passive ciphers, disconnected from their rich histories. Each semester I struggle to disabuse my students of these simplistic assumptions. Soyinka's memoir provides a powerful way of dislodging them and introduces students to more nuanced, variegated perspectives on colonialism in Africa. And although *Ake* is not, of course, a novel, Soyinka relentlessly blurs distinctions between the imaginary and what "actually" happened to develop a genre that he has subsequently called "faction" (Soyinka 1994: ix). This deliberate interweaving of fantasy, opinion, and reality can also provoke students to tackle questions about the historical interpretation of memoirs.

In this chapter, then, I will elaborate why and how I have used Soyinka's *Ake* in undergraduate courses. I begin with a brief summary of the work and my justifications for using it, and then describe the contexts in which I have used it. I explain strategies for teaching the work, and conclude with suggestions for further reading.

AKE: THE EXPANDING
TIME AND SPACE OF CHILDHOOD

Soyinka has elegantly crafted *Ake* around a series of events that broaden his childhood world both temporally and spatially. The memoir commences as the adult Soyinka recalls his family compound in the Ake parsonage, comparing its once lush gardens to its present "depleted landscape, full of creaks, exposed and nerveless" (p. 7). But then he draws the reader into this past time and place with a vivid description of his mother's remembrances of her brother, the tree demon, continually interrupted by a young Soyinka's incessant questions. The first chapters center on the Ake parsonage, where Soyinka engages with his parents, siblings, his parents' foster children, servants, and parsonage visitors. Eventually, however, the space of Ake appears smaller and smaller to Wole the child; his world expands to include the grammar school that he attends, the markets, the Alake's palace, his father's home village, Isara, and its environs, and even beyond Abeokuta. The memoir culminates with a rebellion, led by the Women's Egba Union (created by his mother, her friends, and acquaintances) against colonial authorities—especially the Alake of Abeokuta—over taxation. Soyinka uses it to illuminate his own growing awareness of women's authority, the limits of colonial power, of Nigerian struggles against British colonial rule, and indeed of broader African struggles against colonialism. *Ake* ends just before he sets out to attend the prestigious Government College in Ibadan.

In the very first pages, the reader catches beguiling glimpses of a passionately curious, imaginative, and sometimes exasperating boy and encounters some of the most powerful presences in his life. His mother, whom he has startlingly named The Wild Christian, is a devout Christian, an energetic shopkeeper, a commanding woman, sometimes indulgent, sometimes impatient. He never explicitly elaborates the reasons for her name, but instead describes her recollections of the early Christians in Nigeria, who possessed "Faith and— Discipline. That is what made those early believers. Psheeaw! God doesn't make them like that any more" (p. 11).

His father is also a compelling presence and possesses an equally astonishing name: Essay. Soyinka explains that his father's friends often called him by his initials (S. A.), which the boy transmogrified into a name that evoked his father's meticulousness and elegance. "It did not take long," Soyinka observes in one evocative passage,

> for him to enter my consciousness simply as Essay, as one of those careful stylistic exercises in prose which follow set rules of composition, are products of fastidiousness and elegance, set down in beautiful calligraphy that would be the envy of most copyists of any age. His despair was real that he should give birth to a son who, from the beginning, showed clearly that he had inherited nothing of his own handwriting. He displayed the same elegance in his dressing. (p. 17)

Essay is an exacting disciplinarian, but also possesses penetrating insight into Soyinka's childhood world. When young Soyinka suffers a head injury and discovers that his blood has soaked into his *dansiki*, Essay recognizes his son's anxiety about his blood loss and reassures him by suggesting that he has already replaced the lost blood: "It's all back in there, while you were asleep. I used Dipo's feeding bottle to pour it back" (p. 31). As Soyinka grows older, Essay indulges, challenges, and cultivates the boy's developing intellect; clearly, his later successes are as much a product of his own talents as his father's creative and demanding interventions.

Eventually, Soyinka makes his way out of his family compound to the parsonage school and the surrounding town, with the guidance of a host of other attentive "parents." The schoolteacher, Mr. Olagbaju, takes seriously and encourages his precocious enthusiasm for school, but also becomes an avid partner in pounded-yam consumption. Mrs. B, the bookkeeper's wife, feeds the Soyinka children, protects them from Essay and Wild Christian's punishments, and carries them on her "capacious, soft and reassuring" back that "radiated the same repose and kindliness that we had observed in her face" (p. 18). Soyinka ventures farther from the parsonage in Ake and encounters other influential adults who take charge of his education. Having outgrown the parsonage school, he attends Ake's Grammar School, run by his Uncle Daoudu, who inculcates a sense of discipline in Soyinka, as well as a mistrust of British ways. Soyinka also visits his father's home in Isara, where his grandfather (whom he calls Father) subjects him to a scarification ritual to protect him from malefactors and teaches him how to deal with adversaries in the adult world.

Children are less compelling than the adults in Soyinka's memoir. I make this point not as a criticism, but rather as a contrast to his portrayal of adults. To be fair, in his early years, Soyinka struggles with predictable rivalries with his elder sister Tinu and his younger brother Dipo. He witnesses and only partly comprehends the tragic illness and death of his year-old sister, Folasade. He befriends many children, including an older boy, Osiki, who is responsible for two accidents that Soyinka suffers. But other children seem more fleeting in this work; Soyinka does not develop nuanced depictions of the children with whom he played, argued, and went to school. Tinu and Dipo (later renamed Femi) seem to drop entirely out of the picture a little over halfway into the work. A host of "siblings" inhabit his family compound, but Soyinka never seems to name or describe them. Wild Christian and Essay foster numerous children from the families of kin, friends, and acquaintances, sometimes as many as twelve at a time. Soyinka seems less than enchanted with the ceaseless flow of children, particularly with the resulting sleeping arrangements in Essay and Wild Christian's home. Indeed, he describes in memorable terms Wild Christian's bedroom, where all the children slept on their mats at night:

> On waking up in the middle of the night, the sounds in the room approached the sounds in the Blaize Memorial Canning factory where we were once taken to watch the grapefruits, oranges, guavas, and pears being cleaned, sliced, pulped, canned by a series of monstrous guillotines, motors and flapping belts, pistons and steaming boilers which spluttered, belched, spat, thundered and

emitted measured jets of liquid that went into the cans and bottles.
(pp. 82–83)

Soyinka spends a good deal of time describing his efforts to flee
Wild Christian's bedroom for the relative peace of his father's,
though he ultimately doesn't succeed. It seems odd that a memoir of
childhood would take so little time to develop depictions of other
children. Soyinka the writer seems most concerned with distinguish-
ing his childhood self from those of other children.

USING *AKE* IN THE CLASSROOM

As a pedagogical tool, *Ake* can accomplish many things. I have used
it in my African history survey, but find that it is also appropriate for
an upper division course addressing the history of West Africa. In
these courses, I assign *Ake* to shed light on Africans' changing social
relations under colonial rule, on their responses to Western education, and on the different ways that they reckoned families. This
work helps me to cajole students into questioning assumptions that
they often seem loath to give up. Often students want to fit Africa's
colonial history into a set of dichotomies: colonialism was the event
by which Europeans imposed their authority on Africans, and in so
doing they brought modern ways of working, living, and learning to
a static, tradition-bound people. For these students, colonial history
pivots around a single conflict between powerful Europeans and passive Africans, between the modern and the traditional. When these
students encounter elite Africans who borrowed European education
and other cultural and social practices, they describe them as "brainwashed."

Ake doesn't allow students to get away with such simplistic
interpretations. Soyinka has peopled his memoir with complex characters who do not lend themselves to easy categorization. Soyinka's
father, uncle, and their friends, for instance, are all Christian,
Western-educated men who use their knowledge and intellect to
actively question each other, Christianity, and colonialism. Wild
Christian, her kin, friends, and acquaintances also embrace Western
education, ultimately using it as a tool in their struggle against the
injustices of colonial taxation. Education not only provides rural
women with a better understanding of how to manage their monies,
but also allows them to gain a self-awareness and confidence to

protest excessive taxation. And though the Alake, the "Native Authority" of Abeokuta, owes his position to the British and sometimes seems like little more than a yes-man for the British, he still must also answer to Yoruba subjects, who are kin, friends, and acquaintances. Indeed, the Egba Women's Union pushes for his abdication. In short, nothing in Soyinka's childhood universe suggests that educated, Christianized Africans in the 1940s had become passive, brainwashed British clones.

Soyinka's depiction of African families is equally startling for many students. They expect, as I have mentioned, that colonialism destroyed African families, rendering them a withered nuclear version of their once expansive form. But students discover that Soyinka identifies many adults as his parents, for they contribute significantly to his upbringing. He also claims many siblings, because Essay and Wild Christian's compound hosts many foster children. And though his family compound is in Ake, Essay and his children retain powerful ties to Isara, where his own father and other kin live. Clearly, this is not the depleted, fragmented African family that undergraduates expect to find. "Family" here constitutes a broad, flexible category incorporating a vast range of social relationships.

Ake destabilizes undergraduate assumptions about African social relations under colonialism in other ways, calling into question their monolithic understandings of colonialism itself. Soyinka gradually reveals the influences of British colonialism on the people of Ake. It comes as a shock to many students that colonialism does not intrude on Africans' everyday lives in the dramatic ways that, say, one sees in Buchi Emecheta's *The Joys of Motherhood* (see Chapter 10). Emecheta's long-suffering main character, Nnu Ego, embodies women's vulnerability under British colonialism: she and her husband work for a British colonial official, only to lose their jobs and to fall into impoverishment; her husband is forcibly conscripted into the British army during the Second World War, and she struggles endlessly to find food and to educate and clothe her children in Lagos. In contrast, Soyinka allows the reader's awareness of the British colonial presence to unfold as his own consciousness of the broader world develops. During Soyinka's early years, he hardly encounters British officers. The heightened British demands on African labor and production that Nnu Ego feels so acutely seem indirect and even abstract in Soyinka's childhood. Only later does Soyinka begin to see the ways in which colonialism impinges on everyday lives, how local elders and chiefs participate in indirect rule yet still remain implicated in other networks of political power, or how market women suffer under the burdens of heavy taxation.[2] This gradual unfolding of colonialism's influences is the work's strength as a teaching tool; it illuminates the hardships and injustices of colonialism but importantly reveals that not all Africans participated in or were affected by it in the same ways.

Finally, for any history course, *Ake* can raise questions about historical interpretation and the complexities of historical truths and fictions. The work problematizes the relationship between historical truth and fiction on several levels. Students are aware that Soyinka would have considerable interest in presenting himself in the most favorable light; they find his portrayal of young Wole, who attends school before the age of three and displays extraordinary intellectual abilities throughout his youth, both endearing and self-serving. This fairly cursory observation, however, leads to more fundamental questions about truth and fiction. On one hand, Soyinka's memoir makes a claim to truth about his childhood. And yet *Ake* is premised on the fiction that it reveals the expanding world of a growing child. Readers know, of course, that an accomplished novelist, playwright, poet, philosopher, and political critic actually animates this child. Indeed, the adult Soyinka at times can scarcely keep himself from intruding on this childhood narrative. In one lyrical description of the culinary delights in the evening market, for instance, the adult Soyinka interrupts with a bitter tirade against Kentucky Fried Chicken, bubble gum, and contemporary music.

This shifting narrative voice and the blurred truths and fictions pose real interpretive challenges and can lead students to confront several questions: How does one interpret this work in a history course dealing with colonial rule in Africa? As one glimpse into a colonial past, experienced by a boy growing up in an elite household? What generalizations, if any, should students take from Soyinka's clearly privileged upbringing? Or, rather, should they interpret the work as the product of the nostalgic adult Soyinka, who wrote the work in the 1980s? In their efforts to interpret *Ake* as historical evidence, students must consider how to juggle the claims to truth and the fictions upon which Soyinka has premised the work.

STRATEGIES FOR TEACHING *AKE*

I have used Soyinka's work in a survey of modern African history (1800 to the present), and in the History of West Africa. The survey course has an enrollment of sixty students, mostly freshmen and sophomores, while the West Africa course contains thirty-five upper-division students, some of whom have had previous exposure to African history or anthropology. In both of these courses, I incorporate *Ake* into later sections of the course addressing the social changes occurring in the 1940s and 1950s, after students have acquired a solid foundation concerning economic and political changes taking place in Africa (or West Africa) from the late nineteenth century to the early 1950s. In an effort to contextualize Soyinka's childhood, I normally give lectures concerning colonial education. I illustrate European intentions in introducing Western education. But I also spend a considerable amount of time addressing African education in the nineteenth century, African demands for Western education, and the varied results that Western education produced, as it helped to contribute to new grounds upon which Africans claimed authority and developed the cadres of elite Africans who articulated the intellectual grounds for African independence.

As part of this section concerning the social changes taking place in the 1940s and 1950s, I also explore changes among African families. I use a set of lectures and Soyinka's work to counter widely held notions that colonial rule totally depleted or destroyed African families. Through these lectures, though, I illustrate that various economic and social interventions under European colonial rule did have significant effects upon the ways in which Africans organized their familial relations. I also assign additional readings in the course texts so that students have a sense of the broader context in which this work occurs.[3]

Discussions of *Ake* itself seem to require few teaching pyrotechnics—the manipulative pedagogical practices to which I frequently resort to compel student participation (such as debating, working in small groups, or engaging in roundtable discussions). Students are enthusiastic about discussing the work. The memoir is often a favorite reading over the semester, no doubt because of Soyinka's lively, vivid depiction of Ake's people and his past childhood world. Of course students are drawn to the inquisitive, charming, and brash young Soyinka, but they also find compelling his personal vision of the colonial past. It is the lack of this personalized quality that so many students find alienating about African history courses in general.

I usually draw up a set of open-ended, interrelated questions that ultimately bring students to consider the ways that the people of Soyinka's memoir actively sought to shape the relationships and circumstances in which they lived. I invite students to reflect upon the different sources, forms, and uses of Soyinka's education, and upon the diverse grounds on which men and women, elders and juniors, Europeans and Africans claimed authority in Ake. I particularly encourage them to focus on the authority that women exercised both within and outside their families, and the ways in which women used Western education to express their grievances against the colonial administration. I ask them to think about relations between elite and rural Africans and to speculate about how such relationships might play out in anticolonial struggles of the 1950s. I often request students to consider how Soyinka defined "childhood" and "family" while growing up, and how his memoirs could cast doubt upon the assumption that European colonialism caused African families to disintegrate. And, finally, I ask them to address the interpretive challenges of using Soyinka's memoir as historical evidence. Sample questions for these discussions include:

• What type of family does Soyinka belong to? How do his family members make a living? Who lives in Soyinka's family compound? What relations, if any, does he have with people outside his compound? What does he call these people? Whom does Soyinka consider to be part of his family? Why? How does his depiction of "family" resemble or differ from your understanding of African families during colonial rule?

• What period of life does Soyinka write about in this memoir? Why do you think he limits his "childhood" years to just before his departure for Government College?

• What different types of education does Soyinka receive? And from whom?

• What does Soyinka tell us about colonialism and its influences on Africans in 1940s Nigeria? What do the people in Ake think about the British and colonial rule? In what ways does Soyinka's depiction of British colonial rule resemble or differ from what we have heard or read about so far in this course?

• What was the women's uprising about? What were their grievances? Who participated in the uprising? Who led and who followed? How did women protest, and against whom? What significance did this rebellion have for Soyinka's education, his conceptions of childhood, and his childhood world?

• How is *Ake* structured? How does the Ake parsonage appear to Soyinka in the beginning? How does it change over Soyinka's childhood?

- What genre is *Ake*? With what different "voices" does Soyinka speak in this work? Is it, by definition, "the truth"? What do you suspect might be fictionalized in Soyinka's account? If you were writing a history of Nigerian elites under colonial rule, how would you use this work?

I have required writing exercises on *Ake* as well. In the survey, I ask students to write a one- to two-page journal entry, in which they identify and explore a particular question that interests them. This loosely defined assignment provides younger, less-experienced students with some much-needed discipline, so that they think carefully about the work before we discuss it in class. It gives them an opportunity to ask questions that they did not ask in class. And it provides me with a sense of how they interpret *Ake* in the context of the course.

In the West Africa course, I have required students to write a five- to seven-page paper addressing the interpretation of the work. One version of this essay question is as follows:

What can Soyinka's *Ake: The Years of Childhood*, tell us about the influences of British colonial rule on Africans' conceptions of and practices surrounding childhood, family, and/or education? Note that you will need to consider how we should interpret this autobiography as a historical document. You should address the broader historical context in which this work took place.

This broad question initially stymies some students, so we usually discuss the work at length (both in class and during office hours) before the paper due date. I ask students to develop one well-defined argument for the paper. The advantage of such a broad question is that it provides students with the freedom to do what they want with the work, but simultaneously to tackle head-on their assumptions about elite African responses to British colonialism. The essay question has generated some well-argued responses about the varied experiences of colonialism and the difficulties of interpreting autobiography as historical evidence.

SOYINKA'S LIFE AND CAREER

Born in Western Nigeria in 1934, Soyinka attended University College in Ibadan and then, at the age of twenty, left for England, where he spent the next five years. He earned an honors degree in English language and literature at the University of Leeds and then trained with the Royal Court Theatre in London. Returning to Nigeria in 1960, Soyinka taught at different universities, traveled extensively, and was involved in a wide range of theatrical productions, directing and producing his own plays and those of others. His political activism brought him into increasing conflict with the independent Nigerian government, and Soyinka spent several years in detention during the time of the Civil War. Although he returned to his position as head of the drama department at the University of Ibadan after his release, Soyinka went into self-imposed exile in the 1970s. He later returned to head the Comparative Literature Department at the University of Ife.

Winner of the Nobel Prize for Literature in 1986, Soyinka has produced a substantial body of work, including critical essays, poetry, plays, novels, and memoirs. It is primarily as a playwright that he is known, however; the best known of his more than twenty plays include *The Lion and the Jewel* (1963), *Kongi's Harvest* (1967), *Madmen and Specialists* (1971), and *Death and the King's Horseman* (1975). While his work often uses themes from Yoruba history and culture as context, the genius of his writing is to highlight the universal tension that results from man's dual potential for creativity and for destruction.

CONCLUSION

Teaching *Ake* can inspire students to think in more complex ways about the social and cultural changes under colonial rule. But using it does require a counterbalance; Soyinka's prose is so engaging and persuasive that students often need reminding that he grew up in a relatively privileged household, and that European colonial interventions in Africa could produce far more upheaval and brutal injustices than Soyinka apparently witnessed as a child. Undergraduates should not emerge from an African history course believing that colonialism was a benign event in Africa's past. To gain an alternative to Soyinka's vision of colonialism in Nigeria, students could also read Buchi Emecheta's *Joys of Motherhood*—a novel that fairly bludgeons the reader with the woes of one Lagos woman during the same years as Soyinka's childhood (see Chapter 10). *Ake* and *Joys* together can illuminate contrasting experiences and perspectives of men and women, elite and nonelite, rural and urban, and child and adult of colonialism, Western education, childhood, family, and Christianity. In reading both works, students might at first feel compelled to give credence to one interpretation over the other. But with guidance, I think that they can ultimately consider both works as evidence of Africans' wide-ranging experiences and interpretations of British colonial rule.

NOTES

1. Bishop Samuel Crowther was the first Anglican bishop in Africa. Rescued from a slaving ship bound to Brazil, Crowther converted to Christianity and later worked extensively to spread Christianity to the interior of West Africa. See Curtin 1997 and Ajayi 1969.

2. Soyinka explores the effects of the Second World War on Nigerians in *Isara: A Voyage Around Essay*, a meditation on his father and the times in which he lived. See Suggestions for Further Reading.

3. Like most of my colleagues, I have experimented with several textbooks, and prefer to keep the text readings relatively simple. For the History of West Africa course, I use Boahen, Ajayi, and Tidy 1995. And for the survey, I have most recently used Shillington.

SUGGESTIONS FOR
FURTHER READING AND RESOURCES

Background Reading for Teachers and Students

Ajayi, J. F. Ade. 1969. *Christian Missions in Nigeria 1841–1891: The Making of a New Elite*. Evanston: Northwestern University Press. This is an old work, but nevertheless will provide instructors with a solid history of the nineteenth-century expansion of Christianity in Nigeria. Ajayi argues that the creation of a Western-educated elite was absolutely crucial to the nineteenth-century spread of Christianity in Nigeria.

Ajayi, J. F. Ade, and Michael Crowder, eds. 1995. *History of West Africa*, vol. 2, 3rd ed. London and New York: Longman. This two-volume set is probably the most comprehensive overview of West African history available. Teachers will find this work absolutely essential in helping them to develop lectures that will provide a broad historical context for *Ake*. Several chapters, written by leading West African, European, and American historians, detail the economic, political, and social history of colonial West Africa, the Second World War, and the independence movements. Undergraduates, however, find these volumes rough going and frequently complain that they are "dry."

Boahen, Adu, J. F. Ade Ajayi, and Michael Tidy. 1986. *Topics in West African History*, 2nd ed. London: Longman.

Curtin, Philip, ed. 1997 [1967]. *Africa Remembered: Narratives by West Africans from the Era of the Slave Trade*. Prospect Heights, Ill: Waveland Press.

Emecheta, Buchi. 1980. *The Joys of Motherhood*. Portsmouth, N.H.: Heinemann. See Chapter 10 of this collection.

Gibbs, James. 1986. *Wole Soyinka*. New York: Grove Press. A study in criticism and interpretation of Soyinka's work.

Jones, Eldred Durosimi. 1988. *The Writing of Wole Soyinka*, 3rd ed. Portsmouth, N.H.: Heinemann. An authoritative study of Soyinka's life and writings through the 1980s.

Mann, Kristin. 1979. *Marrying Well: Marriage, Status, and Social Change Among the Educated Elite in Colonial Lagos*. Cambridge: Cambridge University Press, 1985. Mann effectively describes the ways in which Lagos elites selectively appropriated practices associated with Christianity and western education, but combined them with a variety of older concerns and made them their own. Individual chapters of this monograph work well as collateral reading for students.

Peel, J. D. Y. 1995. "For Who Hath Despised the Day of Small Things— Missionary Narratives and Historical Anthropology," *Comparative Studies in Society and History* 37, 3: 581–607. Peel is primarily concerned with the role of narrative in social transformation, but instructors will find an interesting analysis of the interplay of Christian missionary narratives and those of Yoruba communities.

Shillington, Kevin. 1995. *History of Africa*, rev. ed. New York: St. Martin's. I find it a bit slim for the colonial period. Students, however, appreciate the pictures in Shillington, which means that they open this text more frequently than they do other textbooks that I've used.

Related Works by Wole Soyinka

Soyinka has produced a substantial body of work, including critical essays, poetry, plays, novels, and memoirs. Teachers and motivated students may want to consult the following writings that also address Soyinka's own and his father's pasts:

Soyinka, Wole. 1990. *Isara: A Voyage Around Essay*. London: Methuen. A semibiographical, semifictional meditation on his father and his friends. The work begins as his father and his friends are young men, confronting the changes, new opportunities, and constraints introduced by British colonial rule and negotiating their relationships to the people and village of Isara. *Isara* overlaps temporally with *Ake*, but offers a strikingly different adult perspective on these years.

———. 1994. *Ibadan: The Penkelemes Years: A Memoir: 1946–1965*. London: Methuen. Soyinka calls this work "Son of *Ake*." In the aftermath of the aborted 1993 democratic elections, Soyinka returned to the subject of his own past, evidently as a means of making sense of his

"love-hate relationship" with Nigeria. Soyinka calls *Ibadan* "faction"—
a "much abused genre which attempts to fictionalise facts and events,
the proportion of fact to fiction being totally at the discretion of the
author" (p. ix). The work begins when "Maren" (Soyinka) returns to
Abeokuta from England, where he has been attending university and
staging his own plays, but it does not proceed in chronological order. It
explores Maren's continuing education and his relationships with Essay,
Wild Christian, his grandfather, and other kin and friends. It also focuses on Maren's engagement with the politics in the newly independent
Nigeria.

———. 1999. *The Burden of Memory, the Muse of Forgiveness*. New York:
Oxford University Press. A recent volume of essays reflecting on the
responsibilities carried by an artist who is politically active and socially
aware.

23

Moyez G. Vassanji's
The Gunny Sack

Jamie Monson

THE GUNNY SACK OF M. G. VASSANJI'S 1989 NOVEL IS OLD
and mysterious, filled with the treasures and memories of the past.
As the novel's narrator Salim Juma removes the contents of the sack
one by one, he recalls his family's stories for us, just as his grandaunt
Ji Bai once did for him. Vassanji is a masterful storyteller, and the
evocative imagery of this novel brings East African history to life for
my college students. He lets us in on family secrets, allowing us to
hear not only the voice of Ji Bai the grandaunt but also other voices
and stories. The result is a textured, multilayered narrative. This is a
historical novel, covering approximately 150 years of East African
history through the experiences of one extended Tanzanian Asian
family. It helps students of history to contextualize the material covered in class lectures, readings, and discussions. The novel integrates
several themes that are central to understanding East African history:
oral narrative, collective memory, cultural identity, race, gender, and
nationalism.

I use this novel throughout my introductory-level survey course
on East African history. Because the novel incorporates so many historical periods—the later nineteenth century, German colonialism,
the two world wars, British rule, and independence—it can be used
in group discussions over a succession of class periods.
Alternatively, it can be used at the end of the course to synthesize the
course material. Normally I have an enrollment of approximately
thirty students in this introductory survey, and I teach using a combi-

Moyez G. Vassanji, *The Gunny Sack* (Portsmouth, N.H.: Heinemann, 1989).

nation of lecture and discussion. The course is open to students from all levels, so I look for materials that can provide a challenge for upper-level students while still remaining accessible to first-year students. *The Gunny Sack*, because of its many layers of stories and meaning, is an ideal novel for this audience.

As *The Gunny Sack* opens, Salim Juma is writing from exile on the occasion of the funeral of his grandaunt Ji Bai. His reminiscences about life in East Africa begin when he inherits her old gunny sack. "Now for some history," he exclaims as he reaches back in time (and into the depths of the sack) to the village of Junapur in India. From this village his earliest remembered ancestor, Dhanji Govindji, set off for Zanzibar, the jewel of Africa, to seek his fortune in the 1880s. Govindji settled in a mythical coastal town south of Bagamoyo, where he set up shop as a retail trader in 1885. The *mukhi* (or village leader) offered him a store, some goods on credit, and a slave woman (Bibi Taratibu) to take care of him. In time, Bibi Taratibu gave birth to their son, Huseni. This union and its offspring become the first of two dark secrets in the Govindji family, and introduce the conflicts of East African identity and racial origins that are developed throughout the book.

Families in India react against these interracial relations, decrying the "half-castes littering the coast from Mozambique to Karachi." Govindji must therefore arrange a formal marriage with the daughter of a Zanzibari widow, and Bibi Taratibu is sent to the edge of the forest. In the next four chapters of the novel, Huseni grows up straddling the "civilized" culture of the South Asian immigrant community and the "barbarian" culture of up-country Africans (*shenzis*). Vassanji describes the historical events of this time period in vivid detail: the baskets of gum copal bartered for cloth, beads, and wire in the 1880s; the arrival of the *mdachis* (Germans) and their plantations; the Maji Maji rebellion against colonial exploitation. Huseni eventually marries, and his wife bears him a son, Juma. Yet against his father's wishes, Huseni continues to visit his mother, Bibi Taratibu, at the edge of town. This sparks a final confrontation with his father, who shouts, "You are descended from the Solar Race! What do you have to consort with slaves for?" Huseni leaves, never to be heard from again. Thus begins the second dark secret of the family: Dhanji Govindji, who is now the *mukhi* of Matamu, stole the money the community had entrusted to him in a desperate and futile quest to find Huseni. This was the greatest sin, the deepest shame, that haunts the family throughout the book: Govindji stole from his "own" people for the sake of his half-African son.

The gunny sack reveals the stories of the growing lineage of this immigrant family: "our catalogue of names, where history moves in a noisy parade wearing faces like masks" (p. 60). Four generations of Tanzanian Asian experience spill out, interwoven with the historical events swirling around them. During the First World War, the family evacuates the coastal town and treks inland to escape the fighting. Juma, the son of Huseni, ends up in Nairobi with the family of his mother. There Juma is treated as a second-class citizen because of his mixed-race heritage. His divided loyalty is revealed in a bad memory, a "pang of conscience" spit out by the gunny sack. Like his father, young Juma finds solace in friendship with an older African woman (Mary), a mother figure. During the Mau Mau emergency, however, Juma and his wife Kulsum betray her.

The remainder of the novel takes place in Dar es Salaam, where Kulsum moves after the death of her husband. These are the years of the narrator Salim Juma's childhood, and they are illustrated primarily through his own stories and memories. Kulsum first settles her family in Kariakoo, the African section of Dar es Salaam, setting up shop in one of the many Asian *dukas* along Msimbazi Street. We gain an intimate look into the history of Kariakoo, its "thousand faces," through the eyes of the growing Salim and his siblings. We are introduced to more relatives—cousins, aunts, and uncles—the growing cast of characters in the neighborhood of Kulsum's shop. The shop was located not in the Indian quarter, but on the Kariakoo side of the Mnazi Moja ground, just inside the African quarter. Here again, Salim finds himself on the boundary between the "civilization" of the Asian community and a "maze of criss-crossing, unpaved streets lined with African huts" (p. 85).

Salim Juma's adolescence coincides with the development of nationalist politics, Legislative Council elections, and the early years of independence under Julius Nyerere. We view these events through the experience of the Asian community. Despite fears of an anti-Asian backlash, independence itself was "painless." But Kulsum's expert tailor, Omari, uses the threat of the labor union to claim years of back pay for an inadequate salary. We learn of the Zanzibar revolution through a story told to Juma by a Zanzibari girl. Several characters express their fears of assimilation, Asian-African intermarriage, and the nationalization of businesses.

The first impact of independence on Salim Juma himself is the obligation for all Tanzanian youth to perform National Service. At Camp "Uhuru" Salim comes of age, dealing significantly for the first time with his identity and his past. Most Asian youths were stationed close to Dar es Salaam, where their mothers could bring them curries on Sundays. Because Salim Juma has an African surname, however, he is sent to a distant camp north of Bukoba. He is ridiculed for bringing a heavy trunk loaded with amenities, and reflects, "We Indians have barged into Africa with our big black trunk, and every time it comes in our way. Do we need it? I should have come with a small bag, a rucksack. Instead I came with *ladoos, jelebis, chevdo.* Toilet paper. A woollen suit. And I carried them on my head like a fool" (p. 204). The National Service teaches Juma rigorous physical discipline. He also learns songs of revolution, the importance of building a new nation, and the evils of capitalism.

At Camp "Uhuru" Juma falls in love with Amina, a fiery African intellectual. Amina introduces Juma to radical politics, and they take on the task of political education at the camp. They continue their relationship back in Dar es Salaam, where they engage in political work through a student activist organization. In this final section of the book, the theme of interracial relationships returns with added intensity. Salim reflects, "To have met in the jungle and fallen in love there, among people we did not know, on the banks of a stream under a tree, how easy it was. No sooner were we back in the city than we started carrying the burdens of our races" (p. 228). Salim's thoughts echo the past: Dhanji Govindji and Bibi Taratibu lived together in the 1880s when the coast was still sparsely settled, and interracial families could be anonymous. With time, and the development of towns, Bibi Taratibu was sent to the forest edge. Throughout the book, the distinction between forest and town, jungle and civilization is a metaphor for racial difference in East African society. There is ongoing tension between those who inhabit both worlds—Huseni, Juma, Salim—and those who do everything in their power to maintain their distinction.

Salim Juma ultimately leaves East Africa, following his brother Sona to the United States and then moving on, probably to Canada. In the final paragraph of the novel, Salim vows to cease "the cycle of escape and rebirth, uprooting and regeneration" that has characterized his own family and others of the Indian diaspora. Here M. G. Vassanji addresses the theme of South Asian migration, placing *The Gunny Sack* within the larger genre of South Asian diaspora literature. He reminds us that this story of Dhanji Govindji's lineage is tied to multiple memories and multiple histories, not only of East Africa but of the larger world of Asian migration and resettlement.

M. G. Vassanji is perhaps best known as a South Asian Canadian writer, having served as editor of *The Toronto South Asian Review* and the *Review*'s book series. He has edited a book in that series, *A Meeting of Streams: South Asian Canadian Literature*, in 1985, which contains a chapter by him entitled "The Postcolonial Writer." Vassanji's short story "A Tin of Cookies" is set in Canada and appears in a 1994 anthology, *The Whistling Thorn: An Anthology of South Asian Canadian Fiction*. While Vassanji's work is commonly located within this South Asian genre of Canadian literature, however, *The Gunny Sack* is very much an East African novel. As Peter Nazareth notes in a review essay, "Just when [Vassanji] is being recognized as a Canadian author, he has published his first novel as an African" (Nazareth 1990: 129–133).

MAJOR THEMES AND DISCUSSION QUESTIONS

I find *The Gunny Sack* to be a very helpful novel for teaching my East African history survey. It raises questions about historical experience in East Africa that connect directly to our class lectures and discussions. It also provides rich material for student essays. Perhaps the most important initial question, one we engage from the first day of the course is, What is African history? (see Sarvan 1991). In *The Gunny Sack*, history is constituted from events (colonial conquest, the world wars, independence) and from memory. Vassanji shows that events are experienced in different ways by different groups of people—and are remembered in equally diverse ways. The gunny sack urges us to begin history "at the beginning"—but whose beginning? Where? If history is made up of reconstructed memories, collected in the jumble of the gunny sack, what can history offer in the way of truth or objectivity? As Vassanji writes, "The past is just this much beyond reach, you can reconstruct it only through the paraphernalia it leaves behind . . . and then who would deny that what you manufacture is only a model" (p. 127). Students can discuss the novel as historical text—does fiction make history more "real" through the development of characters, settings, and stories? Does this novel change the way we think about historical reconstruction and narration?

Other themes that come out in our discussions of *The Gunny Sack* include those of identity, race, gender, and nationalism. The themes of identity and race are quite prominent in the novel and provide an easy launching point for class conversation. Students are quick to notice the more obvious elements here—the tensions between Asian and African identities, the unique experience of the South Asian community in East Africa, the problems of racial exclusivity and multiracialism. Once these have been established, students can be challenged to look deeper. For example, there are very few European characters in the novel, despite the pervasive presence of colonial rule in the lives of the protagonists. The appearance of whites is fleeting and their characters remain superficial. Why is this the case? What is the meaning of the *absence* of European experience in Vassanji's book?

Another important theme is the metaphor of the forest. The forest edge is the home of Bibi Taratibu and a forbidden space for her half-caste son Huseni. Here the forest represents the home of black Africans, or *shenzis,* in the novel. Similarly, the forest is the home of the Mau Mau fighters, described as "Kikuyu" (ethnically and racially different) by the Asians in Nairobi. The forest during the emergency is a place of danger, grisly and menacing. After independence the forested Uhuru camp, far from coastal civilization, is the meeting place for the Asian Salim Juma and the African Amina. It is a place of transgression, where Salim and Amina develop their own radical political ideology as well as their love affair. Other spatial metaphors correlating with race and identity abound throughout the book, and once students get started, they enjoy searching them out.

Gender is another significant theme in *The Gunny Sack*. The narrator of the novel is a young man, Salim Juma. History begins with the migration of his male ancestor, Dhanji Govindji, to Zanzibar. Yet the novel itself is organized into sections bearing the names of the three prominent female characters: Part 1 is "Ji Bai," Part 2 is "Kulsum," and Part 3 "Amina." What does this tell us about the role of women in the novel? This novel is filled with stories about strong women, detailing their influence in the family and community.

Kulsum was sixteen when she married Juma, still "the naive daughter of a Mombasa mystic." In the home of her husband's family in Nairobi, Kulsum occupies the lowest rung of the household hierarchy—she is a poor in-law and the wife of the orphaned half-caste Juma. Unable to endure this position and the abuse that accompanies it, she plots to free herself and Juma from the arrangement. She uses devious means, first violating the family rules and then going on a hunger strike. "The first guerrilla was surely a woman," the narrator muses, "the ways of a woman are softer but surer" (p. 70). He acknowledges that such methods of resistance only result in isolated victories—but in this instance Kulsum triumphs. This scene is a good one for exploring the power relationships between men and women in the novel. It can also be used to discuss the topic of resistance more generally. Vassanji sets up the initial arguments for this debate—Kulsum's tactics can be seen as "surer" in the struggle against oppression, or alternatively as piecemeal and ineffective. When the experiences of other women in the novel are brought into the discussion, students see that there is no uniform female strategy. Ji Bai, Kulsum, and Amina all represent different experiences and different tactics in taking on male-dominated power structures. This material produces lively debate among students about the nature of female power and agency in the novel and in East African history more generally.

Finally, the theme of nationalism is a good one to take up in class discussion of *The Gunny Sack*. Vassanji writes, "Independence was painless. A man's colour is no sin in Tanganyika" (p. 156). These two sentences reveal the anxieties of racial identity for Asian East Africans during the establishment of independence. Independence may have been painless, but the ensuing uncertainties of new nationhood and the expansion of socialist politics in Tanzania led many Asians to emigrate anew. This is the fate of Salim and two of his three siblings, who resettle in North America and in Britain. To what nation, then, do South Asians born in Africa belong? Are they a people without a nation, or a nation of migrants? Salim Juma vows that the cycle of "uprooting and regeneration" will stop with him: he will live in the present, not in the past. Ji Bai, on the other hand, makes a pilgrimage to her childhood home in Bajupur, India, the place where her family history began. She finds that the area has changed drastically, but the house she lived in as a girl still remains.

This novel is full of rich detail and description. It is peopled by a large number of characters, many of whom have similar names and similar destinies. The narrative is made up of stories and memories that weave together distant places and time periods. Some of my students, therefore, feel lost as they struggle to keep track of the many people, places, and events. For this reason, I normally assign the novel relatively late in my survey course. Alternatively, I have students read individual sections of the novel as we cover the relevant content material in class. Then we have a general discussion of the entire book at the end of the course. I also remind my students to consult the aids provided by Vassanji—there is a helpful glossary of Swahili and Cutchi-Gujarati terms at the back of the book. At the beginning there is a family tree showing all the descendants of Dhanji Govindji and a map of East Africa.

RELATED READING AND STUDENT ASSIGNMENTS

The events covered in *The Gunny Sack* are central events in East African history and would normally be covered in any introductory survey course: nineteenth-century trade, German colonialism, Maji Maji, British rule, nationalism and independence, postcolonial East Africa. There are several useful textbooks that can be used to teach this material, along with a number of scholarly articles. There is also a growing body of scholarship on East African Asian history that can be used with *The Gunny Sack*. The most helpful textbook for Tanzanian history during this period is John Iliffe's classic *Modern History of Tanganyika*. This book begins in 1800 and covers roughly the same time period as Vassanji's novel. It is a lengthy and detailed study, both thorough and well documented. The size and scope of the book may initially put off undergraduate students, but Iliffe is a master of synthesis and a fluid writer. The pairing of Iliffe's book and *The Gunny Sack* gives students two wonderful tools for learning about East African history. An earlier text, Kimambo and Temu's *History of Tanzania,* is another useful overview. More general textbooks on African history are also available. I have found it helpful to assign Abiola Irele's "Narrative, History and the African Imagination" to accompany a discussion of the novel and its relationship to history.

For teaching this particular novel, I have students read something about East African Asian experience. A recent volume by Robert Gregory, *South Asians in East Africa,* covers Asian activities in Kenya, Uganda, and Tanzania during the same time frame as Vassanji's book. New research by Richa Nagar in Dar es Salaam has resulted in a number of articles, several of which can be used for teaching this novel. A bibliography of scholarship on Asians in East Africa, published by Christian Kiem, contains additional resources. Vassanji's edited volume, *A Meeting of Streams*, can be used to place the novel in its literary context as a postcolonial, South Asian Canadian work.

My students normally write a five-to-seven-page essay on *The Gunny Sack*. I ask them to use the novel to explore one of the themes we have discussed in class—for example, identity, history, gender, or nationalism. I give them a fair amount of latitude in these essays, but I do require them to refer to the historical materials we have covered in class lectures, discussions, and readings. I usually assign this essay toward the end of the course, after we have covered the early independence period and after we have discussed the novel together in class. In their course evaluations my students repeatedly mention *The Gunny Sack* and this essay assignment as enjoyable and valuable components of the course. Most of my undergraduate students come into my East Africa survey without any previous knowledge of the Asian African experience. M. G. Vassanji's novel opens up new ways of understanding African history: students see the complexity of identity, the salience of memory, and the difficulties of reconstructing the past. The essays they turn in at the end of the course show me how much they have learned and how *The Gunny Sack* helped them to get there.

SUGGESTIONS FOR
FURTHER READING AND RESOURCES

Gregory, Robert. 1996. *South Asians in East Africa: An Economic and Social History, 1890–1980*. Boulder: Westview. Covers Asian activities in Kenya, Uganda, and Tanzania during the same time frame as Vassanji's book. Unfortunately not available in paperback, but excerpts can be assigned to students, and the book can serve as a helpful guide for teachers.

Iliffe, John. 1979. *A Modern History of Tanganyika*. Cambridge: Cambridge University Press. The most helpful textbook for Tanzanian history during the nineteenth and twentieth centuries.

Irele, Abiola. 1993. "Narrative, History, and the African Imagination," *Narrative* 1, 2: 16–72. Provides a useful framework for a discussion of the African novel and its relationship to history.

Kiem, Christian. 1993. *The Asian Minority in East Africa: A Selected Annotated Bibliography*. Forschungsschwerpunkt Entwicklungssoziologie, Universität Bielefeld.

Kimambo, I. M., and A. J. Temu. 1969. *A History of Tanzania*. Nairobi: East African Publishing House. An edited volume covering the major themes in Tanzanian history from earliest human settlements through independence. A new edition is planned but not yet available. Copies of the original are available in the United States through "Books on Demand" in Ann Arbor, Michigan.

Nagar, Richa. 1998a. "Communal Discourses, Marriage and the Politics of Gendered Social Boundaries Among South Asian Immigrants in Tanzania," *Gender, Place and Culture* 5, 2: 117–139. Looks at marriage and migration patterns of South Asians in Tanzania from a gendered historical perspective. Covers the same time period as the novel, with helpful maps and illustrative vignettes. The author's discourse analysis approach is best suited for upper-level undergraduates and graduate students.

———. 1998b. "The South Asian Diaspora in Tanzania: A History Retold," *Comparative Studies of South Asia, Africa, and the Middle East: A Journal of Politics, Culture, Economy* 16, 2: 1–19. An excellent article to assign undergraduates as background to the novel. A useful, concise summary of South Asian history in Tanzania, covering roughly the same time period (1890s to 1990s) as the novel. Shows how class and religious differences among Asians affected attitudes toward migration and interracial marriage. Also discusses the spatial segregation of racial groups in the colonial period, and the effects of independence and the Zanzibar revolution on Asian families.

Nazareth, Peter. 1990. "The First Tanzan/Asian Novel," *Research in African Literatures* 21, 4: 129–133. A short review of the novel, discussing it in relationship to other East African and Asian fiction.

Sarvan, Charles. 1991. "M. G. Vassanji's *The Gunny Sack*: A Reflection on History and the Novel," *Modern Fiction Studies* 37, 3: 511–518. A useful review of Vassanji's novel in a special issue on postcolonial African fiction.

Shillington, Kevin. 1989. *History of Africa*. New York: St. Martin's. A good overall African history textbook for general background. Has helpful maps and illustrations, and works well in undergraduate survey courses.

Vassanji, M. G. 1985. *A Meeting of Streams: South Asian Canadian Literature*. Toronto: South Asian Review Publications. Helpful in placing *The Gunny Sack* in its literary context as a postcolonial, South Asian Canadian work.

———. 1989. *The Gunny Sack*. Portsmouth, N.H.: Heinemann.

———. 1991. *Uhuru Street: Short Stories*. Portsmouth, N.H.: Heinemann. A collection of short stories based on South Asian life in East Africa.

24

P. T. Zeleza's
Smouldering Charcoal

Melvin E. Page

HOW TO LEND A FEELING OF AUTHENTICITY TO MY
teaching about the troubles that plagued so many African countries
after they had grasped the prize of independence from their colonial
rulers? My solution has been to have students read Paul Tiyambe
Zeleza's novel, *Smouldering Charcoal*, concerning postcolonial
problems in Malawi. Of course, other novels capture similar themes;
Zeleza himself has noted that "African writers, almost from the dawn
of independence, knew that the masses were dissatisfied and hungry
for meaningful change" (1994: 478) and has suggested the work of
numerous others. Among those Zeleza has singled out are Ousmane
Sembene, whose 1960 novel, *God's Bits of Wood*, is well known (see
Chapter 21), as well as *Petals of Blood* by Ngugi wa Thiong'o and
Bessie Head's *Maru*. He also acknowledges the debt he and other
authors have to Peter Abrahams's pioneering *A Wreath for Udomo*
(see Chapter 1).

   Zeleza's own writing both reflects those postindependence
themes very well and extends such artistic expression into the era of
postcolonial atrophy in many African countries. *Smouldering
Charcoal* also lays out these sentiments much more clearly and
forcefully, and with greater aesthetic appeal, than the previous novels
of such Malawian exiles as David Rubadiri (*No Bride Price*, 1967)
and Legson Kayira (*The Looming Shadow*, 1968, and other works),
who have nonetheless received more critical attention than has
Zeleza (Chapman 1996: 273–274).

P. T. Zeleza, *Smouldering Charcoal* (Portsmouth, N.H.: Heinemann, 1992).

Generally Malawian writers have chosen the forms of poetry and, to a lesser extent, drama as the mediums for expressing such ideas and convictions. The celebrated poetry of Jack Mapanje, Steve Chimombo, and others has often been held up as the authentic "popular voice" in Malawian literature. Most of their work owes inspiration to a successful Malawian Writers Group organized at Chancellor College of the University of Malawi in the 1970s. The intellectual ferment of that group encouraged the development of a Malawian literature frequently characterized by "elaborately-coded social protest" (Chapman 1996: 273).

Zeleza himself was associated with this group, and although he did experiment with poetry, his best early writing tended to more narrative forms (Roscoe 1977: 25, 215). *Smouldering Charcoal* represents an intellectual and artistic pinnacle in his work, bringing together many of the themes that others expressed poetically. And as a novel, it has a decided advantage—certainly for the purposes of teaching—in having a sustained narrative voice and powers of description useful in presenting a historical understanding of contemporary Africa.

For this reason, *Smouldering Charcoal* is one of several works of African literature I use when teaching a survey History of Africa course. My general intent has been to give voice to African perspectives and emotions that might not otherwise be represented in my course. With an enrollment of usually about twenty-five students, a multiracial mix of sophomores through seniors, the course offers a good environment for class discussion of each work and a variety of issues suggested in the texts. Because *Smouldering Charcoal* deals with the postcolonial period in Malawi, the book offers clear insights into many of the dynamics of that contested part of Africa's recent past.

Set principally in a large city, which really can only reflect Malawi's commercial (but not political) center, Blantyre, the action spills over to surrounding communities on the edges of the rural countryside. This urban and periurban focus, of course, rings very true to much of the dispute-ridden contemporary history of the continent. The major protagonist is Chola, a young, American-educated journalist who is disillusioned with his job and the increasingly meaningless news he is expected to report. "Just concentrate on the usual things, . . . report the facts, that's all," he recalls his editor telling him. Yet Chola understands that this means little more than stories extolling the nation's leader, "coupled with repetitive reports of the latest development achievements" (pp. 20–21). For him the result is an unsettling sycophancy that he increasingly cannot endure.

The story initially revolves around an independent strike at the largest local commercial bakery in the city, an unusual event in this African country, one that would nonetheless normally be ignored by Chola's newspaper. Only inadvertently learning about the strike plans, Chola is determined to report on the action of the workers against the state-owned corporation that has taken over the bakery. Yet the strike, and its effect on a few of the workers who participate in it, is not really the principal focus of the novel. Unlike *God's Bits of Wood*, for example, Zeleza's story cannot be considered a "strike" novel, nor is it primarily a labor-focused story; its trajectory is much broader than that.

Among the bakery workers, Mchere is the key figure whom we meet. His life seems to be spiraling out of control into deepening disaster, and although he sees the strike as an echo of his late father's preindependence activism, this latest protest only seems to promise Mchere more of the same woes as those already plaguing his life. Drawn to the strike as a means of protesting to achieve what Zeleza has elsewhere described as "meaningful change" (1994: 478), Mchere also knows joining the strike may mean an end to even this inadequate job, furthering his own suffering and that of his family. Without exactly knowing why, Mchere senses what the Western-educated Chola can more clearly articulate: "In Africa we have the trappings of power and little or none of its substance. . . . our former colonial rulers constantly smile all the way to the banks" (p. 22).

A number of coincidences bring Chola and Mchere together in several situations at just the time when Chola's closest friend, the activist attorney Dambo, is found dead in a nearby river. Dambo's apparent murder precipitates a crisis in Chola's life. He is determined to take a new direction, to fight the forces undermining his country, even if from exile, and to write a book "about himself, about Dambo, Mchere, their families, and about many other people, their inadequacies and frustrations, their lives and struggles to break out of the monstrous concentration camp that is independent Africa" (p. 106). For Chola, the issue is less the political prisons into which political opponents of the state have disappeared when they have not been killed outright. It is more the sense that he is living in a prison without bars, a country in which he has only the most limited freedom to move about and even less to exercise his mind and express his ideas.

Clearly the manuscript of *Smouldering Charcoal* is the result of Chola's determination to tell this story, but this novel is more than that. By the end we realize that the story is narrated by Catherine, Chola's former fiancée, who admits she is presenting the work with added "experiences pertinent to the story" (p. 181). She is writing from exile in a nearby country where she has gone after Chola's death in prison. Like so many others, Chola had been caught up in the paranoia of a state determined to root out any dissent, however mild, or any suspicion of disaffection. While imprisoned, Chola is a key figure in organizing a hunger strike that prison authorities determine must be ended. Their efforts to do so include extremes of torture (which Zeleza briefly but graphically describes) and ultimately an arrangement in which a fellow prisoner beats the severely weakened Chola to death. "If the Chief Superintendent had any regrets," Catherine as narrator reflects on the death of her fiancé, "it was that Chola had died before making a confession" (p. 159).

It is clear that the added material Catherine has brought to the story concerns not only Chola's prison experiences and death, but also reflections on the role and place of women in the country's postcolonial life. She confesses to having once angered Chola with an accusation that he was, indeed, "just like other men, selfish and bossy" (p. 108). Even more, the extremes of both financial and emotional poverty in which women are often trapped by their husbands, who seem more interested in their own pleasures than in their families, is sensitively outlined in Zeleza's examination of Mchere's wife Nambe and their children.

In the figures of a priest, unwilling to help Nambe when her son is injured, and the prison guards who shun her attempts to communicate with her husband, incarcerated as a striker, we see how the coincidence of male domination and institutional disdain further marginalize women in this society. Their frustrations—not only with the broken dreams of independence, but even more with the unfulfilled promises from the men in their lives—give the novel an especially poignant character. The contrasting yet complementary actions of the groups of men and women in dealing with the problems of their postindependence world offer a vital gendered perspective on this period in recent African history.

As an example of African fiction, *Smouldering Charcoal* certainly displays the qualities of African writing Zeleza himself has called a "creative imagination . . . not encumbered by the strict discursive structures of the academic enterprise" (1994: 486). But it also benefits from his skills as "a historian, not a social scientist who studies the present or tries to crystal-gaze into the future" (1994: 478). In several early short stories, for example, written while he studied both history and literature as an undergraduate at the University of Malawi, Zeleza was keen to embrace oral traditions and reminiscences in his fiction. He went on to graduate study in history at Dalhousie University, followed by teaching positions in the West Indies, Kenya, Canada, and also Malawi. Since then he has established himself as a fine economic historian of Africa, with the first volume of his *Modern Economic History of Africa* winning the 1994 Noma award for publishing in Africa. He is also a perceptive critic of writing and scholarship about the continent, with some of his views culminating in the 1997 *Manufacturing African Studies and Crises*. He is presently director of African studies at the University of Illinois, Urbana-Champaign.

Certainly there are many sections of *Smouldering Charcoal* that clearly reflect the descriptive power that only personal experience can provide, an area where Zeleza outshines his Malawian novelist predecessors. His experiences in Malawi, both as a student and later as a university lecturer, permeate the fiction he creates. His skills at historical observation are obvious and evident, as is his appealing and convincing style; the situations he describes are presented with a drier and much less captivating voice in David Williams's historical treatment of the same period, *Malawi: The Politics of Despair*. There are, for example, certain institutional settings—such as the university and the hospital—which, from my own experience as a Fulbright lecturer in Malawi during the early 1970s (when Zeleza was, in fact, one of my students), ring uncannily true in Zeleza's prose. Similarly, having Zeleza as a colleague for a semester at Kenyatta University during the mid-1980s in Kenya reaffirmed my sense of his connection with the postcolonial debates and conflicts swirling in Malawi.

This awareness, of course, has affected my teaching and use of the novel in my history classes, but only to the extent that I am convinced of its authenticity in portraying the recent African past. My approach has generally been to have students read about the postindependence period in Africa in a standard history text; frequently this has been Basil Davidson's *Africa in History*, but I have also used others from time to time, including Kevin Shillington's *History of Africa* or John Iliffe's *Africans: The History of a Continent*. After lecturing on the same period for one or two class periods and discussing the treatment of it in the text with the students, I then ask them to read *Smouldering Charcoal*. I generally offer little introduction, other than to say it is set in Malawi during the 1970s and/or 1980s and to ask them to consider what the author has to say about postcolonialism in Africa.

When we turn to consider the novel directly, usually in one long or two short class periods, I begin by answering questions about the novel. Students have many useful queries concerning all manner of details. They want to know, for example:

- Was there really a bakery strike? (Not as described.)
- Were prison conditions truly so terrible; were people tortured and killed? (Others who have been in those prisons have described it so, as have Amnesty International reports.)
- Was there really was such sycophantic allegiance to the party among some people? (Most definitely! And this has also been true in other African countries.)
- Are women treated so badly by men? (All too often, yes, reflecting both sexism and culturally different roles.)
- And was the Youth Militia (Young Pioneers) really so insistent on enforcing loyalty to the party and the state? (Yes; not only motorists but also poor market-goers were often similarly harassed.)

Then it is my turn to ask the questions. Does this description of what happened to the promise of independence ring true? What about the place of the state? Is Zeleza's analysis correct when Ndatero, the university literature lecturer imprisoned alongside Chola, says

> You know what the problem is? We worship the state, even those of us who attack it. I suppose we caught the bug under colonialism when our reverence for the state began. Independence did not alter this conditioning. . . . it grew under the new rulers . . . that's where [even] radical movements go wrong. They concentrate all their energies on capturing the state machine. And when they do the state swallows them up and they become reincarnations of the ousted regimes. (p. 151)

Does Ndatero speak for Zeleza himself in this passage? Here Zeleza the novelist clearly reflects the perspectives of Zeleza the historian on the legacy of the past. This usually prompts a lively discussion about the history of colonialism and its legacy.

Finally I ask the students if they see any indications of hope for the future in the novel's account. At some point, one or more of the students usually points to Catherine's final observation, on the promise of the movement in exile: "The future has begun" (p. 182). We discuss this prospect, which I intend as an introduction to the final section of my course, on the "democratic transitions" in Africa. At that point I feel constrained to share Zeleza's own more recent assessments. Catherine's statement, he has written, is one of "defiant simplicity" (1994, p. 488). Of course, this further observation introduces a thorny problem, perhaps best, as Zeleza says, left to crystal gazing rather than to history.

My usual practice is to ask students to prepare a report on this and each of the other works of literature they have read. I give them four options for these reports: (1) a traditional book review; (2) a reading journal in which they record their reactions, observations, and questions about the book; (3) a character study of one of the chief characters in the story; or (4) a work of art (painting, poetry, drawing, music, whatever) that illustrates or exemplifies the major theme they have derived from reading a particular work of literature. They must vary their report choices, and in each case, my expectation is that they will consider the particular literary work in the context of African history we have been studying.

Perhaps not surprisingly, I get few works of art based on reading *Smouldering Charcoal*, with the exception of some poetry. Most students seem to prefer character studies when considering this novel. I believe this is because Zeleza's characters are sharply drawn and seem to voice fairly clear impressions about their circumstances. This often gives the class an opportunity to discuss individual African reactions to the promise of independence lost or under threat. Such discussions also help to highlight the varied nature of African responses even as there were many common general expectations of both independence from colonial rule and the problems that have unfortunately plagued postcolonial Africa.

At the end of my course I ask students informally which of the works of literature they have enjoyed the most. For the most part, *Smouldering Charcoal* is not among those they mention, and often they tell me it is because the events in the story are so depressing. Perhaps this is because their expectations of literature are entertainment rather then enlightenment, and, indeed, Zeleza acknowledges that his primary concern was to reach an African, not a Western, audience (1994: 485–486). Recently, however, I have been surprised that several students have made a vociferous case for *Smouldering Charcoal* as their personal favorite. Their reasons are that it spoke to them more clearly than their text, or their instructor, about the difficulties experienced by Africans in the recent past. If that is indeed true, then I am certain my choice of *Smouldering Charcoal* for use in my classroom has been a good one.

SUGGESTIONS FOR
FURTHER READING AND RESOURCES

Beahan, Charlotte, and Melvin E. Page. 1986. "Some African and Asian
    Fiction for Teaching Modern World History," *Teaching History* (The
    Historical Association of Great Britain) 44: 26–29. Written before
    Smouldering Charcoal was published, this essay gives some idea of my
    early thinking on the use of novels in teaching history.
Chapman, Michael. 1996. *Southern African Literatures*. London: Longman.
    Though sometimes frustratingly incomplete, this is probably the best
    treatment of literature from southern Africa.
Chimombo, Steve. 1994. *Napolo and the Python: Selected Poetry*.
    Portsmouth, N.H.: Heinemann.
Davidson, Basil. 1992. *The Black Man's Burden: Africa and the Curse of the
    Nation-state*. London: James Currey. Considers some of the key prob-
    lems of postcolonial Africa in terms similar to those presented in
    Smouldering Charcoal.
———. 1995. *Africa in History: Themes and Outlines,* rev. ed. New York:
    Scribner.
Forster, Peter G. 1994. "Culture, Nationalism, and the Invention of Tradition
    in Malawi," *Journal of Modern African Studies* 32: 477–497.
    Describes creation of the postcolonial sense of nationalism cultivated in
    Malawi by President H. Kamuzu Banda, which underpinned the politi-
    cal culture described in *Smouldering Charcoal*.
Iliffe, John. 1995. *Africans: The History of a Continent*. Cambridge:
    Cambridge University Press.
Kayira, Legson. 1968. *The Looming Shadow*. Portsmouth, N.H.:
    Heinemann.
Mandala, Elias. 1990. *Work and Control in a Peasant Economy: A History
    of the Lower Tchiri Valley in Malawi, 1859–1960*. Madison: University
    of Wisconsin Press. An analysis of agricultural change in southernmost
    Malawi from about 1860 to 1960, before independence. Though not
    directly related to themes of the novel, nonetheless interesting for those
    wanting to have a sense of the rural economy.
Mapanje, Jack. 1991. *Of Chameleons and Gods: Poems*. Portsmouth, N.H.:
    Heinemann.
Roscoe, Adrian. 1977. *Uhuru's Fire: African Literature West to South*.
    Cambridge: Cambridge University Press. A former University of
    Malawi lecturer, Roscoe was in a position to comment on Zeleza's
    skills well before the publication of *Smouldering Charcoal*.
Rubadiri, David. 1967. *No Bride Price*. Portsmouth, N.H.: Heinemann.
Shillington, Kevin. 1995. *History of Africa*, rev. ed. New York: St. Martin's.
    One of the most accessible history textbooks for undergraduates.
Theroux, Paul. 1971. *Jungle Lovers*. Boston: Houghton-Mifflin. Early novel
    by a now celebrated writer who was a Peace Corps volunteer in imme-
    diate postcolonial Malawi. Although in many ways overly caricatured,
    Theroux's novel does offer some additional literary insights into the
    nature of Malawian society, even though not suitable for a comparative
    reading assignment.

White, Landeg. 1987. *Magomero: Portrait of an African Village.* Cambridge: Cambridge University Press. While not specifically concerning the urban setting of the novel, *Magomero* does offer exceptional insights into the history of a small community not far from Blantyre.

Williams, T. David. 1978. *Malawi, The Politics of Despair.* Ithaca, N.Y.: Cornell University Press. Although published some time ago, Williams's book treats historically some of the same themes Zeleza considers in *Smouldering Charcoal.*

Zeleza, Paul Tiyambe. 1976. *Night of Darkness and Other Stories.* Limbe: Montfort Press. Two stories, "The Wrath of Fate" and "The Soldier Without an Ear," particularly reflect elements of Zeleza's commitment to the oral transmission of historical information.

———. 1993. *A Modern Economic History of Africa,* Vol. 1: *The Nineteenth Century.* Dakar: CODESRIA. Winner of the Noma Award 1994 for publishing in Africa.

———. 1994. "The Democratic Transition in Africa and the Anglophone Writer," *Canadian Journal of African Studies* 28: 472–497.

———. 1997. *Manufacturing African Studies and Crises.* Dakar: CODESRIA. In this most recent work Zeleza lays out his views, as a multidisciplinary Africanist, on the creation of knowledge about Africa in the West.

Novels by Region

Region/ Chapter	Author and Title	Setting
23	Moyez G. Vassanji's *The Gunny Sack*	Tanzania
24	P. T. Zeleza's *Smouldering Charcoal*	Malawi

Southern Africa

8	Tsitsi Dangarembga's *Nervous Conditions*	Zimbabwe
9	Modikwe Dikobe's *The Marabi Dance*	South Africa
13	Elsa Joubert's *Poppie Nongena*	South Africa
14	J. Nozipo Maraire's *Zenzele: Letters to My Daughter*	Zimbabwe

Novels
by Principal Themes

Anticolonial resistance: chapters 1, 13, 16, 21

Christianity and Christian missionaries: chapters 2, 8, 16, 22

Colonial society, nature and critique of: chapters 8, 9, 10, 13, 16, 19, 21, 23

Indian immigrants: chapters 6, 23

Indigenous religion: chapters 2, 10, 11, 18. *See also* Christianity and Christian missionaries; Islam

Islam, influence and spread of: chapters 4, 5, 7, 17, 20, 21

Postcolonial societies, critiques of politics and society in: chapters 3, 12, 15, 24

Precolonial social and political organization: chapters 2, 7, 11, 17

Rural/village society: chapters 2, 7, 8, 10, 11, 16, 18, 20, 22

Urban society: chapters 1, 3, 4, 5, 9, 10, 12, 13, 15, 19, 21, 23, 24

Women's position/status: chapters 4, 5, 6, 8, 10, 11, 12, 14, 18, 21

The Contributors ⌐

Charles Ambler is professor of history and head of the Graduate School at the University of Texas at El Paso. He is author of *Kenyan Communities in the Age of Imperialism* (1988) and coeditor of *Liquor and Labor in Southern Africa* (1992) and has published articles on the history of colonial Kenya and Zambia. His current work focuses on the history of leisure in Africa and on debates over the use and control of alcohol in British Africa.

Emmanuel Akyeampong is Hugh K. Foster Associate Professor of African Studies at Harvard University. He is the author of *Drink, Power, and Cultural Change: A Social History of Alcohol in Ghana, c. 1800 to Recent Times* (1996).

Misty L. Bastian is assistant professor of anthropology at Franklin and Marshall College in Pennsylvania. She has published a number of articles on gender, popular culture and the media, religious practice, fashion, and political economy in Nigeria. She is the coeditor, with Jane L. Parpart, of *Great Ideas for Teaching About Africa* (1999).

Iris Berger is professor of history, Africana studies, and women's studies at the University of Albany, State University of New York. She has published widely on African economic, religious, cultural, and gender history. Her most recent books are *Threads of Solidarity: Women in South African History, 1900–1980* (1992) and *Women in Sub-Saharan Africa* (1999), coauthored with E. Frances White.

Joye Bowman is professor of history at the University of Massachusetts at Amherst and director of undergraduate studies in

309

the History Department. She has published articles in the *Journal of African History* and the *Revista Internacional de Estudos Africanos*. Her book, *Ominous Transition: Commerce and Colonial Expansion in the Senegambia and Guinea, 1857–1919*, appeared in 1997.

Bill Bravman is the author of *Making Ethnic Ways: Communities and Their Transformations in Taita, Kenya, 1800–1950* (1998). He teaches world history at the Marlborough School.

Barbara M. Cooper teaches interdisciplinary seminars at New York University's Gallatin School for Individualized Study. She is the author of *Marriage in Maradi: Gender and Culture in a Hausa Society in Niger, 1900–1989* (1997). She is currently researching the history of a minority Christian Hausa community in Niger.

Dennis D. Cordell is professor of history and associate dean at Southern Methodist University in Dallas. His interests include the social and economic history of Africa as well as African population history. His most recent book is *Hoe and Wage: A Social History of a Circular Migration System in West Africa* (1996). He is an editor of the *Canadian Journal of African Studies/Revue canadienne des études africaine*s.

Tamara Giles-Vernick is assistant profesor of history at the University of Virginia. Her research focuses on conceptions of environment and history in equatorial Africa, as well as on malaria in West Africa. Her publications include articles in the journals *Ethnohistory* and *Environmental History*. She is currently working on a manuscript entitled, "Cutting the Vines of the Past: Environmental Histories of Loss in the Sangha River Basin of Equatorial Africa, 1894–1994."

Sandra E. Greene is associate professor of African history at Cornell University. She is author of *Gender, Ethnicity, and Social Change on the Upper Slave Coast* and is currently working on a book manuscript that combines her interests in West African colonial history, traditional belief systems, gender, and geography. She recently completed a term as president of the African Studies Association (U.S.A.)

Margaret Jean Hay is associate professor of history and publications editor at the African Studies Center, Boston University. She is editor of the *International Journal of Historical Studies*, and her publications include *African Women and the Law: Historical Perspectives*

(1982, with Marcia Wright) and *African Women South of the Sahara*, 2nd ed. (1995 with Sharon Stichter).

Lidwien Kapteijns is professor of history at Wellesley College. She teaches African and Middle Eastern history and has published widely on the history of the Sudan and Somalia. Her most recent book is *Women's Voices in a Man's World: Women and the Pastoral Tradition in Northern Somalia* (1999).

Curtis A. Keim is professor of history at Moravian College. He is interested in the nineteenth-century history of Central Africa and Western perceptions of Africa. His most recent book is *Mistaking Africa: Curiosities and Inventions of the American Mind* (1999).

Karen R. Keim is currently adjunct professor of English at Moravian College in Bethlehem, Pennsylvania, where she teaches African and comparative literature. Her research and publications have focused on the trickster in Cameroonian literature.

Martin A. Klein is professor emeritus of history at the University of Toronto. He has taught African history for thirty-four years and has often profitably used novels. His most recent book is *Slavery and Colonial Rule in French West Africa* (1998). He has also edited *Breaking the Chains: Slavery, Bondage, and Emancipation in Africa and Asia* (1993), and *Slavery and Colonial Rule in Africa* (with Suzanne Miers, 1998).

Beverly B. Mack is associate professor of African studies at the University of Kansas. She has lived and worked in Kano, Northern Nigeria, where she conducted field research and taught African literature at Bayero University. Her recent publications include *The Collected Works of Nana Asma'u 1793–1864* (1997) and *One Woman's Jihad: Nana Asma'u, Scholar and Scribe* (forthcoming).

Jamie Monson is associate professor of history at Carleton College and St. Olaf College. She has published articles on the agricultural and environmental history of southern Tanzania and on the Maji Maji rebellion in such journals as *African Economic History* and the *Journal of African History*. Her current research project is a rural social history of the TAZARA railway.

Mary Montgomery is a Ph.D. candidate in history at the University of Maryland, College Park. Her dissertation concerns the triangular relations among Ghana, Great Britain, and the United States in the 1950s and 1960s.

Melvin E. (Mel) Page is professor of history at East Tennessee State University and formerly Fulbright professor of history at both the University of Malawi and the University of Natal (Durban). He teaches the history of central and southern Africa and has published numerous articles on the twentieth-century history of Malawi. He is editor of *Africa and the First World War* (1987), coauthor of *Discovering the Global Past* (1997), and author of the forthcoming *The Chiwaya War* concerning Malawian experiences during the Great War.

Jeanne Penvenne is associate professor of history and core faculty in international relations and women's studies at Tufts University and a research fellow at the African Studies Center, Boston University. Her recent publications include *African Workers and Colonial Racism* (1995) and the chapter on Mozambique in *The History of Central Africa: The Contemporary Years* (1998).

James A. Pritchett is assistant professor of anthropology and assistant director of the African Studies Center at Boston University. His research focuses on the ways in which social change is interpreted and validated according to local beliefs. He has recently completed *Lunda-Ndembu: Style, Change, and Social Transformation in South Central Africa* (forthcoming).

Richard Rathbone is professor of modern African history at the University of London and teaches at the School of Oriental and African Studies. A specialist in modern political history, his most recent books are *Murder and Politics in Colonial Ghana* (1993) and *Nkrumah and the Chiefs: The Politics of Chieftaincy in Ghana, 1951–1960* (1999).

Kathleen Sheldon is an independent historian who is a research scholar at the Center for the Study of Women at the University of California, Los Angeles. She edited *Courtyards, Markets, City Streets: Urban Women in Africa* (1996) and has published articles on Mozambique, many focusing on women and work, in the *International Journal of African Historical Studies, History in Africa, Signs, Women's Studies International,* and several edited collections.

Janice Spleth is professor of French at West Virginia University. She has taught francophone African literature for a quarter century and has published numerous articles in that field. Her volume on Léopold Sédar Senghor (1985) was recognized as an outstanding academic book by *Choice* magazine. Her most recent book is *Critical Perspectives on Léopold Sédar Senghor* (1993).

Farouk Topan is senior lecturer in Swahili at the School of Oriental and African Studies, University of London. He has taught at the universities of Dar es Salaam and Nairobi, introducing the teaching of Swahili literature at both universities. He has published two plays in Swahili, has edited two volumes of essays in Swahili literary criticism, and has written a number of articles on Swahili literature and culture.

About the Book

Some of the best college teachers have found novels to be extremely effective assignments in courses addressing various aspects of African studies. Here, two dozen of those teachers describe their favorite African novels—drawn from all over the continent—and share their experiences in using them in the classroom.

Each contributor discusses why a particular novel works well with students and what specific topics it addresses. Information provided in each case includes: details about the course in which the novel is used, the plot line and major characters, the historical and social context of the novel and how that fits into the writer's life and literary production, course asignments and suggestions for further study, topics that enliven class discussion, and any problems the students have encountered.

Indexes listing the novels by region and by theme further enhance the usefulness of this practical resource, which is a perfect companion to *Great Ideas for Teaching About Africa* (edited by Misty Bastian and Jane Parpart, 1999).

Margaret Jean Hay is associate professor of history and director of publications at Boston University's African Studies Center. Her books include *African Women South of the Sahara* (coedited with Sharon Stichter) and *African Women and the Law: Historical Perspectives* (coedited with Marcia Wright). She is also editor of the *International Journal of African Historical Studies*.